JOHNNY GINGER'S
LAST RIDE

TOM FREMANTLE

JOHNNY GINGER'S LAST RIDE

PAN BOOKS

First published 2000 by Pan Books
an imprint of Macmillan Publishers Ltd
25 Eccleston Place, London SW1W 9NF
Basingstoke and Oxford
Associated companies throughout the world
www.macmillan.co.uk

ISBN 0 333 37692 6

3 5 7 9 8 6 4

A CIP catalogue record for this book is available from
the British Library.

Typeset by SetSystems Ltd, Saffron Walden, Essex
Printed and bound in Great Britain by
Mackays of Chatham plc, Chatham, Kent

Acknowledgements

This book owes a great deal to my agent Barbara Levy and my editor, Mari Evans, for their patience, enthusiasm and particularly for patching up the many punctures in my rough-and-ready prose.

A big thank you to all my sponsors, who between you, managed to convert a loafer's whim into something far more worthwhile. The sustained support of Chris Catton and Pauline Downs at Stoke Mandeville Hospital and the team at Mix 96 in Aylesbury was especially valuable. Thanks also to the *Bucks Herald* newspaper and to the ever helpful Ann Parry, author of *The Admirals Fremantle*.

Many of my family and friends have been an inspiration. My sisters Betsy and Fanny, Iain Duncan-Smith, Shaun and Martin Stanley, Jim Fry, Tom and Sue Finchett, Patrick and Sarah Westropp, Yorkie and Caroline Holdroyd, David Fox-Pitt, Virendra Anand, Ali Kwan, Amar Grover, Cath Mendiaux and Tessel Van Oudenhoven all deserve a special mention. Many more of you have the dubious honour of popping up elsewhere in these pages.

Most importantly, to all those strangers with generous hearts who offered me friendship and fresh insights on the road, I thank you. I only hope my story does you justice.

ACKNOWLEDGEMENTS

Where necessary in the book I have changed people's names to protect their privacy and guard them against any political repercussions.

This book is dedicated with love to my parents: two people who understand the world of Johnny Ginger better than I ever will.

Thus the butterfly had entirely forgotten that it was a caterpillar, perhaps it may in turn so entirely forget that it was a butterfly that it becomes a fish. The deeper natures never forget themselves and never become anything else than what they were.

Søren Kierkegaard

CONTENTS

CONTENTS

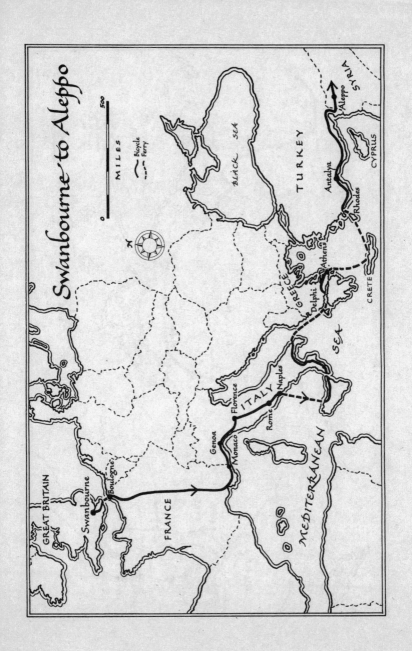

Swanbourne to Aleppo

GREAT BRITAIN

Swanbourne

Boulogne

FRANCE

Genoa

Monaco

Florence

ITALY

Rome

Naples

MEDITERRANEAN

BLACK SEA

TURKEY

GREECE

Delphi

Athens

SEA

CRETE

Rhodes

Antalya

CYPRUS

SYRIA

Aleppo

MILES

0   500

Bicycle
Ferry

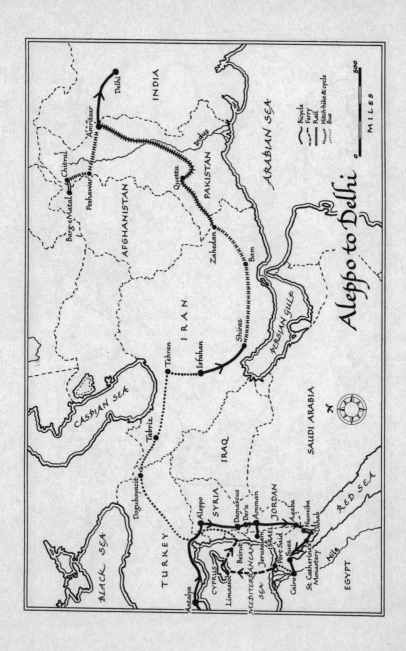

Aleppo to Delhi

Bicycle
Ferry
Rail
Hitch-hike & cycle
Bus

500
MILES
0

INDIA
Delhi
Amritsar
Chitral
Barg-e Matal
Peshawar
PAKISTAN
Quetta
Indus
AFGHANISTAN
ARABIAN SEA
Zahedan
Bam
IRAN
Shiraz
PERSIAN GULF
Isfahan
Tehran
Tabriz
CASPIAN SEA
Doguboyazit
SAUDI ARABIA
IRAQ
TURKEY
Aleppo
SYRIA
Damascus
Dera
Amman
JORDAN
Aqaba
Nuweiba
Taba
ISRAEL
Port Said
Suez
Jerusalem
Beirut
CYPRUS
Limassol
MEDITERRANEAN SEA
Antalya
BLACK SEA
Cairo
St Catherine's Monastery
EGYPT
Nile
RED SEA

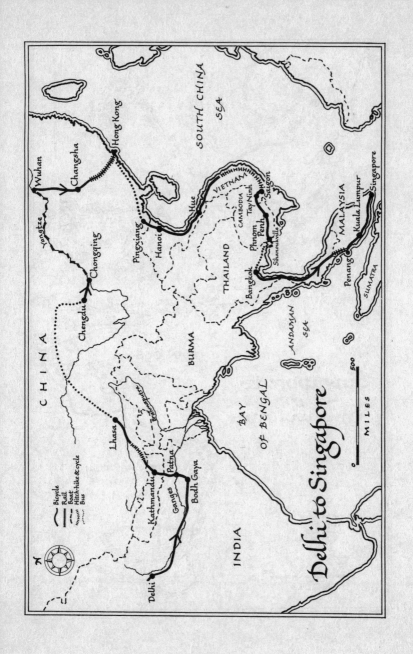

Delhi to Singapore

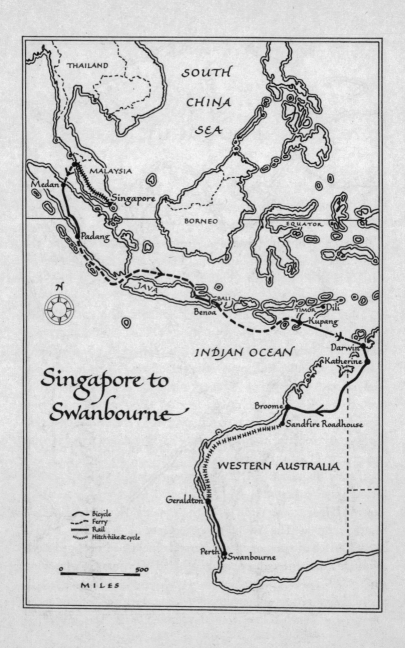

PROLOGUE

Swanbourne: Winter 1978

Talking to Johnny Ginger was always interesting, but the conversation I had with him that January morning on Cemetery Hill when we spoke of Captain Charles and duck-billed dolphins turned my world upside down.

Johnny was a fat, cherry-faced gardener who cycled every day through Swanbourne, my home village. His route never varied. He pedalled from his thatched cottage past St Swithun's Church and under the ancient avenue of lime trees that flanked the stately frontage of Swanbourne House. Once there, he would spend his days raking leaves, shooting pigeons and absorbing, with quiet serendipity, the choicest of pastoral gossip. Everybody in Swanbourne knew Johnny Ginger; but never as well as he knew all of them.

If anything happened in Swanbourne then Johnny Ginger heard about it first. He could tell you if Jack the shepherd was courting Lisa from Aston Abbotts, if Gary Hawsler drank too much cider at The Swan, if the badger at Ivy Farm bred a record litter of cubs or if old Bert Sheffield had dropped dead while his Bakelite radio played 'When The Saints Go Marching In'.

Johnny loved Swanbourne: he loved it with the calm wisdom of Atticus Finch's love for Maycombe, with the innocence of Diggory Venn's love for Egdon Heath and with all the unrequited intensity of Heathcliffe's love for the dark moors fringing Wuthering Heights. Throughout his life Johnny never spent a single night away from the village and even the sleepy town of Buckingham just up the road seemed an exotic and sophisticated colony to him. Swanbourne was his world.

Rumours persisted about Johnny Ginger. Some said he was over seventy years old, others that he was only forty. Some said he had once loved a girl in the village who had eloped to High Wycombe, while others thought the only woman in his life had been the imperious mother he had dutifully nursed to the grave. Several others imagined he could pick Derby winners, shoot rabbits from the hip, make elixirs from dandelions and even read the stars.

As with most village gossip, few of the rumours were true. Few were ever malicious either. If he had lived in a city Johnny Ginger might have been cast as a loner or a drunk; in Swanbourne, though, he was a mythical figure. Villagers respected consistency and no one was more consistent than Johnny: his permanence was a comfort.

The locals saved their waspish gossip for the freshly arrived commuters with their urbane airs and large, shiny cars. These were the people who skewed the concept of a bucolic idyll; while Johnny Ginger enhanced it. He may have been a simple, clumsy talker but when Johnny spoke of Swanbourne his words achieved a magic fluency, soothing like balm a community increasingly bewildered by the world outside.

I still have vivid memories of the day I spoke to Johnny Ginger on Cemetery Hill. I was eleven years old. The ground was carpeted with snow and my school friend, Simon Knocker, and I were pulling a toboggan past Elm Copse. A gaggle of Canada geese flew over, their wings swishing leisurely through frozen air. Johnny Ginger cycled past and doffed his cap. I dropped the toboggan's reins, ran to my bicycle and pedalled after him. 'Hey Mr Ginger, Mr Ginger.'

Johnny dismounted and began pushing his bike over the brow of Cemetery Hill. Under the chequered cap, which he never removed, his face was puce and beaded with sweat, his breathing laboured.

'Why don't you buy a car?' I asked.

'A car!' puffed Johnny. 'A car! What would I want with a car? I never leave Swanbourne. Besides, I hate cars. The world's a better place without 'em. I go everywhere by bicycle.'

'But you can't go everywhere by bicycle.'

'Swanbourne is everywhere to me, Tommy,' he said, offering me a walnut from a bag in his trench coat pocket.

'What happens if you want to go to Australia?'

'Why would I do that? I know your ancestor, Captain Charles, sailed there all those years ago. But why should I?'

'Well there are kangaroos and duck-billed dolphins and snakes that move faster than Mrs Clark's lurcher . . .'

'I don't want any of 'em. Swanbourne has enough for me. You just can't see it, can you, Tommy? Take a good look around you.'

He put his arm over my shoulder and pointed towards Swanbourne House. 'You see the sand at the end of the drive? That's my Sahara. The stream running by the football pitch, that's my Amazon and the one by Brises Barn, my Mississippi. Those little hummocks near Hoggeston are the Himalayas. The War Memorial, look really hard now, clearly it's the Eiffel Tower and the village pub, that's right, Tommy, the Ritz.'

To Johnny Ginger the grass was never greener than in Swanbourne. To me it was simply dull, a tiny cricket pitch that had become worn out by too much play in summer. I wanted to travel, the farther and wilder the better. To Johnny Ginger Swanbourne supplied enough dreams to last a lifetime and although he proved that a small world can boast a wide horizon I always wanted more.

'What about savages?' I demanded.

'Savages,' said Johnny. 'Well, I just talk to the vicar. He'll do – he speaks a different language altogether.' He imitated the vicar's voice and we both laughed.

'I'll bet you, Tommy,' he said, suddenly serious. 'I'll bet you I've already cycled to Australia. I've pedalled through this village more times than you've fired that catapult of yours. Thousands of miles. Even more than your Captain Charles. I'm fat now but I used to be as fit as a trout. It will be a long time before you catch up with me.'

'Well, I'm going to bicycle to Australia,' I said. 'Right now.'

'Off you go then. Here, you'd better take another walnut. Watch out for those savages.'

Of course I didn't go. I made it as far as Home Farm and stopped to have a snowball fight with the Wallace twins. But Johnny Ginger sparked an idea I was never able to shake and from that day on I was convinced it would only be a matter of time before I set off for Australia again – this time for real.

By some strange irony, the least travelled man I've ever met inspired me to pedal a push-bike halfway around the world.

INTRODUCTION

CASTING OFF

At my leaving party, drunk and surrounded by friends, I imagined myself in a kaleidoscope of gung-ho scenarios. Dodging mortars on the West Bank, coasting up and down Himalayan peaks, slaloming through Oriental traffic jams and finally breasting the finishing line in Australia.

My friends were more sceptical. Many saw my trip as rash, a last-ditch attempt to postpone growing up. They were right, of course, but this only fired my desire to make it a success, and all of them, however dismissive, liked the idea of chasing a dream. At the party, though, the insults were playful.

'Long haul cyclists often suffer from impotence, mate,' said Ed, 'but Alexandra tells us that won't make much difference.'

'Why not ride a motorbike, darling?' purred Ali. 'Much sexier. You could look like Marlon Brando instead of Jacques Tati.'

'Tom is twenty-nine years old,' shouted Napoleon, standing on his chair and playing to the crowd. 'He tells us twenty-nine is the perfect age to travel. The same age as his Captain Charles when he sailed to Australia. The same age as Buddha when he set off in search of nirvana. Captain Charles found a port, Buddha found enlightenment.'

5

'And, don't tell me,' I interrupted. 'I'll find myself.'

'You, you plonker, will be lucky if you find St Albans.'

Now, on the eve of departure, the boozy optimism had faded and I found myself sick with worry. I opened Alexandra's goodbye card which had become illegible after repeated readings. 'I'll be riding pillion with you every mile of the way,' she had promised when she last telephoned from her office in Hong Kong. But she wouldn't. I was on my own. That was the way I had wanted it – but I wasn't so sure now.

Outside, snow was falling, soft as ashes, forming glistening dunes on the roadside. I had chosen February as my leaving date so that I could conquer the Himalayas before they froze over in November. Bicycling through London in winter would be uncomfortable, but hitting Tibet at the wrong time would be suicide.

TIBET. From where I was sitting now, log fire crackling, Motown on the CD, it might as well have been on Jupiter or Mars.

My maps were splayed over the floor, a road-scarred tapestry of desert, mountain, jungle and red dirt. Then there were the cities – Paris, Rome, Athens, Damascus, Jerusalem . . . Like Monopoly street names I could reel them off in sequence without thinking. I had studied my miniaturized world meticulously, but now the time had come to fold it up and confront the real thing.

I inspected my 24-gear Condor Heritage, a robust touring bike with reinforced wheels made in Belgium, and Kevlar tyres. 'Kevlar is the stuff bulletproof vests are made from,' Monty at the cycle shop in Grays Inn Road in London had boasted. 'Not even sniper fire will deflate it.'

I had plumped for a tourer rather than a mountain bike because it would be so much faster on paved roads; a mountain bike would be more suited to the rough tracks of Nepal or

Sumatra, but these were only small sections of the route. I had to think about my journey as a whole.

That evening, without thirty kilos of panniers hooked on to it, the bike looked fragile and bare, like a yacht with its sails furled. But what a beast it would become tomorrow.

The bike, however, was the least of my worries. My mind was crammed with last-minute anxieties and potential disasters. It was illegal to ride a bike through China, the doom-mongers had warned me. In Syria I would be kidnapped by the Hezbollah or, if not, sold off as an Occidental love slave in a Damascus souk.

As usual, the best advice had come from Johnny Ginger. 'If you asked ten different villagers about Swanbourne you'd hear about ten very different places,' he once told me. 'The only way is to find out for yourself.'

I sat down at the dining room table with several newspapers spread out in front of me. The world news made grim reading: Israel tense after Yitzhak Rabin's assassination . . . Taiwan and China on the brink of war . . . Kurdish terrorism in southern Turkey. These previously distant events, the sort I would tut-tut about over morning coffee, were now linked to my fate; in fact I had started to take them almost personally.

If the nationals made for daunting reading, the local paper was even worse. My picture, morose and multi chinned, stared out from page five.

Journalist Tom Fremantle leaves Swanbourne, Buckinghamshire tomorrow to cycle to Swanbourne, Australia.

The English Swanbourne is the village which has been home to Tom's family for 200 years. The Australian Swanbourne is a tiny district on Australia's isolated west coast.

His 12,000 mile route passes through twenty countries and is expected to take a year. Tom intends to cycle all the way, apart from the obvious sections where he will hitch rides on boats.

12,000 miles, twenty countries, cycle all the way. Could these fantastic statistics really apply to me?

'Tom is setting out on the trail of his ancestors . . . capturing the spirit of his seafaring forebears.'

I looked around at the portraits of my motley ancestors lining the dining room walls. There was noble, square-jawed Admiral Thomas who fought with Nelson at Trafalgar. His wife, Betsey Wynne, a buxom matriarch and famous diarist hung beside him. Betsey's father, Richard, once described by Casanova as 'the most decadent young man I know' smiled down, rakish and puffy eyed, from above the wine rack.

But the ancestor most relevant to me now was Captain Charles Fremantle. There he posed above the fireplace, dripping with medals, sideburns the size of mole pelts; by turns a brilliant sailor and philandering rogue. I was grateful to him: it was Captain Charles who had provided me with a route for my bike ride.

The local paper continued:

In 1829 Tom's great, great, great uncle, Captain Charles Fremantle sailed to Western Australia, and the port of Fremantle – now a famous yachting venue – was named after him. Tom will be following loosely in his wake, cycling at least fifty miles a day. Swanbourne is only two miles away from Fremantle, near one of Australia's premier nudist beaches – just one of the many things that have changed since Captain Charles's time.

So that was it. The grand idea: Swanbourne – sleepy English village famed for its Norman church – to Swanbourne –

antipodean suburb famed for its under-dressed sunbathers. Hardly El Dorado or the Holy Grail but what the hell, it had a certain ring to it.

Like any journey, mine balanced uncertainly between the magical and the absurd. I had to realize its absurdities but also understand it was a chance in a million, a trip that so many dream of but never have the chance to fulfil. More than anything else, I had to be true to all those dreams.

Travellers over the years have pursued quests for the strangest reasons. William Dalrymple went on a pilgrimage to Outer Mongolia to pour sunflower oil over Kublai Khan's ruined palace; Bruce Chatwin wandered Patagonia in search of dinosaur hair; Sir Richard Burton had himself circumcised as a way to infiltrate Mecca; and Beowulf travelled in the hope of a glorious death.

All I wanted was to pedal halfway round the world to a place called Swanbourne. Once there, I would tear a postcard of Captain Charles to shreds, cast the pieces into the sea and watch them spiral, like skittish ghosts, into the depths. Then I would throw in a walnut, like the one Johnny Ginger had given me on Cemetery Hill. The time had come to lay my heroes to rest.

CHAPTER ONE

PROBLEMS WITH POTENCY

The final pannier clicked into place. I mounted my bike and pedalled down the gravel drive towards my parents who were waiting by the road. They looked vulnerable somehow, frail and silver haired, bracing themselves against the cold; my mother in a cardigan and tatty plimsolls, my father, an ex-naval commander, in a tweed jacket and a tie decorated with kingfishers.

'Good luck, old boy,' said my father, slapping me on the back. He's called me old boy since I was seven years old. The three of us stood looking at each other with nervy smiles of reassurance.

'Well, better be off then,' I said, brushing a coating of frost off my gloves. 'I'll write from Paris.' I pedalled fast out of Swanbourne – away from my waving parents, away from the legacy of Captain Charles, away from the world of Johnny Ginger.

'I'M RIDING A BLOODY PUSH-BIKE TO AUSTRALIA!' I shouted, punching the air. It was a huge relief to be off at last. My main fear had been delay – even the day before the roads had been choked with snow – but now it was bright and the sun's rays carved through the mist. The landscape was still familiar: I had cycled through the hills to Stewkley many times with my childhood friend, Simon Knocker. In summer we used to stop, throw our bikes into a ditch and climb up hay ricks, or catch red admirals in jam jars. One winter we made a snowman, and old Mr Reeve, the gamekeeper, kerpowed it with his shotgun . . .

Stop daydreaming, Tom. Focus on the big ride. I looked down at my digital milometer. 0003.00. Only another 11,997 miles to go. I began to sing. Everything was going to be just fine. SPREEEESPREEEE. A rasping noise was coming from my back wheel. No, no, no. Not today. Not now. The shame would be unbearable. 'Cyclist Tom Fremantle rode just three miles yesterday before returning home, his trans-world dream in tatters . . .' I pushed my bike on to the pavement and ripped off the panniers in dismay. As there was a payphone nearby I decided to call Phil, my mechanic.

'In trouble already, mate?' he asked sleepily. 'I'm sure this didn't happen to Captain Charles. God Almighty, what time is it?'

'Sorry Phil, but the bungee tying down my tool kit has coiled round my sprocket.'

'Painful. You'll have to cut it – but be gentle; mind it doesn't twist your derailleur and whatever you do, don't panic.'

The first time I met Phil, a portly man with a Lord Kitchener moustache, he was sitting in an oil slick surrounded by bicycle entrails, listening to 'The Boys Are Back In Town' by Thin Lizzy. But Phil's muddled workshop belied a very tidy mind. He had taught me, the king of the cack-handed, to fix any puncture with the dexterity of a master surgeon.

As I worked on the bike, various early risers, including Roger, the manager of Swanbourne Post Office, pulled over to offer their assistance. It was all most embarrassing. After chopping free the bungee with my nail scissors I began reloading. 'Know your panniers,' Phil had told me. 'Think of that bicycle as your home.'

I had two small panniers attached one each side of the front wheel. The left one contained my camera gear: a Canon EOS 500 with a single 28–80mm lens and a dozen slide films. On top of this were two brand new, buckram diaries in which I planned to write my journal. This pannier would be my memory trove, irreplaceable, the most valuable room in my mobile home.

The front right pannier held my books: *Don Quixote* by Cervantes, Ted Simon's *Jupiter's Travels*, a pocket SAS survival guide, Captain Charles's journal and some torn-out pages of Lonely Planet's *Western Europe on a Shoestring*. This was my least disciplined room: what lunacy let me pack a thousand-page novel about a hapless Spanish knight which weighed more than all my shirts put together?

In my handlebar bag I kept ready-to-use or miscellaneous items: my bike's Allen keys and puncture repair kit, a torch, a lighter, two biros, a mug, the map I was using that day, a photo of Alexandra, some aspirin, a woolly hat, a packet of Fisherman's Friends, my sewing kit, Swiss Army penknife, compass and a bog roll.

The right back pannier contained clothes for every climate, a frugally filled sponge bag and a special camping towel the size of a chess board. The opposite pannier held a goose-down sleeping bag, an inflatable mat and a North Face Tadpole – a very light, pitch-wherever-you-like tent. Under all this were my mess tins and XGK stove which could burn at high altitudes with all sorts of fuel – kerosene, petrol and, if desperate, whisky.

Bungeed to the back rack was my tool kit and spares including an emergency tyre coiled in a figure of eight. On top of this was a small rucksack full of medical kit – bandages, syringes, antibiotics, iodine tablets to purify water, cloves to chew for toothache and a twelve-pack of condoms. (In emergencies they can hold up to two litres of water, so the SAS told me.)

As I hitched my panniers back on I realized that a large part of every day would be spent packing and repacking this unwieldy new home of mine. But it was worth it. Extensive kit would enable me to be self-sufficient, to travel with an edge of spontaneity like the explorers of Captain Charles's generation, not knowing what loomed on the horizon. Unlike most modern travellers I had the privilege of time. I could shun aeroplanes or any other hasty transport that blurred the landscape. I wanted to coast along, swallowing beetles in the wind, alive to all the earth's subtle pulses.

I finally reached my sister's home in north London late in the afternoon and joined the family for steak and chips. After a glass of red wine I fell asleep at the kitchen table.

Fanny, Shaun and their baby, Theo, waved as I pedalled into the morning dark towards Swiss Cottage. It was raining but my Gore-Tex jacket and freshly fed belly did an admirable job of fending off the cold. My shoulders were aching already and my backside, despite generous padding, felt blistered.

I freewheeled down to Hyde Park Corner; cycled past Boadicea and over the Thames until I reached Peckham where I stopped for tea in a café full of road workers in Day-Glo anoraks. They were laughing over a story in the tabloids about Scandinavian men having higher sperm counts than their British counterparts. Being both British and about to spend a year with my testicles imprisoned in Lycra I was surely bottom of any potency league. Depressed at this chilling thought I cycled out of the capital.

Journal – opening entries:

9 a.m.   My mood is fine. I only have to make it to Tonbridge today – about thirty-seven miles. I am feeling strong and focused. My vigorous training, all those trial runs to Milton Keynes and Drayton Parslow village hall, has paid off. By tomorrow I will have clocked up well over 100 miles. The rain has stopped and the wind is light. Passing lorry drivers wave at me in encouragement. I sing 'My Way' with great animation.

11.30 a.m.   What the hell made me go through with this débâcle? I've never taken so long to cycle up a hill. A storm is brewing, the sky resembles Michelangelo's *Last Judgement* and I need a piss. I'm too fat and probably already impotent. I sing 'My Way' with great rancour, when my laboured, high-pitched breathing allows.

Eventually, I reached Badsell Park, a rare-breed farm near Tonbridge owned by my cousins, Simon and Celia Preston. Once inside I drank some tea, draped my sodden clothes like bunting across a variety of radiators and sank into a hot tub with Cervantes. Much later I awoke, shivering, *Don Quixote* face down in the tepid suds.

The following morning I was stirred by the distinctive hiss of a sizzling breakfast. It reminded me that soon the luxury of hot baths and home cooking would be over. In Dover I would have no relatives or friends to stay with – I would be alone and the trip would finally begin. But today I was going to be joined by Nic, a hard-smoking Greek friend. He arrived at dawn in a bobble hat and Chelsea football scarf.

As we set off up the rough farm drive, the front pannier containing my camera bounced off. The wind, the cold and a preoccupied mind meant that I did not even notice and Nic had to stop and collect it for me. This was upsetting – not even out of England and almost a pannier short. 'Stay sharp, Tom,' said Nic. 'Tomorrow, there will be nobody to pick up the pieces.'

As we headed east there was still evidence of snow, little cusps of white on the ploughed land. Near Dover we confronted a steep hill which twisted wildly, like a helter-skelter. We slogged up it and passed a child in a red balaclava flying a kite. At the summit Nic took a picture of some plump hill ponies before we gingerly freewheeled down to the main road.

With chilled sweat and chattering teeth I looked ahead at Nic weaving along on his mountain bike. I framed a mental picture of him tonight with his wife and baby, sitting in a warm room, reading a newspaper. Lucky bastard. What the hell did I think I was doing? I could just jack this whole sorry episode in, surrender to a life of security and routine. Why was I forever riding against the wind?

The East Cliff Hotel was impossible to miss with its flaky pink façade. Outside the front door was a disused phone box luxuriant with moss and weeds and inside a set of multi-pronged deer antlers perched above the check-in desk. Fifteen quid a night – over budget but I was soaked and couldn't face camping. I said farewell to Nic and dragged my bike indoors.

'My gott, my gott, look at yoos, just look at yoos!' said a large, weather-beaten woman, grabbing my bicycle. 'There is no room but never mind. Never mind!'

She pushed my bike through the dimly lit hallway and into a bedroom with a kangaroo doormat and a collage of Aboriginal faces above a double bed. I took the panniers off the bike – each had been insulated with a dustbin liner so luckily my gear was still dry. The woman, a deadringer for Giles's cartoon

Grandma, started to peel off my jacket. I wondered where this was heading.

'Is, um, this my room?' I asked.

'No, no. This is my son's room. He is Hungarian.' She hung up my jacket and tried to pull off my jumper.

'Oh, fine, so, um, surely we shouldn't be in your son's room?'

'Yes, of course. He is my son. This is his room.' My jumper was removed and she gestured to my damp tracksuit bottoms.

'Yes, quite so. Is your son, um, used to sharing a bed with strangers?'

'My son, yes, yes.'

She loosened her hair and looked in the mirror. I quickly stammered an explanation about my trip and told her I was pedalling to Australia. My mind was racing. This was my first night alone. I was dog-tired and about to be seduced by an elderly Hungarian on her son's bed watched by a posse of magnificent Aborigines caulked in ochre paint.

'Yoos cycling to Orstralia! Oh, yes. This room is yoos, all yoos. My son, Victor, is motorbike to Orstralia right now.' She gestured towards a photograph of a swarthy youth astride a Harley-Davidson. Victor started off in a group of twenty riders, she explained, but due to crashes, disillusion or sickness only four of them made it to Sydney. 'I know what it is like for yoos. Tonight I pretend yoos my son.'

Once I realized her affection was maternal, I relaxed. Her name was Vicki Neuberger. She had set up the East Cliff over fifteen years before to provide Dover with some budget accommodation and insisted, bless her laddered tights, that I stayed for free.

'Yoos must live cheap,' said Vicki. 'My Victor spend so little on his journey.'

My budget was between £3,000 and £5,000, depending on how long I travelled. This would include everything – food, lodging, visas, boat rides, post and camera film. I had decided to carry no more than £500 in travellers' cheques at any one time and had sewn a credit card into the lining of my sleeping bag in case my money belt was stolen.

Although my travels were self funded I had received the odd discount on my equipment because I was riding in aid of Stoke Mandeville Hospital in Aylesbury. I had no connection with the hospital other than it was close to Swanbourne and its crusading work on behalf of spinal patients had always impressed me. Stoke Mandeville had set up a trust fund specifically for the bike ride and we hoped to raise £20,000 to buy hi-tech wheelchairs.

The trip, though, was very much a selfish one: I was doing it principally for myself, not Stoke Mandeville. In some ways the charity angle was simply a way to assuage the guilt of over a year's freedom, but it did lend the trip an added focus and during my darkest hours would provide a fine incentive not to give up.

Vicki had left and I was lying in her son's bed reading *Jupiter's Travels* by Ted Simon. Simon is a journalist who spent four years roaring around the world on a motorbike. Doing the same had crossed my mind. It would certainly have been a faster option aping Simon and the host of other adventure bikers. There was Che Guevara who cruised a Norton 500cc through Latin America in the 1950s; Lawrence of Arabia, when not on camel back, vroomed across the Syrian deserts; biker journalist Hunter S. Thompson spent a year blazing around California 'like Ghengis Khan on an iron horse', tailing a gang of Hell's Angels.

Bicycling by contrast is more the domain of fitness nerds and country vicars, but the sport also has its travel heroes. A favourite of mine is doughty Thomas Stevens who spent three years riding a penny-farthing around the world back in the

1880s. Then there was Dervla Murphy. In 1963 she cycled from Dunkirk to Delhi on a dilapidated single gear bike armed with only £65 and a pistol to shoot wolves. Even in the intense heat of Pakistan's precipitous Karakoram Highway she would sometimes clock up over one hundred miles a day and here I was, struggling with the gentle humps of Kent.

The bicycle won the day for me because of its simplicity. A bicycle can be tied to a fishing smack or dragged over a landslide, it needs no special permits and is simple to fix. It also offers a physical challenge, that strangely appealing chance for the traveller to prove, in the words of the Prophet Mohammed, that 'a journey is a fragment of hell'.

Jupiter's Travels was keeping me awake. I was intrigued to know how Ted Simon would sum up his time on the road. What does a journey that long do to a man? Can it be justified?

Psychologically, my mileage was a major worry. I simply couldn't get my head round it. Like the Eskimos, who measure distance in *sinik*, or 'sleeps' – the number of nights a journey requires – my trip could not be gauged by conventional methods. The distance was too huge to be imagined all at once. So I decided that every night, whether it be one mile clocked up or a hundred miles I would view it as a little triumph, a valuable part of a much larger equation. Not 11,876 miles to conquer but 124 miles defeated. I felt the need to play by my own rules – my own *sinik*.

The journey was firing up my senses, especially tonight: the ochre face paint of the Aborigines above my bed almost seemed to glow, the mineral stink of the mud on my bike tyres was rich and pungent, Vicki Neuberger's smudged lipstick and generous heart had touched my long-dormant soul. Every nuance seemed relevant now. I had not expected this sort of experience in England – maybe I had just never looked for it before. Whatever, it was clear my trip had finally begun.

I glanced up at Victor's photo, wondering how he was coping now that his quest was over. What curious fate to be lying in the bed of a stranger who was at the other end of the world, 12,000 miles away. A stranger who in two months would be back in this same bed, looking up at the Aborigines, his head spinning with impossible memories.

CHAPTER TWO

HITCH-HIKING JESUS

The ferry docked at lunchtime. I unlocked my bike from its hawser and sped down the gangplank towards the cobbled streets of Calais. Cobbles are bad news on a bicycle. Even wearing Lycra shorts (which usually incubate one's bouncing groin so reliably) makes no difference on cobbles. It feels like tap dancing naked.

To add insult to injury, Calais was a hole, its ancient centre blighted by stunted tower blocks and advertising billboards. Calais was the last place in France to be surrendered by the British in the sixteenth century. At the time, a bereft Queen Mary said the port, then in its heyday, would stay forever engraved on her heart. If she could see Calais today she would insist on a bypass.

The beach area however was a slight improvement. I stopped, for sentimental reasons, in a café called L'Alexandra and ordered a hot chocolate. I had forgotten what fun French cafés can be. The barman, wearing a kepi and smoking a cheroot, poured a cocktail with languid panache. A young boy shared a milkshake with his gap-toothed mother, while opposite them a couple of jolly girls in leather trousers battled with the pinball machine. There was an atmosphere of mild hedonism, never to be witnessed in England on a wet, weekday afternoon.

After draining the chocolate I weaved my way on to the coastal road. The sky was grey and hazy, the wind strong. A line of black overalls flapped like restless crucifixes, on a farmhouse washing line. Bare-branched oaks cast long shadows while stone angels with blunt swords and sharp wings sprouted from the hillside marking the graves of the war dead.

One of the dead was my grandfather's elder brother, Halford. Eighteen-year-old Halford, a fine looking Eton scholar with an exceptional gift for poetry, had landed at Boulogne in May 1915 eager 'to repel the Boche'. He was killed four months later on the Western Front, lacerated by shrapnel. A fellow officer described Halford's final battle in a letter to my great grandfather, its noble words a pathetic testimony to that unimaginable time: 'It is wonderful to look back and see how well Halford did his job at eighteen-years-old, when he should have been at Sandhurst instead of commanding troops in this grim war . . . over 430 men fell with him . . . The Company Sergeant Major told us never had a battalion fought so gallantly against such heavy odds. Webb and myself were the only two officers left, and we feel ashamed of being alive.'

Halford was not killed instantly: he had been convalescing for several weeks, and, had septicemia not set in, would probably have returned home. His parents visited him in France before he died, but he was too weak to move: he was never to see Swanbourne again.

At least Halford was dead, not 'missing'. At Thiepval near Amiens there is a memorial arch in honour of 73,367 Allied soldiers who went missing, either drowned in mud or blown to irretrievable pieces. Thankfully, Halford's fate was known, his memory lives on still in his faded school photograph, his letters and poetry. His name is chiselled forever in Etaples's military cemetery and Swanbourne's ancient church.

Although it is easy to romanticize war victims, especially those who died in the Great War, Halford was perhaps the last of a generation of unshakeable patriots. He loved his country in a way many teenagers would find risible now, sharing the heroic naivety of his soon-to-be-slain contemporary, the poet Rupert Brooke. I am proud to think Halford will always be 'some corner of a foreign field/That is for ever England . . ./In that rich earth a richer dust concealed . . .' Although today's England would no doubt be a 'foreign field', compared to the one he left behind.

The day was fading fast by the time I reached Wimereux, an elegant village fringed by a wide, purling river. Several trees on the high street were lit up with strings of gently pulsing fairy lights and the delicatessen had a brace of mallards hanging from its front wall together with ripe smelling cheeses the size of cannon balls.

It was a pretty spot and I was tempted to stop, pitch my tent and retire to the warm glow of one of the local taverns, perhaps to join in a game of cards with the regular barflies or write some letters by the fire. But somehow it seemed important to reach Bolougne where Halford, then aged only eighteen, had first landed in France. I pressed on into the twilight, freewheeling into the port centre an hour or so later.

It didn't take too long to track down a cheap hotel; and the one I finally opted for described itself as *très jolie* on its door sign. Indeed it was *jolie* in every way – the décor, the waitress, the music. The only weak link was the boss, perhaps the least *jolie* fellow I'd ever met, who leaned against the reception desk, sipping a green liqueur, eyeing me up like a lugubrious spaniel. I hauled my panniers upstairs, ate a *baguette* and fell asleep fully clothed, helmet included. It was an uneventful first night overseas.

Two days later I was on the outskirts of Paris, having pedalled through the flat, misty farmland of Picardy. It was a stretch of road Flaubert described as 'a bastard land where the accents of the people and the contours of the ground are characterless'. I agreed with him although I had no complaints about the characterless contours; I suspected they were far easier to pedal across than charismatic ones.

Paris traffic is always a frightener – even more so on a bicycle – and it took me several hours to reach my friend Sandrine's studio on the Quai de Jemmapes, weaving the bike through the suburbs of Saint-Denis, negotiating the one way streets, the four-lane highways and the cobbled roundabouts. Acting on a misguided whim I had also decided to pedal via the Arc de Triomphe for a photocall. It was early in the trip and I was anxious to obtain photographic proof for my sponsors, however awkward the setting. Place Charles de Gaulle Étoile, though, was a traffic war zone; thirteen roads converged on it from all directions and so I leant my bike against a bollard at the top of the Champs-Elysées, ran the gauntlet of deranged Vespas, clicked the camera, remounted and pedalled off down the Quai des Tuileries. No sweat!

Soon I was in a long tunnel. Cars and lorries flashed their lights and drivers shouted abuse; it was obvious I wasn't supposed to be there but it was too late to turn back. The bicycle sped along straight and furious, as if stuck in a high-speed Scalextric. The darkness, the confined space and the magnified roar of engines were utterly terrifying. Finally, puce from hard pedalling and exhaust fumes, I was flushed out into the light. Tunnels would remain a phobia for the rest of the trip.

After another hour of Parisian traffic I finally tracked down the tranquil Quai de Jemmapes, bisected by a thin, cocoa-coloured canal. Sandrine buzzed the intercom and I shoved my bike into the flagstone hallway, staggered up six flights of stairs and flung open her plyboard door. Sandrine's studio walls were lined with a selection of dog-eared Tintin posters and Eric, her boyfriend, had left his drum kit strewn all over the floor.

My body was still fizzing with surplus carbon monoxide. Never, I vowed to myself, would I inhale such a chestful of fumes in a single afternoon again. I walked over to the window, picked up a potted hyacinth and breathed in the blossom.

Sandrine emerged from the kitchen. 'Salut Tom,' she said, pecking me three times on the cheeks in the charmingly protracted way Parisians do. Her hair smelt of lemons. A vintage radio, the size of a bread bin, crackled the news in the background.

It soon became clear that I could not have chosen to visit Sandrine at a worse time; her father had died a month before and she was clearly still tired and shaken. We sat down with a tray of tea and she reminisced in prolix bursts about her childhood, from time to time gesturing to a photo of her father, a Lear-like character with a pallid complexion and explosive beard. 'He looks a little wild, don't you think?' asked Sandrine, smiling with affection.

'He looks like you,' I replied.

'Shh, ssshhhh.' Sandrine suddenly lifted a finger in the air. She was listening to the news on the radio. 'That liar Chirac,' she said. 'At least my father will not have to suffer him any more.'

'What's happened?' I asked.

Her dark eyes blazing, Sandrine savaged the French premier's politics. She was still bristling over the rail strikes the previous winter, as, like many Parisians, she had been forced to ride a bicycle. But her true bête noire – and the subject of the broadcast – was the recent French nuclear testing in the Pacific, an issue she felt had tarnished her country's reputation on a global scale. I assured her that Chirac's nuking of New Zealand waters had sparked fury everywhere, even in Swanbourne. One local eco-warrior had threatened to drive a muck spreader to Paris and spray a ton of dairy slurry into the River Seine.

'Good,' said Sandrine, grinding her Gauloise violently into the hyacinth pot. 'Our leader speaks bullshit, now he can drink some too.'

She stood up and turned off the radio.

'You and me, however, we will drink something much finer,' she announced. 'Let's go to the pub.'

In Quai de Jemmapes, after the frivolity of my first evening, I spent a surprising amount of time on routine chores: washing clothes, writing postcards, cleaning the bike. It had not been the joyous reunion I'd anticipated. Sandrine was kind and hospitable towards me but it was easy to see she was still very cut up about her father's death. She was also struggling to find photographic work and my presence was hugely intrusive – my bicycle and sleeping bag alone occupied much of her *bijou* studio.

To give her some space, I spent my time wandering old haunts.

'Don't trust Paris,' Sandrine warned me, as I set off the first morning. 'It has more faces than a pair of dice.'

But Paris looked beautiful in a bleak, melancholic way: the silver birch rendered with mire, the starlings chattering, a tramp blowing plangent scales on his harmonica. I walked along the Seine, watching the *bateaux mouches* pass by or peeking at the work of the icy-breathed pavement artists. None of it bought back any fond memories and even Notre-Dame's familiar, gargoyle-topped façade was distorted by scaffolding, its huge doors bolted.

It was only when I reached the steep steps leading up to Sacré-Coeur that I was finally warmed by nostalgia. I had last visited it as an eighteen-year-old, backpacking abroad for the first time. My companion at the time had been James Fry, my oldest friend. Sitting on those crowded steps, cushioned by rucksacks, high above the world, I had told Jim about the bike ride. It was the first time I had mentioned it to anyone and Jim jumped at the idea. We plotted the wildest route possible on a map at the back of his diary, thinking nothing of traversing the Burmese Golden Triangle or the wastes of Siberia. We shook hands and toasted each other with duty-free Finnish vodka. We even lit a candle inside Sacré-Coeur's distinctive dome to christen our dream.

Although time did not diminish our friendship it did snuff out the idea of a joint adventure. Jim is an engineer for London Underground, slowly climbing the greasy pole of promotion. He is not madly ambitious but a year-long break would have been impossible. 'My dreams have changed, mate,' he told me. 'I'm sorry. I'm just not eighteen any more.'

Don Quixote successfully teamed up with Sancho Panza, Phileas Fogg with Passepartout and Candide with the ever-optimistic Pangloss but, deep down, I always knew my trip would have to be solo.

Once again I lit a candle in Sacré-Coeur's dark chancel.

The two weeks after leaving Paris were psychologically the worst of the trip. Odysseus warned his crew that 'the time for supreme vigilance is at the very end of a journey', but to my mind the beginning of a trip is the most vulnerable time.

You set off full of confidence and brio, imagining life on the road as a long rose-tinted adventure, but reality sets in when you find yourself riding every day through a miasma of mist and drizzle. The daily grind of packing and balancing your damp panniers becomes increasingly draining while the flat roads, the dark cathedrals and the ranks of stunted vines do nothing to stir your soul. The hostels and campsites are largely deserted and your confidence deflates like a slow puncture.

But worst of all, you realize that this is how life will be for the next year. You desperately want to gloat over the poor souls you watch driving to work, to enjoy a glowing sense of *schadenfreude* as you compare their humdrum lives with your adventure-filled days. But secretly all you want to do is join them. You cannot see through the mist towards the sunshine and the mountains, nor can you anticipate the lively camaraderie of the road that awaits behind that persistently opaque skyline. How true it is to say that without a clear horizon the traveller despairs.

Thankfully this phase did not last too long. In these sloughs of morale, not just in France but throughout my journey, somebody always seemed to be there when I needed to lift my spirits. In Valence that somebody was Hugh. I met him in the youth hostel dormitory, where, other than a reclusive Norwegian, we were the only two guests.

There was something strange about Hugh. He was about forty, very pale and he spoke with the calm authority of a man who knew things that I clearly did not. He told me he was driving to a friend's house in St-Tropez where he planned to spend his time hitch-hiking around the coast.

'Why hitch-hike when you have a car?' I asked him, over dinner. He sounded like an alternative Johnny Ginger.

'I have an isolated job,' he replied, in a brittle Glaswegian accent. 'Hitching helps me meet people. But best of all, it's based completely on trust.'

'What is this isolated job of yours?'

'I'm a priest.'

'A *priest*!'

'I belong to an order called the Priests of the New Heart of Jesus,' he explained, amused at my surprise. 'We remind people that Jesus was human, a teacher not a god. That he wept and felt fear like one of us.'

Hugh became a priest at the age of twenty-four and had been a determined celibate ever since. He confided though that he had fallen madly in love just before taking his vows and it had put his faith to the ultimate test: he had had to choose between the girl or Jesus.

'Why couldn't you have chosen both?' I asked.

'Love that strong can only be directed one way,' replied Hugh, sipping his cassis. 'Believe me, it tore me apart for a while. The girl was so real compared with Jesus who I'd never seen; but I still loved him more. Sometimes, if I watch a romantic comedy like *When Harry Met Sally*, I wonder what I'm missing. I mean, that Meg Ryan is *gorgeous*. But someone told me if you've made love once, you won't ever be able to stop.' Hugh laughed nervously, afraid he had said too much.

'Do you miss this girl?'

'Every day,' said Hugh wistfully. 'But I'm still sure I made the right choice.'

'Well, this is the first time I've spoken to a priest who hitch-hikes and chats about his love life,' I told him. 'It's all very refreshing and you haven't even accused me of being a worthless pagan!'

'God will find you in his own way,' said Hugh, with calm assurance. 'I don't believe in preaching fear and guilt. Besides, it's good for me to speak to people who don't belong to the monastery. If Jesus was here today he'd have hitch-hiked his way across the world as a means of staying in touch with his followers. He might even have ridden a bicycle.' He paused, his face wrinkled in thought. 'Actually no, that's just ridiculous.'

The next morning I pedalled off early towards Avignon. I was delighted to discover that the mist had evaporated and, with sunlight lancing through the roadside conifers, finally I could see the road ahead. Hugh drove past me in his hatchback. He pulled over and cranked down his window. 'God bless you, you crazy Englishman.'

'Watch out for Meg Ryan,' I shouted back. 'I hear she's got a thing for holy hitch-hikers.' Hugh tooted his horn and was gone. Whether it was his faith or his frankness, I don't know, but chatting to him had certainly lifted my spirits.

Some of the farmland I was passing resembled the hedge-rowed patchwork of the Home Counties. Elegant, silver-coated Charollais cattle occasionally came into view, chomping on sugar beet or turnips. But it was not pure country: many of the fields were dotted with pylons, and industrial chimneys occasionally scarred the horizon.

Once I skirted the Roman arch at Orange I was pleased to see the attractive, hodgepodge farmland of Provence unfolding around me.

It was almost dusk by the time I reached Avignon, the City of Popes. I quickly set up my tent at the campsite. The single green dome seemed lonely amid the camper vans. After drinking some soup I huddled in my sleeping bag and watched my frozen breath plume upwards, the opal crescent of the moon glinting thinly through the canvas.

The following morning I pedalled over the River Rhône and past the imposing Palace of the Popes whose sharp, grey turrets dominated the skyline. It amused me to think that in the fourteenth century this little town had usurped Rome as the centre of the Catholic faith and, if it had not been for the outstanding debauchery of several of Avignon's popes, the Papacy might have stayed in France to this day.

I cycled on in glorious sunshine through quaint but crowded Aix-en-Provence, and then down to Marseilles, France's second biggest city, in time for my thirtieth birthday. THIRTY YEARS OLD. 'The promise of a decade of loneliness, a thinning briefcase of enthusiasm', as F. Scott Fitzgerald put it. But surely this did not apply to me; I had no need to analyse my place in society. No home, no job, no wife and thankfully no briefcase. Not a care in the world barring thousands of miles of potentially inhospitable terrain and an increasingly dodgy sperm count.

At the sprawling youth hostel in Marseilles I met Lesley Iwai, a half-Japanese girl who lived in Utah. Lesley was tiny, quiet, very pretty and weighed down by a rucksack so new and shiny that it glowed like a beetle carapace. She was attending a Swiss finishing school but had escaped for the weekend. I could not have fallen in with a more perfect companion with whom to celebrate middle age.

Together we walked along the frenzied main street, La Canebière – nicknamed 'can o' beer' by British sailors – and down to the old port. It was hard to imagine that over 2,000 years ago some creaky Greek galleons had landed here and founded what was now this elegant rash of concrete surrounding us. I breathed in, inhaling the briny stink of the sea, the appetizing wafts of fish frying on the harbour-front skillets and, best of all, Lesley's musky perfume. You're a lucky soul, Tom Fremantle, I thought to myself.

Suddenly, behind us, there was the clip clop of hooves. A frisky piebald horse was being ridden by a girl holding a trident. The girl had long jet black hair and was crowned with a tiara of red carnations, her muscular physique encased in a shining bronze cuirass. She looked fearsomely brazen and reminded me of a picture I had once seen of Hippolyte, Queen of the Amazons.

Lesley and I ran over to see what was happening. Hippolyte was heading a procession; behind her were dozens of bicyclists wearing blue wetsuits and tailing them were saxophonists in top hats, children in white masks, clowns juggling apples and even the occasional semi-naked limbo dancer wielding a fire-brand. It was a scene straight out of Rabelais – we had hit the city's annual carnival.

Lesley and I were gathered into the swirl. We surged through the crowds, firing off our cameras, dancing to the drum beats – the nautical smells now drowned out by the stink of burgers and marijuana. Marseilles is best known for its mean streets, its violence and crime, but the carnival had put everyone in a good mood, all tensions burnt off in the sweaty tide of revellers.

After a couple of hours we peeled away from the hordes and headed up to Basilique Notre-Dame de la Garde, the highest point in the city and a place still pock-marked by rifle fire from the war. As we peered down, Marseilles appeared to be awash with colour, some houses bleached moon-white, others glowed with bright amber or green. Purple tresses of bougainvillaea hung from the decaying balconies. How wonderfully incongruous this vibrant, sprawling mess of a city is compared with the manicured fleshpots that dominate so much of the French Mediterranean.

Marseilles acts as a colourful crucible for immigrants from France's old colonies. Like bouillabaisse, the city's celebrated seafood stew, the human population of Marseilles boasts a mass of distinctive ingredients: Algerians, Moroccans and Tunisians are seasoned with migrants from Martinique and Guadeloupe and a peppering of Portuguese and Jews.

This racial jumble produces great cultural dynamism but inevitable tensions. While the Arabs are worried about the lack of mosques in the city despite the massive Muslim population, the French are more concerned that certain areas of Marseilles are turning into exclusively North African ghettoes. The immigrant population grows day by day. According to Lesley's guidebook, by the year 2015, over one third of births in France will be to non-European parents.

Later that evening Lesley and I stopped off in an Arab bar in the west of town. The owners were Algerian and poured us glass after glass of red wine, gritty with tannin. All the customers were Arabs, including one mustachioed Tunisian who regaled us with increasingly slurred tales of Hannibal before proposing marriage to Lesley and passing out on her lap. Abla, the jolly bejewelled barmaid, danced to a snake charmer's pipe while Omar, her hangdog husband, smoked a hookah. It was a fine birthday.

Lesley and I arrived back at the hostel smashed. We wavered on the doorstep looking at each other. 'You're thirty, you're *so* old,' she said, searching my eyes for the crow's-feet of an Old Testament prophet. She kissed my cheek, then lurched away and headed for bed in a steady zigzag. I fell asleep in one of the youth hostel's deckchairs and woke up feeling as if my head had been attacked by a posse of ham-fisted acupuncturists. Thirty years old. Jesus Christ. I popped three Anadin Extra and headed for the shower.

Five days later I was in very different surroundings, winding my way up the palm-fringed corniches of the Cote D'Azur. It didn't get much more glamorous than this: a coffee and watermelon breakfast in the hills above Cannes, lunch on the pebbly beach at Nice watching the rollerbladers swoop along the promenade and a siesta in the refreshing shade of an orange grove.

Near Monaco, exhausted by the corniches, I stopped to rest on an isolated bluff. Below were villas stuck to the slope like swallows' nests, their gardens bright with blossom and postage-stamp-sized swimming pools winking in the sunlight. The odd racing cyclist, luminous in Lycra, flew past before corkscrewing down towards Monte Carlo.

Monaco is a hard place to take seriously. Tucked between rocky outcrops, the pint-sized principality has a population of only 30,000 – less than half the capacity of Wembley Stadium. A mere 5,000 of these are locals or Monégasques. Not only does this lucky minority pay no taxes but they have the highest per capita income in Europe.

It is an attractive place, in an ostentatious sort of way, with beautiful boats, skyscrapers, casinos, people – but, like all fabulously affluent places, it lacks a sense of reality.

In fact, Monaco reminds me more of Hong Kong than any European port; both are modern, dynamic, slightly tacky and have the world's most stunning harbours. In each case this beauty stems from extravagance; but while Hong Kong could be compared with a savvy young entrepreneur battling for success, Monaco comes across more as a spoilt heiress, complacent with wealth.

At the time of my visit to Monaco the future of both places was equally nebulous – Hong Kong was soon to be returned into the gloating hands of mainland China and in Monaco a treaty was signed to the effect that if no heir was produced the principality would be absorbed into France. The Monégasques continue to hope that Prince Albert, a confirmed bachelor in his early forties, will eventually marry and secure the Grimaldi family's 700 year inheritance.

The Monaco youth hostel certainly boasted its own share of glamour in the shape of Tecla, Ami and Vanessa, three New York art school graduates. They waltzed into reception, suitcases on leads, sunglasses on heads, like strays from the catwalk. Tecla, the leader of the trio, was half Italian. Her Latin looks were offset by an accent more nasal than Ratso in *Midnight Cowboy*.

'We gotta sleep in a dawmitary!' she said, opening the door, her *retroussé* nose twitching. 'Why does it smell like a moose just died in here?'

I spent the afternoon wandering around Monte Carlo with the three of them. They were comical and fun to be with, excited by everything around them. In the posh Hotel de Place we all touched the bronze fetlock of Louis XV's horse which was supposed to bring gamblers luck, and ran out past the top-hatted doorman.

The girls were all nineteen years old and high on life. They didn't care where their journey led them, as long as it was fun. They were like leaves in the wind blowing wherever destiny intended them. That evening we were all blown back to the youth hostel.

Sitting in one of the armchairs was a gaunt, yellow-skinned man, his hair as tangled as a rook's nest. He picked his thumbnail with a penknife while Ami and Vanessa played chess. Tecla dabbed moist patches of cotton wool over her eyes.

'Where are you from?' I asked the man.

He looked up at me with eyes so still and sunken I thought he might be blind.

'Croatia.'

'Gosh,' exclaimed Tecla. There was a brief silence.

'I hitch-hike up to Italy from Dubrovnik, then across France,' said the man, sounding almost too tired to speak. 'I fighting four years. I want get away. Find work on the boat here. I sailor before the war.'

'What about your family?' I asked.

'All dead,' he replied softly. 'My wife and me in prison camp together for six month. She die two week before I let free. I return to my parents. They look after my baby daughter. Their house bomb. All dead.'

Tecla groaned and put her hand to her mouth. Her cotton wool patches had fallen to the floor.

'My brother killed at beginning of war. I no one left now. That why I here. Find work. Sail away. Start new.'

He was crying but his face expressed no emotion; the tears could just as easily have been raindrops or beads of sweat. Tecla put her hand on his back. None of us could think of anything to say. Vanessa offered him money but he turned it down, explaining that the youth hostel had agreed to let him stay for free. Slowly he stood up, nodded goodnight and shuffled off to the dormitory.

For a while we remained silent, absorbed in thought. Then Ami and Vanessa resumed their game of chess while Tecla riffled distractedly through an old magazine. I walked through to reception and nosily opened up the youth hostel ledger to look for the Croatian's name. It seemed important somehow. He had simply written Serge and the date, 22 March 1996. Under the section COUNTRY he had written Croatia, but his address he had left blank.

I suddenly felt ashamed of my earlier doubts. If a man like Serge could lose everything he loved in this world and still have the spirit to hitch-hike hundreds of miles to find work, it made everything seem possible. I vowed that on my return home, if I saw a hitch-hiker while driving, I would think of Serge thumbing his way to a new life or Hugh hitching for the sake of a simple chinwag, and, unless the hiker looked especially thuggish, would pull over.

It was raining as I approached the Italian border the following morning. This really would be a milestone – completing my first foreign country. I had been on the road for exactly one month and had pedalled over 1,000 miles. My confidence was swelling and I was excited about seeing Italy for the first time.

'YAHHHOOOO!' A voice echoed in the mist. 'WHOA HEY, WHOA!' I looked around, saw nothing and cycled on. 'HEY, COME ON. WHOA! Slow down.'

I braked hard, squinted through the mist and a hulk of a man came towards me, flailing his arms like an impassioned referee. He had a beard so impressive it looked as if he was midway through swallowing a small bear.

'WHOA THERE, WHOA THERE!' he howled. 'What are you, German or something?'

'No, I'm English.'

'Well, you act as though you're German; those guys never stop. The Japanese are even worse, they just shoot past like banshees.'

'I'm not surprised. Do you always get so excited when you see someone?'

'Tour cyclists should always stop for each other,' he said sententiously. 'It's good manners. My name's Dave. How long you been riding?' His accent, once calm, was an American drawl.

'I started in England and I've just finished France,' I replied. 'How about you?'

'Well, I been riding almost twenty years now. Had an office job in the States before. Used to sit there all day just dreaming of a long bike ride. So I decided to quit and started pedalling full-time in 1979. I guess I haven't stopped since.'

Dave had an aluminium mountain bike, its frame as scratched and dented as an old saucepan. He wore a blue T-shirt, rugby socks and well-worn cycle shoes. He usually camped rough, made a fire and washed in rivers, his one luxury a short-wave radio with which he listened to the BBC World Service.

This was a man who had cycled around the world several times. I – having merely crossed France – was trussed up in Gore-Tex, a reflective Sam Browne belt, a flashy helmet and five bulging panniers. I was like the new recruit fresh into the fray, compared to Dave, the battle-seasoned nomad.

'I'm not like you, Tom,' he said. 'I cycle exactly where I want – if there's a boring section I'll stick my bike on a bus. Cycling is my favourite transport but I'm not on a quest.'

'What do you do for money?'

'I don't need much,' he replied, flicking free a pebble lodged in his front tyre. 'I usually stop about every three months and land some building work. I'm not a bad artist and in summer make money in Switzerland painting portraits at the roadside.'

'Don't you ever want to settle?' I asked.

'I'd love to find a woman, a kindred spirit,' he mused. 'But I've become too self-reliant now and no woman wants a wanderer. I simply don't fit in with the nine-to-five world. If I stopped moving I'd probably die.'

He looked westward, his eyes glazed with sudden reverie. Perhaps he was thinking of past lovers, of all those lost chances of settling down, of painting seriously or starting a family. Perhaps he was just thinking of his next stretch of road.

'Why are you heading to France?'

'France,' he said, snapping out of his daydream. 'Oh, I love the French. They're so goddam intellectually arrogant – it's great. In America we elect presidents because they're good ol' boys, one of the people. Carter, Reagan, Clinton. In France they like 'em to be all haughty and superior like de Gaulle or d'Estaing and even Chirac; he may be a bit of a yob but he's still on a pedestal and the French love him.

'American presidents play down their intellect.' Dave tapped his temple with his forefinger. 'Bush spoke fluent French but didn't dare to as he might be seen as a grandee. The only French-style politician we had was Adlai Stevenson. When told he had the vote of every thinking man in America, he replied, "Oh hell, then I'll never be elected."'

Dave talked on. He had been on the road for years but his passion for travel was still fierce, his imagination as bright and frenzied as a string of firecrackers. He was happy to reminisce about his cycling highs – the King's Highway in Jordan and the hills of Crete. We could have talked for hours but the rain began to lash down and we both packed up. He gave me a book, *Roumeli* by Patrick Leigh Fermor and in return I gave him a dog-eared map of Provence.

'Quite soon, Tom, are some hills called Passo Bracco. They're tough. If you can make it up them, you might just manage the Himalayas. *Bon courage.*'

We parted in opposite directions. As I approached the Italian border I thought of Swanbourne; of Johnny Ginger pedalling along in his trench coat and chequered cap. Johnny Ginger and Dave, what a disparate pair; now I knew two people who had cycled as far as I intended to, albeit around two very different worlds.

Chapter Three

Black sheep, gold pig

It soon became apparent I was in Italy. Overloaded cars pulled alongside to cheer me on; scooter riders wore no helmets and balanced bambinos on their spluttering machines. The scent of pine and lavender was in the air. It all made a refreshing change from the relentless glamour of the Cote D'Azur.

My first port of call was San Remo where I stopped off to buy some oil at a cycle shop. An elderly customer, zipped up in yellow Lycra, came over to inspect my bike's Campagnola gearing. He slid a finger over the cog teeth, the veins on his forearm sticking out like bad wiring. He had the grave, fleshless look of a seasoned racing cyclist.

'Italy has the best cycle equipment in the world,' he told me. 'And some of the best riders.'

'Absolutely,' I agreed. 'But I thought French or American riders usually won the Tour de France.'

'Often, yes,' he replied, a touch defensively. 'But Italians too. Fausto Coppi won it twice back in the fifties and then, of course, there was Pierre Brambilla.' He whistled in approval.

'Brambilla was a great cyclist and such a gracious loser. In 1947 he lost the Tour de France on the last day. He ended up coming third but even so, he never stopped battling. That crazy Spaniard, Miguel Indurain, may have won five times in a row but there was nobody like Brambilla. An extraordinary Italian.'

I had read about Brambilla before and there was no denying he was an extraordinary Italian; but a mildly deranged one too. When not performing at his best the intensely competitive Brambilla would shout at himself, smash his thighs with his bike pump, slap his own face or starve himself of water even if there was plenty left in his bottle. Despite all this self-punishment he never achieved his dream of winning the Tour de France and, legend has it, ended up burying his bike in his garden as a sign he was no longer good enough to ride it.

The old man had started to talk about his own Herculean fitness schedule and I began to worry about the obsessive nature of cyclists. Was it contagious? Would it happen to me?

Take the story of Sean Kelly, the legendary Irish rider. During one Tour of Spain, Kelly developed the scourge of all racing cyclists, a boil on his bottom. If he visited the tour doctor Kelly knew he would be pulled out of the race, so he secretly had his backside sewn up by a local surgeon. Despite excruciating pain Kelly carried on riding until finally, while ploughing his way up a mountain, his severely strained stitches burst. The wound bled profusely and Kelly was forced to withdraw.

The intense dedication of cyclists is perhaps best exemplified by hard man Tommy Simpson, the first Briton to win the coveted yellow jersey for a stage of the Tour de France. Simpson, his brave heart revved with amphetamines, collapsed and died during the 1967 Tour. His last words: 'Put me back on my bike.'

I didn't know whether I should be impressed or appalled by such antics, but at this stage of my journey I certainly had no intention of beating myself with a bike pump, having my jacksie tampered with or even becoming a posthumous martyr to my sport. I decided to stick with the Johnny Ginger philosophy of cycling: if knackered, push. I knew my mettle was soon to be put to the test though, Passo Bracco was looming . . .

I navigated my way past Christopher Columbus's birthplace in Genoa and reached the Bracco's preliminary stages. This was the moment I had been dreading. If I was unable to conquer these cruel undulations surely the Himalayas or even the steppes of eastern Turkey would be beyond me. Maggots of fear began to eat away at my gut.

The first ascent started gently and I clicked through the gears as the incline steepened. The art of climbing hills is to forget. Forget the ache in the arch of your back, the sweat beading your eyes, the cramp in your fingers. You have to think of a million other things to distract your mind from your straining limbs. Anything will do – your all time favourite meals, your top five Beatles songs, even 'What would I be doing now if I wasn't pedalling up the mother of all gradients in a pair of tight shorts?'

But as the road twists up towards another acute corner, all you can focus on is the pain. You are already in the lowest possible gear and have at least another fifteen minutes to go before reaching the top. You no longer care whether 'Let It Be' had a slight edge on 'Hey Jude' or if Sichuan aromatic duck outflavours roast lamb served with redcurrant jelly. Even the sweeping coastal views have lost their allure.

All that matters is to crest the hill. You crave the glide down the other side; the cool air, the still pedals, the whoosh of speed. But this is all a long way off. You must grind on and on and on. You start to shout at yourself, to swear at yourself, to question your sanity as you whisper 'go, go, go' and shake your fist at a passing seagull; you bash your handlebars and groan for mercy when the next set of switchbacks unfurls.

Then suddenly it's over. You are at the top, high above the russet cliffs and ultramarine sea. The pastel-coloured houses of a distant harbour shimmer invitingly up ahead.

You wipe the sweat, tears and snot from your face, your rage subsides and you laugh as you torpedo downhill, slaloming wildly from side to side as the wind stretches your face. You eat a slab of chocolate and then sing as if it's opening night at La Scala; you free the brakes a little more, stick out your legs as you *schuss* through a puddle, shouting 'YES, YES, YES' in a rhapsody of relief.

But already the next hill is approaching. Your belly knots in anxiety; you accelerate to gain the best possible lead up the rise; you feel the bike slowing; you click the gears down and pedal hard again, your legs whirring around like a wind-up toy; but the bike is crawling as you cry out 'please, God, please'. The heat seems to pulse in your head. The pain sharpens. You want to be anywhere but here. *Anywhere.*

Until suddenly you *are* here. At the top. Without pushing once. You have managed to slave your way up and over two hills. No, not hills, mountains. *Two mountains.* Mountains that one month ago would have seemed unclimbable. Passo Bracco. It sounds almost friendly now. You check the map and know the gradients are easy from here on. Elated, you dismount and fire your camera *down* at the carpet of ragged clouds far below. You brew some coffee, lean back in the grass and savour victory over your noble enemy: the mountains.

As the adrenalin begins to dissipate you realize this was only a warm-up, that next time they'll destroy you, leave you for dead. But, right now, with the sunshine on your face and the coffee glowing in your belly like a fine wine, you don't give a damn.

I spent the night after my conquest of Passo Bracco in a lodge at Mattarana, a mountain village, and the following morning peeled back my curtains on to a swathe of heathery pasture studded with black goats. An old woman leaning on a crosier was chivvying a plump terrier through a fence. She seemed at one with the landscape, her swarthy face the colour of the ploughed earth beneath her

I set off late, freewheeling into the diaphanous cloud, inhaling the cool mountain air. Within an hour I was back on flat ground. After the harsh beauty of the Bracco the road from La Spezia to Pisa felt tame and straight; it was lined with soulless motels named Casa Beverly or Villa Serena. The wind was on my side today, blowing me forward in a blustery trajectory, and by early afternoon Pisa was in sight.

I spotted a group of prostitutes soliciting in the woods north of the city. They were wearing miniskirts and fishnet tights. A white Fiat picked one girl up, a tall, elegant black woman in a spangled top. Her rejected friend, a heavy-limbed mamma powdered up like a pierrot, sat spreadeagled on a tree trunk smoking a cigarette. 'Hey little cherry, hey cherry boy,' she hissed playfully as I rode past.

I found the roads on Pisa's outskirts confusing with the added complication of a tangled one-way system, and it took some time to reach the Field of Miracles, the heart of the town, dominated by the huge, cream-coloured cathedral. In front of the cathedral cupola is the famous leaning tower, now over fifteen feet out of true and cordoned off while builders try to remedy the cockeyed foundations.

I flopped down on the grass of the piazza and watched the crowds drifting around. Until now, my trip through Italy had been so rushed that I felt I wanted to soak up some atmosphere, meet the people, scratch beneath the surface of this seductive country. Perhaps my cousin, Richard Fremantle, who had lived in Florence for over twenty years, would help me.

After a night in Pisa's deserted youth hostel, I pedalled east past the ochre façades of the houses lining the River Arno. The roads were busy and the landscape bleak, but there were still sights to cheer me on the way: a farmer shooing along a parade of ducks, a heron flapping low over the roadside poplars, a low swollen cloud in the shape of Australia. It might seem sad, but when you are glued to a bicycle saddle, things like this can make your day.

The city of Florence, like the concentric growth rings in a tree trunk, reveals its age to you the further you penetrate. The modern, inchoate suburbs sit on the fringes, next you encounter the increasingly clogged streets and classical architecture before homing into the cathedral of Santa Maria del Fiore highlighted by Brunelleschi's heart-stopping dome. This central area is known as the Piazza del Duomo, and much of it would still be recognizable to the poet, Dante Alighieri, who lived here in the thirteenth century. Except for one thing: the tourists.

If a prescient Dante had set his masterpiece, the *Divine Comedy*, today, the ninth circle of hell would undoubtedly have been Ponte Vecchio during rush hour. This beautiful bridge, the oldest in the city, used to be lined with silversmiths and artisans plying their trade. Now I found it groaning with a jam of tourists the like of which I had never seen. Adding to the mêlée above the murky Arno were dozens of immigrant hawkers and gypsies.

A Japanese man bumped into my bike. 'Bloody tourists,' I grumbled, conveniently forgetting that I was one of them. Florence's annual ratio of tourists to locals is an extraordinary fourteen to one. Thankfully, my home town of Milton Keynes will never suffer such a fate. It attracts only a tiny number of tourists each year, who come to marvel at its celebrated herd of concrete cows. Perhaps if the man made Friesians had been sculpted by Donatello, instead of resembling a herd of papier mâché buffalo with rickets, Milton Keynes would be similarly invaded with admirers.

However, the tourists were nothing to get upset about, and after weeks of soggy campsites and hostel dormitories, the idea of staying at Cousin Richard's flat on Via Matteo Palmieri was as appealing as Dante's paradise.

'Welcome,' said Richard dramatically, unlatching his portcullis of a front door. He hefted my bike on his shoulder and headed up a narrow spiral staircase. I had not seen my cousin for years. He had a shock of white hair and a tanned face offset by bulging, kindly eyes. He resembled a raffish angel.

Later that evening, Richard took me out for some pasta to a café opposite. Via Matteo Palmieri was a lovely cobbled street – cobbles are fine when walking – lit by antique street lamps. A violinist was busking on the corner and his plaintive chords wavered in the night air.

Everyone knew Richard in the café. He smiled and winked at the waitresses from our corner table.

'So what do you want to do in Florence, Tom?' he asked, once I had updated him with the family gossip.

'My washing,' I said. 'Then maybe a few trivialities like the Uffizi, the cathedral, perhaps the Medici tombs.'

'You said you wanted to see the real Italy,' said Richard, spearing his cannelloni. 'Who cares about the Uffizi? Every traveller has seen Botticelli's brush-strokes. You need to focus on the Italians, not the sights. You should be an *original* traveller.'

'But I'm positively ordinary,' I protested. 'I've already met a hitch-hiking priest, an American who has cycled around the world three times and a heroic Croatian who I can't even begin to describe.'

'Listen, you come from a family of great traditionalists –

admirals, colonels, vicars and county do-gooders. Then look at yourself; you're unusual, like me. A Fremantle outsider.'

'I'm not an outsider!'

'Tom, you're riding a push-bike to bloody Australia. That is not normal behaviour, believe me. You need to decide what this trip means to you. Is it a physical test, a chance to live up to your ancestors or are you just travelling for the hell of it?'

'I'm doing this trip to find myself,' I said firmly, struggling to keep a straight face.

'Balls! What will you do when find yourself? Say, "Hello there, newly found Fremantle, nice to meet you," and fly home? We find ourselves every day, we don't need to pedal our arses halfway round the world for that. Besides, if you're intending to cycle to Australia you'll need to have a pretty good knowledge of yourself already, otherwise you'll never make it.'

We polished off another carafe of wine and then a fearsome nightcap known as a *Bella Donna*, so called because it contains a trace of deadly nightshade. Richard slapped me on the back. 'Come on, let's go home. Your wicked cousin is poisoning your mind as well as your muscles.'

The *pièce de résistance* of Richard's sixth-storey flat is the room at the top – his 'grotto in the stars'. It has no electric light and is illuminated purely by candles. I noticed a skeleton hanging in one corner and a couple of batik puppets, named Giuseppe and Esmerelda, lying in embrace on an old treasure chest. There were masks and vases and family photos in brocaded frames. Richard and I chatted for hours up there in front of a fire crackling with olive branches. Outside bats flittered in the moonlight.

As I wandered around Florence the following day I was staggered by the creative frenzy that had gripped the city six hundred years before. The masterpieces of Botticelli and Cara-

vaggio in the Uffizi, Cellini's open-air statues and the green
and white marble work of Santa Maria's baptistry made me
want to burst into spontaneous applause.

A decrepit tour guide evidently felt the same way. He had
jam jar spectacles and spat and spluttered like a scalded frying
pan as he lectured, but nevertheless there was great dignity in
his enthusiasm.

'Look, just look.' He gesticulated towards the richly frescoed
cathedral dome. 'Such beauty. LOOK. LOOK.' He was shouting now. 'When I was young I LOVE girls, now I am old I
LOVE architecture.' He closed his eyes. 'I LOVE this. THIS
DOME. Let your dreams fly up to it.' He flapped his arms
vigorously like a swan taking off from water. 'UP, UP, UP.'
His audience stared at him, eyes wide in horror; some giggled,
some clapped. 'UP, UP, UP.' This bespectacled old drama
queen was the perfect guide, I decided; none of his group
would ever forget Santa Maria del Fiore.

In the evening, I walked back to the flat via the crowded
Piazza della Signoria. Mounted policemen were clip-clopping
around in lazy circles while hucksters braided the hair of
teenage girls with baubles and ribbons. Above all this activity,
pigeons, cooing furtively to the gods, roosted on the pale
statues.

When I arrived back, Marina, a friend of Richard's, was
cooking dinner. She was a voluptuous grandmother with a big
smile and dismissive gestures.

'Oh Italy, my poor Italy,' she complained. 'Sometimes I
despair of my country.'

'Why?' I asked. 'To me it seems the friendliest place on
earth.'

'Oh no, it's all one big theatre,' she replied while stirring a
saucepan with Oscar-winning gusto. 'I have just returned from

England; in London I can mooch around in jeans and baggy jumpers. It's so relaxed. I can be grumpy and look like hell, but here I have to dress up and be charming.'

'Perhaps pretending to be happy is a good thing,' said Richard. 'It leaves a good impression on naïve visitors like Tom.'

'Oh, it's all right up to a point,' she countered, rolling her eyes, 'but when you have to go to the funeral of a bitchy relative and pretend to cry hysterically, it all becomes a bit much. And Italians are not so friendly in any case. Look at poor Roberto Baggio, that footballer who missed the penalty in the World Cup final. One minute he was a hero, the next local people were ripping up his posters and showering him with abuse. We Italians can be very fickle.'

I remembered the famous observation after Mussolini was lynched that one day forty million Italians were Fascists, and that overnight forty million Italians discovered they were anti-Fascist.

'Why do you stay in Italy, Richard?' I asked.

'I live for art. It's all that really matters. Italians are brought up with great art all around them. They respect the Bohemian way of life and I rather like their ambiguous, over-the-top nature. It beats the dourness of other Europeans hands down.'

Richard is a respected art historian, writer and teacher whose interests have been heavily influenced by his father, Christopher, my grandfather's younger brother, who had been born at Swanbourne but spent most of his life in New York.

Christopher was always the odd Fremantle out: while the rest of the family dutifully pursued conventional, often military, careers Christopher chose to live in an East Manhattan garret with Umi, his literary wife, and paint abstract canvases. He was a sweet-natured spiritual man and an ardent conscientious objector, having seen the agony his parents went through after Halford was killed in the Great War.

But to me the most remarkable thing about Christopher was his dying wish: to be buried at Swanbourne. Here was a sophisticated dreamer who had lived in the most dynamic city on earth but who longed to rest quietly among the crocuses and cow-parsley of the family plot. His tombstone now lies next to my grandfather's on Cemetery Hill. Throughout his life Christopher had been an outsider, and only in death had he wanted to belong. I wondered if Richard would one day be the same.

'You are cycling to Naples, Tom,' Marina was saying as we ate our spaghetti in the candle-lit grotto. '*Madre Mia*. You must be crazy, it is such a dangerous place. There is a saying in Italy: "Brave men and good wines last a short time."'

'Just as well this wine is from Bulgaria,' quipped Richard. 'Don't worry, Tom. All Tuscans have this fear and prejudice about the south. You'll be fine. If you can survive Marina's bolognese you can survive anything.'

He refilled his wineglass and stood up clumsily. 'A toast, everyone.' We raised our glasses. 'To Swanbourne,' he shouted. Then added in a barely audible whisper, 'Here's praying you make it back there, cousin.'

Italian breakfasts are the best in the world. The coffee is as pure as malt whisky and courses through your system in an invigorating stream. The pastries also make fine bicycling fuel, especially the croissants stuffed with custard. After one such breakfast, heavy-bellied with dough and light-headed with caffeine, I was finally ready to make my march on Rome.

Richard had kindly agreed to lead me out of Florence on his creaky bicycle. We drained our cups and headed south at sunrise, rattling over the Via Matteo Palmieri cobbles. After ten minutes we passed the golden statue of a pig. Richard slammed on his brakes. 'Touch its snout,' he insisted. 'It means you will return to Florence.' Chastened, I touched the pig's already burnished nostrils.

'Now you have touched the golden pig, you must embrace the black sheep too,' joked Richard, kissing my cheek. 'Ciao, cousin, you better go before I get too Italian on you. *Buona fortuna.*'

Alone, I pedalled on south. I hoped I would see Richard again some day; if my cousin considered himself a black sheep, then he was a talented and amusing one, not bitter or uptight; a rare breed who wore his fleece with pride.

It took me three days to reach Rome. On the third day, I set off from Aquapendente, an isolated hill village veiled in mist. I was desperate to reach the capital as my money had almost run out, but a headwind blew me to a standstill; it was raining and I still had over eighty miles to cover. I was cursing my luck when the strangest vision appeared: an ostrich.

I'm cracking up, I thought. An ostrich. In Tuscany. The bird shuffled its damp feathers and goose-stepped through a gap in some wire netting to join its friends. There were about a dozen of them, looking at me, all long necks and bug eyes. I felt like Gulliver seeing the Yahoos for the first time, knowing the real world was temporarily on hold. The memory of this feathery mirage continued to spook me for several hours as I freewheeled through the graffiti-scarred suburbs of the capital.

Rome is a wildly sprawling city but has so many distinctive buildings I could hardly go wrong. The serpentine River Tiber also provides a useful guiding artery.

Soon after dark, I reached the flat of my relatives, Susan and Cesare, which lies south of the pastel-shaded houses on the

Trastevere hills. Susan, a larger-than-life director for Sony, was still at work when I arrived, but Cesare her laid-back husband, a songwriter, was busily cooking. Cesare and I cracked open a couple of beers and chinwagged about my trip. Susan swept in half an hour later, her heavy bracelets jangling.

'God, what a week,' she said, crashing down a huge portmanteau on the table. 'I've got Tony Bennett coming tomorrow and then Bruce Springsteen immediately after him.'

Susan has the perfect temperament to deal with celebrities. She can deflate egos quicker than a pin can puncture a balloon and has no care for the consequences. This has won her much respect in an industry known for its pussyfooting and hypocrisy. Nobody messes with Susan.

I noticed that all around the sitting room were photos of Susan: Susan with the Rolling Stones, Susan with Michael Jackson, Susan receiving the Pope's blessing. But the biggest photo was of her father, a distinguished fighter pilot, standing next to his Spitfire during the Battle of Britain.

Susan first arrived in Rome in the 1960s as a teenage backpacker with her sister Jean. The sisters had big plans to travel the world but Susan met Cesare, Jean met Gerald and they have both lived in Italy ever since.

'Make yourself at home – you are one of the family,' said Susan. I was very distant family, her sister-in-law's brother, but this was Italy where all blood ties, however tenuous, are cherished. 'We've got two dinner parties lined up for you and a radio interview, and then of course there's the Springsteen concert.'

I had once loved the sound of Springsteen's guttural, emotionally charged voice. Yet somehow here, in the heart of this ancient city, I could think of nothing worse than hearing him growl about unemployment in Nebraska and girls called

Wendy and Bobby Jean. But now was not the time to dwell on such things. I was safe, warm, happy and among friends. All I wanted was some sleep.

Lots of people are rude about bicycles but the satirist PJ O'Rourke more than most. In his essay 'A Cool And Logical Analysis Of The Bicycle Menace', he rants:

> Bicycles are topheavy, have poor brakes, and provide no protection to their riders . . . Bicycles are dangerous things.
> Bicycles, however, are dangerous without being any fun. You can't shoot pheasants with a bicycle or water-ski behind it or go 150 miles an hour or even mix it with soda and ice. And the idea of getting romantic on a bicycle is alarming. All you can do with one of these ten-speed sink traps is grow tired and sore and fall off it.

There were times on my trip when I agreed with him. But there were also occasions when a bicycle could be great fun, and Rome was one such instance.

Imagine. You have just pedalled 1,500 miles on a push-bike laden with heavy panniers. For the first time you remove those panniers, and then you can race that push-bike, which now flies, around the most visually overwhelming city in the world – listening to Mascagni's *Intermezzo* at full volume – as the sun rises.

You fly past the Colosseum, home to all those bloodthirsty gladiatorial bouts, you fly past the Pantheon, its first-century columns as sturdy as when Nero made his interminable speeches there. You fly past the Spanish Steps, Keats's house and down Via Cavour faster than Marcello Mastroianni on his Vespa in *La Dolce Vita*. You fly over bridges decorated with gargoyles and saints. You stop at the Trevi Fountain, throw in a coin and believe that, this time, your wishes really will come true.

On arriving in Rome in 1786, Goethe said: 'I now realize all the dreams of my youth.' I felt the same. It excited me in a way no city had done before. It made me think anything was possible. And, what's more, it was Easter Day.

By mid-morning, thousands of Catholics from all over the world had converged on Saint Peter's Square: French missionaries and Brazilian students, nuns in wimples and priests in black hats, gaggles of Filipina maids strumming guitars.

Pope John Paul spoke Latin over the tannoy in a halting voice that was not without authority. Gentle applause rose from the audience and it struck me that I was standing outside St Peter's, the largest church in the world, listening to the most revered living Christian. Not many of the congregation were actually listening; they were rocking babies, shooting photos, playing cards and enjoying the buzz of the crowd. It was interesting and fun, but not in the least bit moving.

What was moving, however, was the nearby Sistine Chapel which I visited after the Pope had retreated to his cloistered lair. I stayed two hours marvelling at the genius of Michelangelo and the other artists – Botticelli, Perugino – whose dazzlingly precise brush-strokes covered the walls.

Michelangelo took over three years to paint the ceiling's intricate biblical scenes and when that was completed he set to work on the cupola at St Peter's, even though by that time he was well into his seventies. I remembered the Hollywood epic with Charlton Heston as Michelangelo swinging from fresco to fresco like a Manhattan steeplejack. Jaw jutting, eyes asquint, Heston made it all seem so easy – as though he could complete the entire ceiling in a couple of hours and, after a quick espresso, polish off *The Last Judgement*.

I had forgotten my glasses and, like Charlton Heston, had

to squint up at the famous central fresco of *The Creation of Adam* which seemed a little blurred. In fact, it looked to me as if God's finger, rather than on the verge of making contact, was actually touching Adam's. For some inexplicable reason – I am not a very religious man – it sent a shiver down my spine.

I had a fine time in Rome. The city had reinvigorated me and I made what proved to be a vital contact in Munir Jurdi, a Lebanese antique dealer.

'My parents live in Beirut,' Munir told me during one of Susan's dinner parties. 'You might need to go there one day. Here, have my card. I mean it – you never know.'

At the time, I took his card merely to be polite; I had no intention of going anywhere near Lebanon. But on a trip like this, anything could happen.

I also had a chance meeting with a man called Walter Veltroni while wandering around the markets near the Piazza Navona with Susan. We had stopped for a rest at Bernini's *Fontana dei Fiumi*, an unusual masterpiece depicting four naked river gods, and were leaning against the railings eating ice creams which were melting over our hands.

'Walter,' Susan shouted suddenly, waving into the crowds. 'Walter, Walter.'

A neatly dressed, avuncular-looking man came over with his pretty wife and child in tow. Susan introduced us and I shook his hand, smearing it with sticky ice cream in the process. I smiled blankly while he and Susan rattled away in machine-gun Italian.

'He's out campaigning,' said Susan, as the elegant family walked away.

'What do you mean?'

'It's the general election later this month. If Berlusconi loses, which I think he will, Walter will become the next Vice Prime Minister of Italy.'

Sure enough, two weeks later, while staying at a farmhouse in Puglia, I would see Susan's prophesy fulfilled.

On the morning of my departure, Cesare agreed to guide me out of Rome in his Renault. He drove slowly with his hazard lights pulsing, so that I could follow him on to the southbound coastal road. Convoys are well known for being the most dangerous way to drive and this occasion proved no exception, especially as Cesare was taking bites from a pizza the size of a satellite dish balanced precariously on his steering wheel. I stayed close behind him, at times shooting red lights and kerb hopping to keep him in sight.

Once I had made my escape from the capital's complex bitumen, it only took two days to reach Naples. I enjoyed an attractive ride past vineyards and strawberry fields which was marred only by intermittent showers and the countless dead dogs by the roadside.

Dead dogs are as synonymous with Italian roads as speedy drivers. One afternoon *en route* to Naples I counted eleven slain mongrels of which one, a sort of hyena hybrid, was mown down right in front of me. The guilty van did not even slow down as the little carcass ricocheted down the road like a hockey puck.

As I pedalled into the centre of Naples, I saw that the city lives up to its bi-polar reputation. The Bay of Naples is as beautiful as I had imagined but the city itself, with its over-populated housing estates, is equally as grim. Semi-naked children chased each other through the poorly paved alleys while ranks of laundry suspended between balconies blocked out any trace of sunlight.

I checked into a doss-house called Pensione Columbo which really was a dive. A pair of fat prostitutes — one black, one white — sat chewing gum in the reception. The manager, a spiv with neat greasy hair and a paltry moustache, handed over the room key. I felt like hell, my guts were bubbling and I had a headache. I knew I was in for a bad night.

However, to my enormous surprise, Pensione Columbo proved to be the most homely place I'd stayed in since leaving Vicky Neuberger and the East Cliff Hotel. The spiv was called Luco and the girls Gabriella and Sal. They nicknamed me 'Mista Mafia' when I told them I was catching a ferry to Palermo the following day.

With the incompetence of the Marx Brothers, the girls dragged my bike up the stairs, crashing it into my room; they brought me cups of tea, headache pills, slices of toast, all with no ulterior motive. They only prodded my bike's milometer buttons, laughed a lot and told me that Naples was 'the best' in their hopeless English. Maybe not the best, I thought, but the beleaguered city clearly had some hidden qualities.

Naples, I should explain, is of great historical importance to my journey. It is the city where Admiral Thomas Fremantle fell in love with Betsey Wynne – a union which in due course produced Captain Charles.

In the late eighteenth century young Betsey had been travelling around Italy with her father, Richard Wynne. Wynne, a friend of Casanova, was a charming and irresponsible rogue described by the historian Christopher Hibbert as: 'A man of unpredictable moods, suffering from gout, piles and rheumatism and much given to practical jokes such as placing a bat on the dancing-master's mirror.'

Wynne had inherited a property in Lincolnshire which he sold in 1786. For the rest of his life Wynne, reveals Hibbert, travelled around 'wherever his fancy drew him ... with an enormous suite, which on occasions numbered almost twenty people, not to mention numerous horses and dogs'. Included in this motley group were Richard's five daughters, of whom Betsey was the second.

Wynne was also a dreadful coward. When the French began to infiltrate Italy in 1796, he fled with his family to Leghorn to seek the protection of the British fleet. The family boarded the *Inconstant*, a frigate commanded by a certain Thomas Fremantle, one of Nelson's 'Band of Brothers'. Betsey, then a mere eighteen years old, immediately fell for my ancestor – finding his 'fiery black eyes quite captivating'.

Fremantle, thirty years old and something of a roué, was cautious. In a letter to his brother, William, he described Betsey as 'short', 'not particularly handsome' but 'otherwise a very good humoured sensible dolly'.

Betsey was more spirited than Thomas had bargained for and her tomboy charms finally overcame him. They were married in Naples at the house of the British minister, William Hamilton, whose wife, Emma, later became Nelson's celebrated mistress. Betsey was given away by Prince Augustus, the youngest son of George III; her indecorous father was probably either too drunk or too busy flirting with a bridesmaid to do the job himself.

Betsey proved a good match for Fremantle and enjoyed spending time at sea with him. Within a few months, though, she almost lost both her husband and Lord Nelson. During an ill-fated attack against the Spanish at Santa Cruz, Nelson and Thomas were hit in their right arms by musket balls within minutes of each other. Nelson's arm was amputated and cauterized soon after the injury but Fremantle's limb, wrapped in a poultice, was saved. The wound, however, continued to plague him for the rest of his life.

'God Bless you and Fremantle,' Nelson wrote to Betsey the following day, words which are thought to be the first penned by the now one-armed admiral with his left hand.

On their return from Spain in 1798, Betsey and Thomas

moved to Swanbourne and Fremantles have lived there ever since. It was a happy marriage and the couple produced ten children of whom the first son, Thomas, became an MP and the Chairman of the Board of Customs; the second, Henry, died of influenza aged eighteen and the fourth, William, became the Dean of Ripon. The third son was Captain Charles.

Thomas put Charles to sea at the age of ten and noted that he climbed 'the rigging as if he had been in the navy for years'. Little did he realize that twenty years later this footsure but seasick lad would sail to Australia and have a port named in his honour.

Sadly, Thomas, who was later promoted to admiral, never lived to see that day. He fell ill during another posting to Naples and died suddenly of 'an inflammation of the head and stomach . . . which rapidly exhausted his vital powers'. He was buried with full military honours in Naples military cemetery rather than being tipped into the city's murky bay. A memorial stone was later erected in Malta, the chief Mediterranean naval base at the time.

I was looking into the Bay of Naples now as my ferry steered towards Sicily. I could understand why Thomas had chosen to be interred in the earth. It always amazed me anyone wanting to be buried at sea, left there swirling in the cold, briny murk. Even in the most stagnant waters how could the spirit ever settle? It would eventually be smashed on the rocks of a thousand different shores.

That is not the way Thomas wanted it. He preferred not to leave his soul to the tides, but submerged in the immutable clay of Naples, waiting in vain for his beloved Betsey to lie beside him.

I watched the flickering lights of Naples fade away and then unfurled my sleeping bag on the floor of the lounge. The only other passengers without a cabin were two Scandinavian girls who were sleeping on a row of linked chairs, using their backpacks as pillows. They had a better night's sleep than me and were still inert when we docked at Palermo the following morning. Dawn had just broken and flecks of purple cloud hung above the island's ancient towers and craggy mountains.

Sicily was a blur. After my prolonged stopoffs in Rome and Florence, I was very behind time and pedalled across the island as fast as I could. I loved what little I saw: the prickly pear cacti with stems like canoe paddles, the old men sitting on benches arguing the pros and cons of Berlusconi and the cafés with jukeboxes containing every scratched forty-five from Harry Belafonte to the Sex Pistols.

My fondest memory is of the tiny village of Gioiosa Marea. I arrived mid-morning and found a brass band marching up and down the road, with every member wearing a beret and sunglasses. I was reminded of a New Orleans funeral cortège but the village was, in fact, celebrating the Festival of St Nicholas. I asked several people why a festival in honour of Santa Claus was being held in Sicily, but nobody understood my confusion. I can only imagine that there are two saints called Nicholas: one a tanned Mediterranean with a tuba, and the other a ruddy-cheeked Laplander with a sleigh.

For me, the highlight of the festivities was witnessing a round of *scopa*, Italy's number one card game. A number of card-sharps sat around a table, some dressed in dark baggy suits, others looking more like wine-flushed Yahoos from a Hogarth painting. I understood very little of the tactics except that each player had to shout *scopa!*, *Madonna!* or *Mama!* loudly and at regular intervals. It is a game that openly encourages cheating and has a famous rule book that begins, 'Always look at the opponent's cards.' The book was written by a man from Naples.

Buoyed by the spirited camaraderie of the festival, I rode furiously along the entire northern coastline and reached the ancient town of Messina within two days. While Sicily may have a chequered Mafia-influenced history, across the water from me now lay Calabria, which had the most wretched reputation of all the Italian regions.

Even the crossing from Messina to Calabria had a terrible reputation. This is the sliver of water where Homer's six-headed, multi-tentacled monster, Scylla and her dastardly neighbour, Charybdis, a whirlpool, swallowed many of Odysseus' crew. But this was the stuff of myth, and our ferry plied across the most tranquil of seas, finally decanting us in Reggio, Calabria's dowdy capital.

Poor Calabria has recently been dubbed Italy's 'disaster to beat all disasters'. Over the years it has been devastated by earthquakes, hit by a colossal tidal wave and become the kidnap capital of the country. Geographically the toes and sole of Italy, Calabria also has the highest murder rate in Europe – at least one a day, almost all of which are Mafia related.

Cycling through the region I could see neglect everywhere – roads were pitted, signs inaccurate and the building construction shoddy. Run-down industrial sites stood on land which had once been fertile with citrus groves. The people were decent enough but there seemed little hope of relieving the poverty – just a sad, pervading lassitude. Crime and corruption had destroyed the place; perhaps only God could help now.

It was a relief to reach Alberto Mannarini's olive farm at Manduria in the lush neighbouring province of Puglia. Alberto was a friend of Susan, a great long-legged crag of a man with the sort of presence that wins quick respect. The wrinkles on his face told a story far richer than the lines on any palm, and his boots were scuffed enough to have journeyed through several lifetimes.

The Mannarini homestead was a curious place; part farm, part castle. There were shotguns and flintlocks propped up in a glass-fronted cabinet, dogs asleep at the hearth and a cauldron of stew bubbling on the stove. I was introduced to a sea of richly tanned faces, each one with a wonderful name: Marcello, Francisco, Maria Victoria, Donatella.

Discussion at the dinner table centred on the following day's general election. For the last week Italians everywhere had spoken of little else. There were three main contenders: hard-nosed Silvio Berlusconi, a media mogul who headed a right-wing coalition along with his straight man, Gianfranco Finni; Romano Prodi, and his Christian Democrats; and Umberto Bossi, the loose cannon, who wanted to divide Italy into three self-governing states. His eccentric speeches made Screaming Lord Sutch sound like Gladstone.

'I respect Berlusconi as a businessman but I think he is an arrogant politician,' pronounced Alberto gravely. 'Prodi is a clown and Bossi is crazy. It's Italian politics as usual.'

'Prodi is not a clown!' retorted Maria Victoria, Alberto's pretty niece. 'He's the only honest politician to have appeared in Italy for years. People in the south tend to be conservative and so they prefer Berlusconi, but I think he is dangerous and vain, just using his TV stations to spread propaganda. Prodi has decency on his side.'

Italy is no stranger to volatile politics. The country has endured over fifty changes of government since World War Two with many of its prime ministers coming to tragic or ignoble ends. Aldo Moro, one of the more popular leaders, was kidnapped and shot dead by the Red Brigades in 1978, while long-serving Giulio Andreotti was charged with having Mafia links only a few years back. Andreotti once famously remarked, 'Power only tires those who do not have it.'

'Our politics have always been a shambles, Tom,' continued

Maria Victoria, 'and that's why the family is so strong in Italy. Italians can't trust politicians, judges, lawyers, shopkeepers or sometimes even the Pope. The only people Italians truly trust are their *mamas* – their own flesh and blood! But politicians, to hell with them.'

Later that evening Walter Veltroni, Prodi's dapper second in command, who I had briefly met in Piazza Navona with Susan, appeared on the television news. He looked nervous. No wonder – tomorrow he was to become the Vice Prime Minister of Italy. One could only wish him luck.

The following day Alberto took me on a tour of the farm. We strode across his front lawn which had an ancient thickset olive tree at its centre. In the bright sunshine the olive's bark looked so gnarled and solid it might have been petrified.

'This tree is over a hundred years old,' said Alberto, placing his hand gently on the trunk, 'but that's nothing. In Israel, some olive trees date back to the time of Jesus Christ. The first olives appear in mythology; they were created by the Goddess Athena as a gift to the Greeks.'

But for all their divine origins, olives are clearly not the easiest of enterprises. Three years before, a springtime snowfall had decimated Alberto's harvest. An especially warm sirocco followed, causing the melting snow to burn through the branches, leaving the wood susceptible to canker.

'The government were supposed to compensate us,' said Alberto, shrugging his shoulders. 'But nothing came of it. I do this job for love, not money.'

Alberto had previously lived in Rome working as an executive for Alitalia, but had always dreamt of a country life and out here one could see why. The two of us were looking out over a field of trees, symmetrical as a military parade. Dragonflies and yellow butterflies careened in the breeze and in the distance a team of men were coppicing the olives with hatchets.

'I use old men for the coppicing,' said Alberto. 'They enjoy the work and I pay them less. It's also better for tax. Last year I had to pay fifty-three per cent tax. Fifty-three per cent! Only in Italy.'

Later we dropped in on Alberto's brother, Marcello, and his German wife, Barbara. Marcello and Barbara lived in a part of the house which incorporated a number of holiday rooms to let out. One of the rooms was occupied by Ralph Steadman, the former *Private Eye* cartoonist, and his wife. They joined us for tea.

If you put Ralph Steadman in a room with 1,000 other people you would immediately know he is a cartoonist. He has a fleshy face, flushed and friendly, with tufts of white hair sprouting from the back of his pate. He looks like a man who drinks far too many cups of coffee.

I half-expected Steadman to resemble one of the outrageous, wild-faced freaks he created for the Hunter S. Thompson books, but he was far too benign for that. In fact, it was hard to believe that the gentle artist before me was famed for drawings of bloodstained reptiles, vomiting monsters and a host of other goons and weirdos.

At high tea – red mullet and a bowl of spaghetti – Steadman doodled speedy and surprisingly flattering caricatures of Marcello and Barbara. I wanted to stay but had a ferry to catch later that evening. It was time to move on again and Alberto came to see me off. He said nothing, simply rang my bike's bell with several inquisitive flicks, then turned and walked slowly back down the farm track leaving big footprints in the sand.

I pedalled through the peach orchards to the nearby port of Brindisi and that evening boarded the ferry to Greece. The only passengers were a gang of French lorry drivers playing poker. I bivouacked on deck, exhausted but unable to sleep. A light wind soughed over the dark restless sea and, up above, the opal-coloured moon was hanging between a necklace of winking stars.

'Italy,' I whispered to no one in particular. Like my ancestors before me – Admiral Thomas, Betsey and that lovable poltroon Richard Wynne – I had fallen hopelessly in love.

CHAPTER FOUR

NAVEL GAZING WITH
THE GODS

Greece was the smallest country I needed to traverse. It was only 160-odd miles from Patras, my drop-off point, to the port of Piraeus on the edge of Athens, and from there I could catch a ferry to Turkey. Three days' cycling. Piece of cake.

Many of the road signs were written solely in Hellenic script but there was no need for me to decipher the alphas and omegas as I was already on the main road east and simply had to follow my nose, via Delphi and Thebes, until I spotted the pillars of the Parthenon. I was pleased that, so far, map-reading hadn't proved too much of a problem and, in fact, it seemed the further I cycled, the simpler my route became. Embarrassingly, the most tricky stretch had been from London to Dover, with its busy, jumbled threads of bitumen. Athens, admittedly, was still to come.

I reached Nafpaktos, a beautiful port studded with plane trees, by mid-afternoon of my first day in Greece. I wheeled my bike down to the beach and dozed in the shade of a wrecked fishing boat, listening to the soothing rhythms of the surf.

It was hard to believe that, over 2,000 years earlier, this sleepy harbour had been one of the country's most powerful naval bases. Since then it had been occupied by the Romans, Byzantines, Venetians and, of course, the Turks.

As I looked out over the water, I tried to picture the cannon blasts and rough waves of the Battle of Lepanto, fought here in 1571, during which a combined European navy defeated the ambitious Ottoman fleet. The swashbuckling Spanish author, Miguel de Cervantes, lost an arm fighting in that battle and, had he not been wounded, might never have settled down to write his masterpiece, *Don Quixote*: my front right pannier might also have been considerably lighter.

I walked back to the port centre at dusk and was struck by how lovely it was. The fifteenth-century castle was illuminated by a tiara of white lights, teenagers were buzzing by on mopeds and a priest in Orthodox garb stood solemnly primping his beard. He was watching an old widow crank some clothes through a mangle.

'Hey, my friend, over here.' A voice rang out from behind me. 'Come here, make yourself at home.' The voice belonged to Thomas, the town's travel agent. Within seconds he had grabbed my arm, ushered me into his office and handed over a saucer of small dark olives.

'I don't need your help,' I explained. 'I have a bicycle.'

'No problem. I just like to talk to tourists about the world.' He paused and winked. 'The world outside Nafpaktos.'

The travel business was not faring well, Thomas told me, gesturing towards some posters of the Giza Pyramids above his desk. The previous week a bus party of eighteen Greek tourists had been mown down by Islamic fundamentalists in Cairo; apparently the gunmen had thought the unfortunate sightseers were Israelis. Understandably, the Greeks had decided to give Egypt a wide berth.

'How terrible for the families of the dead,' I said.

'Of course. Fate can be cruel sometimes. But we must make the best of this strange life.'

Thomas looked and sounded out of place in little Nafpaktos.

He wore a blue suit, Paisley tie and shiny brogues. His manner was friendly and sophisticated but he could not understand the purpose of my bicycle ride at all.

'My God, you are cycling for *over* one year,' shouted Thomas. 'But your family will forget you, your friends will forget you. I would not do such a thing if you paid me a million drachma.'

He pointed to a photo on his desk which showed three glamorous girls arm in arm. 'See this? These are my daughters: one is a doctor in Athens, one a lawyer in Rome and the youngest an art student in Florence. Beautiful, huh? They come back to see me at least once a year.'

It was easy to see what made Thomas tick. In Nafpaktos he was a big man – well heeled, well travelled, well respected. In Athens he would be just another fat cat but here, spinning out his twilight years in breezy Nafpaktos, here, he was somebody.

'Why should I care about a bit of lost business?' he said. 'Life is too short to worry about such things. Drink some ouzo, my friend. Come, let us sit outside and watch the harbour lights.' What a good man, I thought, as Thomas chattered about Nafpaktos and his faraway daughters. Somebody who lived by his own rules, who would die with few regrets. A man at peace with himself.

Johnny Ginger in a suit.

Delphi is known as the Navel of the World but this is a complete misnomer. A navel conjures up images of travelling down towards a thimble-like dip in the undulating terrain of one's belly. Granted, the occasional navel breaks the rules and rises to a small bump, but the word certainly doesn't suggest a gradient as steep as the one I was about to cycle up. Delphi should be called the Nipple of the World.

Long ago, this site was carefully chosen by Apollo. The sun god released two eagles from the farthest points of the earth and pronounced that where the two birds met would be the centre of the world, the belly button of the universe. Apollo noted the grid reference and discovered that it pinpointed Delphi with startling precision.

Eagles still glide high above the mountain, as I noticed while struggling up the testing switchbacks. It took me several hours to reach Delphi and finally I collapsed in a heap at the entrance to the campsite. The view was undeniably fit for the gods: a rolling landscape, craggy but lush, stretching out towards Mount Parnassus, the jangle of goat bells all around.

Delphi is all about setting. If the ruins had been unearthed in a potato field near the Albanian border it would attract scarcely any visitors. Sadly, the popularity of Delphi almost overwhelms the place; dozens of coaches snake up and down hills where gods once played, and tour groups in matching baseball caps swarm over the Sanctuary of Athena and the ancient theatre.

I made my way to the museum where I tagged on to a posse of Americans, whose flamboyant guide was spouting some crowd-pleasing sound bites including the legend that Amazon warriors would cut off their own breasts to enhance their fighting performance.

The most impressive exhibit amid the terracotta pots and crude weaponry was a life-sized charioteer, reins frozen in his hands. The statue was made of bronze and dated back to around 500 BC. The charioteer had been animatedly sculpted with impressive attention to detail – in all the other statues the eyes were simply voids but this young hero had coloured, glinting stones in his sockets – and I found that it brought him dramatically to life.

I tagged along with the American group until we reached Delphi's notorious oracle. From what I could understand, the oracle had been little more than a hallucinogenic old crone who spoke on behalf of the god Apollo; nevertheless, vital political or military decisions were taken on the basis of her highly ambiguous and specious predictions.

The guide continued his monologue. 'Above the Oracle was a sign: KNOW THYSELF. It reminded visitors that they were human, not immortal; that no man can escape his destiny.'

Know thyself. I remembered cousin Richard drunkenly telling me I had to know myself if was going to make it to Australia. Perhaps it was in the lap of the gods after all.

One man whose fate was predicted by the Delphic oracle was King Oedipus. I was pedalling through his country now as I had just reached the town of Thívai, once known as Thebes. It seemed a grey and dismal place, quite unlike the bustling centre I imagine it must have been before the birth of Christ.

The action of Sophocles' famous tragedy takes place during a single day in Thebes. By the day's end, the once noble King Oedipus, solver of the riddle of the sphinx, learns that he has unwittingly killed his father, Laius, and married his mother, Jocasta, and so, in a melodramatic fit of despair, the hapless monarch gouges his own eyes out.

I found it surprising that the little town of Thívai had not cashed in on its notoriety as the location of one of the world's great tragedies, but the locals had sensibly decided that the noble science of farming was more worthwhile than pandering to tourists. They evidently wanted to control their own destinies.

I pedalled on towards Athens thankful the oracle had not delivered me any baleful prophecies – cobbles, punctures, a Sean Kelly-style boil – that sort of thing. But the gods were clearly still playing havoc with the weather.

Greece was proving to be a climate of violent extremes. *En route* from Delphi I cycled through a mountain town called

Arahova where snow was falling in heavy flakes, dusting the slopes. The locals were wandering around in fur-lined jackets with sunglasses and woolly hats; some were even brandishing skis and I found it necessary to stop and put on my thermal long johns.

However, freewheeling down towards Athens, the heat was blistering again. I pulled over at a roadside café and stripped down to T-shirt and shorts. A waitress named Anastasia came to take my order; she was a dark rangy girl wearing a white cotton top that revealed her midriff.

'Where are you heading?' she asked, returning with my coffee.

'Australia,' I replied, prattishly.

'Wow. I'd love to go to Melbourne; I've got friends there. But not on that.' She pointed at my bike and giggled. 'I am Greek. We don't do that sort of thing.'

She sat down and told me she wanted to study English literature – she loved Jane Austen – somewhere in America but to save money she needed to work here at her father's café during the week, and at another restaurant in Athens at weekends.

'My father only recently bought this café,' said Anastasia. 'He used to work hard but now he is turning into a slob. He sits around drinking with his friends while my sister and I do all the chores. But this is Greece – I have to do as he says. It is a patricidal society.'

'I think you mean patriarchal. Surely you don't want to kill him?'

'Oh no. Not yet anyway.' We both laughed. Her English was exceptional on the whole, including the accent.

'Where are you going next?' she asked.

'Turkey.'

'Turkey! I hate the Turks. All Greeks do.'

'It sounds as though you hate the Turks just because you're Greek.'

'No, I would hate the Turks if I was British, German, whatever,' she insisted, the colour darkening in her face. 'They are maniacs. The Romans invaded Greece but they showed us respect, the Turks just destroyed everything. Look at Cyprus — the Turks should get the hell out — and there is another dispute now over a little island called Imia near Rhodes. I would like to go to war with Turkey on this issue, even if it is only a lump of rock.' She picked up a pebble and threw it hard towards the road.

'Have you ever met any Turks?' I asked.

'No. Why should I? They are not human.'

I could scarcely believe what I was hearing. This pretty Jane Austen reader was willing to wage war on her Muslim neighbours. It was clearly a deep-rooted hatred which, rather than declining through the generations, was rising to new levels. One could sympathize up to a point; after all the Ottomans had occupied her country for centuries before the Greeks were finally able to push them out in the 1830s at the tail end of the War of Independence. Perhaps the humiliation of this occupation rankled more than all the contemporary squabbles.

'You must watch out in Turkey,' warned Anastasia, without a trace of humour. 'They will kill you without thinking.'

We were both silent, looking out at the dusty road. Anastasia had finished her drink and was aggressively clinking the ice cubes at the bottom of the glass. It saddened me that this broad-minded teenager had, when it came to Turkey, opinions as fallow as the parched hills that surrounded us.

The Greeks have the highest death rate on their roads of all the countries in the European Union and, cycling through Athens, I could believe it. Athena, the goddess of wisdom, may once have lived in the city but her cerebral gifts had clearly not been passed down to the city's drivers. By the time I reached Syntagma Square, I had experienced more near misses than during the rest of the trip put together. At least I would have died with the Acropolis in eyeshot.

On several occasions in the traffic-choked streets, I had caught glimpses of Pericles' masterpiece high above the capital. It was the most grand of views: the distant, salt-white pillars of the Parthenon glinting in the sun. When I later inspected the pillars close up, it was disappointing to discover they were the colour of a cheesecake past its best.

After a tortuous slalom through a final, asthma-inducing traffic jam, I checked into a dormitory at Festos Hotel in the Plaka, the heart of the capital. Athens was clearly heaving with backpackers as my bed was the last available. I dumped my bike, showered and strolled out into the milling crowds.

The Plaka area is renowned for having the highest concentration of tourist shops in the world. As far as I could make out, these kiosks of kitsch stocked just about every worthless trinket in the book from Socrates ashtrays to tea towels mapping out Corfu and Cephalonia. The strangest item I saw was a Dionysus corkscrew, which depicted the lusty god of merriment as a midget with a gigantic twirling penis three times his own height.

On the fringes of the Plaka is Syntagma Square, a pitiful spot. The grass was jaundiced, the flower beds empty, drunks were asleep on graffitied benches and a solitary preacher, wild with a combination of faith and sun, was evangelizing to an imaginary congregation.

Athens was a city in transition with construction sites all around. Skyscrapers were springing up from the rubble, drills tearing at the pavements and a Pandora's box of fumes and smog soiled the air. It was easy to see why pollution had been one of the main reasons the capital failed to secure the 1996 Olympics. But this resilient city, which not so long ago had endured German occupation, civil war and devastating famine, was once again full of life.

It was 1 May, Labour Day – an occasion that Athens, with its history of poverty, still takes seriously. All around Areos Park were parades of workers holding aloft posters of Lenin and Marx. There were Kurds burning posters of Saddam Hussein and Christians handing out leaflets emblazoned with the face of Christ. Hi-fi speakers the size of refrigerators blasted out pop music and a tramp pumped his accordion. The event was a rally of friendly solidarity and there was no violence in the air.

But back at my hotel the atmosphere was quite different. Poor Ulrika, the Swedish receptionist, was in tears; apparently a man wearing a black mask had dashed in and pushed her to the floor shouting, 'Kill the foreign bastards.' Later, a bomb had gone off in the workers' union building nearby and, although nobody was hurt, several guests were tearful and shaken. The motive remained a mystery.

That afternoon I had planned to cycle over to see the Battle of Marathon tumulus where the Athenians had trounced King Xerxes' Persian army in 490 BC. It was a twenty-six-mile ride. I knew this because the first ever marathon had been run by the messenger who carried the news of victory back to Athens. But I simply couldn't face pedalling through the capital again, especially after the bombing, and so, to my shame, I retreated to the restaurant and watched some diverting trash on MTV.

In the evening, shortly before leaving for my ferry, I met Lisa, an Australian girl who gave me a hand hauling my bicycle down the narrow stairway of the Festos. Lisa had a butterfly amulet around her neck, which she kept snagging in my front wheel spokes. She joked that the butterfly was supposed to signify freedom, even though it was usually imprisoned in her cleavage. She was attractive in a kooky way with multicoloured 'Dockers' on her feet and long tousled hair. I asked her where she was from.

'Western Australia,' she replied. 'Perth.'

'Do you know Swanbourne?' I asked.

'Swanbourne, of course. I live about one mile from there.'

My jaw slackened in disbelief and I gabbled a long explanation about Johnny Ginger and Captain Charles. She listened with remarkable patience, then wished me luck and scribbled her telephone number on my forearm, encircling it with two perfect butterfly wings.

'Maybe see you in Swanbourne,' she said. 'Small world, hey?'

'You must be joking,' I replied. 'I've still got 10,000 miles to pedal.'

Sailing to Turkey was not so easy. First I had to island hop to Crete and then on to Rhodes before I could reach Marmaris on Turkey's south coast. I was not too put out about the detour although I was disappointed to learn that Crete's chief attraction, Knossos, the centre of King Minos' kingdom and the site where Theseus slew the Minotaur, was closed due to a strike.

The ferry moored at Crete's dreary capital, Iráklion, at daybreak. After a swift breakfast I decided to pedal up to the Lassithi Plateau, a landscape of legendary beauty where it is claimed Zeus once lived. I had two days to kill before my ferry to Rhodes and knew that, unlike Knossos, mother nature would not be on strike.

It was a hard ride but well worth it. Unlike many parts of mainland Greece, the Lassithi was still primitive with no John Deere machinery or sophisticated irrigation systems to be found. Here the farmers till the patchworked land using yoked oxen or antique Sama tractors. They are at one with their surroundings, the rusty hued earth engrained in their hands and faces.

I camped on Mount Dhíkti, near the cave where Zeus was supposed to have been born, and the following day joined the tourists trudging up the slope in search of the king of the Olympians. Our guide, possibly the only man on Crete not on strike, led us into the darkness. With his cascading grey beard he could have been as old as Zeus himself.

'These stalactites grow downwards,' he wheezed, flashing his torch at the cave's roof. 'One centimetre every hundred years. But the stalagmites grow up, one centimetre every three hundred years.'

It occurred to me that I could snap off one of these gnarled fingers of rock as easily as an icicle and destroy 1,000 years of growth. Perhaps some of them had even been there since the time of Zeus. But my attention was beginning to stray; it was a cold dingy nook this, no matter who had been born here, and I wished I was outside in the sunshine looking down at the glorious valley.

However, the cave does have a colourful, if improbable, history. In legend it had first been inhabited by the wicked cannibalistic king of the Titans, Cronus, and his wife, Rhea: the parents of Zeus. Cronus was a consummate baddie who began his career by cutting off his father's penis with a scythe and went on to eat his own children, with the exception of quick-thinking Zeus who managed to hide in a recess of the cave. Zeus later overthrew his monstrous father and banished the Titans from the area. Atlas, the leader of Cronus' army, was famously condemned to hold the heavens on his shoulders.

Zeus might have been an improvement on Cronus, but his reign was also stormy, full of jealous feuds and bloody recriminations. Zeus' morals were very shaky and he committed rape on several occasions by disguising himself as a swan, a bull and even a cuckoo. He ruled by guile rather than compassion, which ultimately led to his downfall.

Our guide joked that many of Greece's recent rulers had inherited the arrogance of Zeus – especially the Fascist colonels who took over from King Constantine in the late sixties, and ruled for seven tyrannical years. But, deities or despots, it seemed destiny always caught up with them in the end.

I cycled back towards Iráklion, past the sailed windmills and the maize fields of the Lassithi Plateau. I could see why Crete was Dave's favourite cycling terrain: other than the odd tourist-saturated pocket it was an island as magical as Prospero's and as full of life as Zorba's. For sheer natural beauty it had been one of my finest rides to date.

Before boarding my evening ferry to Rhodes I checked to see whether Knossos was still on strike. It was. The myth of Theseus and Ariadne, a golden thread and a half-man, half-bull would remain in my imagination. After my disappointment at Zeus' dingy birthplace, perhaps it was better that way. Crete was a wonderful island, with or without its legacy of bickering immortals.

The following evening the ferry docked at the old walled city of Rhodes. I was only to spend a single night here, but it was to prove a memorable one, thanks to the offer of a free retsina at a seafront kebab restaurant. The manager, a heavy-jowled man with large animated eyes that never seemed to blink, was called George. He was in combative mood.

'Give me the name of a famous Greek,' he demanded, carving from a slowly rotating, grease-beaded torpedo of kebab.

'Hercules.'

'No, no. A normal Greek; not one who strangles lions.'

I frowned in an effort to extract some trivia from my sun-burned skull.

'Spiro Agnew, Nixon's Vice President.' Thank God for pub quiz nights.

'I suppose he'll do. Next please.'

'Maria Callas.' She had to be Greek, or maybe either Spanish or Italian . . .

'Good choice.'

I managed two more: Aristotle Onassis and the poet George Seferis, but then came a cropper. George did not allow Alexander the Great, claiming he was Macedonian, and neither would he agree to Socrates or anyone else who lived in ancient times.

'Pampadroo.' I guessed.

'Who is Pampadroo? A dancer? A circus horse?'

'He's a politician, isn't he?'

George laughed. 'You mean Papandreou, my friend. George and Andreas Papandreou. Father and son Prime Ministers. The father, George, is very famous. He had an affair with an air stewardess. It made world headlines.'

So that was my lot. I could only name four Greeks and was unable even to remember the country's most important political dynasty this century. I challenged George to name some famous Brits. He, of course, just reeled them off – politicians, pop stars and about two dozen footballers.

'OK, you win,' I said. 'But I could tell you many more names from when Greece was a superpower. America is the superpower now and we could both name thousands more famous Americans.'

Bulky ponytailed Alexandros, who was smoking at the counter, pointed at my route map of the world.

'Look at Greece,' he boasted. 'It is still the middle of the world. All civilization stemmed from us. Who needs names?'

'You could pick any country and claim it was the middle of the world,' I said, shifting my finger around the map. 'How about Venezuela, Papua New Guinea or even Macedonia?'

'Macedonia, pah. Don't talk to me about Macedonia.'

Mentioning Macedonia always seemed to spark a reaction.

Many Greeks had harsh things to say about their northern neighbour, largely due to the Macedonians' continuing push for independence.

'The Macedonian struggle is dangerous for Greece,' added Alexandros. 'It is dragging our country down.'

Alexandros did not seem to trust any foreigners apart from the Serbs, whom he described as 'Greece's best friend' because they share the Orthodox faith. He clearly detested both Turkey and Europe and the idea of the two together appalled him.

'Turkey might soon be part of Europe,' he ranted. 'That's crazy. They have nothing in common with us. They are Muslims and they have big problems with the Kurds. Turkey is a mess and will make Europe a bigger mess than it already is.'

'What about Greece?' I responded. 'Your country is Orthodox and has all these problems with Macedonia. In fact, hasn't Russia recently recognized Macedonia's independence?'

Alexandros suddenly lunged forward, grabbing my shirt collar with his pudgy, kebab-stained fingers. I knew Macedonia's desire for independence was anathema to him, but he seemed to be going a bit far. He looked at me through dark, retsina soaked eyes and for a moment I thought he might head-butt me. There was a terrible silence.

'Listen,' said Alexandros gently. 'Throughout history, Greece has lost thousands of lives saving Macedonia from the Turks. It is Greek and always will be Greek. OK?' He smiled, loosened his hold on my collar and walked away.

I was shaking with a combination of fear and anger, but perhaps Alexandros was right to bully me. What did I understand of Macedonia, barring the odd fleetingly scanned newspaper article? If he came back I would talk about somewhere less contentious, somewhere closer to home; Milton Keynes, perhaps.

'I can't stand all this Greece is best stuff,' George whispered when Alexandros was out of earshot. 'It's crazy. We are a tiny country, very poor; just a Balkan state but still so proud. Greek people are waiting for another Alexander the Great, but Alexander believed he was a god and he would not last five minutes today. Our pride is like a disease.'

But was this proud attitude so unusual? I asked myself. Any country that has at some point dominated the world suffers from these delusions. The British still bask in the afterglow of the Empire, the Spanish become misty-eyed at the thought of their conquistadores, the Romans are far prouder than their fellow Italians and the Portuguese still sing haunting songs about their explorers.

Ancient Greece is the oldest and perhaps the most impressive of all these civilizations. Once, at the time of Alexander, it was an empire whose territories stretched through Turkey, Iran and Afghanistan out to the plains of India. Now it has been reduced to a small and troubled state, happy to be neither Balkan nor European, struggling to stay in one piece and at loggerheads with its neighbours.

Yet many modern-day Greeks still have the pride of the Olympians who once, in legend, ruled over them. In a strange way, you have to admire them for it; in fact, I found their atavism and charming self-importance strongly reminiscent of Swanbourne.

CHAPTER FIVE

COMPANY

Through the years Turkey has proved a testing, at times fatal, environment for long-haul cyclists.

When Thomas Stevens, the American who spent three years touring the world on a penny-farthing, arrived in Constantinople he was greeted by 'a most undignified mob ... wild and riotous with excitement, flinging their red fezzes at the wheels ... and more than one stone comes bounding along the street, wantonly flung by some young savage'.

After braving the Turks, Stevens went on to cycle through Iran, Afghanistan, India and China – where he ate fricasseed kitten – and finally made it back to San Francisco's Golden Gate Bridge, his starting point, in one piece. Considering the punishing terrain, volatile politics and the discomfort of perching on a rock-hard saddle, it was quite an achievement.

Unlike most travellers of 1884, who would have been equipped with an entourage of porters and trunks, Stevens travelled very light. He carried no sleeping bag and used his poncho as a makeshift tent. The solid tyres of his penny-farthing meant that he had no need even for a puncture repair kit. His one luxury was a .38 Smith and Wesson revolver which he holstered for self-defence and in the hope of bagging wild animals. Although he was stoned by mobs in Turkey, Stevens never resorted to drawing his gun.

Dervla Murphy was less fortunate during her 1960s cycle tour to India. *En route*, in Dogubayazit, a Turkish town near the Iranian border, she was forced to fire a warning shot at a horny Kurd.

'I awoke to find myself bereft of bedding and to see a six foot, scantily-clad Kurd bending over me in the moonlight,' she recalled in her book, *Full Tilt*. 'My gun was beneath the pillow and one shot fired at the ceiling concluded the matter. I felt afterwards that my suitor had shown up rather badly; a more ardent admirer, of his physique, could probably have disarmed me without much difficulty.'

On the same trip Murphy shot dead a couple of wild dogs that ambushed her near Belgrade.

More recently, south-east Turkey proved a sticky spot for a trio of British round-the-world cyclists. In 1995, they were kidnapped by guerrillas from the PKK, the Revolutionary Kurdistan Workers' Party. All three were released without incident but, as William Dalrymple noted in his book, *From the Holy Mountain*: 'the hostages were forced to live for three months on snake tartare and raw hedgehog'. Dalrymple added a stark warning from his Turkish hotel receptionist. '"The tourists should consider themselves lucky. If it had been Turkish soldiers that had fallen into the PKK's hands they would have had their dicks cut off . . ."'

One cyclist who was to pedal his last in Turkey was Frank Lenz. Inspired by Stevens, twenty-five-year-old Lenz left New York in 1892 to follow the course of the sun on an early pneumatic-tyred bicycle. Lenz had been cycling doggedly for two years when disaster struck. What happened still remains a mystery but fragments of his bike were found near Erzurum in north-east Turkey. It is thought he had either been set upon by Kurdish bandits or devoured by wolves.

This is Lenz's final sad diary entry: 'I must confess to a feeling of homesickness. I am very tired of being a stranger. I long for the day which will see my wanderings at an end.'

It had crossed my mind to pack a weapon in order to avoid a Lenz-like fate. One friend had offered me a rape alarm canister, which screeched like a cockatoo when activated, while another handed over a flick knife bought from a market in Seville. My mother had suggested throwing a bag of pepper and cinnamon into the face of any would-be attacker.

'Sure, Mum,' I said. 'A grenade of mixed herbs will really have them quaking in their boots.'

'David beat Goliath with a sling,' she countered.

'Just take a bloody twelve-bore,' added my father gruffly from behind his newspaper.

Apart from my three-blade Swiss Army penknife (including corkscrew, nail file and toothpick) I had decided to shun all weaponry. Even if I armed myself to the gunwales like Robert De Niro in *Taxi Driver*, somebody could still do me in if they wanted to. A weapon would provoke suspicion at Customs and generally prove more trouble than it was worth. Besides, I took a t'ai chi lesson once.

Travel is never fair. Lenz had carried over 140 pounds of equipment, had been meticulously organized, but never made it home. The more carefree sparsely equipped Stevens survived his penny-farthing odyssey and went on to trek through Kenya – where he met the explorer Henry Morton Stanley – and then cantered across Russia on a mustang, each time completely unscathed. Versatile adventurer though he was, it was undoubtedly Stevens' 13,500-mile penny-farthing record breaker that remained his finest hour. His journey, despite the fact that penny-farthings were outdated by the time he returned in 1887, grabbed the attention of people across the world including the writer Leo Tolstoy, who learnt to ride a bike aged sixty-seven, and Queen Victoria, a keen tricycle collector.

Dervla Murphy's trip likewise sparked the imagination of a new generation of cyclists, some of whom followed in her wake. Murphy has since become an increasingly ambitious traveller, riding a mule across Ethiopia, trekking with her six-year-old daughter through the Pakistan wilderness and more recently, now in her sixties, cycling 6,000 miles across post-apartheid South Africa.

But despite these legends of the road I have to confess my principal inspirations still remain a cherry-faced gardener and an ancestor with outlandish sideburns.

Of course Johnny Ginger never went anywhere near Turkey but Captain Charles was posted there towards the end of his career. He did not like it.

In 1854, at the start of the Crimean war, Britain joined with France and Turkey against the Russian army, which was clearly intent on expansion in the Balkans at the expense of the Turks. Captain Charles, who by then had been promoted to admiral (for convenience, I'll still refer to him as Captain), spent brief spells in the Bosphorus but was mainly stationed in the Crimean port of Balaclava, where he was instructed to sort out the chaotic harbour.

Captain Charles found the Turks a tricky race to deal with. He was in charge of importing grain from Turkey's Danubian provinces, straw from the Sea of Marmara and donkeys from Antioch.

'They have 12,000 animals, with such a set of scoundrels of all nations to manage them (mostly Turks) I never saw before,' Fremantle wrote in a letter back to Swanbourne. But, for all his grousing about Turks, Captain Charles did a fine job. The correspondent of *The Times* wrote in one his despatches:

'Admiral Fremantle displays the greatest energy and zeal . . . he has brought the harbour of Balaklava into as good order as any dock in London or Liverpool.'

For his efforts Captain Charles became a Knight Commander of the Bath. One of his hardest tasks was still to come, persuading Florence Nightingale to leave Scutari with her nurses on one of the evacuating ships. From his diary he clearly found the redoubtable nurse something of a battleaxe. 'It is very desirable that she [Nightingale] should go away, but Ladies are difficult to persuade, particularly this one,' he wrote. Fremantle refused to wait indefinitely and by July 1856 had sailed home to the safety of Swanbourne.

Clearly Captain Charles had little affection for Turkey; Frank Lenz was killed there and several of his fellow cyclists harassed. Martin Luther had once prayed to be delivered from the World, the Flesh, The Turk and the Devil. Just what sort of country was I entering?

Marmaris, my first port of call in Turkey, was not the best place to experience the mystique of the Middle East. It was full of bars called Rick's Cafe or Blue Lagoon playing Pink Floyd and Bryan Adams. The restaurants had misspelt menus which offered 'Startings' followed by 'Main Curses', while the postcards flashed sandy breasts and buttocks promising 'No Problem In Turkey' or 'Pamukkale OKAY!'

The locals were not the swashbuckling Ottomans of yore but rather effete earnest folk, selling boat rides and leather jackets. Marmaris's only distinctly Turkish qualities were the tulip-shaped tea glasses and the odd scruffy copy of the Koran amid the second-hand Jilly Coopers.

It even boasted a youth hostel.

I was sharing a spotless dormitory with two brothers, Andy and Matt Johnstone. They were as American as blueberry muffins: big, bronzed, God-fearing Chicago boys on a month's holiday mountain biking around Greece and Turkey.

The brothers were a friendly pair with steady jobs and even steadier girlfriends. Matt was a trainee surgeon and Andy a salesman for a product called Sky Chair, an extraordinary item of furniture that looked like a levitating sofa. I knew this because Andy carried a wodge of business brochures. As is often the case with home-loving career people, the brothers were anxious travellers, rattled by the unfamiliar.

They had not enjoyed their time in mainland Greece and moaned about rude locals, unhygienic hotels and poor food. But they had liked Rhodes.

'What did you think of Rhodes, Tom? The walled city was so pretty.'

'I don't know,' I said. 'I only spent one night there.'

What *did* I think of Rhodes? Yes, the old walled city had looked impressive and the palace of the Grand Masters too. But the thing I remembered most about Rhodes was Alexandros's fingers at my throat, the same way I remembered Valence because of Hugh's vision of a hitch-hiking Jesus and Dover for Vicki Neuberger's kindness. It was always the people who stuck most in my mind.

Sometimes the transience of my trip was deeply frustrating, never getting familiar with anywhere; but in other ways it was fun to be in a state of permanent goodbye. Memories stayed simple that way, innocent of the confusions of time. The first sip of wine is always the freshest and only after a bottle do things become blurred.

'So how about we ride together tomorrow, Tom?' said Matt. 'Could be fun.'

'I'd love to.' I'd been hoping they would ask me but had been reluctant to push myself on them.

'Good, I'll set my alarm for dawn.'

We lost Andy within five minutes. Matt and I cycled along the harbour past the ranks of bobbing yachts and fishing skiffs while Andy headed for the town centre. We eventually found him after a long search through the labyrinthine streets.

'Dang it, Andrew, why are you always floating around with your head in the clouds?' said Matt. They both used phrases like 'dang' and 'flipping gum trees' instead of more earthy swear words. I felt like a character in a Hergé cartoon. But once we were up in the hills, we were all on a high.

For a while the conifers offered shade but soon we were out in the open, exposed to a nascent but powerful sun peeking over the citrus groves and dewy fields of corn. It was early May and the scents of summer were already in the air – the damp waft of the forests and the fresh sweet smell of pasture. Russet-coloured TURK FIAT tractors were crawling across the land.

I struggled to keep up with Andy and Matt, partly because their bikes were much lighter but also because they had perfected the art of SMT. SMT was their abbreviation for Slow Moving Trucks. Whenever the gradient became too steep the boys would grab hold of one of the wheezy timber lorries as it crawled up the hill and give themselves a tow to the top.

They would overtake me shouting, 'Grab hold, man.' I pompously told them I couldn't because it would be cheating. This was a blatant lie. I would happily have been towed up every hill to Jerusalem but I simply didn't have the co-ordination for such a manoeuvre. Every time I lunged out at a truck tailboard, I would topple over. I tried repeatedly, some-times grabbing hold for a few seconds before capsizing on to the grainy bitumen, my panniers cushioning the fall.

All morning we raced along, taking it in turns to lead. I found it was fun to have some company and the hours flew by. We stopped regularly to shower under garage hosepipes or to eat dried apricots in the shade of tamarisk trees. By lunchtime we had reached Koycegiz harbour, wet with sweat and itchy with the heat blisters on our forearms.

From Koycegiz it's possible to take a short boat ride across to the isolated cove of Dalyan and so, after a swim, we hired a boat and strapped our bikes to its prow. The walnut-faced boatman was clearly stoned but it didn't matter, the water was flat and our vessel as stable as a punt.

Once in the boat I felt very drowsy. The sun was so fierce the palm trees seemed to shimmer in slow motion, as if they were underwater. The outboard was humming away and I lay there listening to Matt and Andy talk about their Swedish grandfather. They wanted to telephone him. He was in hospital. They remembered camping with him one Christmas when it snowed . . . and then I was back in Swanbourne singing 'Silent Night' with the village carollers, sitting on a bale of straw with my sister on the back of a silage trailer, snowflakes swirling . . .

I woke with a start. It was very quiet apart from the softly lapping water all around. I looked at Matt. Fast asleep. I looked at Andy. Fast asleep. I looked at the boatman. Fast asleep. Good. I closed my eyes and then opened them again fast. The boatman. THE BOATMAN IS ASLEEP.

I glanced ahead. We were heading straight for an alarming cluster of grey rocks, protruding from the water like stepping stones. I shouted at the boatman and hit his arm. He opened eyes rheumy with sleep and instinctively grabbed hold of the rudder. The rocks surrounded us but were well spaced and our slow speed enabled us to chicane our way through them. By this time Matt and Andy were wide awake and we all laughed wildly — especially when our baggy-eyed captain fell asleep again only minutes later.

In Dalyan we were lucky to find a room for three in a guesthouse surrounded by whitewashed walls with trellises of honeysuckle and wild rose. We took a brief siesta beneath the erratic breeze of our overhead propeller fan before heading out to explore.

Matt was keen to buy a Turkish rug so we made for the town centre. There were carpets all along the high street, fleecy shagpiles, coarse-haired kilims and silken handmade rugs. Many seemed too dazzlingly intricate to have been the work of human fingers; some hung like royal pennants while others lay on the dusty pavement.

Ramazan, a roguish-looking man with remarkably hirsute eyebrows, was the first salesman to corner us. He was very charming but with a patter so polished you could see through it a mile off.

'Hello, my dears, let me tell you all about carpets,' he said, having lured us into his Ali Baba cave of woolly furnishings. 'Carpets are the Turks' way of telling a story. A man cannot reveal his feelings to a girl in words, it would be too forward, too upfront. So he gives her a carpet as a more subtle sign of his love.'

Each carpet dye is made from a different substance, explained Ramazan, while pouring us tea from a multi-spouted samovar. The crimson dye comes from crushed beetles, the green from pulped reeds, black from tree bark and blue from an indigo flower. Many of the carpets in his shop were covered with animals, especially those made by nomads, as a mark of respect for their livestock.

My favourite was a huge off-white rug the size of a boxing ring. It contained a variety of wools: camel hair stuck out from the fringes, grey goat's fleece dominated the middle while the bullseye was an aureole of snow-white lambswool criss-crossed with mulberry juice.

'This sort of thick simple carpet is used by a woman on her wedding night,' Ramazan told us, stroking it. 'The first time of love-making can be painful so a carpet is preferred to a bed. All Turkish women should be virgins before they marry. In the Koran there is even a description of paradise in which beautiful women have their virginity constantly renewed,' mused Ramazan wistfully. 'But on earth this is sadly not the case.'

'So it's OK for you to sleep around but not the lady?' huffed Andy in mock outrage.

'Of course,' said Ramazan, dismissing the question with a flick of his brilliantined hair. 'The woman is only the receiver of the seed. It is the man who is the provider, he needs experience.'

'Where do you get the experience?' I asked.

'I'm lucky because I travel. I even repair carpets for the Victoria and Albert Museum. I can meet girls from all over the world. My fiancée is English. I met her when she was seventeen; she is twenty-one now but she is definitely a virgin.' He paused, smiling. 'At least that's what she told me.'

We spent the rest of the evening quizzing Ramazan about Turkish carpets and sexual mores. He was a most patient and informed fellow but considering not one of us bought even a bath mat, perhaps not the best of salesmen.

The following day I left the Johnstone brothers at the coastal resort of Fethiye. They had only two weeks of their holiday left and wanted to relax a little, covering thirty miles or so a day. I, on the other hand, had to crack on. It was my job to crack on. It may have been the most happy-go-lucky job in the world, but I still had to see it through.

I was really enjoying the trip now. It had been fun spending time with Andy and Matt but I preferred being on my own. I could set my own rules, stay wherever I wanted to and take risks without having to consider anybody else. Other than the vague time strictures I was obliged to observe for my sponsorship, it was the most freedom I have ever known.

The south coast of Turkey made perfect cycling terrain. Not too much traffic, some challenging roads and plenty of diversions to be had in forested hills. I had 800 miles to cover and the forthcoming mountainous stretch might be tough, but I was cruising now. Three weeks max.

The great thing about being on a bicycle is that your senses are alive to everything around you. I could hear frogs burping and chirruping among the banana trees; I saw mountain hares and ruined Seljuk castles; I was frequently startled by the high-pitched klaxons of passing trucks and chased by children selling strawberries. Sometimes they would follow for miles on their rusty bicycles. 'Mista, mista!' One evening I stopped cycling and found a crystallized dragonfly stuck to my leg. It was as blue as the sky but just one touch and it turned to dust.

In the lush plain of Demre I saw the Church of St Nicholas. Santa Claus again. The nomadic Laplander had first appeared in Sicily, now here he was in Turkey: but this time it really was the famous one.

Legend has it that Noel Baba – Santa Claus in Turkish – was a generous fourth-century bishop who would help out poor village girls by dropping bags of money down their chimneys. Thanks to his kind deeds he later became St Nicholas, patron saint of virgins, sailors, pawnbrokers and Holy Russia among other things. The largely derelict church at Demre supposedly housed his tomb. I spent a lunch break there leaning against the crumbling pillars and eating wild nasturtiums.

It took me a week to reach the south coast's biggest resort, Antalya. On arrival I was dog-tired and before braving the town centre, I decided to stop off at a beach thick with sunbathers. I dragged the bike down towards the sea and was soon stretched out in the hot sand. A topless middle-aged woman with peroxide hair lay next to me; her skin was so pale she looked almost transparent. The swimming was a let-down as the sea was irritatingly unrefreshing, a bit like wading through saliva. This miserable experience served to remind me why I've always hated resort towns. Fine with family or friends, but alone, a crowded beach is one of the saddest places on earth.

The outskirts of Antalya are grim. Concrete skyscrapers rear up like giant harmonicas above the congested streets where crowded buses terrorize the pedestrians. I could see children in the municipal park swinging from a set of vandalized goal posts and knew that all I wanted was to find somewhere to sleep. I'd had enough.

As I pedalled along, a custard-coloured bus pulled up directly in front of me. It was belching the usual toxic fumes and I cursed my bad luck. I stopped the bike abruptly, shouted 'Dang' (a habit picked up from Matt) and pushed off again to get clear of the wretched vehicle.

A minute later the same bus pulled up ahead of me. I skidded to a halt, this time my bike colliding with the bus's rear bumper. In a fury, I pulled away, overtook the tiresome obstacle and cycled smartly off. Within no time it roared past and cut me up again. By now I was white with rage; the bus driver was clearly trying to wind me up. It was time to give him a piece of my mind. I trawled my memory for the appropriate words in Turkish.

'AAAAAAAAAAAAAAAAHHHHHHHHH,' I screamed.

I pulled the bike up on to the pavement, remounted and pedalled like a dervish until I reached the driver's door. I waved my fist and flew into a stream of violent expletives. Flipping gum trees was certainly not one of them. The Turkish passengers palmed the dirt from their windows to get a better view of the ululating Englishman. They were looking at me with grave concern while the bespectacled bus driver glanced nervously about.

'YES!' I shouted, cycling away. 'That will show the bastard.'

But yet again, the custardy bus swerved in front of me. I was speechless, on the verge of apoplexy, when a young boy who had been touting tickets jumped off the bus. He approached me, cowering beneath his baseball cap. I threw down the bike and glowered at him; he had something in his hand which looked familiar. Very familiar. It was my map, my map of Turkey.

The blood drained from my face and my sweat chilled as I looked at my back pannier. The Velcro strap which had held my map was empty. It must have fallen out and the bus had been pulling over to stop me. The poor driver had simply wanted to give me back my map.

I was overcome with embarrassment. The little tout held out the map and I took it from him gently. 'Sorry,' I whispered. Then I jumped up on board the bus and shook the driver's hand as passionately as Stanley must have shaken Livingstone's. He just smiled as if to say, 'No problem.' Such polite people, the Turks.

I walked up the aisle gesturing to the passengers. 'Me crazy man,' I said, twirling my fingers around my temples to denote lunacy. 'Me crazy man. Me very sorry.' I said it so many times it almost became a mantra. They looked at me, some doubled up with mirth, others increasingly bemused. I put my hand on my heart in a hopelessly tardy gesture of humility and walked back to my bike in shame.

I had acted with stupefying arrogance and had been an obnoxious ambassador for my country. I was even wearing a Swanbourne T-shirt, a grid reference to my guilt.

Swanbourne, said the T-shirt, Western Australia.

*

I discovered it was a mistake to write off Antalya as an eyesore, for the old Roman enclave of Kaleiçi was serene and attractive with its tiled fountains and cascading vines. I checked into the popular Pensione Sabah. The beds were all taken, but I was allowed to pitch my tent on the roof terrace. It was a commanding spot, high above the jaunty ginger-tiled roofs of the neighbouring houses and the distant minarets. I was paying less than two pounds a night for the best view in town. After a shower and a catnap, I wandered around the cobbled streets. Down by the harbour was a busker with a crew cut. He sang beautifully and gave a spirited rendition of 'Norwegian Wood' by the Beatles. His name was Terry – a Geordie who had been working in a restaurant in Istanbul but found life as a troubadour more fun. He was hoping to learn Turkish.

'I just wanted to get the hell out of England,' Terry said. 'I love Newcastle but there's no work, man, no quality of life.'

I had met lots of travellers over the past couple of months like him. Brits busking, manning bars, teaching English, picking grapes. Many were simply travelling, happily bumming around, but others like Terry were looking to rediscover a sense of purpose. I left him leaning on the harbour wall singing Simon and Garfunkel's 'The Boxer'. As I walked away, I noticed that his battered guitar had a tiny Union Jack stuck to its neck.

Kaleiçi boasted a winning combination of crumbling weed-infested ruins and tastefully revamped restaurants and shops. A film poster advertising Emma Thompson in *Sense and Sensibility* shared wall space with anti-Kurdish propaganda. It reminded me that the port of Alanya, less than a hundred miles down the coast, had previously been targeted by PKK terrorists.

On the main street, the usual ranks of carpet and postcard sellers were hunkered down beneath a canopy of jasmine and vines.

'Hey, you, Mr Sportsman.' A tiny, bald, grey-stubbled man stood in front of me. 'Yes, you. Mr Bicycle. I saw you earlier today.'

'Hi.' I shook his hand.

'You know what? I climb Mount Ararat with my bare hands,' he said. 'Look at them.' He thrust his palms in my face. 'These are nomad's hands – they work hard. Look at yours. Pah. Like velvet.' He gave me his card. Deniz Kosaz, Gabi Enterprises.

I wondered if this was a new way of selling carpets. Most of the other vendors I'd encountered had been polite to the point of irritation but here was horny-handed Deniz publicly lambasting me.

'Mount Ararat. That's near the Iranian border, isn't it?' I said.

'Pah. You bloody tourists. You come here. You know nothing. Just flash your tits around. No respect. Mess up our country. Where's Mount Ararat? Pah. You disgust me.'

I found him fascinating. His English was faultless even if he had been touched by demons.

'Is this how you usually sell your carpets?' I asked.

Fortunately, Deniz laughed at this. He poured me a glass of raki, adding water from a chipped terracotta pitcher, and the liquid clouded to a milky white.

'You are a weak man,' he said. 'Look at your eyes. You are frightened of me.' Too right, I thought.

'But me, I fear nothing.' He gurgled his raki. 'You think you are better than me. More clever. Pah. I speak perfect German too, you know. Anyway, what are words? Words are nothing. Allah is silent. He is like a mountain, completely quiet, but still he spurts out waterfalls. He rules over us all.'

What impressed me most about Deniz was that he had not

mentioned carpets once. He was in an evangelical mood and harped on about Cat Stevens, the seventies pop star who had reinvented himself as Yusuf Islam, a high-profile Muslim proselyte. Conversation moved on to the newly veiled English rose, Jemima Khan, now living in Pakistan and then to several servicemen who had joined the ranks of Allah during the Gulf War.

Deniz held the conviction that humanity was running out of time. He warned me that eighteen signs appear in the Koran which are supposed to herald Armageddon. Ten of them are subtle signs that have already occurred on Earth: sins like drink, drugs, gambling and casual sex. But there are eight big signs due to appear any day – you know the sort of thing – the sun will change direction, clouds will envelop the earth, Jesus will reappear and lead a terrible apocalyptic war against the forces of darkness.

'The Koran mentions Jesus,' said Deniz, looking me in the eye. 'We respect him as a prophet but do not believe that he was the son of God. Our Prophet Mohammed never tried to be anything other than human. He married a widow and after her death took ten more wives. Mohammed led a worthy life and then simply died; no ridiculous rising again.'

'But ten wives!' I said.

'The Koran says a man can have a maximum of four wives but Allah made a special exception for Mohammed.'

I pointed out that Jesus never married, probably so that he could focus on his spiritual work. Deniz countered by mentioning the wise King Solomon who had 700 wives and dozens of concubines.

'Mohammed is mentioned in the Bible, you know,' said Deniz, gulping on his raki. 'The Saint Barnabas version.'

'I'm afraid I've never heard of Saint Barnabas.'

'It does not matter, his gospel was much later than the others. What is important is that you remember Mohammed lived in the sixth century. He was the last prophet.'

'Are you saying the Koran is more believable than the Bible because it is more recent?'

'Exactly, no updates like your Christian gospels. This is the *very last* word. When humanity is destroyed all Muslims will be replanted on a separate paradise. For those who are not Muslims there will be eight tiers of hell. The worst tier is for those who say they believe but who do not really.'

'What about you Deniz? You are happily drinking raki!'

'Before I die I will make the *hajj* to Mecca. That gives me, how do you say . . . a clean plate. After the *hajj* I will never drink again.'

'What happens if you die before that? It's a long way to go for a confession.'

'I will not. I am going to be a *hajji* very soon. I will fly on this carpet. Whooosshh.'

He plucked a sprig of jasmine from the cascading plant and breathed in deeply. Tears were welling in his eyes and I was beginning to feel very uncomfortable.

'Give me some money,' he suddenly snapped.

'No.'

'Give me some money.' His demeanour had changed radically and he began to look a little crazy; his moustache was beaded with white specks of alcohol and his eyes were dilated like a doll's.

I gave him a 50,000-lira note, about one pound sterling. He put it in his mouth, masticated aggressively and spat it out.

'I hate money, Mr Bicycle man. Hate it.' He began to laugh, a phlegmy cackle. 'Don't worry. I am just a crazy old Turk, but I have more faith and less fear than you ever will. Leave me, you bloody tourist. Leave me on my flying carpet.'

The south coast of Turkey is divided into two clear halves: the coastline west of Alanya contains the holiday resorts; but when the sand runs out so do the tourists, and suddenly the mountains take over.

I found the lack of urban comforts in the mountains daunting at first, but after spending a couple of nights with local families I began to savour it. Conversation was hopeless but I would draw pictures in my diary and they would sing folk songs accompanied by the *saz*, a sort of elongated banjo. We ate omelettes with flat bread accompanied by yoghurt so piquant it made the eyes water.

The bicycle was a great ice-breaker. I was a vulnerable absurdity, coasting along with my multicoloured panniers, and I posed – apart from a blunt Swiss Army penknife – absolutely no threat. The generosity and utter lack of suspicion demonstrated by so many people astonished me. I began to understand that the finest aspect of travel is not a transcendentally beautiful building or a breathtaking landscape but the simple trust of strangers.

My hosts varied enormously in character. In Alanya, the last tourist bastion, I was put up by Rolf, an elderly German who had sold his schnitzel restaurant in Munich and retired to the sunshine. In Anitli, I stayed with a sad-looking farmer who fed me aubergine mush and let me sleep in a string hammock and in Silifke a posse of teenagers in baseball caps invited me to an open-air concert by Haluk Levent, a Turkish pop star. Levent, an Anatolian Rod Stewart, crooned valiantly as fireworks exploded up above.

But it was only when I reached the province of Hatay that I

felt I had truly arrived in the Middle East. Hatay is the nub of land in south-east Turkey that borders Syria, and cycling though the province's cotton fields and pistachio trees I saw many more men sporting the *keffiyeh*, the Arab headdress. My presence began to arouse more curiosity. In the remote village of Serinyol, as I rested in the shade of a fig tree, an elderly farmer dressed in a jellaba touched my sun-bleached hair with great suspicion while his wife studied me bashfully, her pretty face framed by a black cowl.

It struck me as bizarre that three weeks earlier, 800 miles away at the opposite corner of Turkey, I had been in Marmaris with Andy and Matt, sitting in bars that boasted naughty postcards, Bon Jovi on video and Carlsberg on tap. In Marmaris they talked of Europe and America but in Hatay they spoke of Kurds, Syrians and Saddam Hussein. I could scarcely believe I was in the same country.

The only consistent feature I had noticed in the various provinces I had pedalled through was the pictorial presence of Mustafa Kemal, popularly known as Atatürk, the founder of modern Turkey. Although he died from a raki-drenched liver in 1938, Kemal's image is still ubiquitous – the mustachioed hero's statues and photos are displayed all across the country, in high streets, houses, shops and restaurants – from Hatay to the Hellespont.

Atatürk entered Turkish history at a time when the country was on the verge of collapse. The once mighty Ottoman empire, which 400 years earlier had stretched to the gates of Vienna, had shrivelled. At the beginning of the twentieth century the 'Sick Man of Europe' was dying. Mustafa Kemal was determined to revive him.

After defeating Allied forces at Gallipoli in the Great War and ejecting the Greek army from Smyrna in 1922, Atatürk made it his life's mission to drag his country kicking and screaming towards Europe. The Latin alphabet replaced Arabic, polygamy was banned and even the bright red fez, Turkey's distinctive national hat, was branded as primitive; Atatürk wore a panama instead. By the time of his death Mustafa Kemal had achieved his dream: he had united the country and restored pride to his people. Under his leadership the Sick Man of Europe had achieved a near-miraculous recovery.

A few years ago *Time* magazine named Mustafa Kemal 'The Man of the Century'. Kennedy, Churchill and Mahatma Gandhi, among others, were controversially deprived of the accolade by a comparatively unknown Turk, who, even fifty years after his death, is revered throughout his country. As Jeremy Seal observes in his book, *A Fez of the Heart*, Mustafa Kemal is 'the pic 'n' mix icon ... every Turkish constituency can find something in the man of which they approve.'

At Iskenderun, I pitched my tent on a beach near a restaurant with a sweeping sea view. The reassurance of nearby humanity – the lights, the voices – was a comfort but the restaurant looked a little too plush for my budget and so I set off to find a *kebabji* up the road. Two men on a motorbike called out to me.

'Hey, brother, you must join us,' the driver said. 'We are eating here. We will treat you.' The barbecue hissed tantalizingly in the background. Why not? I thought.

The biker was called Akkan, his friend Sedat. They were both twenty-three, clean-shaven and slickly pomaded. They were professionals: Sedat was a TV cameraman and Akkan worked for his parents' advertising company. Akkan spoke good English, Sedat hardly a word.

We had an excellent meal of grilled sardines washed down with weak Amstel lager. The two talked about films; they liked Eddie Murphy and Julia Roberts. I asked them if they had seen *Midnight Express*.

'Of course,' said Akkan. 'It's shit. So are all those films about the Middle East. That film *Not Without My Daughter* was the worst. Even if it is set in Iran it makes all Muslims out to be monkeys. We are modern people. Only the Kurds are like that.'

Akkan winked at Sedat who, it transpired, was half Kurdish. 'I am only joking, Tom,' Akkan whispered. 'So many people hate the Kurds, but to be honest, they are our brothers.'

I asked them about the attacks on Turkish tourist resorts by Kurdish terrorists.

'It's the same with terrorists all over the world,' said Akkan. 'They try to spread fear. It's a shame but the Kurds have had a hard time, not only from our army but Saddam Hussein too. They just want a little more recognition, no more being pushed around. I can understand that.'

Akkan explained that the Kurds had once fought side by side with the Turks against both the Armenians and the Greeks, but with the advent of Atatürk's New Republic they were marginalized. They have been fighting for improved rights ever since and, as a result, south-east Turkey remains a war zone.

I asked Akkan what he thought of Atatürk whose picture was – inevitably – tacked to the restaurant wall.

'He was the greatest Turk of all,' said Akkan. 'Yes, he was hard on the Kurds, but to unify a country you cannot please everyone.'

Later, we sat on the beach. Akkan and Sedat chain-smoked, flicking their fag ends towards the sea. The gunwales of a wrecked ship, gleaming in the moonlight, protruded from the gently lapping surf.

The beer had gone to Akkan's head and he was getting carried away with his patriotism.

'Saddam Hussein is a madman. We have to ignore him.

Turkey is the most modern part of the Middle East. Remember, we are the only Muslim country to have had a woman prime minister. We are truly modern now.'

'Yes, Turkey now allows female prime ministers,' I agreed, 'but what about your problems with Syria and Iraq over the damming of the River Euphrates? And what about the Refah party preaching that a strong Muslim regime is the only way to save Turkey? And what about the Kurds?'

But none of this fazed Akkan and it was heartening to see his unshakeable optimism. He wanted Turkey neither shackled to the austere policies of its Muslim neighbours nor labelled a European Union stooge. He wanted the best of both worlds: a Turkey that was modern and independent. Sedat, however, just wanted to go home.

'We are a modern nation,' slurred Akkan as he straddled the bike. 'I go to Europe on business. Your newspapers just print stuff about under-age English girls marrying Turkish waiters. Who cares? Europe thinks Turkey is still backward. But we are forward. We are just as modern as you. Tell your people that.'

'OK,' I said. 'But we are far from perfect.'

The two friends could no longer hear me over the roar of their bike. They gave a thumbs up and sped off into the night towards Iskenderun, Alexander the Great's old city. Akkan and Sedat had been good company and I felt happy and flushed as I walked back down the beach.

The restaurant was still rowdy. I unzipped my tent, tumbled in and lay in my boxer shorts trying to ignore the racket above me. As I dozed, I noticed a bright light overhead. Must be a firefly, I thought until it began burning the fabric, and I realized it was a cigar butt.

Before I could react, the nib of hot ash had eaten through the canvas and landed beside me. I picked it up fast, peeled back the tent flap and stubbed it into the sand.

The party in the restaurant were all too drunk to heed my shouts of complaint. One waiter tried to help but clearly understood no English. Besides, I must have looked ridiculous in my underwear waving around a frayed cigar butt. I draped my towel over the newly perforated tent and dozed off again.

The next morning I managed to fix the cigar hole with a puncture repair patch. After a swim and a quick breakfast I pedalled off into a searing headwind towards Antioch.

Biblical Antioch was one of the world's most important cities – a stronghold of piety and honest commerce. St Peter preached there as did St Paul, prior to his martyrdom in Rome. Later, St Simeon Stylites the Younger, a hermit with remarkable powers, erected a pillar near the city on top of which he lived for thirty years. The dust from St Simeon's clothes was reputedly able to cure leprosy and constipation, revive dead livestock and turn rough seas to calm with a single sprinkling.

Sadly, there was not enough of St Simeon's holy dust to go around and, in time, Antioch became the most depraved city in the Roman Empire. I cycled through the town (now known as Antakya) in the late afternoon and it certainly appeared to boast none of its former glory. I found it to be little more than a litter-strewn backwater flanked by barren hills.

It was my last night in Turkey. I lay in the guest house cubicle clapping at the mosquitoes and suddenly noticed a cockroach the size of a tablespoon head scuttling across the floor. I threw *Don Quixote* at it. Direct hit. The cockroach buckled, lay still and then shot out under the door. It had been hit by the equivalent of a meteorite and had hardly noticed.

The mosquitoes were driving me mad so I pitched my little tent, which could be erected without pegs, on top of my bed. I zipped myself inside the bug-free canvas and lay down, sweating profusely. I tried to imagine what the province of Hatay must have been like in its heyday, when it had been the nucleus of the ancient world. How could it have collapsed so spectacularly? But then I thought of Russia, not so long ago a superpower, now a fragmented mess.

The cockroach returned, crawling across my outspread map of the world. I unzipped my tent, threw *Don Quixote*, missed and turned out the light. In the darkness, I could hear the frightened insect quickstepping off to a fresh bolt-hole.

CHAPTER SIX

MOVEMENT AND MEMORIES

As I approached the Syrian border, deserted machine-gun nests cordoned off by barbed wire appeared amid the scrubby biscuit-coloured hills. Blinded by the sun, I pulled over to put on my sunglasses. They proved futile; in the phosphorescent light not even a welder's mask would have offered much protection.

I stopped at the Turkish checkpoint, a prefab with a poster of Jean-Claude Van Damme tacked to the wall. The guard gave my passport a cursory stamp. I nodded my thanks and pushed off into a desolate no man's land littered with rusted jeep chassis and smashed furniture. At the roadside, a crow pecked at the dusty viscera of a long-dead cat.

Only after several miles did I reach the border with Syria marked by a large whitewashed office. There my passport was scanned by a torpid youth in relective sunglasses wearing a green uniform. He leaned back on his chair, chewing gum and flicking his worry beads. In the background, a portable TV showed Boris Becker diving for a volley.

The office was dominated by a portrait of Syria's President, Hafez al-Assad, a sombre middle-aged man in a jacket and tie. He had the forehead of an Egyptian pharaoh, dark eyes, an indistinct moustache and a tight smile. It was the face of an ersatz saint and an overworked dictator, a face which has haunted Syria for almost thirty years.

The young official waved me off and I hauled my bike into the shade of an acacia tree. A gust of wind teased the surrounding sand and puffed out my map like a spinnaker. I pinned it down with some rocks and dug out my Lonely Planet's *Middle East*. It was time to do a little homework before setting off on the remaining few miles to Aleppo.

I turned to the bicycling section.

'While there are many places and occasions in the Middle East where a bicycle would be useful, there are many more where it would be a distinct liability. The distances, the climate, the terrain and the politics all make cycling a most improbable method of transport.' Ho hum. And the good news?

'Usual dress restrictions are not waived for cyclists. Ones who wear shorts for example are likely to have stones thrown at them'. Oh well, at least I could finally ditch my rubber shorts. If nothing else, I reassured myself, Syria would double my sperm count.

I pedalled off into the desert. The undulating, pale golden landscape had a biblical feel to it. It was easy to imagine trains of spice-laden camels filing towards Babylon or pilgrims with cascading beards wandering around in search of Christ. Sandstone igloos and drystone walls were scattered across the jaundiced earth. The time warp would have been complete were it not for a New Holland combine harvester parked in a nearby cornfield.

I stopped to buy some cherries at a corrugated tin shack. The woman who weighed the fruit had milky grey eyes which looked as if all colour had seeped from them. A muslin hood brocaded with coins shadowed her withered cheeks. She handed over the cherries and watched me as I ate them. They were yellow, sour and delicious.

An hour later I cycled into Aleppo, Damascus' northern rival, well known for its conservatism. For a callow Arabian tourist such as I, it was an overwhelming place. In Turkey the haunting call of the muezzin had often sounded unnatural but here, in what is perhaps the world's oldest inhabited city, the call has been rallying Muslims almost since the time of the Prophet Mohammed.

But, amid the dusty confusion, what mesmerized me more than anything was the sight of a woman enshrouded completely in black. No part of her skin was visible, there were no eye slits in her yashmak and even her hands, despite the shocking heat, were encased in gloves of dark chiffon. I became so transfixed by her that I was almost run over by an old white Chevrolet, a relic of the French Mandate, which tore across my path. By the time I had recovered myself I had lost sight of the woman's spectral figure in Aleppo's crowds.

After a brief skirmish in the city centre I made a beeline for the Hotel Yarmouk, at the guidebook's suggestion, but was informed by the concierge that it was chock-a-block with Russian businessmen.

My homeless status was changed by a shifty-looking tout with a limp, who grabbed my bicycle and pulled it through a chicane of shoe-shine boys to the Hotel Zahert Al-Rabit. The reception office was dimly lit and filthy but the staff were almost certainly the friendliest bunch in town. I was embraced by a variety of Yasser Arafat lookalikes and ushered into a £3 a night room with a cat asleep on the pillow.

It was going to be an interesting couple of days.

Aleppo has been the site of so many sieges and massacres it is hard to keep track. The blood of Philistines, Persians, Greeks, Romans, Arabs (who infiltrated the city by masquerading as goats), Mongols and Ottomans has stained its fiercely coveted streets.

But, for all its cruel history, it has also acted as a valuable haven for refugees fleeing Turkey, especially Armenians. Between 1915 and 1918, it is estimated that 1.5 million Armenians were killed in eastern Turkey by Ottoman troops. Those left alive fled towards French-ruled Aleppo and only a lucky minority survived.

The Armenians, the vast majority of whom are Christian, have a thriving business community in Aleppo. Coco Maslumian, the elusive proprietor of the city's legendary Baron Hotel, was at one time the most famous Armenian in the city. That evening, I decided to pay the hotel a visit in the hope of witnessing a little of the magic of Coco's heyday.

But the Baron was a shabby ghost; its halcyon days were long gone and its leather armchairs had faded and ruptured over the years. Ignoring the fusty atmosphere, I tried to visualize the celebrities who might have propped up the Baron's bar in days gone by: how about Agatha Christie, sipping a Martini after a long haul on the Orient Express (Aleppo was once the train's last stop); or Theodore Roosevelt, flushed from a day's wildfowling on the Orontes marshes, quaffing a vintage malt; perhaps even T. E. Lawrence (his unpaid bill still hangs on the bar wall) insisting on a revolting desert elixir.

But it was hard to imagine such distinguished barflies today. Tonight there was a party of four taciturn Dutchmen, an old lady asleep on a rocking chair and me. I finished my beer – my first and last in Syria – and went in search of somewhere to eat.

I tracked down a little restaurant in the Jdeide Quarter and tucked into kidneys marinated with mint and yoghurt. Jdeide is the Christian neighbourhood. The streets are narrow and lined by medieval houses with balustraded ivy-threaded balconies. Nearby, church bells were ringing.

The following morning, fuelled by several cups of cardamom coffee, I visited Aleppo's famous souk.

If the Baron stood as a vestige of colonial days, the souk was a throwback to *The Arabian Nights*. All accounts I had ever read of the souk described it as deafeningly loud and so I was astonished by how quiet it was. Some of the stall holders were even asleep. There was a little haggling going on but nobody was hectoring the crowds with an aggressive sales pitch. Each of the souk's dark vaulted alleys contained specific merchandise. There was a spice section which smelt overpoweringly of aniseed; there were glass blowers, butchers and honey sellers too. The stall holders were as varied as their wares: blue-eyed, green-eyed, dark-eyed, clean-shaven, moustached, bearded and some bearded but not moustached – favoured by the most austere Muslims.

One of the noisier sections was crammed with copper smithies and gold jewellers. Many were Armenian, I discovered, as by Koranic law Muslims are forbidden to work with gold. Donkeys occasionally trotted past and I saw boys struggling with wooden wheelbarrows brimming with apricots from Turkey or dates from Iran. A moped revved past with several anxious guinea fowl riding pillion.

I poked around all morning, sometimes coming across the khans or caravanserais, the courtyard inns that had provided shelter and stabling for medieval merchants. There was never any pressure to buy in the souk. It was possible to chat for up to half an hour and still walk away with a flurry of smiles and backslapping.

'Hey, mista, mista,' shouted a voice. 'Scarf, silk scarf.' It was the most aggressive sales pitch I had been confronted with all morning.

'I am Aladdin. I show you best silk scarf.' A manic-looking youth with dark bouffant hair and blue eyes grabbed my arm. 'Where you from, my dear?'

'From England.'

'Yes, England,' he said. 'Look at you. You are a very pale man.'

'So are you,' I replied. His skin was as sallow as candle wax.

'Of course, I live down here all day,' he pointed up at the tiny, randomly spaced portholes of daylight. 'This is our only light.'

Aladdin displayed his different coloured silks, some plain, some shot with silver. He was quite a salesman, flashing his scarves around with the panache of a matador. A crowd began to form around him.

'You know Paul Tearoo?' Aladdin asked me at the end of his performance. 'He is USA travelling writer.'

'Theroux. Yes, I've read his book about England. Some of his fiction too.'

'He is lying man,' said Aladdin. He reached into a cardboard box and pulled out some photocopied pages from Theroux's book, *The Pillars of Hercules*. Aladdin handed the pages over. A yellow marker highlighted several paragraphs which reported an entertaining dialogue between Theroux and Aladdin in which the former clearly implies that Aladdin is gay.

'So are you gay or not?' I asked.

'Oh yes, very gay,' he confessed. 'But Tearoo wrote that I say women smell like omelettes. I did not say this.'

'What did you say?'

'Octopus. Women smell like octopus.'

I laughed.

The travel book is a funny thing. I remember reading long ago in quick succession Theroux's *Kingdom by the Sea* and Jonathan Raban's *Coasting*. Both books were interesting, filled with spiky observations and written about the same subject, England. Most illuminating though were the sharply contrasting accounts of the authors meeting each other in Brighton. Two of the world's most respected travel writers with a clash of memory – not of politics, religion or literary style, but memory. Yet to me the books seemed very honest; each had been telling the truth as he remembered it. It made me realize that memory, honest memory, is a traveller's most important asset.

I left Aladdin clowning around with a new group of tourists and headed out to the citadel which is built from huge tawny slabs. From street level it looks impregnable. Beyond the tall arch of the citadel gates are two badly eroded lions: one happy, one sad. The happy one depicts the thrill of victory, my guidebook informed me, but the sad one reminds triumphant soldiers that death is never far away.

The guidebook's most astonishing revelation was that among all the medieval ramparts and crenellations is the tomb of St George, England's patron saint. His body is at rest in a dank burial chamber deep inside the citadel. Apparently St George was a Christian soldier, martyred during the third century in Palestine. My book even suggested that he might have slain the dragon in a country as far away as Libya.

Surely not! This could not be true. St George. The very epitome of Englishness. I had always imagined him cantering around somewhere up in the Lake District. Now I was being told, categorically, that England's patron saint got no nearer Penrith than Saladin or Tamerlane. If nothing else, this trip was proving an effective way to shatter my often bigoted preconceptions.

The road from Aleppo to Damascus runs flat and straight and is flanked by a carpet of pale sand. The occasional poplar tree or the ribcage of a dead animal breaks the monotony. As I cycled along, I thought it would be like this until I reached the Suez Canal. A beautiful, barren and infinite desert.

The desert is often compared with the sea. Cycling through it, I could understand the comparison. The only way to stay sane when confronted with extreme isolation is to keep your thoughts buoyant. When travelling solo, on a boat or a bicycle, your memory is all you have for company; allow it to become too dark or troubled and it will destroy you.

Great nomadic adventurers like Wilfred Thesiger and Bruce Chatwin thrived on the isolation of the desert. 'Here in the desert I had found all I asked; I knew that I should never find it again,' Thesiger wrote after his last harrowing journey through the Empty Quarter of Arabia, one of the most inhospitable stretches of sand on earth. Chatwin felt much the same way after living with Sudanese nomads. 'I never felt safer with anyone or, at the same time, more inadequate,' he admitted. Thesiger is now too frail to travel far and Chatwin is dead.

Chatwin's most famous book, *The Songlines*, contains many gems – some lucid, some downright weird – on the pros and cons of nomadic life.

My favourite is from Robert Burton, an Oxford don, who after years of dedicated research, decided life in one place spelt depression. 'The heavens themselves run continually round, the sun riseth and sets, the moon increaseth, stars and planets keep their constant motions, the air is still tossed by the winds, the waters ebb and flow . . . to teach us that we should ever be in motion.'

I remembered Round-The-World-Again Dave predicting that if he stopped moving he would probably die. At the time it had sounded absurd but now I could understand what he was talking about.

Of course my nomadic lifestyle on the bicycle was wildly happy. I was a traveller, a stranger, my only responsibility to cycle fifty miles a day. Out here in the desert I did not worry about career prospects, about my social life, my weight, my future wife, my role in the big scheme of things. It all seemed so irrelevant. I hadn't once felt homesick and my only attack of loneliness had been at the very beginning of the trip when Alexandra's smile and the comfort of routine had still been fresh in my memory.

But then I thought of Johnny Ginger – the man who turned these nomadic theories on their head – a happy man who had stayed in one place all his life. Would his life have been improved if he had roamed the deserts and sailed the seas? Would he have been happier, more fulfilled? I doubt it.

But in some ways Johnny Ginger was a nomad, or at least had the vision of a nomad. By comparing Swanbourne with the world, he had turned himself into a cerebral traveller. He had found happiness exploring a world within a world. In this way he was of one mind with Thesiger and Chatwin: they shared a belief in the rapture of simplicity.

The Syrian desert was often bleak but, unlike the sea which frightens and unsettles me, I found its dramatic nudity calming. Despite the seeming desolation, there was always somebody or something about – a goatherd, a nomad, a passing truck, the road signs which warned MAKE LIGHT SPEED, A PLACE FULL OF INHABITANTS – to break the monotony.

In the blazing midday sun I would often stop off and siesta in one of the roadside tents, where I would be spoilt rotten with slivers of watermelon and cups of translucent tea. The Syrians were as instinctively generous as they were laid-back. From the souks in Aleppo to the roadside desert shops, there was a universal lack of urgency.

One person who doesn't quite seem to share his countrymen's easygoing approach is President Assad, whose smile looks the very embodiment of anal retention. The man has the word uptight practically tattooed on his forehead. I have never been to a country where the leader has such a pervasive presence. The man makes Madonna look like a recluse. Assad is *everywhere*, whether hanging ten feet tall from the façades of skyscrapers or sculpted on to roadside milestones. A Big Brother who never blinks.

Assad posters were certainly out in force in the desert town of Hama but what a dreamy place it appeared to be. Enormous wooden water wheels creaked round, churning the muddy River Orontes. Children balanced precariously on the rotating blades and divebombed off. I saw rhododendron leaves drifting slowly downstream while swallows swooped over the water. It had the feel of an English university town, an Arabian Oxford, the perfect place to unwind after the two-day ride down from Aleppo.

But Hama's genteel appearance is only a veneer. The city was the site of Syria's most violent uprising against Assad's tightly controlled Baathist regime. Assad is an Alawite, a follower of an obscure branch of Islam, and from the start his faith and policies have been opposed by the fundamentalist Muslim Brotherhood based in Hama.

In 1982 Assad took radical and brutal action. Troops under the command of his brother, Rifaat, assaulted the city and between 10,000 and 30,000 inhabitants were killed. There are reports of blocks of flats being pumped full of cyanide and tanks shelling indiscriminately. Even now, amid the modern white concrete buildings, it is not difficult to find smashed or pock-marked masonry.

Assad has always been ruthless with his opponents. In 1980, members of the brotherhood tried to assassinate him in Damascus. Two grenades were thrown. Assad kicked one away and his bodyguard dived on the other. In retaliation, Assad ordered the killing of dozens of prisoners in Palmyra.

To be fair to Assad, an ex-airforce commander, he assumed control of Syria in a time of turmoil and since 1971 has charted a steady, albeit blinkered, course. He strengthened ties with the West by assisting with the release of the Beirut hostages and, more recently, offered support to the Allies during the Gulf War. However, the West's continued links with Israel — Syria's chief enemy — mean that a relationship with Assad can never be more than fragile at best.

I never invited negative comments about Assad during my time in Hama but was nevertheless astonished not to hear a single complaint, however ambiguous, about this controversial leader. According to Amnesty International, there are eight levels of secret police in Syria and that may well have had something to do with it.

My route did not take me to Syria's premier tourist attractions: Krak des Chevaliers, possibly the most impressive Crusader castle, and the mainly Roman ruins of Palmyra, Queen Zenobia's beautiful lost city. But the road to Damascus provided other distractions, the most surprising being at a roadside café just outside Hama. It was a grubby, flyblown place with butterflies and flowers daubed on the shabby walls. A sweet-looking girl in a purple cowl served me tea. I drank it quickly and, after a fifteen-minute catnap, walked back outside.

I froze, my heart thumping behind my rib cage. THE BIKE WAS GONE.

I panicked. NO, a voice screamed inside me. NO, NO, NO. I was in a state of shock. As the trip progressed, I had become increasingly trusting. Who the hell would steal my bike here? Nobody even used bikes, so surely mine would look completely incongruous. I dashed down the street, poking my head through latticed shutters shouting, 'BICYCLE! BICYCLE!' I was almost in tears.

And then, emerging out of the shimmering heat like Omar Sharif on his camel at the beginning of *Lawrence Of Arabia*, came my bike. At first it resembled a dark blob but then, as it came closer, the silhouette of the panniers gave it away. I sprinted over to it. The boy pedalling was about fifteen and laughing like a jackass. He had my helmet on back to front, my sunglasses askew and had smeared his face with sun block. I could not possibly be angry, it was clearly a case of high jinks. Besides, I was ecstatic to see my home again.

I think if the same thing had happened to me in France I would not have cared less, but now I knew by the way my heart was pounding that this trip meant far more to me than ever before.

The rest of my route to Damascus was plain sailing. I slept in a dormitory of Syrian soldiers in the remote desert town of En Nebk and pedalled off the following morning as a dramatic dawn, streaked with magenta clouds, filled the sky. On the approach to the capital I passed road signs warning of wild camels and others that indicated MECCA, MEDINA and BAGHDAD. It amazed me that it had taken only five days to ride here from Aleppo – to span the bulk of Syria.

Damascus did not look like a beautiful city from my bicycle saddle resembling a gigantic building site studded with flyovers and industrial zones. After getting hopelessly lost among the old American taxis and horse-drawn carts, I headed for Martyrs' Square along the Barada, a once gushing river now reduced to a toxic ditch full of styrofoam and cigarette butts. The sweltering June heat was putting me in a terrible mood.

Nevertheless, at the Al Haramein Hotel I managed to find an oasis of calm. The hotel's cool reception led through to a blue mock-Iznik fountain swirling with plump, multi-finned goldfish. Geraniums and aspidistras lined the courtyard walls and a wonky staircase led up to a four-bed dormitory which was cooled by a fresh breeze. Outside, a canary trilled in a bamboo cage.

On one of the hospital-style beds lay Takka, a Japanese chef. He was a wild looking man with shoulder-length black hair, a nose ring and ears weighed down with all manner of lobe adornment. On the opposite bed was Dan, a New Zealand actor, who was six foot five at least; he wore calf-length Doc Martens and stripy purple trousers. He would have been cast perfectly as Malvolio.

Dan was heading straight out, so I dumped my gear and tagged along with him. We ran the gauntlet of the relentless main-road traffic and threaded our way through the vegetable markets back to Martyrs' Square. There we sat on wooden stools drinking mango juice and turning down repeated offers to sleep with Russian and Bulgarian prostitutes.

Dan, who had travelled extensively in the Middle East, clearly loved Damascus. He told me his father had been a lecturing engineer in Saudi Arabia. Every holiday he had taken Dan and his two brothers to different parts of the region, including Iran, Syria and Egypt. Dan still spoke passable Arabic.

Clutching our juice cups, Dan and I made our way through a maze of streets to the Umayyad Mosque, one of Islam's finest monuments, which has a dazzling façade of cream-coloured tiles. The courtyard which leads up to it is as attractive as a Florentine piazza, and has the same flocks of restless pigeons. I took off my shoes while Dan struggled with his bootlaces.

In the mosque's cool interior I was struck by the relaxed atmosphere. In a building that has been held sacred for many centuries I expected oppressive austerity. There were families lounging under the arches with one man even stretched out and snoring in staccato splutters. Children played tag around the famous marble fountain, supposedly the midway point between Istanbul and Mecca, while a tour group moved through the prayer hall past the shrine containing the head of St John the Baptist.

After dozing in the mosque's shady interior for a while, Dan and I wandered back out into the courtyard and tracked down a coffee house. Dan ordered a *nargile* pipe and sat cross-legged on a hard chair, puffing away regally like the caterpillar in *Alice in Wonderland*. I had a try. Being both an asthmatic and a non-smoker I was surprised at how easily I inhaled. The smoke tasted good, a little blossomy, and fuzzed my head with positive thoughts.

'It's because you're inhaling smoke through water,' explained Dan. 'It's less rough.'

A shaven-headed soldier with rotten teeth came and sat next to us. His name was Mohammed, he was twenty-two and on leave from the Golan Heights.

'I live Aleppo,' he said. 'But it too far to go for one week holiday. I stay Damascus. I no friend here.'

'How long have you been in the army?' asked Dan.

'Seven month, less than year to go now,' he said, flashing his ruined dentistry. 'I no fire my gun yet. I hope I never do. We hopeless gun from Russia, Israel get good gun from Britain and America. I no want die.'

I wondered if it was safe for him to talk so openly, but he did not seem to care. He had not mentioned Assad yet.

'Why your country support Israel?' he asked me, suddenly angry. 'The Golan Height belong us. All the crazy fighting.' He stopped and spat at the floor, then asked Dan more calmly, 'You fight in army in your country?'

'We don't have to fight anybody,' said Dan. 'There's only

three million New Zealanders and we live miles from nowhere. It's a beautiful country, but no one can be bothered to disturb us, except for the French and their bloody nuclear experiments.'

A party of smart-looking Syrians entered the café, one dressed in a leather jacket talking on a mobile phone. Mohammad turned away from us, swigged his coffee and walked briskly away down an alley thick with vines and creepers.

Our final visit was to Saladin's tomb. It is a modest mausoleum for Islam's greatest military hero, so modest in fact, we had to ask repeatedly where to find it. Once inside the little crypt we inspected the two sarcophagi, one of rotting walnut – from when he died in 1193 – the other a beautiful marble slab, draped with a sheet the colour of snooker baize and covered in Kufic characters.

I had always imagined Saladin, who was of Kurdish descent, to be a sabre-wielding butcher. But in fact he was a man of some compassion. When he stormed Jerusalem in 1186, wresting it from the Crusaders, he freed many of the Christian survivors and was even rumoured to have shed tears over the slain knights. It was a display of extraordinary tolerance towards the Crusaders who had captured Jerusalem and slaughtered Muslim women and children in the streets less than a century before.

On the way back to Al Haramein Dan and I passed a hammam – a Turkish bath – and could not resist trying it out. Within minutes we had been stripped, swaddled in towels and pushed into a room where steam belched from what looked like an old bus exhaust pipe. Soon Dan and I were weak with perspiration. A giant, bare-chested man walked in. He looked like one of Cleopatra's eunuchs and had a belly so impressive a small rodent could have hibernated in his navel. He led me off to a side room and told me to lie face down. I gingerly prostrated myself on the chipped lilac tiles. My corpulent tormentor began by dousing me in icy water; he then slapped my thighs, hard, as a sign for me to turn over. He was holding what looked like a baseball pitcher's glove coated with sandpaper which he planed roughly over my heaving chest. Little flecks of skin, like miniature woodchips, peeled off my body.

After this undignified scouring, he lathered me roughly as if basting a turkey, pulling and karate-chopping at my soapy limbs. The worst part involved having my toes cracked, one by one, from their sockets. I gritted my teeth and whimpered stoically. After twenty minutes he stopped. I lay on the tiles, panting with relief. The silent masseur helped me up and swaddled me in half a dozen towels. Ten minutes later I was sipping tea on a pile of plump cushions, having never felt so relaxed in my life.

Dan appeared soon after.

'Bloody oath,' he said. 'I feel like a snake that's just shed its skin. I could do with another of those tomorrow. How about you?'

I leaned over and whispered. 'I'm off to Jordan first thing – then on to Disneyland.' What I wanted to say was Israel but, as Syria's long-term enemy is a strictly taboo subject, Disneyland had become a widely used travellers' euphemism. I had been warned before my trip that anyone thought to have been to Israel or even expressing a desire to go there would be instantly expelled.

'The Syrian secret police are hardly going to be sitting in a steam room,' scoffed Dan. 'Bloody Disneyland. What does that make Netanyahu, Mickey Mouse?' We both laughed at my paranoia.

'Where are you heading next then?'

'I think I'll stay in Damascus for a while,' said Dan. 'I really love it. And the Al Haramein is so cheap I could probably live there for years, eat nothing but felafel and still make a profit!'

Early the following morning I headed off to the border. The sky was still dark and a warm breeze tickled the sand. I was hoping to reach Jordan that night so that I wouldn't need to stay in Der'a which, like many Middle Eastern border towns, has a terrible reputation.

After the high spirits of Damascus and the friendship with Dan, I suddenly felt flat. Here we go again, I thought: another border, another currency, another language, another round of postcards. Fling Damascus on to the jumbled scrap heap of memory along with Aleppo, Rome, Paris, Swanbourne. This moody limbo always seemed to hit me as I was leaving a country but as soon as I had pedalled my first few miles, I would be on a roll again.

After a painstakingly slow ride against the wind, I did not arrive at Der'a until early evening; reaching Jordan was out of the question. The guidebook's only hotel was a dud. It was a hovel with pebble-dashed walls, a locked door and a couple of broken windows. It did not look as though anybody had stayed there for years.

In desperation, I asked around for an alternative and was shown to a rickety wooden stairway at the back of a grocery. There was no sign, so I clambered up to inspect the premises. The place smelt like a school changing room and in the foyer was a man, naked but for a pair of maroon underpants. We both looked as surprised as each other.

'You want girl?' he asked.

'I want sleep,' I said, putting my hand on my cheek and tilting my head.

He shouted across to a room. A tarty-looking girl in orange

tracksuit bottoms appeared. She dissolved in hysterics, as did the man in the pants. I made to leave.

'No,' he said quickly. 'I show you.' The man took my hand and led me into a dormitory. The beds were grim, wobbly and grey-sheeted. 'You sleep. Two-fifty.'

I haggled him down to 150 Syrian pounds (about four pounds sterling) and collapsed on the bed. Later the orange-trousered houri appeared with a bag of chips which she chewed listlessly. She had a hard, pock-marked face and a boyish figure. She started to dance. She was clumsy and graceless, gyrating about like a lapdancer. Soon she became bored with my embarrassment and swanked off to the balcony.

I found I was itching like mad, probably from bedbugs. I walked to the shower and poured a bucket of cold water over my head. Back in the dorm, I unfurled my sleeping bag and endured a fitful night listening to the whine of mosquitoes interspersed with the muffled sounds of strangers making love.

The following morning, the proprietor, still in his underwear, helped me downstairs with my bike. He could not stop smirking. Perhaps it was the bike. Perhaps it was the fact I had slept in a brothel alone, in a sleeping bag rather than in his bedbugged linen or with his orange-trousered lapdancer. Perhaps it was his maroon underpants. I'll never know.

Der'a is famous for its connection with Lawrence of Arabia. During the Great War Lawrence was a liaison officer with the Arabs and led them in some daring guerrilla raids against the Turks. In 1917 he led a reconnaissance mission to Der'a to check its defences. He was captured soon after his arrival. In his classic memoir *The Seven Pillars of Wisdom*, Lawrence skirts around this humiliating episode, but a year after the publication of this book he exposed the full story, telling of the horror of being gang-raped by the town's Ottoman governor and his lackeys. Lawrence admitted this violent experience had greatly traumatized him but, more worryingly, that it had also sparked in him 'a fascination and terror and morbid desire . . . like the striving of a moth towards a flame'.

After the war, disillusioned by the way the Allies had carved up Turkey, Iraq and the Levant for themselves, Lawrence returned to England where he joined the RAF.

Robert Tewdwr Moss, in his book *Cleopatra's Wedding Present* (so called because Syria was given to Cleopatra by Antony), notes that Syria is a land that lures detached and enigmatic people like Lawrence. Other Brits from the same stable include the explorer Richard Burton, who after his Mecca and Tanganyika escapades became a consul in Damascus. Then there was the beautiful impetuous Jane Digby, who after three marriages, five children and an affair with the King of Bavaria settled down with a Bedouin sheikh. Moss was something of an enigma himself. The day he finished *Cleopatra's Wedding Present*, his first book, he was found murdered in his London flat by an Arab rent boy.

Lawrence met his fate in equally mysterious circumstances after losing control of his motorbike near Bovington Camp in Dorset. It was 1935 and he was forty-six years old. The inquest recorded a verdict of accidental death, but the facts remain unclear. One theory is that the hero of the desert swerved to avoid a cyclist.

CHAPTER SEVEN

QUITE A SHOW

Before tackling Jordanian Customs I was careful to hide any incriminating evidence of my imminent visit to Disneyland. I stuffed my route map, which had Jerusalem clearly marked, in among a pile of ripe laundry. A soldier in a red beret and gravy-coloured uniform prodded my back pannier with his machine gun.

'You have drugs?' he asked.

'No.'

'Then go,' he ordered, waving me on.

For one of the world's most sensitive checkpoints it was a very perfunctory search although, to be fair, a blond push-biker in a Tom Petty and the Heartbreakers T-shirt was never going to be a Hezbollah prime suspect.

After the rash of Assad pictures in Syria, it was good to see a fresh face on display. King Hussein looked much more benign. On his poster at the money changer he was dressed in regal finery, festooned with medals and linking arms with his glamorous American wife, Queen Noor. Both were beaming like Colgate models. I changed fifty dollars into Jordanian dinars and pedalled off towards Amman.

Before long the pale sand darkened dramatically and an industrial chimney came into view emitting a plume of grey, wind-tugged smoke. A pair of buzzards circled high above in a sky the colour of faded denim. A westerly side wind buffeted me, constantly threatening to capsize the bike, but like a sailor changing tack I now knew exactly at which angle to lean into the wind, how to streamline my body and which gear to flick. Those first unsteady days in Swanbourne were long behind me; the bicycle was now part of me.

Within five blustery hours Amman was in sight. From afar the Jordanian capital looked like a mass of upturned cardboard boxes interspersed with the odd minaret. King Hussein had insisted all the buildings be constructed from the same local limestone which gave the city its stark, amorphous quality.

The streets were choked for miles and it was hard work swerving around the livestock trucks, the motorbikes and the French hatchbacks. I repeatedly hailed pedestrians to ask them the way downtown.

Eventually I found my hotel down a narrow alley shaded by hanging laundry, where an old man in a green tarboosh was playing chess against himself. A couple of lovebirds twittered on a perch above his head.

As with so many budget hotels the Cliff was on the top floor. I dragged my bike up five flights before crashing into reception. A mêlée of football fans congregated around a flickering TV screen: it was the European Championship. The Jordanian staff seemed as excited as the tourists. 'Steve Mc-Manaman, vary goowd,' the receptionist assured me.

I dumped my bike in an airless three-bed dormitory, then walked out on to the hotel balcony, high above Amman's pale flat roofs. It was here that I met Tanya. She was a sprite-like Bostonian, dressed in bell-bottoms. She looked up at me from her notepad.

'Are you pedalling around the world?' she asked, eyeing my bicycle helmet.

'Just to Australia.'

'Trying to break any records?'

'Too late for that,' I confessed. 'I think the fastest around-the-world cyclist was an Israeli. He took something like seventy-seven days. It took me that long to reach Turkey.'

Tanya, a Harvard history student, was working as a writer for a travel guide over her summer holidays. I told her it sounded like very exciting work, especially being posted somewhere like Jordan.

'You must be joking,' she said, yawning and curling her legs beneath her like a cat. 'There's this romantic myth about writing travel guides but I spend most of my time checking out the budget hotels. Whether there's cockroaches in the bathrooms, lice in the beds – that sort of thing. It's hardly crusading journalism.'

Tanya was a conscientious note-taker, scribbling into her diary whenever she had a chance. She appeared streetwise enough, wearing a loose neutral-coloured shawl and sporting a wedding ring – although she was single – to fend off unwelcome suitors.

We chatted until the last blip of crimson sun dipped below Amman's hills and then meandered over to the open-air street stalls opposite the Cliff. I plumped for a bowl of hummus while Tanya chose *fuul*, a dish of broad beans, garlic and lemon. We dunked our bread and gossiped.

Many of the Jordanians were in suits or chinos and check shirts, swigging on bottles of Coca-Cola. A picture of King Hussein in a leather jacket and jeans decorated the fridge. I mentioned to Tanya that Jordan felt much more westernized than Syria.

'Of course,' she said. 'The Jordanians are far more liberal. The papers here are even allowed to criticize King Hussein up to a point. Syria is a dictatorship whereas Jordan is a monarchy

– it's very different. Don't forget this is a country ruled by a man who used to play all sorts of team sports with his friends. I think the only person Assad plays with is himself.'

'And his people,' I said.

'Syrian people never complain about Assad but many hate him. Jordanian people always complain about King Hussein but mostly love him. That's politics.'

We had finished the main course and moved on to ice cream. As with most ice cream in the Middle East, this was gooey and elastic, like licking wet Plasticine. Tanya told a joke about King Hussein and President Assad.

It went like this.

Assad and King Hussein are standing on a balcony looking down on a military parade. To prove the discipline of his troops, Assad proposes to throw a feather over the balcony. When the feather hits the ground, he brags to King Hussein, all the Syrian troops will shoot each other. Sure enough, Assad barks out his orders and throws the feather. It floats down and when it lands the Syrian troops all shoot one other. Assad looks on proudly. 'How's that for obedience?' he says. 'I challenge your army to do the same.'

King Hussein has no choice. He braces himself, a look of regret on his face, and throws a feather down to his Jordanian troops. It glides down, skittish in the breeze, further, further, further. Then suddenly it flies up a little, and then up again. The Jordanian troops are all blowing dementedly, trying to keep the feather afloat. To demonstrate, Tanya puffed out her cheeks like a rainforest toad and blew her napkin in the air.

'That's the difference between them,' she said, catching the napkin. 'Assad expects blind devotion, whereas Hussein just expects a bit of respect. By blowing the feather in the air his troops did not have to die, but they did not have to disobey their king either.' We sat writing our diaries as darkness fell. I was writing about Tanya, while she was probably writing about the Cliff Hotel's cockroach population. At the end of the evening we exchanged addresses in the meaningless 'See you in Boston' way people do even when they are unlikely to see each other again. I headed for bed and left her in the moonlight, feverishly scribbling down fresh information.

The following morning I secured my Egyptian visa – very straightforward – and wandered around town. Tomorrow I would head for Jerusalem but this evening I had arranged to meet Muna and Darwish Aweidaii, two more contacts from Susan's bloated address book in Rome.

I could not work out Amman. At times it looked so spick and span with its Intercontinental Hotel, Pizza Huts and American high-rises but then I would come across a grubby old shop selling flintlock shotguns or a tumbril of grapefruit pulled by a scrawny mule.

The capital shows little trace of the twenty-odd years of British rule. In many ways the British in Jordan – the Union Jack was lowered in 1946 – proved as impotent as the French in Syria. King Hussein may have been educated at Harrow and Sandhurst, but his capital has a distinctly American flavour. The only evidence of the Empire I spotted was a solitary red postbox.

By mid-afternoon I was pole-axed by the heat. I returned to the Cliff, washed my clothes, wrote some postcards and fell into a deep sleep. At dusk, bleary-eyed from my extended siesta, I turned up at Muna and Darwish's travel agency. It was in a quiet, palm-fringed suburb to the north of town. Their office walls were very avant-garde, decorated with a combination of Jackson Pollock splotches and antique maps of the Levant and Asia Minor.

Muna, a buxom woman with immaculate geisha-style hair, caught the lift with me down to the office car park where

Darwish was waiting in a rusty Citroën. They both looked desperately tired. I suddenly realized what an inconvenience I was to them. These people had never met me, all they knew was that I had ridden a bicycle from England to Amman. Poor souls. Now they had to drop everything and take a grubby stranger out for the evening at the request of a faraway friend.

We drove to Zaman Kan, a swish touristy restaurant up in the hills. It was the sort of place that sold multicoloured sand in test tubes and charged Himalayan prices to dress you up as a bedouin and take your photograph. The high-pitched skirl of *urbeh* – Jordanian bagpipes – permeated the room as we entered. Effeminate men in white robes with red cummerbunds pranced around the tables like morris dancers on amphetamines.

Muna, Darwish and I sat in a candle-lit corner. Darwish was very quiet all evening. He was a strange-looking man, with no eyebrows and dark flaky skin. His scalp was almost tonsured, surrounded by clumps of silver hair. Muna did most of the talking as we ate our salads. She had studied tourism in Paris and then worked in Egypt conducting tour groups around Karnak and Abu Simbel. Darwish had managed a hotel in Saudi Arabia before returning to Amman to set up his own travel agency. The couple met when Muna applied for a job there.

'Were you born in Amman?' I asked Darwish. There was a palpable silence.

'I am a Palestinian,' he said, tipping the ash off his Marlboro. 'When I was a child I lived in Jerusalem; the east of the city belonged to our people then. During the 1967 war with Israel my parents had to pack up everything and flee. They walked with me and my seven sisters towards Amman. I was ten years old.

'We walked for hours and hours. The heat was severe and my feet became badly blistered. We had just crossed the King

Hussein bridge when KABOOM!' Darwish clenched his hands. 'An Israeli bomb blew it to pieces. Several of my school friends were killed.

'Another stray bomb hit our family. We were engulfed in flames. Two of my sisters were killed – one was fifteen, the other only three. I was so badly burnt I passed out. All I remember is the explosion, the heat, the screaming, the awful smell of my skin. I was in a coma for months. When I woke up I looked much worse than this.' He pointed briefly at his damaged face. 'I was lucky; the doctors did wonders.'

'Do you still feel Jerusalem is your home?'

'There are thousands of Palestinians in Amman. It is home now. I don't want to go to Jerusalem again. I have only been back as far as the ruins of the bombed bridge. Of course there's a new one next to it now.'

'Are you angry?'

'No, not now,' replied Darwish softly. 'The Jews and the Arabs are cousins, you know. In the Bible, Abraham had two sons with two different wives. One son was Isaac, the father of Judaism, the other was Ishmael, the father of Islam. So you see, the Jews and Arabs are related.' He interlaced his fingers, as if about to pray. 'During the Gulf War Jordan had no choice but to support Iraq; Israel was still the enemy then. But now things are improving. Israelis can visit Jordan for the first time in years. I'm glad.'

Darwish had told his story quietly, without sensation or bitterness. Muna must have heard it countless times but was still almost in tears. It was touching to see this gentle dignified man complimenting the people who had killed his two sisters and disfigured his own face.

'Have either of you made the *hajj*?' I asked, wanting to change the subject.

'Oh no,' said Muna, her voice still crackly with emotion.

'Once a woman makes the *hajj* she is expected to wear a permanent veil and never talk to any man other than her husband. I would not have been able to talk to you tonight. You are never supposed to drink alcohol again, either. Neither Darwish nor I are in too much of a hurry to reach Mecca.'

After the meal, we walked out into a star-spangled night. The odd flash of neon blinked out from the valley. 'Amman is nowhere near as beautiful as Jerusalem,' said Darwish. 'But it has been far kinder to me. Jerusalem only has sad memories.'

'I can't believe that tomorrow I'll be cycling there.'

'You'd better get some rest,' replied Darwish. 'I can assure you it's a long way.'

I woke at 4 a.m. The Cliff's insomniac door attendant rolled off his divan and helped drag my bike down the stairs. I sat on the pavement and breakfasted on biscuits and orange juice. The hummus stall opposite was already stocking the fridges with Coke for the day.

Amman is a city of hills. It had been an easy freewheel coming down from Syria, but cycling out towards Israel would be the reverse; I clicked into low gear and prepared for a hard ride. Some road workers, huddled around a brazier, whistled and whooped as I rode by.

After an hour I forked off the main road down towards the Dead Sea. Town was magically transposed to country, uphill to downhill. One minute I was hemmed in by a phalanx of white concrete as I struggled up a smooth three-lane highway, the next I was freewheeling down a wonky track lined with poplars and palms.

For the last twenty minutes before the Israeli border, I descended a steep series of spiralling switchbacks. It was an exhilarating ride; my face was jellied by the g-force and my eyes were streaming as the bike nudged 40 m.p.h. This was

Dual inspiration: Johnny Ginger outside the
Swanbourne House potting shed (reproduced
by kind permission of Swanbourne House
School) and Captain Charles Fremantle with
his mole-pelt sideburns at the age of 29.

Vanessa, Tecla and Ami manage Colgate smiles despite the fact that their Monaco Youth Hostel dormitory smells 'like a moose just died in there'.

A marcher holds high a placard in Athens on Labour Day (May 1). Later a bomb exploded in the capital's Plaka area. Fortunately nobody was hurt.

A common road sign in the Syrian desert, but I saw very few wild camels in the Middle East. The country with the most feral camels in the world is Australia.

On arrival at the King Hussein Bridge border crossing between Jordan and Israel.

Having freewheeled from Amman down into the Dead Sea valley (over 350 metres below sea level), I then had to confront Jerusalem's many hills. The last ten kilometres to Damascus Gate in the Old City were largely pushed.

The road signs in Sinai were often irrelevant.

Mr and Mrs Jurdi with Abraham in their garden in central Beirut.

Faranak outside the Armenian museum in Jolfa, Esfahan. Her traditional black chador helped to shield her blue jeans and Puma training shoes.

One of Ghafor's many 'uncles', taken near the shepherds'
bothy where we spent our first night in Nuristan.

Pakistani cycle wallah transporting his canteen
of parboiled Coke cans towards the Indian border.

The Sikhs' holiest shrine, the Golden Temple at Amritsar,
a spectacular copper-gilt 'cricket pavilion'.

Punjabi man disguising his bicycle as a genetically modified leek.

Sporting a turban outside the gurdwara in Patiala.
To my far left is the splendid Kuldeep Singh.

Above: Not so far from the madding crowds – everywhere in India, even in the remotest villages, the bike would be converged on by crowds of curious onlookers.

Left: Mrs Anand imprints a tika dot on my forehead at my Delhi leaving party. As a sign of good luck Mr Anand later smashed a coconut over the frame of the bike.

not surprising. I was plummeting towards the tip of the Dead Sea, the lowest point on earth. Shortly before the border, a thuggish soldier in mustard combat fatigues pulled me over. He grabbed my passport, studied it intently – holding it upside down – and thrust it back, the purple EU cover splashed with his palm sweat.

The King Hussein Bridge was sealed off by a fence of tangled barbed wire. THE HASHEMITE KINGDOM OF JORDAN – WELCOME, THE LAND OF PEACE, read one of the signs. A grey bus with a farting exhaust was waiting to cross over.

I pleaded with the border guards to let me ride my bike across the bridge. I explained I was not permitted to take any public transport – that I *had* to cycle. I dug out Captain Charles's diary and a faded *Bucks Herald* newspaper article to prove my point. I may as well have shown them *Don Quixote*.

'This is the West Bank,' said one of them. 'If you go over the bridge on a bicycle you will be shot. It's simple. There is only one way over – by bus. It takes a few minutes.'

I skulked off, unhinged my panniers and gave my bike to a luggage boy who threw it into a boot at the rear of the bus. My reflector light clipped a suitcase handle and shattered. Shards of vermilion plastic fell on to the road. The boy shrugged his shoulders and walked off.

My nerves were frayed but not as badly as Peter's, the fidgety German sitting next to me. The poor fellow was a study in *angst*. He ran his fingers through his pudding bowl hair and picked his sunburned nose. On his lap was a Good News Bible.

'I cannot have an Israeli stamp on my passport,' he said. 'Otherwise I will not be able to see my girlfriend for months. She is working in Damascus.'

I tried to reassure him that all he had to do was ask for his Israeli stamp on a separate piece of paper. I did not want an Israeli stamp either. If my boat ride to India fell through, my only other option would be through Iran. If Iranian Customs saw an Israeli stamp in my passport, it would mean an instant *fatwa* or a one-way ticket back to Milton Keynes.

'But I have heard of the most terrible mistakes,' Peter wailed. 'And if you are not careful the Israeli guards will stamp you out of spite.'

'Come on,' I said. 'It can't be that bad.' His hysteria was starting to worry me.

'*Kaput*,' groaned Peter, filling in his Israeli entry form. 'Why did I decide to visit the Holy Land? *Kaput*. I tell you. *KAPUT*.'

When the bus arrived, Peter held my bike while I loaded up the panniers. We walked towards Customs. A Japanese man in blue-tinted sunglasses was in front of us.

'You, come here.' A female voice. I looked behind. 'Yes, you.'

A girl in uniform walked up to me. She was wearing an olive-green shirt and a thick black belt which enhanced her slender figure. She frisked me with a wooden baton then wheeled my bicycle off to an X-ray machine. Another guard, a gamine blonde brandishing an M16, ordered me through to Customs. The place seemed to be run by a militia of stern Amazons.

Peter was already on the other side of the barrier giving me the thumbs up and waving his separately stamped piece of paper.

'No stamp please,' I said. The squinting official glanced at me and bashed his fist down four times, very hard as if trying to swat a fly. Fortunately, he missed my passport, as requested. After its X-ray, my bike was wheeled back by the sour-faced Hippolyte. I saddled up and said farewell to Peter. Within thirty seconds I had been stopped again.

'You cannot ride a bicycle for the next two miles,' barked a young soldier at the checkpoint. 'It is no man's land. If you bicycle you will be shot.'

'By who?' I asked.

'By me,' he replied, but I could tell he was joking. I wanted to tell him about my bulletproof tyres but decided against it.

'So what do I have to do?'

'The minibuses won't take you with a bicycle. You'll have to hire a taxi.'

'A taxi!'

I unloaded the panniers again, unhitched my front wheel so the frame would fit into a taxi boot and haggled to be driven through the deserted two-mile stretch of desert. From the taxi window it seemed an eerie landscape, no shades of red, or pink, or yellow, just the wan washed-out colour of dead skin.

The taxi driver dropped me off. He threw the panniers out on to the road while I snagged the front wheel back on my bike. An Israeli soldier, gun at his hip, sat chewing gum as I struggled to put the panniers back on. Gone was the goofy obliging friendliness of Jordan and Syria; in Israel I was clearly on my own.

The West Bank, the buffer zone between Israel and Jordan, is a frightening place to cycle. To me the land looked sick and abused and the few cars I saw never waved or honked, they just thundered past. It was hard to believe, in this wasteland of bullet-dimpled signposts and broken glass, that I was near the road where the Good Samaritan had once walked.

What's more, it was the very worst time to cycle: the heat was at its mid-morning zenith and I was fighting a vigorous headwind. After an hour, near the Jericho turn off, I stopped at a white smut-stained tent where a friendly hunchback sold terracotta pots. I poured several buckets of water from his tank on to my overripe face.

Further south, the road began to rise but it was the wind that really slowed me the most. The occasional gust would even batter me to a standstill. I tried to focus solely on the road ahead, which at times was flanked by craggy monoliths of dark striated rock. I cycled in ten-mile bursts – each taking me over an hour.

Finally, I reached a sea-level sign which displayed a zero. I had already climbed almost 400 metres and had only just made it to sea level. How depressing. I felt like a mountaineer who has conquered a false summit and found a new peak protruding from the clouds ahead.

My skin was on fire. The wind was subsiding but the heat coupled with the relentless gradient was enervating. Apart from the odd juniper bush or brambly thicket there was little shade. I was only able to cycle in short bursts now. The small of my back ached terribly, I had no energy left and had to shout at myself to keep going. But there was something promising up ahead.

JERUSALEM 10 KM

I collapsed in the thin shadow of the sign and poured the remaining water from my bottle over my head. As I dozed, a colony of ants marched in a wavy procession up my forearm. It took several minutes to summon up the energy to brush them off.

From there on, I took it in turns to push and ride. I had been going uphill for hours now. The high-speed sprint down to the Dead Sea seemed like a lifetime ago. My long hair had matted into sweaty dreadlocks and I was desperate for a cold shower.

The first sight of Jerusalem was a real disappointment. The suburbs looked parched and neglected and developments of reinforced concrete sprung up from the haggard pine-studded hills which rolled like waves out towards the Mediterranean. Despite the busy traffic, there was no hard shoulder and I was regularly blasted by the airstreams of passing lorries. This was not the triumphant entry I had envisaged.

I pushed the bike, by now as heavy as a wheelbarrow of bricks, uphill until I reached the first major intersection. Confident that I was now high enough to glide down to the city centre, I remounted and kickstarted off into the wake of an open-backed truck filled with young shaven-headed soldiers. The initial coolness offered by the speed was invigorating. 'Alleluia,' I whispered as the sweat blew off my face. After an afternoon of incessant climbing, the downhill run felt sweeter than ever.

Then the pale ramparts of the old city appeared before me and the Dome of the Rock's golden cupola glistened – a triumphant beacon beneath the falling sun. Minutes later, I skidded to a halt among the crowds outside Damascus Gate.

Jerusalem. The ultimate pilgrimage city, hallowed by Jews, Muslims and Christians alike. Even a pagan like me could not fail to sense the spiritual currents. A young orthodox Jew in a black poncho bumped into my bike. His tousled hair flapped like spaniels' ears either side of his black hat. He scowled and moved on.

I stood for a couple of minutes just savouring the moment, watching the pilgrims swarm into the city which has been labelled everything from wondrous to psychotic. What did they hope to find behind these hallowed walls? Salvation? A piece of Christ's cross? Perhaps a handmade chessboard or a wedding ring?

Once I had snapped out of my reverie, I telephoned my friends, Nadav and Daniella, from a nearby call box. I had met them three years before on a trip to the Far East and was longing to catch up, to hear their news, to talk to people who had known me before this crazy two-wheeled odyssey of mine.

They lived in Tel Aviv and said they would drive straight over. An hour later, they found me slumped against one of Suleiman the Magnificent's sandstone pilasters, clutching my bicycle. I was fast asleep.

The couple of days I spent in Tel Aviv were blissful. Nadav and Daniella were both working and I had their bungalow to myself. I slobbed about eating Weetabix and jiving around to Daniella's Stevie Wonder CDs. As I had been starved of familiar music for months – except for the time I borrowed Cesare's Walkman in Rome – to hear it now was sublime. The other luxury was a hot bath, my first since England, and listening to 'Master Blaster' while submerged in soap bubbles was as near to nirvana as I dared imagine.

I didn't even want to look at my bicycle. I cleaned and oiled it then shoved it in a corner with a sheet on top. We needed a trial separation from each other.

Nadav's house was in Brandeis, a neat suburb of Tel Aviv. The houses are white-bricked and airy, with bougainvillaea and fig trees growing in the gardens. It was only after inspecting the place a little more closely that I realized the whole of Tel Aviv was neat and suburban: a plain functional city filled with the many foreign embassies that still refuse to accept Jerusalem as the Jewish capital.

Walking through central Tel Aviv my first morning I was mesmerized by a Marks and Spencers – a sudden flashback to home. I even began to imagine I was in Milton Keynes until I spotted three guards at the exit, each toting a sub-machine gun. Another time, I was browsing in a bookstore next to a man in a lumberjack shirt and a white yarmulka. His M16 prodded me gently in the ribs. He apologized and carried on trawling the thriller section, his gun slung as casually as a tennis racket over his shoulder.

This was a common sight. An Israeli soldier, even off duty, hangs on to his gun for dear life; if it is lost, he can be imprisoned for several years. Israeli men are conscripted into the army for three years, women for two. Looking after one's weapon is a long-term commitment.

That evening, as we sat eating olives in the kitchen, I asked Nadav and Daniella whether they had enjoyed the army.

'I was lucky,' Nadav said, dipping an olive into a bowl of hummus. 'I missed the action. The war with Lebanon in the early eighties was before I joined and the trouble on the West Bank afterwards. I had a good time. But I didn't have to shoot anybody, that would have changed everything. Most Israelis don't resent spending time in the army. We realize that with our geography and politics we have to know how to fight. Military service is seen as a necessary evil.'

Nadav had none of the machismo bluster of so many of the Israelis I had met on my travels. He was calm, softly spoken and formidably bright. Daniella, his long-term girlfriend, was originally from Argentina, a tall, graceful blonde with occasional flashes of Latin impatience. She too had enjoyed her spell in the military.

'We are both proud to be Jews and proud to defend Israel,' stressed Daniella. 'But that does not mean we are hardline Zionists or anything. I'm not very religious at all.'

'My father visits the synagogue regularly and eats kosher food,' continued Nadav. 'He despairs at my lack of faith. I had my bar mitzvah in front of Jerusalem's western wall when I was thirteen years old. At the time it was an overwhelming experience but now I am sceptical about religion. If anything I am lured by Buddhism.

'As a young Jew I lived a very regimented life, what with Judaism and the compulsory stint in the army. After twenty-one years of discipline, I slung on a rucksack and flew to India. Suddenly I was in a country where you can do *anything* you like. It gave me the most incredible sense of freedom.'

There was a collection of videos about India at the bungalow, which Nadav used for research. He insisted I watch one about a man called Lattan Baba, known as the Rolling Saint. He said it would inspire me to finish my trip. The three of us huddled down on the sofa in front of the telly.

'This is the reason I love India,' Nadav said as the screen blipped to life.

It was the most remarkable documentary I had ever seen. Lattan Baba was a sadhu, a holy man, who had spent his life demonstrating his devotion to God in the most outlandish ways. He wore no clothes other than a dhoti, and his hirsute skin was caulked with ash and orange paste. An explosive beard rolled down his torso.

Lattan Baba's finest hour, and the focus of the documentary, was a marathon roll of over 1,000 miles from his home in Gujarat province to the hills of Kashmir. When I say roll, I mean just that; Lattan Baba lay outstretched on the road and rolled over and over, day after day, through desert and monsoon. As he rolled, crowds lined the streets to watch his tumbling technique. It was remarkable: downhill he was very fast like a ballerina pirouetting horizontally, uphill his pace became more steady, the speed of a slowly twisting kebab. It was pure *Monty Python*, down to the plummy tones of the commentator. At first I laughed at the absurdity but then realized I was watching something quite remarkable. Lattan Baba was achieving an essentially impossible feat – it was beyond human endurance. He had elevated himself to a higher plane: it was his faith alone that kept him rolling.

Dumbstruck Kashmiri villagers would touch his body and fall to their knees. A little band of acolytes tailed him, bashing drums and jiggling tambourines. After several weeks the Rolling Saint arrived at his destination, a temple in the Kashmiri hills. He was placed on a throne of marigolds and jasmine and paraded around his village.

'Wonderful, eh?' said Nadav, ejecting the video. 'But only in India. If Lattan Baba had rolled through Israel we would probably have shot him. Eccentricity isn't something tolerated much here. It's just seen as a weakness.'

'What's Lattan Baba doing now?' I asked. 'Somersaulting to Samarkand?'

'Don't joke, Tom,' said Daniella. 'You should have learnt a valuable lesson from him. Remember, if ever you are about to give up, think how much tougher your trip could be. Remember Lattan Baba.'

On Friday afternoon, Nadav drove me up to a kibbutz on the Lebanese border where his brother worked. It was the first time I had travelled properly by car since leaving Swanbourne but I deemed it justifiable as we were heading north, off my cycle route.

It felt wonderful to sit in air-conditioned comfort, listening to Harry Belafonte croon about sunshine and coconuts. In fact, it was so comfortable I fell fast asleep: a three-hour journey through the Holy Land in complete oblivion. It made a marked contrast to cycling where every nuance of the landscape, every gust of wind and every camber of the tarmac came into play.

At the sprawling Misgav-am kibbutz, we were greeted by Nadav's brother, Achay, his wife Alona and their five children, two girls in their early teens and three younger boys. They were a beautiful family: dark, slim and strong, almost glowing with bucolic vitality.

The kibbutz was in a striking location. Mount Hermon, Israel's tallest peak, juts like a craggy fin from the volcanic hills to the east, while the barren undulations of Lebanon stretch to the north and west. A reinforced chicken-wire barricade, at least ten feet high, marks the border.

The family flat was too small to house Nadav and me so we were billeted in a spartan dormitory opposite the canteen. We dumped our stuff and Achay took us for a tour of the grounds.

The kibbutz had a team of one hundred workers, twenty of whom were foreigners. The main enterprise was fruit, explained Achay gesturing to the avocado and apricot trees sweeping across the valley. There was also a poultry unit, a cotton factory and a small trout farm. It was very much a family kibbutz and the children were provided with a well-equipped school, an indoor swimming pool and a zoo with deer, rabbits, ducks and peacocks.

'It's like a slice of paradise,' I said.

'In some ways you're right,' said Nadav. 'It's an efficient set-up, largely self-sufficient with everybody working for the common good. But you don't see the negative: the bitching, the financial wrangles and the lack of freedom. Everything is for the kibbutz and not the individual.

'The whole system is too claustrophobic for me – like a politically correct labour camp. Achay and Alona have community spirit running through their veins. They don't mind the long hours and low pay.'

The main complaint Achay had about Misgav-am was its proximity to the Lebanese border. That spring, Israel's 'Grapes of Wrath' campaign against the Hezbollah fundamentalists in south Lebanon had put the kibbutz in the front line. Several shells landed in the orchards and, although nobody was hurt, the women and children had been evacuated to a shelter near Jerusalem. Grapes of Wrath came to a tragic end when over a hundred Lebanese civilians and UN workers were accidently killed by an Israeli missile near the town of Qana. International outrage forced the Israelis to cease their bombardment.

After circling the kibbutz grounds we walked back along the border. Abandoned gun emplacements lay amid the Corsican pines and large yellow signs warned of landmines. Achay mentioned that the border's most pressing problem now was not invasion but drugs. Bags of hashish grown in Lebanon's Bekaa Valley were regularly thrown over the border fence at night into the hands of Israeli dealers.

That evening the only sign of life on the border was a pale heavily jowled man wearing Buddy Holly spectacles. He was sitting cross-legged on a grass bank looking out towards Beirut.

'That's Gary,' Achay whispered after we had walked passed him. 'He's about forty, our oldest foreign worker. There are only two kibbutzes in Israel who take on workers over thirty-two years old: ours is one of them.' Achay paused to point to a couple of eagles circling above us in the darkening sky. 'Gary had some high-paid job in London before he came here. Now he only earns two hundred shekels a month – that's about forty-five pounds – but he doesn't care. He loves the sunshine, the physical labour and the fact he's in God's country.'

As we made our way to the kibbutz bar, Achay explained that some of the more religious Israeli kibbutzniks were opposed to employing foreign workers; they considered them outsiders with loose morals who drank too much beer. But generally relations were harmonious and Achay believed foreigners prevented Misgav-am becoming too insular.

The night air was sweet with blossom, cicadas chirruping all around. Little black bats swooped above the swimming pool roof. This tranquillity vanished when Achay opened the bar-room door. The murmur of cicadas was replaced with ear-splitting pop music and the scent of blossom by cheap perfume and spilt liquor. The bar had been designed like a Montana ranch: the walls were made of knobbly slats of dark wood and a timber beam supported the ceiling. Posters of girls in tasselled bikinis advertised peanuts and sawdust carpeted the floor.

It was only 8 p.m. but the dance floor was heaving. Hits by KC and the Sunshine Band and Kool and the Gang throbbed from speakers crackling with static. The Dutch barmaid wore a T-shirt with HOLY LAND written across the cleavage – she had crossed out the Y to remind her of home. Everyone had to shout to be heard. Those dancing ranged from teenagers to middle-aged couples. This was their big night. They worked six days a week and on Friday night let their hair down. They danced in animated pairs, pumping their arms in the air. Sometimes little groups would converge, link arms, shut their eyes and sing together, as if they were participating in a Bacchanalian ritual.

It all looked a bit embarrassing but they didn't care. This was their world. They made no comparisons with Tel Aviv or Jerusalem. This hillbilly seventies timewarp of a bar *was* their Friday night and, what's more, they loved it.

Nadav and I were not part of this tightly knit team. We were only there to make a few cynical observations and get out. But part of me was jealous. Having led such a rootless existence for the past three months, in some ways I longed to join in, to pick avocados all week and have a singsong on a Friday night, to embrace Misgav-am's strange and desperate camaraderie.

The following day we drove off early to the Golan Heights. The morning light was so bright that the country glowed like an overexposed photograph. As we climbed the land became harsher and the citrus trees petered out making way for the hardier olives and tamarisks. Occasionally, military jeeps or armoured cars drove past.

Near the Syrian border, Nadav pointed out a desolate moonscape cut off by barbed wire. It is called the Valley of Sorrows, he explained, after the soldiers who died there during the 1973 war. The Syrians cleverly launched their attack during Yom Kippur, a time when Israel comes to a standstill and many Jews are fasting.

'It was a complete surprise,' said Nadav. 'Had it not been for the Golan Heights, the Syrians would have reached Jerusalem in no time. But the steep hills slowed them down and gave us a chance to prepare a defence force. We were able to fight back.'

The Golan Heights had previously been wrested from Syria during the Six Day War in 1967 when the Israelis also took control of the Sinai desert from Egypt and the West Bank, including East Jerusalem, from Jordan.

'We sometimes have to be aggressive in order to survive,' said Nadav. 'Remember, Israel only came into existence in 1948 after the British baled out. It's still a young country and very small, only four million of us. I would happily concede a little land to the Arabs if it meant peace but with an arrogant fool like Netanyahu in power, there's not much chance of that. He is a puppet of the hardline Jews.'

We entered a Druze village near the Syrian border, a cluster of white shoebox homes on a flat shelf above the plain. Apart from a cluster of Muscovy ducks preening in the sun, there was no sign of life.

The Druze are one of the Middle East's most fascinating and secretive minorities. They are a distant branch of Islam, celebrate their holy day on a Thursday and believe strongly in reincarnation. Their shrinking population of 600,000 is spread through Israel, Syria and southern Lebanon.

'It's very difficult for the Druze here,' said Nadav. 'They are sandwiched in no man's land between Syria and Israel. Sometimes Druze families in the Golan Heights live on both sides of the border, some in Syria, some in Israel. They have to speak to each other with loud-hailers through the wire.'

A Druze farmer in a white tarboosh and with a walrus moustache trundled past on an old Massey Ferguson tractor. Nadav waved.

'What about military service?' I asked. 'Do the Druze have to fight for Israel?'

'The Druze in the Golan are exempt from military service,' said Nadav. 'But if they want to fight then they can. During my time in the army I was posted to a Druze village for a while. I found them to be noble, serious people. But they don't give much away to outsiders.'

'I don't blame them,' I said. 'This Middle East religion is enough to do anyone's head in.'

'Come on, I'll take you to the Sea of Galilee. A swim there will clear your mind.'

We drove south into a lush valley and within half an hour were wallowing in the cold fresh water where Jesus' disciples had once fished. We had parked in an isolated spot on the eastern shore near an isolated Greek Orthodox church.

The coastline was a miniature Eden, dotted with banana palms and peach trees. A white egret perched on a gatepost and russet-coloured crabs scuttled across the smooth grey shingle. At one point, I thought I saw the radiant flash of a kingfisher above the ultramarine water. After a long swim Nadav and I lay on the rocks. I felt great, my wet gritty skin tightened by the sun's rays. Suddenly, a man appeared behind us in dark robes and a cylindrical hat topped with a mortar board, evidently the Orthodox priest. In his hand was a bottle of beer.

'This is for you,' he said. 'I do not drink.' Nadav took the bottle, swigged and nodded his thanks before passing it to me.

The priest was called Erinarchos. His face was dark and emphatically bearded, making him look much older than his thirty years. He told us he had lived there since 1990.

'Don't you get lonely?' asked Nadav.

'Sometimes, yes,' replied Erinarchos. 'It is quiet here. Once in a while another priest might visit or maybe some tourists. But it is isolated. I read a lot.'

'Do you ever go back to Greece?

'The last time I visited Athens was three years ago,' he replied. 'I don't feel Greek any more. I've lost touch with my friends. But my parents visit me here sometimes, which is good of them.'

'You must have strong faith,' I said.

'My faith is all I have and it is all that keeps this church going. Somebody must look after it. I might stay here for ever.' He smiled at us. 'I think you ought to go now. I should not really allow people to swim near here.'

It seemed madness that a young man could allow himself to become so sequestered, I thought, as we all walked to the car. Living like an old man had turned Erinarchos into one. His movements were slow and methodical, his voice soft and melancholy. Walking next to him I felt like a child, with my jazzy swimming shorts and silly questions. I could not believe he was the same age as Nadav and me.

'How could anyone cut himself off like that?' I whispered to Nadav as we waved goodbye.

'This is the Holy Land,' said Nadav. 'People are prepared to sacrifice everything for faith. He is probably not too concerned about this life. He is working towards the next one.'

*

Back in Tel Aviv I was greeted with bad news. Daniella had found out from a friend who worked in Customs that my passport would definitely be stamped in south Israel. The only place where I could avoid an Israeli exit stamp was the King Hussein Bridge, known to the Israelis as the Allenby Bridge – the same way I had come in.

I could not risk a stamp. My boat to Bombay might easily visit Saudi Arabia or Port Sudan, and neither place was tolerant towards Israel. I had no choice: I would have to backtrack to Amman and pedal through Jordan. Once I reached the coast I could catch a boat from Aqaba across to Sinai and then cycle on to the Suez Canal.

And so the following day, 24 June, was my last in Israel. By mid-morning I had dealt with all my practical needs – new travellers' cheques, camera film, socks – and decided to catch another glimpse of Jerusalem. Daniella dropped me off to the west of the city near the Knesset, the Israeli parliament, which sits on a flat ridge shielded by conifers.

By chance my one day in Jerusalem was an historic landmark. The Israelis were celebrating the 3,000th anniversary of King David's establishment of the city. Star of David flags were fluttering everywhere and a huge firework display had been planned for the evening.

I walked along Jaffa Street in the New City, where Mexican buskers in sombreros and orange ponchos were strumming to an appreciative crowd. Rollerbladers swished past while professional types sipped cappuccino and gabbled on their mobiles. This was young upbeat Jerusalem, an escape from the tug of God and a place to relish the secular: the cafés, the movies, the cheeseburgers. I loved what I saw but my time was short and the Jerusalem of King David and Nebuchadnezzar, of Herod and Suleiman, of Jesus and Mohammed was just down the hill, sucking believers and cynics alike into its compelling spiritual vortex.

I entered the Old City through Jaffa Gate which is flanked by the robust beige masonry of King David's Tower. Rather than head straight for the major pilgrimage sites, I decided to break myself in gently. Of all the city's eleven gates, Jaffa is the worst place to do anything gently. Tourists and hawkers were jockeying for position among the bags of salt from the Dead Sea, the Yasser Arafat T-shirts and the Jesus dolls with revolving eyes.

I shouldered through the scrum into a quiet alcove and took out my map. The Old City was divided into four overlapping quarters: Armenian, Christian, Jewish and Muslim. Right now I was sandwiched between the Christians and the Armenians. But the whole area seemed surprisingly compact and I decided to wander where chance took me.

Before long I was in the thick of the Muslim Quarter. I checked the map and found I was standing on Via Dolorosa, the Street of Sorrows along which Jesus pulled his cross. Dolorosa is a typical Jerusalem street, narrow and flagged with ashlar blocks which have been rubbed smooth by the tread of a million sandals and Nike training shoes.

I traced the Messiah's final footsteps then ducked down an obscure side street which was narrow and darkened by awnings. A mustachioed man selling mother-of-pearl backgammon boards and Aladdin lamps beckoned to me. A mynah bird squawked from its perch on a stunted fig tree.

At the end of the street some children were scavenging through a rubbish pile topped with rubble and old tyres. Several of them latched on to me. The most persistent, a cocky snot-faced Artful Dodger, made a grab for my money belt. I shouted at him and quickened my pace. Just as I thought I was clear, something smashed into my back. I looked down; it was a potato. I ran fast until I was back on the crowded Via Dolorosa where I stopped and spreadeagled myself against the ancient brickwork, my heart pumping. It was the first aggressive begging I had come across on the trip and the least expected, as I was in the middle of the holiest few acres on earth.

After a while, I composed myself for a visit to the Church of the Holy Sepulchre. I had spent so many compulsory hours on a church pew as a boy and so few as an adult, I wondered if a glimpse of the site of Christ's tomb and resurrection would fire up my faith.

If anything, it did the reverse.

The Church of the Holy Sepulchre, with its blond-stoned multi-tiered façade clutched by a tight fist of shops and houses, could win the prize for the most dysfunctional monument in Christendom.

The church is run by an uneasy confederation of Roman Catholics, Greek Orthodox, Armenians, Syrians, Copts and Ethiopians, the latter actually living on the roof. As you enter the church, it is easy to forget you are in the presence of God. The stone cloisters are cluttered with scaffolding, the masonry and pillars are graffitied with tiny crosses and crudely scratched 'I love yous'. Brown-cowled Catholics and black-robed Orthodox priests shuffle among the gaudily dressed tourists while votive candles flicker all around.

I branched off up a long dank alley to the east of the church. At the end was a chapel with a picture of St Helena above the lectern. (St Helena first pinpointed the Holy Sepulchre site in AD 346, although the church has been destroyed and rebuilt countless times since.) The chapel was tiny, filled with lilliputian pews and badly flaking paintwork. Nobody was inside.

Beyond was a flat area of the church roof, adorned with vines and luxuriant pot plants. I was led by an elderly scruff in plimsolls through a wooden door and down a flight of steep uneven steps. After a couple of flights, we reached a ledge which overlooked a well pool of dark water. It shimmered in the candle light. My shaky guide picked up a tin can threaded with string, lowered it and fished it up. He tipped some holy water on to his palm and smeared my cheek.

Back on the hot stone roof was an Ethiopian priest, leaning back on a wicker armchair reading a Bible. With his easy smile and wisp of grey beard, he resembled an ebony-faced satyr. Another of his colleagues was stretched out asleep. The Ethiopians, descendants of Solomon and the Queen of Sheba, have been living in little hutches on the Holy Sepulchre roof since late last century. To me it seemed by far the most serene part of the church.

On the way back down I noticed that Calvary, the site of Jesus' crucifixion, was gridlocked with tourists. I steered clear and headed back down to the ground floor to find Christ's tomb.

It was in a rectangular room the size of a pantry. I ducked under a couple of low arches and crept inside. Twelve copper lamps hung from steel chains shedding dim light on the Stone of Resurrection. Two vases of wilting roses, a variety of crucifixes and a photograph of a little girl holding a kitten cluttered a ledge above.

A Spanish-speaking couple in fortissimo shirts chanted in front of me. They seemed transported, eyes shut, faces tilted heavenwards. I found the whole situation unbearably funny, standing there in Christianity's inner sanctum listening to a woman in a bright-green fedora and a man in a blue baseball cap singing dirge-like incantations to their maker.

For me, Jesus was not here in this chamber. He had been evident on the Sistine Chapel ceiling and in the compassion of the many strangers *en route*, but in the Holy Sepulchre's tangle of incongruous architecture and conflicting sects my faith severely lost its way. In fact, Christianity throughout the city was in a state of decline. It astonished me to learn that Christians, who in the 1920s made up over half the people in Jerusalem's Old City, now comprised less than 2.5 per cent of that same population.

From the Holy Sepulchre I walked up to another bastion of belief, Temple Mount, once the very foundation stone of the world – the spot where God created Adam from a handful of dust.

But in modern Jerusalem the Mount was dominated by the Dome of the Rock, marking the spot where the Prophet Mohammed had ascended to heaven. The building's golden cupola, its façade of peacock-blue tiles, its elegant arabesques and rich internal woodwork made from the cedars of Lebanon, must make it a contender for one of the loveliest monuments in Islam.

For all its outstanding beauty, the Dome offered no spiritual pulse. Yes, it housed some of the hairs from the Prophet Mohammed's beard and yes, the Angel Gabriel's fingerprints (Muslims believe Gabriel was Allah's messenger) were supposedly embedded in its masonry, but to me, it had the feel of a popular museum.

The final stop of the day, however, was electric with faith: Jerusalem's Western Wall, the focal point of Judaism. Of the three sites it was without doubt the least architecturally stimulating, a high rampart built from huge sandstone slabs and weeds sprouting from the stonework. That was about it, but I could immediately tell why it had overwhelmed Nadav at his bar mitzvah.

The whole area echoed with chants from the Torah. Orthodox Jews, their nodding heads bouncy with ringlets, made up the bulk of the standing congregation. But there were Jews from all over the diaspora — Americans, Latins, Eastern Europeans — all praying in black hats or yarmulkas, the women cordoned off from their men in an enclave to the east of the wall.

The Jews at prayer seemed intoxicated with their faith. They stood stock still except for their upper bodies which rocked like pecking birds, back and forth — some with the manic thrusts of a woodpecker, others with slow swan-like grace. One soldier, gun inevitably on shoulder, did not rock or peck at all. He simply slouched forward, forehead pushed hard against the holy masonry.

This was a place of serious and unified worship. The Jews have only had access to the wall since 1967, when they defeated the Palestinians in the Six Day War. The fact that it is such a sacred site and so recently won gave the prayers a desperate quality, as though making up for centuries of lost time. I watched the wall, mesmerized in the mottled twilight. Occasionally, someone would walk forward and stick a written prayer into a crack in the colossal stonework.

It was easy to sense the strength of belief here, especially among the ultra-Orthodox Jews. It was these fierce-looking ascetics with their wild pepper-and-salt beards, not the rest of the crowd, who lent the Western Wall its palpable intensity.

I made my way back to Jaffa Street for a rendezvous with Nadav. It was dark now and the first fireworks in celebration of Jerusalem's 3,000th birthday began to pop. Green and red stars shot fountains out towards the Kidron Valley. Fire crackers spluttered and sparklers hissed. One rocket blasted high into the darkness, exploded and cascaded in a shower of golden tears.

It had been quite a week. I had seen Christ's tomb, the Prophet Mohammed's beard, the Angel Gabriel's fingerprints and a magic wall. A few days before I had seen an Indian roll more than 1,000 miles and now the sky was decorated with fireworks.

If there was somebody up there he was certainly putting on quite a show.

CHAPTER EIGHT

LITTLE PEPPER

Two mornings later, I was back in Amman being woken at the same ungodly hour by the Cliff's same insomniac doorman. Once again I blazed over the pine-lined hills of Amman. But this time, I felt much stronger and more focused than I had done on the way to Jerusalem two weeks before. I freewheeled south, passed a strange billboard which advertised THE LOWEST PARK ON EARTH! and headed out on to the bleakest of deserts.

The road was flat, the wind weak and I powered along, covering ten-mile stretches in forty-minute bursts. At this rate, I would comfortably span Jordan in three days. It was now almost July and I needed to crack on in order to reach the Himalayas before winter.

For the sake of speed, I had plumped for the flat desert highway rather than the more spectacular King's Highway which carved a swathe through a hilly landscape of ancient castles. But the desert highway was not without incident and, on my first afternoon two miles from the village of Al-Quatrana, disaster struck. My back tyre began to deflate. Rather than stop, I sprinted on in the hope of reaching a garage where I could fix the puncture in the shade.

This was only my third puncture of the trip. I had suffered

two in Turkey, but they had been in the front tyre, caused by thorns working deep into the Kevlar, and had been easy to fix. A back tyre involved unloading far more kit and messing around with the cogs and chain.

Al-Quatrana was nothing more than a roadhouse with a garage, a restaurant and a tourist shop. I parked at the garage workshop, ripped off my back panniers, levered off the tyre and coaxed out the inner tube. When I submerged it in water, I found a tiny scar near the valve. I patched it up, hitched back on the wheel and used a narrow stretch of hose to connect the valve to the garage compressor. It inflated the tyre as tight as drumskin. I piled the panniers back on and remounted. The whole process had taken about fifteen minutes. I gave a thumbs up to the mechanics and rode off.

What a breeze. The afternoon light had given the sand a beautiful pinky hue, the colour of salmon flesh. The sky was a clear cloudless blue. Life was just great. All those doubts I had harboured before starting the trip were dissolving with every mile I covered. My mind drifted into a triumphant daydream. TTSSSHHHHRRR SHSHSH BANG. The shock of the explosion caused me to brake, slide forward off my saddle and crunch down hard on to the bike frame like a dislodged showjumper. I turned around to see what had happened. Bollocks. My back tyre had blown up.

I dragged the bike back to the garage, unloaded the panniers and threaded in a new tube. Next to me, a Bedouin in a white pyjama shirt was spot-welding the side panel of a truck. It was late afternoon and I decided to stay at the roadhouse for the night. I propped up my bike against the wall and ordered some tea from the café.

Coach parties on their way to Petra dashed in periodically to relieve themselves or gawp at the tawdry souvenirs and I LOVE

THE DEAD SEA postcards. The roadhouse was run by a suffocatingly friendly man called Mahoot. He was plump and jolly and could not stop asking questions. Why are you alone, sir? No wife or children? Oh, sir, you are a truly lonely man. However, as I was such a sad case, he let me eat as much as I wanted free of charge. Bowls of lamb curry. Chips. Milkshakes. He even pulled in my bicycle from outside and told everyone about it in excited Arabic. The kitchen staff took it in turns to inspect both the bike and my pale hairy legs.

I soaked up the attention with a mixture of relish and growing irritation. When I could take no more I retreated to a laurel bush near the petrol tanks. I inflated my sleeping mat and lay down to read. After a while I must have dropped off; Captain Charles's diary can be crushingly dull in places. When Mahoot nudged me awake it was dark and I had absolutely no idea where I was.

'Sir! Sir!' he shrieked. 'What are you doing? You must come now. England are playing football against Germany. It is the semi-final.'

I was in a state of semi-consciousness: that brief subliminal moment when you wake up believing you are at home, tucked up in a freshly sheeted bed listening to the *Today* programme. Then reality bites. You are a dust-caulked road bum, sleeping against a petrol pump in the middle of the Jordanian desert.

I dragged myself up and followed Mahoot through the gift shop, past a display of wooden dromedaries and into the waiters' dormitory where a crowd was gathered around a tiny black and white screen. They watched with determined concentration; Euro 96 clearly had the whole of Jordan in its thrall. Occasionally, one of the waiters would shout out 'Shearer!' 'McManaman!' or the name of some sharp-shooting German. After a while, I was as gripped by the match as them.

England, in their white shirts, were making an offensive dash. There was a corking pass to the goalmouth and BAM! England scored. I leaped up, fisting the air.

'By the heavens, sir. What are you doing?'

'We scored a goal!'

'No, no,' said Mahoot. 'The white shirts are Germany. England are in the grey ones.'

'But we always play in white shirts.'

'Not this time,' said Mahoot. 'But don't worry. The goal is not allowed.'

Many of the Jordanians were surprised by my ignorance, but out of politeness continued to support England. It was a tense game that ended in a 1–1 draw and the agony of a penalty shoot-out.

I am clueless about football, but one of the few games I had watched in the past was the one in which Stuart Pearce missed a penalty against Germany in the 1990 World Cup. I remembered Pearce well, thanks to his psychotic stare and face like a kicked-in biscuit tin. He must have known that if he missed another crucial penalty it would haunt him forever. However, if he hammered it home, it would show formidable courage. Pearce aggressively struck the ball on target and the England fans roared with relief.

Almost everybody remembers what happened with Gareth Southgate's penalty, so I will spare the details. Suffice to say, when he missed all Jordan groaned in sympathy. I buried my head in my hands.

'Oh, by the heavens, sir,' said Mahoot suddenly. 'This is a beautiful moment.'

'What do you mean?' I shouted. 'The poor bugger missed. We lost.'

'Oh sir, but look at the players. They are all telling him not to worry, that he is hero.'

Sure enough, a gaggle of English players led by Stuart Pearce was consoling the hapless Southgate. Mahoot had a point. If nothing else, England still had the capacity to lose magnificently.

After the match, I had a good night's sleep in one of the spare dormitory beds and at dawn was woken by the noisy ablutions of my room-mates. I ate a breakfast of fried lamb and, before heading on south, was press-ganged by Mahoot into taking several photos of him and his staff, posing with smiles of evangelical intensity, beside the fully loaded bicycle.

I found the hospitality of the Jordanians exemplary, whether staying in a relatively upmarket place like the Cliff or sleeping under the stars at the Al-Quatrana. But the people I feel most privileged to have spent time with are the Bedouin.

In the Middle East the Bedouin are clearly not the force they once were. In previous centuries they provided pack animals to merchants or acted as indispensible guides and trackers to the military. Now, even in the most remote places, camels have been superseded by pick-up trucks and many Bedouin have retreated to the towns; animal husbandry is no longer enough to support them.

But Bedouin culture still has its highlights, as I discovered at the village of Birkhadad Baker twenty miles from the ruins of Petra, when a couple of kohl-eyed youths in green headwraps ran alongside the bike and pulled me over. 'Mister, mister.' I stopped and watched them gesturing to a distant white marquee. A large crowd was snaking out from the entrance. 'Marry!' said one of them, inviting me over.

I dismounted and dragged the bike through the sand, eventually propping it against one of the marquee's straining guy-ropes. Beside the entrance was a row of six sooty cauldrons, licked by flames. A bug-eyed man, his teeth capped with gold, was stirring one of them with a ladle. He wore a white T-shirt

with the curious logo SNOW BOARD — IF YOU AREN'T LIVING
ON THE EDGE, YOU'RE TAKING UP TOO MUCH ROOM. The
rest of the party looked more traditional and many were
sporting the red and white chequered keffiyeh with pale loose-
fitting gowns which draped down to the ankles. One Bedouin
played a two-stringed lyre made from an old coffee tin. A
lupine dog lay by his side. I couldn't see any women at all.

There must have been at least a hundred guests. At first, we
all sat on black plastic chairs which ran in lines around the
perimeter of the tent. I was squeezed in next to a man called
Mohammed. He was a suave businessman from Amman, uncle
to the groom and was clad in a grey high-buttoned jellaba. On
my other side was a dramatic-looking Bedouin with withered
nut-brown skin. The backs of his hands were as ridged as
melted wax and his eyes a brilliant hue of green. He reminded
me of a gnarled and ancient tree, still boasting two unpicked
fruit. Barefoot youths offered us styrofoam cups filled with
viscous gravy lightly flavoured with mint. Mohammed sipped
his cup as if it were claret, whereas the Bedouin downed his in
three or four long glugs, like a pint at closing time.

Mohammed was one of the few guests who spoke English
but telling him I lived near London proved a bad mistake.

'You are Israel's friends,' said Mohammed. 'The British are
no friends of the Arabs.' As usual in the Middle East, these
remarks were not directed personally and were more a general
broadside against the West.

'Saddam Hussein, I like him,' he continued. 'In the Gulf
War most Arabs supported Saddam. Our King Hussein was
weak. He pretended to sympathize with Saddam but he likes
the West really.'

'The West respects King Hussein,' I replied after draining
my cup. 'But I don't think he's a puppet. I've always thought
of him as a brave man.'

'Oh, he's brave all right,' railed Mohammed. 'He's fought off all sorts of assassination attempts and illnesses over the years. My problem with him is that he is not a proper Jordanian. His family originally came from Saudi Arabia, I tell you. Saddam is a genuine Arab. We should all rally round him.'

It was the first time I had heard someone openly praise Saddam in the Middle East – although it is commonly known that he has considerable support in both Syria and Jordan. Many see him as a new Saladin or Nasser, uniting the Arabs against the West, although his critics consider Hitler and Mussolini as more likely role models.

As we talked, tin salvers stacked high with rice and fatty chunks of meat were placed in front of us, each was crowned with a sheep skull. Everyone rose together and hunkered down in circles of six or seven. Mohammed grabbed my left arm in a half nelson to remind me not to eat with it. All conversation stopped as we attacked the food.

Mohammed and I both ate quickly but the Bedouin was a revelation. He scooped up mouthful after mouthful, tearing at the meat with his fingers, occasionally throwing morsels my way. Like a lizard he did not seem to chew the food, just gulp it down. Within twenty minutes we had devoured everything. It was the most remarkable display of gluttony I had ever witnessed but, looking around, very few of the guests were fat. It was probably a rare occasion to eat this well. And, my God, it was good – the lamb tender, delicately spiced and saturated with flavour. The Bedouin belched in approval.

'So when does the wedding start?' I asked Mohammed.

'That was it,' he said.

'But what about the bride?' So far the whole occasion had seemed to be nothing more than a well-mannered stag party.

'The women stay at home,' explained Mohammed. 'The

husband will visit the bride later and there will be another, short, ceremony. There would have been some dancing but an old man died in the village last week. It would be disrespectful to celebrate too wildly. This is also the husband's second marriage. His first wife died. He is forty years old now. If it was a first marriage there would have been more of a party.'

Gradually, the guests started to drift away. Some formed a queue in front of the groom who was a large, sun-baked man who appeared rather uncomfortable with the attention and the endless hugs and kisses. Children were wandering around with pitchers of water for the diners to wash their hands.

I said my farewells to Mohammed and gave *Don Quixote*, which I'd finally finished, as a present to the groom and his invisible bride. Then, emitting minty, contented belches, I pedalled lazily south.

I slept that night in a guest house a stone's throw from Petra and the following day rose early to inspect the legendary civilization of the Nabataeans. Along with hundreds of other expectant tourists, I meandered through the well-shaded corridor of tall rose-coloured rocks leading into the lost world. It did not disappoint.

During the third century BC the ingenious Nabataeans hewed hundreds of elaborate palaces, temples and tombs from the local sandstone. Their efforts created Petra, a city beyond reproach and at one time a potential rival to Rome.

After a brief heyday, this remarkable trading city declined, bypassed by alternative overland routes across Syria and Egypt and sidelined by the increasing use of sea travel. The Nabataeans and their extraordinary capital slipped inexorably beneath a cloak of historical obscurity.

In 1812, more than a millennium later, Petra was rediscovered by the Swiss scholar and adventurer, Jean Louis Burckhardt. It has now become the Middle East's most enticing tourist destination and despite all the hype it is still impossible not to be overwhelmed.

Petra has been lavished with enough superlatives to make a Hollywood diva blush, so I will keep my observations succinct. What I liked more than anything was the sheer scale of the place. It was big enough to lose the crowds and it was possible to look out towards the Shara mountains and imagine the slave caravans and spice mules, the dancing girls and the jangle of ancient currencies. More than anything it made me wonder whether tourists will view the skyscrapers of Manhattan the same way in another thousand years. Will they look up at the glass hulks of Trump Tower or the Empire State and wonder, 'How did they do that?' And more importantly, 'What went wrong?'

The following morning, after being chased over the opening hill by a ferocious mongrel, I comfortably cruised the ninety remaining miles to Aqaba. *En route*, a gentle headwind cooled rather than hindered me. To my west, sadly out of eyeshot, lay the rolling sands of Wadi Rum, where much of *Lawrence of Arabia* was filmed.

The harbour of Aqaba, Jordan's sole port, was filled with oil tankers and bobbing fishing skiffs. A huge aircraft carrier, the USS *Tarawa*, dominated the view, helicopters buzzing around it like flies. I checked into the Petra Hotel on the main street, a curious place with an alfresco rooftop dormitory where hung several cages of dejected grey squirrels.

The ferry to Sinai did not leave until the following afternoon and this suited me just fine. Aqaba is a popular spot with Jordanian tourists and has a relaxed happy-go-lucky feel unlike other more frazzled Middle Eastern cities. I spent much of my time in an American-style ice cream parlour called Mr Cool writing up my diary.

Mr Cool attracted some interesting people. I met a Canadian

couple working on a nearby archaeological dig, a Frenchman hoping to hitch a boat ride to Cape Town and a couple of American navy pilots from the *Tarawa*.

The pilots were twenty-year-old James from Oklahoma and twenty-seven-year-old Cruise from Kentucky. James was fair and short, the youngest helicopter pilot on the carrier, and Cruise was a Hispanic with a bum-fluff moustache. They both considered Aqaba a dud posting. In Bangkok or Singapore it was cheap, they could pick up girls, wear what they liked and stay out all night. In Jordan they were ordered to wear long trousers, suffered very restrictive hours and faced court martial if caught bedding one of the local girls.

'Man,' said Cruise, 'all there is here is rocks. Rocks and sand. Sand and rocks. It ain't healthy for a lonely man.'

The *Tarawa* had a crew of 1,800. It would be spending another two weeks in Aqaba before setting sail for Singapore. James told me he had wanted to join the Navy Seals but, at five foot four, was one inch under the minimum height stipulated for recruits.

'You're not only looking at one of the youngest pilots in the navy,' said Cruise, pointing at James, 'but the goddam shortest too.'

'One Thai girl told me that the little peppers are often the hottest,' said James, smirking at his friend.

'And was she holding your little pepper at the time?' countered Cruise. 'God knows how she kept a straight face.'

Little peppers are often the hottest, I wrote in my diary. I had no idea of the validity of this statement with regard to either James's libido or cooking. But as a description of Israel and Jordan it struck me as spot on. Like Syria and Lebanon to the north, Israel and Jordan are little, hot and, when it comes to politics, potentially explosive.

This theory, however, quickly fell apart in Egypt, my next

destination and a much larger pepper altogether, a plump, shiny cayenne. Egypt boasts the longest river in Africa, the second most densely populated city in the world, one of earth's hottest climates and, forty years ago during the Suez crisis, had produced events explosive enough to rock Downing Street.

It was also the country that would almost destroy my trip.

CHAPTER NINE

SCUTTLED AT SUEZ

On the ferry to Sinai I met a Hungarian razor blade salesman called Zack. I remember him distinctly because he was the only other white face on a deck crammed to the gunwales with Arabs. Zack and I sat in the sun at the prow of the ferry – a sort of creaky, multi-tiered Noah's Ark. Two young Kuwaiti boys in denim jackets crouched beside us, asking excited questions about the Spice Girls and Madonna. Bunched together in sweaty adversity, we drifted along at the speed of a canal barge past the insipid scenery that flanks the Gulf of Aqaba.

The four-hour voyage did offer the odd excitement: murmuring, white-robed Muslims prostrating themselves across the deck towards Mecca, a pair of dolphins flipping up in jaunty arcs to starboard, Zack's observations on the international razor blade market. But, by the time our overpopulated vessel berthed at Nuweiba, Sinai's tiny east-coast port, everyone was champing at the bit to get away.

It was a disaster waiting to happen.

The 500-strong crowd surged down to the lower deck in a determined exodus, rucked up like rugby forwards against the only available exit door. All the other escape routes had been blocked by piles of plastic buckets, stereos, furniture, hessian sacks, ironing boards and masses of other passenger detritus. By the time I reached my bike, which was sandwiched between piles of cardboard boxes, the crowd had run amok. I could have shouldered in, but knew that if I lost my grip on the bike for even a second, it would be trampled into irreparable ruin.

Pandemonium soon turned to outright panic. Zack tried to help me but was washed away, like a spider down a plughole, towards the choked exit. Passengers, frantic to escape the claustrophic mêlée, began a destructive stampede towards alternative routes, climbing over mountains of boxed microwave ovens and computer equipment. Children on the shoulders of their fathers screamed with fear and women shrouded in black fanned their veiled faces with passports. The humidity was unbearable. One old woman broke down in tears and began wailing to herself, lifting her hands in the air as if a winged deity might appear to pluck her away from this inferno.

I straddled my bicycle and braced myself as the crowds battled past, many of them laden with luggage twice their weight. Some yelled at me to move, others smiled in sympathy and rolled their eyes at the futility of it all. The fetid air stank of oil, brine and frightened human beings. From above, we must have looked as frenzied and impotent as a bucketful of eels.

It was at least an hour before I finally tagged on to the stragglers and made my way through the trammelled piles of merchandise to be flushed out into a bright star-spattered evening. It was almost midnight. Zack had waited for me, sitting on his rucksack, and together we trudged off to Customs. There was no queue as we were the only two foreigners.

I was ranting away at him as if I had just survived genocide or civil war. Zack, like most of the other passengers, was being far more stoic. 'Egyptians deal with this stuff all the time,' he said simply.

On our arrival at Customs, a dilapidated X-ray machine juddered to life. I shoved my bike, panniers and all, on the temperamental conveyor belt while a guard in white uniform and black beret watched impassively. The gun he held was topped with a comical bayonet no bigger than a tailor's bodkin.

When the paperwork had finally been completed Zack and I looked for a place to eat. Fortunately, some dockside stalls were still open. I troughed a bowl of chopped liver, onions and chilli which bore an uncanny resemblance to farmyard slurry, while Zack swigged down three bottles of tepid Coke and threw up under a street lamp.

A little later we crawled into the nearby Zahraa Hotel. The staff were polite but the place was a dump. We were ushered into a room which looked as though its last guest had been a semi-house-trained dromedary. The basin had a tap which dribbled rusty water and the toilet was piled high with turds. We collapsed on dusty snot-smeared beds and fell into merciful slumber.

The following day I felt as Hercules must have done after taming Cerberus: my eyes were glued down tight with the early-morning crust of the truly exhausted. It was 8 a.m. and the enervating heat of the Sinai was already starting to take hold. I unstuck my recalcitrant eyelids and rolled out of bed, still in the soiled clothes of the previous evening – things like that didn't bother me much these days. I left Zack in peace, having tentatively arranged to meet him in Dahab, a beach hang-out roughly fifty miles south.

Already the portside braziers were luring early punters with the hiss of frying meat, and a renegade camel was charging about chased by a Bedouin with a stick. I drank several cups of sweet tea, filled my water bottles and set off up the preliminary hills, watched by a pack of skeletal dogs.

After an easy couple of miles I encountered a distressing road sign. It showed a car climbing up a steep hill. So did the next, and the ones after, for the following ten miles. Uphill riding in the coruscating heat is thirsty work, and for the first time on the trip I ran out of water. The three ice-cold litres I started with soon dwindled to two tepid litres, then one hot litre and, by the time the sun was high, a boiled and cloudy half litre.

As my water supply evaporated I rationed myself to a sip every time my mouth became parched. Before long my tongue had turned to fly-paper, my saliva curdled to a viscous paste and I could no longer swallow.

The waves of rolling sand – by far the most attractive desert of the trip to date – and the brilliant blue sky ceased to mean anything. I was running on empty, my radiator drained, my blood pinking with dehydration. I began to picture an array of refreshing beverages: pints of ice-misted lager, tumblers of chilled Italian coffee, jugs of fresh snow-white milk, Bloody Marys tinkling with ice cubes and sharp with the bite of Tabasco and Worcester sauce.

I could not believe how stupid I had been. In Syria and Jordan the landscape had been so flat; the hills nothing more than transient humps. Even the gruelling ride to Jerusalem had boasted several roadside watering holes; three litres had always been enough to keep me going until the next top-up. But riding uphill·in this Sinai wilderness was another matter. It was at least 35 °C degrees with not a breath of wind. My insides were shrivelling like fruit left too long on a sunny window sill. Sweat was running down my spine in rivulets.

Salvation came at the top of the final hill in the form of a wooden refreshment shack run by a friendly tar-black Sudanese boy. The shack walls had been tastefully daubed with white doves, anarchy symbols and Pink Floyd lyrics, possibly the work of Peace Corps volunteers. The boy prised open an icebox which housed a selection of bottles of sugary pop. I glugged down four or five of them with greedy alacrity, followed by a litre of iodinized water. My belly felt like a vat of congealed candyfloss, but at least I had slaked the thirst of Tantalus.

From here on the ride was easy, beginning with a long downhill run which eased off into gentle undulations. The only life I saw in this beautiful wasteland, other than the odd clump of emaciated vegetation, were three roan-coloured camels lying in the middle distance, heads held aloft like hirsute periscopes. These were the first wild camels I had seen all trip.

Most camels in the Middle East are single-humped dromedaries, the majority of which are domesticated and either harnessed up for tourist safaris or bred for their wool and meat. Dromedaries have no problem dealing with the Sinai temperatures as their tough, air-pocketed skin only begins to sweat at 45 °C, a heat which would kill most mammals. They also have the capacity to drink a remarkable 150 litres of water in one sitting.

Interestingly, neither the Middle East nor Asia – with its hardy twin-humped Bactrians – has the world's largest population of feral camels. It is, surprisingly, Australia.

The sand surrounding me now looked as smooth as cake icing. Waves of pale butterscotch spumed out towards Africa. The perfect symmetry of the dunes gave this landscape a softer more refined quality than much of the desert I had previously cycled through. Unlike those early fog-bound days in France, what I was looking at now was probably the clearest horizon I could ever hope for.

But, as I approached Dahab, American-style billboards advertising restaurants and diving clubs began to sprout up. The panorama was further tarnished by Dahab's grim expanses of grey concrete. This, however, was not my destination. Where I was heading, two miles down the road, was something quite different – a legendary backpacker's village.

Dahab village has a long-standing reputation as a lotus-eater's paradise. It is really nothing more than a line of hippy dippy beach shacks with names such as the Blue Pool and Crazy Horse. They are all pretty much identical. You can buy banana pancakes and chilled melon juice; you can play chess or backgammon while sitting on beanbags. The air is fragrant with dope, and the sounds of 'Bad Moon Rising' and 'Walk on the Wild Side' blast out around you.

This sybaritic enclave is controlled largely by Egyptian entrepreneurs but many of the local Bedouin work here too – Bedouin who have forsaken their flocks to lead 'once in a lifetime' camel safaris, mix happy-hour cocktails or run souvenir stalls selling plastic worry beads and SIZZLING SINAI T-shirts. While the history and culture of these once self-sufficient nomads has been destroyed by tourism, ironically their future depends on it.

Tourists in Dahab can be divided into two categories: long-term and short-term. The short-term are holidaymakers, or backpackers who need a few days to recharge their batteries. The long-term are either washed out, incurably lazy or writing their first novel; often a combination of the three. In Israel, everyone warned me if you spend one day in Dahab (thousands of young Israelis holiday in Dahab village every year), you would end up staying at least a month; but, within a matter of hours, I was longing to get out.

What sparked this decision was the sight of a middle-aged woman, stick thin and sun withered, who had clearly lost her mind. In the afternoon, suffering from some sort of fit, she jumped into the sea. Here she floated, face down like a harpooned mermaid, while the Bedouin children threw stones at her. She feigned death for so long a group of us jumped in and fished her out. For a while she lay curled up on the Blue Pool bar floor, pulling at her greying hair, her bikini bottoms at half mast. She shouted and sobbed and scratched her weathered face. She was as low as a human being could go.

Stories were circulating about this woman with no name in the various bars. Some said she was a German aristocrat who had blown her inheritance on high living, others said she had married an Egyptian who had deserted her. To me, she looked like someone who had simply taken too many drugs and lost her way. No family, no friends, nobody was prepared to show her an ounce of compassion. She was one grade lower than everyone else in Dahab – and everyone liked her for that; liked to sneer at this human wreckage, to marvel at the sheer extent of her lunacy, to laugh at her rabid gesticulations.

Dahab was not the place for her to be. Apart from the few Bedouin living in their tin shacks and goatskin tents, it was mainly inhabited by travellers who couldn't give a damn about anything except their own solipsistic agendas, let alone this sad drug-addled woman. And why was I laughing at her along with everyone else?

I would not have laughed if I had been back in Swanbourne, nor would many of the others if they had been at home. But we were travellers. Nobody knew us here in Dahab. We could behave however we liked. We could shoo away the Bedouin and tease the insane – behave appallingly without anybody really noticing.

Maybe I was just getting paranoid. Or maybe it was time to finish another banana pancake, have a good night's sleep and move on.

Something was wrong. I couldn't put my finger on it but something was definitely amiss. Maybe it was Dahab, or too much desert, too much time to myself. Since France my mood on the road had been so consistently upbeat, my mind so entertained, that I had never thought the black dog of melancholy would come nipping at my heels again. But it had, and now it was taking well-aimed bites at my rear panniers.

I had read somewhere that the Pharaohs, in order to test their suitability for paradise, had their hearts weighed by the gods. As I cycled through Sinai, my heart felt as light as a rotten nut, healthy enough on the outside but empty within.

At least the twilight views from Mount Sinai, where I spent the following night, resuscitated my flagging morale a little. From its base, the mountain was a stunning moonscape of grey and red granite. I left my bike at St Catherine's Monastery, where God exposed Moses to the burning bush, and yomped up. Dozens of other pilgrims were on the peak by the time I arrived there an hour and a half later. I blew up my sleeping mat and found a nook in which to bed down. Before long, several other climbers bivouacked nearby. They were within easy earshot.

'This is truly the heart of the Middle East,' said a deep confident voice with distinctly public school cadences.

'I've never understood the term Middle East,' said another more wistful-sounding man. 'I mean how can you have the middle of the east? The east is the east; that's that. You can have the north-east or the south-east but the middle east is just weird.'

'What about the East End?'

'Well that's OK; that's the end of the east. But the middle of the east is like saying the middle of the sea. It doesn't mean anything.'

'Have you noticed you always find trouble in the east of a country?' This time it was a girl's voice, very St Trinian's. 'Think about it. The east of Turkey is where the problems are with the Kurds. Then there's East Timor. The Middle East.'

'Not much trouble in East Anglia though,' said the deep-voiced man. 'Stop talking such bollocks, Kate.'

With such sparkling dialogue in progress, I found it hard to accept that this was the holy mountain where Moses had been presented with the Ten Commandments. In fact, it was even hard to imagine Charlton Heston as Moses, holding aloft his stone tablet while shouting furious truisms to Cecil B. De Mille's cameras.

I snuggled into my sleeping bag to block out the ambient chatter. For the first time in months, up here at over 2,000 feet, the night was cold enough to see my breath. It felt good to be cold, not having to worry about mosquitoes or waking up in a pool of sweat. I savoured the shivers knowing that tomorrow I would be back in the sort of temperatures in which my tyres could spontaneously combust.

At 4 a.m. I was woken by dozens of people singing. Some sang folk songs, others national anthems and one group a rather beautiful madrigal, but I did not wait to see the sun rise with them. A sunrise is a beautiful thing in solitude or intimate company, but not with a mass of mixed nationalities warbling different soundtracks.

I made my way down the mountain in just under an hour. Sturdy mean-faced camels, kitted out with makeshift howdahs, stood in lines ready to transport the rich, the idle or the weak. Most of Mount Sinai is bare rock but on the lower ground, near St Catherine's, the odd robust olive tree breaks through the granite. Bathed in golden light the sixth-century monastery looked more like a fortress than a place of worship; in fact it was built by the Roman emperor Justinian as just that, to protect Sinai's early Christians from attack.

St Catherine's did not open until mid-morning and I had to

crack on before the heat became unbearable. Before setting off – perhaps inspired by the intensely biblical location – I recited the Lord's Prayer, my only audience a flock of white goats.

From Mount Sinai it took two days to cycle up the Red Sea coast. I spent the first night in a deserted convent near Wadi Feiran and the second on a dramatic beach alive with rock pools of bubbling sulphur. The sea had never looked bluer or more comforting, probably due to its proximity to such relentless desert. Occasionally, I would dump the bike and charge into the cold waves just to check they were not a mirage. Within five minutes back on the bicycle my T-shirt, tracksuit bottoms and baseball cap would be bone dry.

Towards Suez, the military checkpoints, manned by guards in pale-green uniforms, became more frequent. The guards were po-faced with boredom and repeatedly asked me for pictures of women, any women, preferably naked. The only solace I could provide was a photo of Alexandra wearing the sort of baggy figure-swamping jumper usually favoured by Hebridean fishermen. One soldier showed great interest and even offered Alexandra his hand in marriage. I accepted on Alexandra's behalf. I would call her later and tell her the good news. It made me wonder: if a passport photo of a snugly dressed German girl could win over officials like this, just think of the red tape a *Playboy* calendar would slice through.

But the presence of these remote love-starved sentinels seemed so utterly pointless, merely serving as a depressing reminder that Sinai, despite being little more than a barren wilderness, was a frequent battle ground. From the time of Moses splitting the Red Sea to the more recent wars with Israel (who controlled the peninsula from 1967 to 1982) Sinai's sand has soaked up the blood of countless armies.

As I pedalled north a different army was on parade: serried ranks of pylons, some shaped like crucifixes others like Saracens' shields, marched over the horizon, hissing to each other along their sagging wires. For hours these sibilant giants and the lapping surf of the Red Sea were my only company. There was no traffic.

Eventually, I reached an isolated roadhouse, its plastic tables hot enough to fry eggs on. I drank several lukewarm sodas and made my way to a pitted side road which was marked with a sign: TO THE BOT. This led to the wharf which would finally launch me across the famous canal and on to Suez, the end of the first section of my journey.

What struck me first about the Suez Canal was how lush its banks looked: there were palm trees, flashes of blossom and knee-high vegetation, the first real evidence I had seen of fertility in Sinai. The canal also looked deceptively narrow but according to statistics was still wide enough to cope with six to seven hundred ships a month.

When I raised my camera to take a picture a soldier grabbed it from my hand. He pointed to a sign in the ticket office: NO FOTO. It was probably something to do with the nearby army depot. I put away my camera and hefted my bike on board the little shuttle boat. Soon we were drifting across the dark waters which had linked the Mediterranean and the Red Sea for over 120 years.

On the other side the banks were even more lush – almost equatorial – and were lined with ramshackle huts on stilts. Barefoot children charged along after the bicycle, shouting with excitement. Skinny men in flip-flops washed cars while dishevelled chickens scratched at the dust. It could have been Thailand or Sumatra.

Within twenty minutes I had reached the city centre. During the Six Day War Suez had been levelled by Israeli bombs. Nowadays it is not the beautiful town it once was, but despite its prefabricated air it has retained much of its former bustle. Unlike Port Said and Ismailia, the other major towns which serve the 100-mile-long canal, business in Suez does not rely solely on shipping fees. The surrounding area is an important industrial zone with petrochemical refineries and fertilizer plants.

But I was in Suez for one thing only: to catch my boat to Bombay. I checked into a topsy-turvy hotel just off the main street. Its corrugated tin roof was alive with the patter of rodents. First thing the following morning I headed for the port.

It was 9 July. The day that would change the course of the whole trip.

The port office was a grey concrete monster, a dimly lit labyrinth resonant with the tappetty-tap of antique typewriters. All morning I was shunted around by the many shipping companies: Damanhour, Assuit, Aswan, Bombay Lines. The feedback was relentlessly negative.

'You may have a bicycle, sir, but you have no seaman certificate. No insurance. No letters. No skills. No hope.'

'You would need permission from the ship owners who live in Korea. It would take months, my dear. You must try the yacht club, try Port Said or Alexandria. Maybe Beirut.'

'By the Prophet Mohammed, we will never allow such things. You cannot take basketball.'

'Not basketball. BICYCLE.'

'Bicycle. Basketball. You are crazy man. You must fly.'

I tried to explain that I was not allowed to fly, that I would write a letter exonerating the shipping company of any responsibility if I drowned. I said I would work on the boat, wash up, swab the decks. I did everything but genuflect and run myself through with a bicycle spoke.

It was hopeless. My only option from Suez, they told me, was to sail to Jeddah (the port that serves Mecca) and catch a boat to Karachi. The problem was that Jeddah is in Saudi Arabia. I would only be able to secure a transit visa for forty-eight hours and if I failed to hitch an ongoing vessel in that time, I would be thrown out. Another passenger boat sailed once every fortnight from Suez to Port Sudan. But this was a non-starter, principally because there was an internecine war raging in Sudan.

I should have done my homework better. This was the area where many travellers have come unstuck. The writer Gavin Young who hitched slow boats from Athens to Peking in the late 1970s managed to get as far as Jeddah. From there he was forced to fly across Saudi Arabia to Dubai where, after a two-week hiatus, he endured a memorably sluggish passage on a cargo dhow to Karachi. Michael Palin, in his quest to make it around the world in eighty days, also shunned a boat down the Red Sea. Instead, he tore across Saudi Arabia in a Toyota Cressida and, like Young, hitched a lift on an eastbound dhow.

A century earlier things had been less problematic. Phineas Fogg and his faithful Passepartout had calmly sailed from Suez to Bombay on the steamboat *Mongolia*. They then travelled through India using a combination of steam train and elephant howdah, even taking the time to save a Parsee bride from burning on her husband's funeral pyre. After a quick stop-off in Hong Kong and across America with a carriage full of Mormon fundamentalists, they still made it back to the Reform Club on time. Fiction always makes it so much easier.

Saudi Arabia was out of the question. I did not have the BBC contacts of Michael Palin or the finances of Phineas Fogg, and Saudi visas were tough to get at the best of times. My only other option would be to obtain an Iranian visa and head overland that way. But I was still determined not to fly. Even if I had to hitch-hike or travel on public transport, it would be preferable to flight. Air travel was not available to Captain Charles in 1829, but he would have been able to go overland if not by car then by horse or stagecoach. Hitching would dilute the meaning of my trip but flying would destroy it. At this rate I would have to dismantle the bike, inflate my panniers and design a bloody pedalo.

The following day I cycled ninety flat miles into the swarming bowels of Cairo, the second biggest city on earth. By the time I reached Midan Tahrir, the city centre, I had vowed never to bicycle there again. Cairo traffic is a terrifying and relentless battle: up flyovers, under arches, across bridges, past frail ponies carting water melons, gardeners attacking grass verges with sickles, buses careering around corners with passengers stuck to the sides like barnacles, soldiers waving, trams chuntering, hawkers screaming, seagulls mewing.

'Hey mister, you want papyrus, you want student card, you want pyramid trip, you want girl?' asked one of the myriad touts. 'You want cheap hotel?'

'It all sounds wonderful, but just the hotel for now.'

Mohammed led me to the Sun Hotel off Midan Tahrir. Before departing he gave me his card. 'Anything you want.' He winked. Like so many Egyptians, he had a fine-looking face but when he smiled his teeth were ruined – no trace of white, just broken brown pellets. I took the lift up to the ninth floor. The hotel was run by a friendly man with an Inspector Clouseau facial twitch and a pate as bald as a cabbage stump. He led me to a neat, six-bed dormitory, mostly occupied by Europeans who were studying Arabic.

Dan, a rangy dark-haired boy, was on the bed next to mine. He was reading *Arabian Sands* by Wilfred Thesiger. Nick, his classmate, a Liverpudlian, was playing a very poor version of 'Wonderwall' on his guitar. After the usual interrogation about the bike ride, I got talking to them about their reasons for studying Arabic. Dan was very serious about his studies and had read large segments of the Koran. Nick was less focused.

'I got drunk one night,' he said. 'Then I stuck up a list of possible language courses on my wall and threw a dart at it. I hit Arabic. If the dart had landed lower I would have studied Apache.'

That evening I met up with the pair of them in a narghile bar in Midan Tahrir. We ate *kushari*, a dish of noodles, fried onions and tomatoes. To wash it down Dan ordered a jug of refreshing blood-coloured tea made from hibiscus leaves and crushed ice.

Later we were joined by Osamir, a young Egyptian with a greasy cow-lick. Osamir had spent his life in Cairo but was desperate to emigrate to Europe or America. He claimed to have bedded dozens of foreign girls.

'I like Dutch girls the best,' boasted Osamir. 'They've got big tits and they're gullible. I slept with one Dutch girl, I forget her name now, for six or seven weeks. I nearly got her to marry me; then I could have arranged a visa and dumped her. But she had a friend who saw through my act and tipped the stupid bitch off.'

Dan had warned me Osamir was a braggart, but that his brags were genuine. Western girls did fall for his smart-talking charms and those of other young visa-hunting Egyptian play-boys.

'Do you love any of these girls or is it purely for visas?' I asked.

'Once I really fell for a girl from Sheffield,' said Osamir, smiling; he still had bright white teeth with no hint of decay. 'She was beautiful, like Cleopatra, dark and strong. Weird voice though. She stayed with me for five days and said she loved me but then one morning just left. No apology, no goodbye note, nothing. She was cruel. She had used me and I cried over her for days. I suppose I love the ones who are a challenge, but they will never marry me. If I ever get out of this place, it will be by seducing a stupid girl. A visa beaver we call them.'

'That's terrible,' I said. 'Egypt can't be that bad?'

'For the Egyptians, yes,' said Osamir. 'It's all right for you to turn up and get excited about the pyramids. We live here. Look what we once had: the Pharaohs, the hieroglyphics, the intelligence, the beauty. Now what have we got? Poverty, despair and tourists. I am a smart man. Why should I suffocate here?' He paused, taking a pensive drag on his cigarette. 'You know something,' he added angrily. 'I have just had a letter from a friend in San Francisco. He's married a California girl. Ugly as a camel but he doesn't care, he'll drop her soon enough. He's only eighteen. The bastard. But I'll get there eventually. I just need a wife. Any wife. Then I'll fly away and never come back.'

The rest of my time in Cairo was spent in a state of despair. No amount of sightseeing could alleviate my frustration. I rode a jagged-spined pony around the Giza Pyramids; saw Tutankhamun's mask and the ossified Pharaohs among the muddled artefacts of the Egyptian museum; and studied the brilliant hieroglyphics at Saqqara, the oldest pyramid, built in the twenty-seventh century BC by the splendidly named King Zigor.

I visited a doctor who tapped my bloated gut as if he were testing for dry rot. 'You have gas,' he told me. 'Stop eating so many kebabs.' To convalesce I sat in the library bar of the Hilton Hotel, surrounded by pictures of nabobs shooting crocodiles and read excerpts from a leather-bound volume of Henry David Thoreau's *Walden*.

I became increasingly worried about the trip, which seemed

to be slipping away faster than the sand in a broken hourglass. I contacted Nile Valley Tours who ran a ferry for Mecca-bound Pakistani pilgrims from Karachi to Jeddah. I hoped I could hop on the return boat east. Sadly, the service did not start until September when the monsoon in north Asia would have abated. It was now only mid July. I could not possibly wait that long.

After dozens of enquiries, the only boat I could find passage on was a cruise liner from Port Said to Cyprus. From Cyprus I could catch a hovercraft to Beirut and then backtrack overland through Syria and Turkey and on to Iran. It was a ludicrously convoluted option but the only one left.

The first step was to secure an Iranian visa. This was never going to be easy. 'Out of the question,' said the official at the heavily guarded consulate. But if I liked, I could fill in a form, pay 180 Egyptian pounds (roughly forty pounds sterling), and wait a month until the bureaucrats in Tehran had decided my fate.

'What are the chances?' I asked.

'Very small and you will not get your money back if your request is refused. I suggest you go to Beirut. It is very easy to get an Iranian visa there.'

The die was cast. Beirut or bust. I secured a Pakistani visa – a prerequisite for travelling overland through Iran – and then prepared to head north to Port Said, the first stretch of my serpentine detour to India.

Until this point, every part of my original route had been covered by bicycle but now I had to accept defeat. If I cycled back to Turkey and then through Iran and Pakistan, it would add months to my journey. I could not spare the time. Reluctantly, I telephoned Stoke Mandeville and explained I would have to use public transport.

I would still cycle at least 12,000 miles between the two

Swanbournes, I assured Chris Catton, the charity co-ordinator at the hospital, and continue to shun flights, but certain stretches would have to be bussed, trained or hitched. It was capitulation of the highest order but my only choice. Chris was very encouraging and said the trust fund had topped £10,000. 'Most people don't care as long as you do your best,' said Chris. I wondered if this was my best.

I arrived in Port Said – by bus – on 19 July, almost five months after I had set off from Swanbourne. My boat to Limassol did not depart until the following afternoon, which gave me some time to look around.

Unlike Suez, Port Said survived comparatively unscathed by the Six Day War and there were still timber-framed porches and stone balustrades from colonial days. When Ferdinand De Lesseps started work on the canal in 1869, Port Said had a raffish reputation, its cafés full of small-time hashish dealers and corrupt ship's chandlers. In 1929 Evelyn Waugh spent a memorable night on the razzle trawling the port's whorehouses, albeit for literary rather than carnal gratification. But now it is a respectable duty-free zone, competing with Alexandria as the north coast's primary lure for tourists.

My formidable ninety-four-year-old grandmother, who was brought up in Karachi, remembers docking at Port Said in 1919 on her steamship from England. Granny is an indefatigable survivor of the Raj. Her animated blue eyes still require no spectacles and enable her to drive her Mini Clubman, albeit appallingly dangerously, around the streets of Rugby, where she has lived for the last thirty years. Although she never remembers to use her indicators she remembers Port Said as if it were yesterday.

'We threw down coins into the sea and the Egyptian boys would dive down like cormorants and fish them out,' she would tell me while zigzagging down Rugby High Street in second gear. 'Then our bags would be carted off on mules which were all named after Edward VII's mistresses. Oh my dear, it was the time of my life.'

Those days are long gone. Port Said is now probably best remembered for its part in the Suez Crisis of 1956 when British paratroopers landed there to resist President Nasser's nationalization of the canal. The action proved a political disaster and was swiftly aborted. British Prime Minister Anthony Eden later resigned while Nasser went on to become Egypt's most prominent leader of the twentieth century.

Port Said no longer attracts many foreigners. The age of cadging a ride on a slow boat to India or China seems to be well and truly over. I was the only tourist sitting on the dockside watching the sluggish container ships glide by, their foghorns sounding off, mournful as old men's sighs.

Before setting sail, I decided to track down a barber for a much-needed haircut. I had begun to resemble one of the Bee Gees. The only barber I could find was an impish fellow operating from a cubby hole near the port office. I watched with mounting anxiety as he calmly singed the errant ear hair of the previous customer with a Zippo lighter. I was clearly in for a thorough exfoliation.

Within ten minutes of sitting down, the lightning-fingered scissorsmith had trimmed my locks down to an uneven stubble and dusted my scalp with talc. After this he performed an operation I had never witnessed before. He rolled a plait of cotton threads between his forefingers, held it taut as a cheese wire and ran it very fast over my upper cheek to uproot the tiny hairs that were too delicate for scissors. It left my cheeks tingling but immaculately smooth.

My journey may have been falling to pieces faster than the Sphinx's nose, but at least I would leave Egypt looking my best.

CHAPTER TEN

VISA TEASER

The *Princess Cyria* was full of formerly pasty Europeans, many of them now sun-baked to alarming shades of bubblegum pink. These overdone adventurers had cruised from Cyprus to Haifa, glanced at Jerusalem, sailed on to Port Said, whistle-stopped around the pyramids and were now heading back to Limassol, shoulder bags heaving with Pharaonic trinkets.

Nasco Tours, the cruise company operating from Port Said, had initially refused to let me on board the *Princess Cyria* unless I paid the full four-day whack: several hundred dollars. I ranted, harrumphed, cajoled and rolled my eyes like a meditating sufi. I needed just one night to reach Cyprus, I begged. Finally, they relented and let me on for fifty US dollars, provided I slept on a pull-down chair on the quarterdeck. This was actually a good deal as, even without a cabin, I still got to eat the same gourmet fodder as the other passengers.

That evening I dined on roast beef, sautéd potatoes and asparagus spears. I felt like a food critic, sat at my table for one; but I had always imagined food critics to be rather stern and I was in a terrific mood, my mouth full of the tastes of home, and my head, which had been a paragon of Middle Eastern sobriety for the past two months, now muzzy on house red. As much as anything I was relieved to be out of Egypt; to be on the move again.

I could see the other guests wondering who the hell I was – this solitary diner masticating wildly and flashing lonely eyes at everyone. I could just imagine their whisperings: Didn't we see him earlier with his bicycle? Strange bugger, all on his tod. Stay well clear. Don't know what rock he crawled from under.

It was always when surrounded by couples or groups – especially if they were British – that I felt a real outsider. I was the only *single* passenger on the whole ship. This status never mattered to me when I was riding the bicycle, or if I was shacked up with local families and other travellers, but on a cruise liner full of conventional holidaymakers I was a definite oddity. I could understand the distrust. What exactly was a thirty-year-old bum in tracksuit bottoms and a ripped lumberjack shirt doing among these fine upright citizens taking their well-deserved annual break? Tonight, however, I didn't care. I smiled at everyone, no matter how warily they eyed me. I was pissed.

But if I stood out from the crowd a little, my ancestor Admiral Edmund was in a league of his own. Edmund was the fourth son of Captain Charles's elder brother, Thomas. He was a severe-looking cove with mutton chop sideburns – *de rigueur* in the 1870s – and a withering glare. A man of undeniable bravery but also acute self-importance, he wrote a vast self-aggrandizing autobiography called *The Navy As I Have Known It*. On the opening page is a portrait of Admiral Sir Edmund R. Fremantle GCB GCVO, as he liked to be called, hung with more medals than a Ruritanian grandee.

The *Princess Cyria* was now moving through waters that were familiar to Admiral Edmund. In 1880, while berthed in Alexandria harbour, my ancestor became well-known for his acts of derring-do. One time he plunged into the sea, sporting a thick beaver-skin frock coat, and rescued a drowning sailor. In an earlier incident, also off the Egyptian coast, he had dived off his frigate the *Invincible*, after hearing the cry 'man overboard'. By the time Edmund, stark-bollock naked on this occasion, had taken the plunge, the crewman had been saved. Sir Edmund had to be hauled up on a rope by a neighbouring ship, denuded of all badges of rank. 'I don't know what the world in general, the Admiralty or my own relatives will say to my going overboard again,' he wrote in his journal. 'But I could not resist it.'

At the time of his Egyptian posting, Edmund had already fought with distinction against the Maoris on New Zealand's North Island and the Ashanti warriors in West Africa. During the latter conflict, in 1873, while recovering from a wounded arm, he had met the explorer Henry Morton Stanley, who was then employed as a reporter by the *New York Herald*. As usual, straight-talking Sir Edmund did not mince his words. 'Mr Stanley who found Livingstone has come out in the Benin and dined with us. He is the most insufferable, self sufficient little snob I could imagine . . .' After a final overseas posting – principally in Shanghai – during the Sino–Japanese war, Edmund returned to England for good in 1895. Within a few months, like Captain Charles before him, he had been promoted to Admiral and invested with a GCB, the Knight Grand Cross of the Order of the Bath. He died in London in 1929.

Edmund's eldest son Sydney, who, remarkably, looks even more imperious than his father and was more facially hirsute, became the fourth, and as it stands, final admiral in the Fremantle naval dynasty. A brilliant gunnery officer, he went down with his dreadnought, the *Russel*, when she struck a mine and sank off Malta Harbour in 1916. Sydney, then a Rear Admiral, stood on the *Russel*'s forecastle as she submerged. Over 120 men drowned but Sydney survived with nothing worse than a dislocated foot. Sadly though, he lost all his possessions which included Nelson's telescope, a family heirloom, given by Britain's great naval hero to Admiral Thomas shortly before Trafalgar: '. . . a precious relic of a very sincere friend'.

By the time Admiral Sydney died in 1958, Britain's navy had been eclipsed by several rival fleets, most conspicuously America's. The Admirals Fremantle – Thomas, Charles, Edmund and to a lesser extent Sydney – served during a time when Britannia ruled the waves, a time since overtaken by the tide of history, preserved only in the cracked paint of Swanbourne's dining room portraits.

I certainly had no nautical blood flowing through my veins. No Mediterranean, no Adriatic, no Swan River filled my gene pool. Swanbourne's duck pond was about my limit. This was one of the reasons why I had decided to follow Captain Charles's route on a bicycle rather than a boat. Even the steady rolling of the *Princess Cyria* made me feel heady and disorientated.

'Why are you alone?' asked the smiling henna-haired man standing in front of me. He was flanked by his family. 'Come and sit with us.'

My mind had been so lost in boozy recollections of my forebears that it took me some time to reply to his invitation. 'Oh, thank you,' I replied, a touch overzealously, grateful for the hand of friendship. I followed my new-found companions down towards the bar.

They were Egyptians, probably the only Arab tourists on the *Princess Cyria*, as much outsiders as me. Adel was a portly bespectacled man with the rubber-skinned, wide-eyed look of a vaudeville clown. He was the only one of the family who spoke to me; his son read a book while his veiled wife and daughter looked down at their shoes, shooting the occasional furtive glance out to sea.

'I am a doctor,' Adel was telling me. 'Egypt is a poor country but medicine is one profession we excel at. I believe your queen Elizabeth has an Egyptian doctor. The fact I am a good doctor makes me feel less guilty about being a bad Muslim.'

'Are you that bad?'

'Not really,' said Adel. 'But my wife and children are far more religious than me. I think Islam can be a little too stern sometimes; it doesn't allow much room for fun.'

'Surely it is possible to be both a happy Muslim and a good one?'

'I think it becomes harder after you have made the *hajj*,' replied Adel, sipping his orange juice. 'I have been to Mecca, but on the way I fell over my suitcase and slipped a disc. I was in agony kneeling in front of the Kaaba. I didn't feel any of Allah's redemption, I can tell you. But it was different for my wife; she was very moved and my son, Ayman, burst into tears.' Ayman peered up nervously from his book but quickly looked down again. His father eyed him fondly.

'Ayman is sixteen now,' whispered Adel. 'A student in Saudi Arabia. He has been back to Mecca three times. He is a very serious Muslim. So serious it worries me sometimes. He can hardly look at girls.' He leaned towards me. 'Between you and me, I hope this holiday will loosen him up a bit.'

A little later a troupe of snazzily dressed couples appeared on the stage. 'Hi everybody. Welcome to the Elite Dancers,' shouted a cockney in a blue-sequined jacket. The dancers were supposed to resemble the Jets and Sharks from *West Side Story* but looked more like rejects from *Saturday Night Fever*. They launched themselves into that old crowd-pleaser, 'America' — 'La la la la la la Amereeeka' — with amateurish gusto. At the end of the song the boys whipped off the girls' knee-length dirndls and threw them, with exaggerated flourishes, into the wings. The girls were now down to cheerleaders' miniskirts and they jiggled their hips coquettishly.

Adel cheered while Ayman recoiled sharply. He looked down at the floor in outraged embarrassment. Watching Ayman's face, his dark serious eyes and knitted brow, he seemed a much older man than his father. In fact, it was hard to imagine he had ever been young.

We docked at Limassol the following morning. It was Sunday, 21 July. Five months on the road and I'd only made it to Cyprus, I might as well have been travelling by donkey. From the deck I gazed out at the new horizon. The island's hills looked parched and uninviting.

Once I had pedalled down the gangplank and was away from the bustle of the dockside, Limassol appeared ghostly quiet, not a soul around except for the occasional cat. I rode off on the smooth wide highway towards Larnaca on the island's east coast, where the next morning I hoped to catch my hovercraft to Beirut. An undulating landscape of scorched sienna and diluted green stretched ahead as I cycled quickly on my way. At times, large corrugated warehouses and distant factories came into view. This was not the island I remembered seeing all those years ago as a bumptious seven-year-old on his first ever trip abroad.

On all previous summer holidays my parents had driven Betsy, Fanny (my two elder sisters) and me up to Pitlochry in Scotland. For twelve hours, we would sit in the back of my father's advocaat-yellow Morris Marina and crunch humbugs while the five family dogs panted and farted in the boot. But that summer of 1973 was such an amazing contrast, a wildly exhilarating departure from the norm.

I don't remember too much about it although the powerful oven blast heat on alighting from the plane, the thunderstorms, the lemon trees, the bluest warmest sea imaginable and the unconditional friendliness of the Cypriots still sticks in my mind. By the time we left the whole world was our friend. We never wanted to leave.

Now I was no longer a doe-eyed seven-year-old just as Cyprus was no longer a childhood Utopia. Both of us had weathered with time, but Cyprus seemed to have a different personality altogether, completely unrecognizable to me.

En route to Larnaca I chatted to as many Cypriots as possible. I wanted to relive that magic summer, but it was not to be. The present-day Cypriots seemed so bitter, so distant, as fed up with the tourists as with the Turks. They had been betrayed by everyone, they all told me in the cafés and on the streets: betrayed by the Greek government who had ousted popular Archbishop Makarios in 1974; betrayed by the British who had washed their hands of the island; betrayed by the tourists who took package holidays in Turkey instead; betrayed by the Turks who had invaded the top third of the island in 1975 and provoked an exodus of 180,000 Greek Cypriots from their homeland.

But not all Cypriots had hatred in their hearts.

Take Doros, a thickset, rusty-skinned carpenter and Maria his petite wife whom I met on Larnaca's dreary beach front. They lived in a village just south of Nicosia and had stopped in Larnaca to pick up some timber.

Maria, a South African policewoman, had originally met Doros while on a summer holiday and had since made Cyprus her home. Doros originated from the north of the island.

'Many of my family used to live in the Kyrenia mountains,' said Doros. 'When Turkey invaded they had to flee south. Nobody was killed but they lost almost everything. What is most hurtful is that they have not been allowed back since. Not allowed back to their own birthplaces. Old men who have lived all their lives in one village kicked out for good.

'Even the bloody tourists can visit, but not the Greeks,' continued Doros, banging down the tailboard of his Toyota pick-up and throwing in a plank of wood. 'It used to make me so mad, but I have become more resigned now. Marrying Maria has calmed me. She has told me about South Africa and other trouble spots. Before, I used to think Cyprus was the whole world. Now I realize our problem with Turkey is not so isolated.'

The trouble in Cyprus was still very real according to Maria. A huge motorcycle rally had been organized for mid August, during which Greek protestors accompanied by foreign sympathizers would ride into the north of the island. Maria, now a policewoman serving in Nikosia, was dreading the event, as it would be her job to hold the bikers on the Greek side of the Green Line. She was worried that if any of them managed to cross over, they would be shot by the Turks.

Maria and Doros invited me back to their home but I declined as my hovercraft to Beirut was due to leave early the following morning. I watched them speed off in their little pick-up, planks of wood wobbling on the tailboard, tyres kicking up the dust.

Over a month later, at a campsite in Islamabad, I heard that one of the Greek motorcyclists had been killed trying to rip down a Turkish flag. I thought of Maria watching in vain as the bikers trespassed on the forbidden side of the Green Line, risking everything for just one more glimpse of home.

Only a dozen people were waiting for the hovercraft the following morning. Most were Lebanese, heading home after visiting friends or family who had fled from Beirut during the seventeen-year civil war. The only other non-Lebanese was a Frenchman in a sharp suit with a laptop computer sitting at his feet like a pet dog. He told me he was visiting Beirut for the first time. His sister had recently married a Lebanese doctor.

'You must be careful,' he whispered to me in the passport queue. 'Beirut is a vury, vury, *vury* dangerous place. Trust me, I've been around.' Been around what? I felt like asking. The maypole? The block? Too long? I never trust people who tell me they have been around, it invariably means they haven't.

Predictably, he ignored my yawning and carried on with his doom-mongering about the Hezbollah and the Phalange, the Israelis and the Americans. Why did I always attract these types? I didn't need this nonsense. For Christ's sake, I was about to bicycle through Beirut. My bowels were in an incipient state of liquefaction.

Three hours later we arrived on Lebanese soil, heads swimming with the washing machine effect of the hovercraft. The Bulgarian cabin steward – many of the ferries on the Mediterranean employ eastern European staff – helped me lift my bicycle out on to the wharf. The sky was grey, the air humid. I scanned my map and pedalled off towards the city centre.

The initial streets were fringed with dirty piles of rubble, as if gigantic moles had burrowed alongside the bitumen. Chevrolets and Corvettes, lorries and Landcruisers tooted with the frequency of a Marble Arch snarl-up. A drainage sluice rattled my bones as I rode over it, almost snaring the bike tyres within its narrow maws.

This was a country that two years previously had been famous for having just a single set of traffic lights. According to one travel guide, the traffic was so anarchic it was only when these lights were manned by armed soldiers that Beirut's drivers took any notice of them.

I finally spotted a solitary yellow sign pointing to Hamra. I knew Hamra was near the city centre, just a step away from the famous Corniche promontory where the likes of Frank Sinatra and Ava Gardner used to stroll when Beirut had been the Paris of the Middle East back in the fifties.

The only celebrities to bless Beirut with their presence now were on the advertisement hoardings – Kate Moss with her chignon hair and oriental cheekbones looking out over a hairnet of wires and aerials, the Marlboro cowboy tipping his ash on a bullet-pitted church, the Lacoste crocodile snapping at the shattered hulk of the Holiday Inn.

Once I reached the Corniche I stopped to get my bearings. I propped the bike against a ragged palm tree next to Uncle Deek's pitta joint. A couple of children were playing badminton on the promenade opposite using a juice carton as a shuttlecock. I ate a chicken *shwarma* and pedalled on up into the nearby Hamra district.

Hamra was the area of Beirut that buzzed, that had made every effort to cleanse its cavities and plug its pockmarks. Smart glass offices glistened with refracted light along the Rue Bliss. Shop fronts displaying swankily dressed mannequins, burnished shoes or strings of compact discs lured Beirut's post-war shoppers. On the hovercraft, one passenger had joked that the only explosions to be heard in Hamra now were those of the silicon breasts of rich débutantes detonating in the sun.

But amid the mobile phones and the Hermès handbags, there were still street children tugging at strangers' sleeves, an old man hawking pistachios from a wooden barrow and a paralysed dog dragging its hind legs in the dust.

A cinema billboard high above the cluttered Rue Hamra advertised *Dangerous Minds* starring Michelle Pfeiffer. It was one of those hand-painted boards that made Hollywood stars look strangely distorted. The glamorous Miss Pfeiffer had metamorphosed into a crabby and decayed *doppelgänger* of Bette

Davis. I pushed my bike along the busy pavements and knew that I would soon have to find somewhere to stay. My only contact in Beirut was Munir Jurdi, who I had met at one of Susan's invaluable dinner parties. The man who had told me, 'You never know where you'll end up.' How right he had been.

I had tried to call Munir's parents from Cyprus and had failed to get through, but before finding a hotel, I thought I'd give them one more shot. I parked outside a Lacoste shop north of Hamra. A place like that was bound to let me use the telephone.

The shop assistant had the long dark lustrous locks of her Arab ancestors, the blue eyes of the Crusaders and the dress sense of Baby Spice. She told me her name was Maria and she was a Christian, a Maronite. She dialled the Jurdis' number and fired off a quick volley in Arabic.

'Your friends live just up the road,' she told me, studying her purple fingernails. 'They will come over in about twenty minutes.'

I could not believe it. The Jurdis had no idea who I was, what I wanted, and yet they had already agreed to meet me. If they could put me up that would make my stay in Lebanon so much easier and more interesting. Beirut was, after all, still one of the most expensive cities in the Middle East.

'Where are you going on that bike?' asked Maria. 'Whatever you do, don't go to Baalbek,' she said before I could answer. 'It might be a wonderful city but it is the HQ of the Hezbollah. The British and American hostages were held there. They were so lucky to be released and not . . . chrrruugg.' She sliced her forefinger across her throat. I remembered the excitement surrounding John McCarthy's release; I had been covering the story as a cub reporter for the local paper in Wiltshire. At the time, Beirut had seemed the ultimate leitmotif for danger and violence.

But in this Lacoste shop, with its John Denver soundtrack and smiling sales assistants, Lebanon seemed far removed from hostages and Hezbollah.

The doorbell jangled and in came Mr Jurdi. I was horrified. He looked terribly stooped and frail. I realized what a liberty I had taken, calling up the aged parents of a distant friend of a distant relative who lived in an even more distant continent. Mr Jurdi grasped my hand. His wrists were as thin as a child's but he shook my fingers with surprising vigour. 'Munir said you might come,' he said, straightening the lapel of his baggy brown jacket with his free hand. 'Come on. Let's take you home.'

He clamped my bicep and led me out of the shop. I stopped to collect the bike and together we wandered up the road. Maria waved from behind her desk. We passed a large grey building crudely fenced off with wire mesh which Mr Jurdi told me was a women's prison and then ducked down a busy side street. A demolition crane was smashing up a tower block. Only one side of the foundation wall remained standing. It resembled a Brobdingnagian gravestone, construction rods sticking from its side like rusty whiskers. Mr Jurdi held a handkerchief to his mouth as he shuffled through the dusty air.

'We live here,' he said, stopping at a metal gate which looked as solid as a freezer door. He fumbled with the lock and then led me through a shady corridor with an awning of vines and honeysuckle. At the end was a large pale-tiled courtyard with a cracked enamel fountain that was home to a shoal of tiny black fish. To one side of this courtyard was an elegant town house with grille windows. On the other side was a small wooden-framed building, about the size of a garage. Mr Jurdi pushed at the plywood door which was shielded by a ripped mosquito blind.

Inside was a self-contained studio. It looked as if it had not been touched since the late 1970s. On the walls were various posters: John Travolta in a white suit, Darth Vader with a light-sabre, a chimpanzee on a toilet seat. An old record player sat in one corner and in the other was a fridge, containing two cans of Amstel beer and a jar of apricot jam (best before 17/4/ 84). There was a double bed, a fan and several rows of well-thumbed books. It was perfect.

'This is dear Munir's flat,' said Mr Jurdi. 'He hasn't used it since he went to live in Rome. He only comes back to Lebanon to see us now. My other son, Emir, liked to visit us more frequently but he died from a heart attack last year. He always stayed in our home though – not here. It would be nice to have somebody use the place again.'

He left me to unpack. What terrific luck to be presented with a flat all to myself in the middle of Beirut. In celebration I cranked up the ancient record player; the stylus hurdled through the opening movements of Grieg's *Peer Gynt* and then lodged itself in the long-neglected grooves. It sounded terrific, crackly and resonant with bass. I took a shower to wash off the grime of the last few days and then waltzed back into the bedroom vigorously conducting 'The Hall of the Mountain King'.

As I was pulling on my tracksuit bottoms the door flew open to reveal an old lady, presumably Mrs Jurdi, and an Indian girl with a tray of drinks. The Indian girl shrieked, turned away and dashed outside, glasses tinkling. Mrs Jurdi shielded her eyes. 'Oh, no, no. *Pardon, mon cher,*' she said. 'When you are ready, please join us for an evening meal. Bring along your washing.' She had a thick French accent – a legacy of the Mandate.

I quickly finished dressing, sprayed myself with a can of Munir's vintage Right Guard and strolled out into the court-yard. The Jurdis were sitting around a table beneath a canopy of jungle vegetation. The Indian maid, who I could now see was a heavily built girl in a green sweat-soaked sari, nervously grabbed my washing and retreated behind the fountain.

'She is a good girl, really,' said Mrs Jurdi. 'Her name is Latta, from Sri Lanka. She has two children back there but has come over here to earn money and learn English. She is a Buddhist. We're a very mixed household. We have another boy who helps out who is a Sunni Muslim and Mr Jurdi and I are Druze. We all get on fine, though, like Beirut's population used to. It used to be such a beautiful place.'

Mrs Jurdi stopped to pluck a date from a platter in front of her. She had a kind deeply lined face inset with dark beady eyes and a dazzling, if transient, smile.

'Yes, so beautiful,' agreed Mr Jurdi, who had reappeared wearing a pair of blue pyjamas. He held a hissing radio to his ear. In his free hand was a book: *Sri Lankan For Beginners*. I remembered Munir had told me that his father, a retired literature teacher, was able to speak several different tongues.

Mr Jurdi was eighty-seven years old and Mrs Jurdi eighty-five, but neither of them looked it. Above all, they exuded a gentle patience. That patience had enabled them to endure the long civil war, and witness all the death and destruction without rancour. There they sat, Mrs Jurdi chewing on a date, Mr Jurdi practising Sri Lankan with a radio held to his ear. In Israel, Nadav had told me the Druze were noble and very private people. Whatever their secret, I was deeply impressed.

'In a couple of days, our nephew Abraham is coming over from Rome,' said Mrs Jurdi, shooing away a hovering dragonfly. 'He will show you around town. He is the one member of the family who likes to come back every year. He is still proud to be Druze. He will tell you many things.'

It touched me how quickly the Jurdis had taken me under

their wing; a stranger on a bicycle who had telephoned them out of the blue and waltzed naked around their flat. They were the most wonderful old couple. I was grateful to whichever star had led me to them. Now all I needed was to secure my Iranian visa and then I would be back on course.

The following morning I was sitting in the sumptuous waiting room of the Iranian Embassy, sunk deep into a plump-cushioned sofa. A picture of a blue-tiled mosque in Esfahan hung in front of me alongside another of a pot of caviar from the Caspian Sea. On the wall behind me were several portraits of the late Ayatollah Khomeini. It occurred to me that the Ayatollah was the only Middle Eastern leader I had seen sporting traditional garb in his portraits; Assad, King Hussein, Mubarak and the Christian Lebanese President Rafiq Hariri favoured the jacket-and-tie look of the West.

I filled out my visa form and had the letters from Stoke Mandeville on my lap. Please God, let me get this visa, I muttered to myself. It worried me slightly that I was the only applicant in the room.

After an anxious half-hour, 'Mr Thomas Henry' was called out from behind the door. How charming, I thought, using my Christian names. This was all going very nicely. The inner sanctum was yet more opulent, the carpet springy beneath the feet, an elegant divan to perch on and coffee cups of bone china laid out on a dumb waiter. I got the impression visa applicants were a rarity here. Perhaps they were just pleased to have a guest. A chance for a good chinwag and to display the embassy china. Such decorous folk, these Persians.

There were two officials, a clean-shaven man in a grey suit and an extravagantly mustachioed beefcake in a black suit. The grey suit was Lebanese, the translator; the black suit was the

Iranian official. My fate was in his hands. He looked friendly enough for a diplomat with a good repertoire of hand-on-the-heart gestures and insincere smiles.

The translator fired a volley of irrelevant questions at me: How old was I? Why wasn't I married? Did I like Lady Diana? What bicycle did I have? Why didn't I have a car? I felt this was small talk, rather like having an interview when you know you have already got the job. Would you like more coffee, sir? More cake? England is a wonderful country, I think. It was all too good to be true.

Grey suit related all my answers to black suit who listened nodding his head and treating us to the occasional nod. After fifteen minutes of rapid-fire questioning and no mention of Iran, I bit the bullet.

'So, my friends, how about the visa?'

The translator gently put my enquiry to the diplomat. There was a long pause. Then a quick reply. Then silence.

'So?' I squeaked, the panic creeping into my voice.

'Mr Henry, we are very sorry but we cannot give you a visa,' said grey suit softly.

'But in Egypt they said I could definitely get one here.'

'Never trust an Egyptian, Mr Henry,' said grey suit, putting his hand on my knee.

'It wasn't an Egyptian who told me. It was an Iranian.'

'Mr Henry, listen to me carefully. You must go to Erzurum in Turkey. There you will definitely get a new visa.'

I pleaded with them. I milked the charity angle, the fact I was allowed no flights. Please, please, make just one exception. *Please*. The smiling diplomat was not for turning.

'So,' I said finally, my voice shaking. 'Where exactly is Erzurum?'

The grey-suited man pulled down a map from an overhead storage cabinet and spread it out on the carpet. It was hopelessly vague, labelled with spidery contours and Arabic script. Both men scanned it for a while.

'We cannot find it, Mr Henry,' said grey suit. 'But it is over here somewhere.' He gestured to a generous area near the Iranian border. 'Somewhere here, or maybe here. Anyway, wherever Erzurum is, you will definitely get your visa there. Definitely.'

I was beginning to understand that the word definitely was not one to be taken seriously. I put my hand on my heart and smiled sweetly, first at black suit, then grey suit – I could have happily throttled the pair of them.

This was a devastating setback and I had to quickly consider alternative plans of attack. I could fly with Gulf Air to Bombay but they would charge me US$250 extra to take the bike. I could fly with Pakistan International Airlines to Karachi, but Karachi was way off route and would mean pedalling through the Sind desert, which would be a royal pain in the arse. Besides, I was still determined not to fly.

I decided to try for Erzurum. One last gamble for the visa. If it failed, I would have to backtrack across Turkey and fly from Istanbul. The trip was so off schedule, it wouldn't make much difference.

In order to pursue this overland option the first thing I needed was another Syrian visa. My six-month multi-entry visa had annoyingly just expired. I walked down to Hamra and stopped off in one of the many travel agents to ask where the Syrian Embassy was.

'Syrian Embassy, pah!' said the heavily jowled travel tout. He looked like a swarthy Falstaff, his lively pug eyes set deep in his fleshy face. 'There is no Syrian Embassy in Lebanon.'

'What do you mean no Syrian Embassy? Syria is your neighbour. She must have an embassy.'

'Yes, I grant you, we have many pictures of President Assad,' he replied, chins wobbling as he handed over a business card. 'And Syrians will no doubt soon outnumber Lebanese. But there is no embassy. Don't ask me why. That's just how it works.'

I put my head in my hands. This must be some sort of cruel joke.

'But I've got to get to Syria,' I said to Falstaff. His name was actually Haleb, a Kuwaiti who had lived for a year on the Edgware Road.

'There is one way,' he said conspiratorially, running his hands over his enormous belly. 'It's a long shot but I might be able to get you a transit visa. I'm a traveller myself. I like a challenge. Once I drove a Landcruiser to Amman.'

Haleb picked up my passport and analysed my Syrian visa. His face suddenly froze as if he had seen an angel playing a harpsichord outside the window. 'I've got it!' he shouted, banging his fist down on the desk and sending a SKI LEBANON brochure flying. 'You can forge the bloody thing.'

'Forge it?'

Haleb explained that my visa had been issued on 16 January. That meant it expired on 16 July. It was now 25 July. But if I changed the issue month from January (1) to February (2) then it would be valid for another three weeks. The main problem was that there were two 2s needing to be forged – an Arabic 2 and a English 2. Changing the Arabic numeral was simple, just a tiny tick. But changing the European digit would be more tricky.

'I can't do this,' I said. 'If I'm caught they'll have my balls off.'

'Pah, you call yourself an adventurer, a traveller!' bellowed Haleb. 'Forget your balls. You have the heart of a woman anyway. The world bicyclist not even able to fool a Syrian border guard. What has happened to the spirit of adventure? Since when did an Englishman worry about losing his balls?'

His chiding worked. I grabbed a pen from Haleb's desk and practised my forging technique. I was only going to get one shot at this, so I wanted it to be good. If I made a mess of it, flying would be the only option. My fingers shook like an aged spinster writing her last will and testament. I took several deep breaths then lowered the pen and quickly carried out the necessary alterations.

'Oh shit,' I said, holding up the passport and surveying my fraudulent figures. 'My English two looks terrible. Not like a two at all. More like a question mark.'

Haleb grabbed the passport from me and held it up to the light. 'Yes, that is certainly a very poor two,' he said coolly. 'More like a seahorse. Don't worry, the only two the passport checker will look at is the Arabic two. You have forged that perfectly. Don't worry about the English two; it will be ignored.'

'What happens if they check up on a computer?'

'A computer!' Haleb guffawed and slapped his navel, sending shockwaves across his seismic gut. 'We are in Syria, not Singapore.'

'Well. What happens if they recognize it's a fake?'

'You already know, my friend,' said Haleb, winking. 'They'll cut your balls off.'

CHAPTER ELEVEN

CHAINS OF FREEDOM

I arranged to meet Haleb in two days. He would fix it for me and my bike to be bundled into a shared taxi and ferried across to Damascus. From there I could catch buses up to Erzurum, secure the Iranian visa and carry on east. 'No problema, amigo,' Haleb promised me as I left. He sounded, if that were possible, even dodgier than he looked.

That afternoon, I wanted to get away from Beirut. I cycled up to a beach near Jounieh, north of the city. It was a flashy place with jet skis revving around and house music pumping from the beach bars. Groups of young Lebanese were kicking beach balls and flinging frisbees. I dumped the bike, ran across the sand and into the surf.

Within seconds, my upper legs were smarting with pain. I let out a mute scream and scrambled for the shore. My left shank felt like it had been chargrilled. I looked down to find that my whole thigh had turned into a gently pulsing bruise.

Two children ran up to me, a boy and a girl, both about ten years old. They pointed to a mound of ice on the beach. At least it looked like ice, but, as I got closer, I realized it was moving. The girl lent down to touch the mass and pulled something out of it. It took me a while to realize that it was a jellyfish. The girl held it in her palm with the utmost delicacy, as if it were a butterfly. Entranced, we watched the transparent creature's subtle death throes before she gingerly put it back down.

'Mister, you put sand on leg,' said the girl. She picked up a handful of sand and rubbed it on to her leg to demonstrate. 'You,' she pointed at my leg. I dutifully picked up a handful and worked it into the wound. It turned an even more inflammatory red but at least the movement took my mind off the stinging. When I stopped rubbing the pain slowly subsided to a dull itch. The sand had acted like a dock leaf on nettle rash.

I thanked the children and they waded back into the sea which, I now realized, was a minefield of burning jelly. As fast as grizzly bears pawing for salmon, the youngsters would snatch at the diaphanous globs with their palms, then walk back, unstung, to the beach to deposit their victims on the twitching funeral pyre. Amid the loud music and thrum of jet ski engines, it was a scene of surprising beauty.

That night Abraham, Mr and Mrs Jurdi's nephew, flew in from Rome. Abraham was a charismatic antiques dealer who combined Mediterranean flair with Druze serenity. Mr Jurdi hugged him for several minutes while Mrs Jurdi and Latta held back tears.

After a while I slipped away. Their reunion had an almost religious intensity and I was beginning to feel like a voyeur. Besides, it was a gorgeous balmy evening, perfect for a bike ride. Although my thighs were still chafing a little from the jellyfish sting, I cycled off down the Corniche, past the American University, the famous Pigeon Rocks and the twittering lovers, past the lunar park with its neon Ferris wheel, past the Raouche cafés and felafel houses, under the fluttering posters heralding the upcoming elections, and then back for a final night in my flat. I ate a bowl of tabbouleh and then settled down to give Munir's old forty-fives another airing.

Abraham woke me early the following morning. He was eager to show me more of Beirut's downtown area before my taxi to Damascus. He made it clear there was no time for breakfast, fired up his Nissan hire car and off we went, driving at breakneck speed towards the awakening city centre.

After a farewell cruise along the Corniche, pulling over occasionally to look out over the choppy blue-grey Mediterranean, we visited a Hamra bookshop. The previous night, I had asked Abraham to recommend the book that best described the Lebenese civil war. He had recommended Robert Fisk's much-lauded *Pity the Nation*. Fisk, something of a Middle East legend, was one of the few journalists to stay on in Lebanon when the fighting was at its most fierce. Abraham said we would have no problem tracking a copy down.

The first bookshop we tried claimed to have never heard of it, the second was shut, and an assistant at the third, a huge underground vault, informed us the book had been banned in Beirut for years.

'Banned!' fumed Abraham as we left. 'Just typical.'

Abraham stopped to buy two cups of sugar cane juice before we jumped back into his hatchback. The plastic seats were already hot and Abraham flinched as he touched the scalding steering wheel. 'I've only been away ten months and half the roads have been re-routed,' he said, winding down his window. 'The driving just gets worse. You should have seen what it looked like before, Tom. Such beauty.' That seemed to be the phrase on everyone's lips.

We pulled into a car park near Martyr's Square, a dusty desolate area surrounded by shattered buildings, some roofless others honeycombed by small-arms fire. Amid this battlescape a huge isolated billboard showed an architect's vision of what downtown would look like in a few years. It resembled a futuristic Milton Keynes, with concrete bollards and manicured trees.

Abraham pulled some postcards from his jacket pocket. 'See this? This is what downtown was like before the war.' The card showed a street scene of pastel-coloured Dodges, of tall palms, big balconies and quirky street lights. It looked charming and confused. The new plans looked soulless – buildings for profit and performance, not for people. It was not only downtown that would be affected. Solidere, the French company engaged to carry out the modernization, also planned to reclaim sixty hectares from the sea.

Abraham pulled out another card showing the glory days of Beirut's glitzy hotel district. 'The Intercontinental Hotel opened on the eve of the civil war.' He sighed. 'Now it looks like a broken cheese grater.'

We entered a huge white stone church. Polythene netting covered what had once been stained-glass windows, plastic chairs replaced the pews, bullets had dimpled the masonry like rampant pox.

'What do you remember about the war, Abraham?'

'This will sound a little crazy to you,' he said, 'but it was beautiful.' Beautiful, I thought, a conflict which spanned three decades and claimed up to 150,000 lives. 'The best time of my life,' he continued cheerfully. 'We were teenagers; thought we were immortal. We would run into Maronite territory just for a laugh. Sometimes we were shot at. It was such a rush, such a high. Oh yes. Life was a carnival, you see. A carnival of rocket grenades and sniper fire perhaps, but a carnival where every day was sacred. People knew how to live. Now we all whinge about the most trivial things. We are all so afraid to die that we forget to live. Yes, it was a wonderful time. You never have friends like those when you are fifteen years old and at war.'

He paused, his animation fading. 'My elder brother thinks of it differently, of course. His best friend was blown up defusing a land mine. When my parents heard, they sent my brother straight to school in America so the same thing wouldn't happen to him. He is bitter about Lebanon now which I can understand. I think I am the only one of our family who wants to come back and live here. I am proud to be Druze and proud to be Lebanese.'

'Who do you think caused the war?'

'You have to remember, Tom,' said Abraham with a heavy sigh as we left the church, 'that Lebanon was once a country with sixteen different religions all living in harmony.'

An army truck drove slowly by, a Lebanese red and white flag with a green cedar tree droopping from a pole on the bonnet.

'The historians claim the war was between the Christians and the Muslims,' explained Abraham. 'This is not strictly true. Yes, the Green Line split the city into two convenient halves: the Christians on the east and Muslims on the west. But the war was much more complex than that. At different times Shia Muslims fought Sunni Muslims, and after first siding with Syria the Maronites later teamed up with Israel. The Druze were sometimes divided too.'

'Who do you think is to blame for the war?'

'It's impossible to say,' Abraham said fiercely. He then nodded his head sadly, his scowl gradually softening. 'I suppose in truth the war was really nobody's fault, but like all wars, everybody lost.'

We passed what looked like a massive bomb crater dotted with wigwam-style tents. Two fair-haired girls in jeans and filthy white T-shirts were burrowing through the wreckage. Several classical pillars were standing like lonely sentinels amid the debris.

'That's the one good thing about the bombing. Underneath some of the smashed buildings archaeologists have unearthed remnants of Roman Beirut. They're supposed to be in very good condition.' Abraham smirked. 'How's that for irony?'

Back at the Jurdis' a farewell feast had been prepared. Grilled lamb, spinach, pine nuts and pitta bread, washed down with glasses of sour home-squeezed lemonade. We sat in the garden, yellow butterflies tumbling around us as we ate. At the end of the meal I mentioned to Abraham my fears about cycling through Iran. He put his arm around my shoulder.

'You should not be afraid, Tom,' he assured me. 'Take a lesson from me. We Druze do not believe in reincarnation like the Buddhists who believe you can come back as an animal. We believe you can only be reincarnated as a human being and only on *this* earth. It cuts out a lot of stress if you know you are coming back. It gives you a very positive attitude towards danger.'

'Do not talk of death to one so young, Abraham,' interrupted Mr Jurdi. 'Tom will be fine. He is free, able to travel as he pleases, but he must realize that freedom can be found in many ways. I am an old man who has lived all his life in one place but I too have known great freedom. You must remember, Tom,' he added gravely, 'that too much freedom, too much possibility, can lead to the same frustration as being in chains.'

I looked hard at Mr Jurdi. His grey eyes sparkled with knowledge and confidence. He seemed that most rare of human beings, one with the faith to know that whatever life threw at him, in death, he would always find the way home.

After my goodbyes Abraham dropped me at Rue Sourati, where Haleb was waiting with the clapped-out black-windowed Mercedes taxi that would take me back to Damascus. Buses from Beirut to Damascus had not run for years, Haleb assured me, and taxi was the only way, even if it cost US$60 for the pleasure. My fellow passengers were a sullen droopy-moustached man holding an empty bird cage and his silent wife wrapped in a black chador. The elderly driver whistled to himself at the wheel.

I was leaving Beirut just as the politics were heating up. Rue Sourati was flapping with innumerable posters; every inch of space filled with images of middle-aged candidates wearing ties and rictus smiles. Like Christmas decorations they hung between palm trees and street lights, or stared obtrusively from tower block windows or restaurant fronts.

'It costs one million Lebanese lira (£4,000) to enter for the local elections,' said Haleb. 'Look at these hopeless self-important fools. They all think they will make a difference. God, it's enough to make me put myself forward. The Up Yours Damascus Party.'

'Catchy name,' I commented but I was barely listening. I was suffering an attack of seahorse-in-my-passport jitters. 'Shouldn't we get going?' I asked Haleb testily, shoving my final pannier in the boot.

'Yes, yes. Off you go. By the way, keep ten dollars handy; you may need to use it as a bribe.'

'A bribe! You promised me there would be no problem.'

'There *will* be no problem,' proclaimed Haleb, waving his fists at me. 'Inshallah, amigo. Be strong.'

As it turned out, crossing the Syrian border could not have been easier. The hangdog guard scanned my visa for all of three seconds – perhaps the longest three seconds of my adult life – and quickly waved me on. The seahorse had served its purpose. Now I had been stamped I was beyond the Rubicon.

The following day and night were spent on buses heading slowly north to Erzurum. The stretch from Damascus to Homs was especially enjoyable, livened up by the fact that Syria had just won their first ever Olympic gold medal. A dainty-looking athlete called Ghada Shouaa had clinched the women's heptathlon title in Atlanta. Her success generated a friendly patriotic *esprit de corps* among the bus passengers.

By the time we neared Adana in southern Turkey the Olympic rapture of the Syrian passengers had been superseded by discomfort and fatigue. Many of them were massaging cricked necks or shaking cramped feet back to life. I, too, had lost my sanguine mien. In fact, the lighter the dawn the darker my mood, as I gazed out at the road down which I had so assiduously cycled two months before. I was now travelling in the reverse direction in a crowded bus. It was demoralizing.

Adana bus station was huge, dirty and very noisy. There were dozens of hawkers pushing plastic worry beads or counterfeit US Army badges. An African boy in a white fez sat cross-legged on the pavement, energetically sharpening a skewer on a whetstone, while irritable backpackers in singlets and baseball caps argued with travel touts over bus tickets to Cappadocia.

To kill time before my late-afternoon bus north, I wrote three long letters: one to my parents, one to Alexandra and one to the local paper, the *Bucks Herald*. In the latter I had to explain to my sponsors why I was temporarily on four wheels rather than two. I began with a moan about the lack of boats and the intransigence of the Egyptians but then crossed it out and rewrote the first paragraph, beginning, 'Sorry, I've cheated.' It sounded rather like an early obituary, as if the trip might soon have to be killed off. Nice try Tom, but it's time to head for home. At this stage it was certainly a serious possibility. Everything hinged on this wretched visa.

The bus to Erzurum finally turned up late. It was one of those old chuggers with strings of fairy lights looping the dashboard and mournful ballads blasting non-stop from antediluvian speakers. The driver had an irritating propensity for pulling over every twenty minutes for piss stops. Still, it did make it to Erzurum for 9 a.m. – the opening time at the Iranian Consulate.

And, even more remarkable, by 10 a.m. I had my visa.

This time, I did not show any letters or newspaper articles; I did not even mention the bicycle. I decided it would only complicate matters. Back in Egypt, Zack had told me that small consulates were usually far more compliant regarding visas than big embassies. The more remote the better. How right he had been. In Erzurum, I simply needed to fill out a visa form, Xerox a couple of papers and pay US$50. BANG. One five-day Iranian visa, sir, easily extendable once in the country. I had travelled hundreds of miles in the wrong direction, braved Beirut's anarchic traffic and risked castration at the Syrian frontier, but it had all been worth it. Now I did not have to fly. I did not have to sacrifice the spirit of Captain Charles and Johnny Ginger.

I sat in a *kebabji* and popped open a bottle of cold Amstel beer. Then I extracted my passport from my money belt, opened it at the page of the Iranian visa, kissed it several times and propped it up in front of my face. I stared at it. No piece of paper could have given me more pleasure – a thousand-pound cheque, a degree in astronomy, a ticket to see the Beatles, a knighthood – right then, right there, five days in Iran was all that mattered. My dream was safe.

That afternoon, I caught another bus on to Dogubayazit, the Iranian border town known to travellers by the less enigmatic sobriquet of Dog Biscuit. The sky was pregnant with dark clouds, and rivulets of warm rain ran down the steamed up bus windows. I noticed a lushness in the surrounding farmland. After months amid the pale shades of the desert, the grass seemed almost luminous. It was the first time I had seen rain in weeks.

As the bus clattered east, it was inspected at several check-points by soldiers in yew-green uniforms. The closer we were to Dogubayazit the more thorough their searches became. On one occasion I had to pull out my panniers from the bus's side vault for inspection.

Dog Biscuit lives up to its name. It is a litter-strewn place of drab concrete buildings, grubby sheep and deranged water-melon salesmen. The only redeeming feature was the magnificent view of Mount Ararat. It had a potent brooding presence and was tipped with snow. According to my guidebook the 5,000-metre-plus peak had been closed to tourists for some time due to a combination of hazardous terrain, ferocious dogs, violent outlaws and, perhaps most relevant, potential kidnap by the PKK. I decided against any mountaineering.

The one thing I needed to do in Dogubayazit was some shopping. That afternoon I bought a pair of cotton hippy trousers with auburn zigzags, perfect for pedalling in post-Ayatollah Iran. I posted home my paperback copy of *Jerusalem* by Colin Thubron, a book which would not go down well at the following day's border crossing. Finally, in a fit of wild extravagance, I purchased a roll-on deodorant called Impulse. It smelt like pot-pourri but was far lighter than the more machismo brands, one of which was called YES! YES! and weighed as much as a jar of jam.

After a good night's sleep in a friendly doss-house and a visit to a backstreet userer to change my remaining Turkish lira into Iranian rials, I was ready to start my last and longest Middle Eastern ride. I was also about to fulfil a promise made back in 1979, the year of the Iranian revolution.

CHAPTER TWELVE

REMEMBERING REZA

When I was ten years old my best friend was an Iranian boy called Reza Vazifekhah.

Reza arrived one evening at Maidwell Hall, my tweedy Northamptonshire prep school. He was holding hands with his younger brother Mohammed. The two boys stood in the school quadrangle, their frozen breath smoky in the darkness, looking up at Maidwell's austere ivy-threaded turrets. A cluster of us watched them excitedly from the library window.

Were the brothers princes? Runaways? Were they from China? The Congo? Jamaica? This was as good as the *Hardy Boys* or John Buchan. The Vazifekhah brothers were about as incongruous at Maidwell as *Just William* would have been at King Darius' court. They knew not a word of English and spoke in phlegmy incomprehensible murmurs. They wore bright silk jackets despite the bitter cold and sported haircuts like medieval pages. They were both impressively small; at the time of their arrival, I was the shortest boy in my year but nevertheless towered over them both.

Over the ensuing months, the transformation of Reza and Mohammed was remarkable. Their Iranian garb was soon replaced by Harris tweed jackets, mustard corduroys and ox-blood brogues. They learned to play rugby, conkers and British

Bulldogs, how to eat marmalade with fried bread and, most astonishingly of all, to speak in the same plummy tones as the rest of us.

Reza and I became the greatest of muckers. We looked out for each other: I helped with his English, he with my maths. I taught him how to play snooker, he taught me to how to inflict first-class half-nelsons and Chinese burns. I nicknamed him Raze; he called me Freo.

As his family never seemed to visit, Reza would come back and spend half-terms and holidays at Swanbourne, while Mohammed would head off to London to stay with the family of his great friend, Bugsy. My parents and sisters became fond of Reza. Every time he turned up at the village he would bring a James Herriot book or a fistful of roses as a present for my mother. At Christmas, he joined in the carol singing at Swanbourne's candlelit church and we gave him an Abba album and a Monopoly set.

I only knew Reza for a couple of years. In that time what impressed me most about him was his uncompromising bravery. I remember one incident especially vividly when the school suffered a summer plague of ladybirds. All the boys thought it was excellent sport to tear around the grounds thwacking the swarms of red bugs with tennis rackets. Reza was appalled. He felled prefects twice his size with rugby tackles in a bid to end the genocide. Naturally, despite plucky resistance, he was beaten up.

The only time I ever came to blows with Reza was at the height of the *Star Wars* craze. Cooky, Reza and I were taking it in turns to play Luke Skywalker, Han Solo and Chewbacca. When Miles Hunt and Charlie Courtauld turned up, we introduced Darth Vader and Princess Leia into the fray. When it was Reza's turn to play Princess Leia he refused point-blank. I told him to stop being such a prat. Without hesitation he threw me into a bramble bush, bloodying my nose and shredding my boiler suit in the process. From then on, to appease our Persian playmate, we dropped female characters and added Obi-Wan Kenobi to the cast instead.

Reza's last few months at Maidwell were not easy for him and he made several attempts to run away. One time he was caught yomping down the road towards Market Harborough, his pockets stuffed with two weeks' supply of tuck. He kept his problems private and I had no idea of the turmoil he must have been going through, but gradually more details about his family life came out. We learned that his father was one of the Shah of Iran's bodyguards and that his mother had died of cancer some years earlier. The two boys were apparently being financed by a guardian in London.

As Reza was my best friend, I became very pro-Shah. Of course I knew nothing about him other than that he had a cool name and was sometimes in the papers. But that was enough. I promised Reza that the summer after leaving Maidwell we would borrow my father's air rifle, fly to Iran and pot off the 'Ayawallah' (despite the fact he was in Paris at the time). Angus Macoulough said we'd never do it, but Reza and I bet him a sherbet fountain and a *Charlie's Angels* calendar that we would.

We lost the bet. In the spring term of 1979, just after the Shah had been overthrown and shortly before breaking up from Maidwell for good, Reza and Mohammed vanished. Their trunks were suddenly packed and gone. Not a word. They had dissolved into thin air like djinns. At first I was distraught. I asked all the teachers what had happened. Some said the brothers' guardian could no longer afford Maidwell's fees, others said that their father had been killed in the revolution and they needed to go into hiding. Perhaps they had been forcibly sent back to Tehran? The departure of Reza and Mohammed had been as sudden and enigmatic as their arrival.

At the age of twelve, you do not pine for long over lost friends; you find someone else to play Han Solo to your Luke Skywalker. You head off for a summer holiday of swimming in Highland lochs, conveniently forgetting your best mate faces danger and uncertainty, perhaps even death. Despite my initial anxiety over him, within a month I had all but forgotten Reza Vazifekhah. Now Reza was propelled once again to the forefront of my mind as I left Dogubayazit, finally preparing to fulfil that childhood promise, nearly twenty years too late, of visiting Iran. I was not brandishing an air rifle however but straddling an overladen bicycle.

Sorry, Raze. Wherever you are now, may the force be with you.

After leaving Turkey for the second time in three months, I waited in the queue for Iran.

Unlike Turkish Customs, which was wallpapered with mug-shots of wanted PKK terrorists, Iran's passport office resembled a portrait gallery of Islam's turbaned elite. As usual, sombre-faced Ayatollah Khomeini took centre stage. His spiritual successor the Ayatollah Khamenei – they looked as similar as they sounded – sat to his right, while his political successor, chubby smooth-chinned President Rafsanjani, was on his left.

The bike was thoroughly dismantled, my clothes and books ripped from the panniers and spread over the floor. It was the equivalent of watching my living room being ransacked. Behind me a sorority of women shrouded in dark chadors huddled together, husking pistachios.

'Why you come Iran?' whispered one of them, stretching across and tugging gently at my trouser leg.

I looked down at her, astonished. She peered up from her cowl. 'Iran bad. You go Turkey.' She had the prettiest face with large greeny-grey eyes and a button nose. I noticed her chador had rucked up her leg a little and Adidas training shoes were peeking out from under its hem. She flicked her eyebrows at me and slunk down again, like a crab retreating into its carapace.

Outside it was noon and the white sun was beating down with sledgehammer force. Several timber lorries trundled past, heading towards the low lightly rusted hummocks up ahead. A flock of birds flew over, chirruping sweetly. Within seconds they were invisible, swallowed up in the parched landscape.

A boy wearing black flannel knickerbockers and a white *shalwar qamiz* top rushed over. 'Excuse me, sir, can I see your bike?' His face was pale and dotted with freckles.

David, was fourteen years old, of American–Iranian parentage. He usually lived in Washington State, he told me, but for the last year had been travelling all over Iran with his Shiraz-born father. David's favourite place had been the ancient capital of Esfahan which he claimed was as 'cool as Seattle', adding that he was leaving Iran now because if he stayed any longer he might be conscripted into the army.

Our conversation was cut short when his father beckoned him to go through the border. 'See you,' said David, shaking my hand. 'Good luck.' The father waved at me. He had a chamois jacket and his hair was brilliantined; on his back was a large blue and red Berghaus rucksack.

'Good luck, buddy,' he shouted out, 'you're gonna love this place.' Hand in hand the father and son weaved through the crowds towards Turkey, the distant peak of Mount Ararat still visible above the cloud.

Later that afternoon I caught a bus east to Tehran. I had to get a move on. My visa expiry date was already fast approaching. Four days to go. An extension was of paramount importance.

The surrounding landscape was mainly desert, livened up by

fields of bleached corn or the odd flash of cultivated sunflowers. It was hard to see through the front windscreen which seemed to dance with an array of gewgaws: an air freshener shaped like a jumbo jet, a gremlin on a string, and a display of postcards.

I was sitting next to a young Canadian called Simon. He was a physics student from Montreal who spoke with a guttural French accent and came across as one of those crusading academic types who wants to help everybody; a well-intentioned dreamer who after spending a week on Kurdish-occupied Mount Nemrut considered himself an honorary member of the PKK. I listened to his diatribes on everything from Quebec's fight for independence to the redundancy of the British Commonwealth. What finished me off was his lecture on toxic waste in the St Lawrence River. Quebec's whales – Beluga whales, finback whales, blue whales – were dying by the thousand, he asserted. I wanted to ask whether he wore a daffodil on St David's Day too. 'You see, man, it's all to do with the migration cycles . . .' Soon I was asleep.

We pulled into Tehran at 5.30 a.m. Simon had chosen a cheap hotel from his guidebook, the strangely named: Iran-No. For convenience's sake I decided to stick with him.

We loaded my bike into the boot of a white Pakyan taxi parked outside the bus depot. Pakyans are small sturdy cars based on an old Hillman model. They had been built in large numbers in Iran in the seventies using parts imported from Britain. Our milometer read 000, frozen like a fruit-machine display panel, probably since the revolution. Meters were a capitalist vestige of the Shah; nowadays haggling was the preferred way to do business. After much hand-wringing and scribbling on scraps of paper, Simon agreed a price and we sped off into the capital.

Tehran defies description. It must be the easiest city on earth to get lost in. All the buildings seem to have been built at the same time by the same architects; it is a bodged-up sprawl of plastic, glass and grey concrete. It was incredible to think the capital had been nothing more than a trifling market town before Agha Mohammed, a eunuch warrior of the Qajar dynasty, chose to make it his capital in 1783. It now contains over ten million people. Where all these millions of people were on my first morning was a mystery. Other than the odd motorbike whipping past, it was quieter than Swanbourne on a Sunday. I felt like I was stuck in an apocalyptic film set. How could a capital founded by a eunuch called Agha be so dreary?

Once we were out of the taxi, things got a little better. From the Iran-No's door it was possible to see the attractive saffron-tinged Albourz Mountains poking up over the north rim of the city. We were also able to pinpoint the huge white satellite dish of Tehran's central telegram office, the capital's only prominent architectural landmark.

Landmarks are vital in Tehran as most of the city maps were utterly baffling. The main problem was that all the street names associated with the Shah – including Winston Churchill Avenue – had been expunged in 1979. Instead, the city's shambolic streets had been given revolutionary titles often longer than the names of Welsh railway stations.

At the Iran-No, we were struggling with names too. The grouchy receptionist was a stickler for detail. He had written my address as 'United Kingdom of Passport', copying it fastidiously into a grubby ledger. He then asked 'Fader name?' and more surprisingly 'Moder name?' Without the passport to copy from he was less thorough. First he scribbled Jun (John), then Un (Anne).

Finally, he handed us a padlock, small enough to fit a tuck box, and ushered us upstairs. We dragged the bike into a two-bedded room on the third floor. The view was not good. Our sole window looked directly out on to a grey and mossy wall.

Still, it was only 10,000 rials (£3.50) a night. One could hardly expect a vision of Xanadu.

On the door was a laminated message.

Dear guests

We welcome you to the Islamic Republic of Iran. Now we would like you to get familiar with some samples of Islamic veil for ladies. Please respect and be observed with Islamic veil always.

A crude sketch of a woman in a dark mask had been drawn below. A waggish previous guest had superimposed a speech bubble with the caption, 'Use your imagination, boys.'

Even by the time Simon and I had freshened up, Tehran still seemed comatose. We parked ourselves on a couple of stools in a nearby *shwarma* restaurant. There was one other customer; a soldier in immaculately creased olive-green trousers, designer stubble and a moustache that could have scoured the grimiest of frying pans. He was sipping his tea from a saucer, Persian style, using a sugar lump as a cooling filter.

'Are you here for Mohammed's birthday?' he asked us, peering over the saucer.

'Mohammed who?' I replied.

'The Prophet Mohammed, of course. It's his birthday today.'

'Excellent,' said Simon. 'What happens?'

'Not much, everything stays quiet. People want to be with their families. It's a holy time.'

'Why aren't you with your family?'

'The army only gives me one day off; I want to have fun, then see the family.' His face suddenly lit up. 'I can be your guide! I love English. I read all the time.' He was gabbling with excitement. 'Please, friends, please, let me talk with you.'

'Sure,' we replied in unison.

'Oh, the Prophet's blessings, what good fun. My name is Davood. I telephone my friend, Hammid, and we show you around.'

Hammid, a cadaverous neatly bearded man, arrived soon after in a blackberry-coloured Paykan. The car had an accelerator shaped like a human foot and an engine with the roar of a small aeroplane. Hammid said he wanted to buy a Renault or a Toyota instead but on a trainee English teacher's wages it was impossible.

'Both of us want to get away from Iran,' said Davood. 'I love to go to England, Canada, anywhere. I like Iran, but it is so strict. For the next two years I waste six days a week in the army.' He sighed. 'How will I find a girlfriend?'

'You are too ugly,' said Hammid. 'You must pay for one.'

The mating game in Tehran was clearly a tricky one. As it was frowned upon to be seen with a woman in public, lovers could only meet behind closed doors. Hammid and Davood were twenty-four years old with no homes of their own. In order to be alone with a girl, they were forced to rely on the generosity of friends who could lend them a pad for the night or weekend. Davood admitted he sometimes slept with prostitutes.

We turned off down a long wide avenue lined with plane trees, the trees tall and healthy unlike the stunted pollution blotched ones we had passed on the way to the hotel. We were in the north of the city, Hammid told us, the affluent part where professional types who liked to ski in the Alborz Mountains at the weekend resided. It was spacious and cool, worlds apart from the poverty-stricken slums of the south.

Hammid pulled over near the entrance to a large park. He hooked a steering-lock over the Paykan's wheel which clunked into place like a rifle bolt. The park was a lively spot. There was a lake on which couples were drifting along in pedaloes, there were flower gardens and fountains and fat droopy palms. Near the centre were cages of parakeets and French partridges; another cage housed a frolicking brown bear. Families were picnicking all around and children ran to and fro, faces full of fun. We bought some cold drinks and lay on the grass.

On the pavement below us a skateboarder in a black suit glided by balancing a tray of drinks on his head. He was being chased by a man with a TV camera. Hammid told us they were filming an advertisement; he'd seen them in the park last week. 'They like to make Iran look rich,' he said, laughing. 'Nonsense people.'

After lounging on the grass most of the morning Davood was keen for us to visit the Ayatollah's Khomeini's shrine. It is ten miles south of the capital on the road to the holy city of Qom. There would be time to drive past the shrine before Davood's rendezvous with his family. We jumped back into the sauna-like Paykan, winding down its creaky windows in a vain attempt to catch the passing breeze.

Hammid sped back to the Iran-No where Simon needed to make a phone call. After weaving through the sorry-looking slums south of the city we hit a highway heading out into the open plains.

'Don't you want to pray today?' I asked Davood from the back seat.

'I am not religious,' replied Davood. '*Allahu akbar. Allahu akbar.*' He imitated a muezzin's yodel. 'Doing five times a day. Oh, no. That is why I have a stubble beard, not a mullah beard. I cannot believe in a God who thinks everyone must look like the Ayatollah.'

'But you must be religious, Hammid?' I asked.

'No, no,' he replied, stroking his face. 'I grow a beard because it looks good, like Farsi pop star.'

Fifteen minutes later, the vast gold dome marking the

Ayatollah's resting place came into view. The most outstanding thing about the dome is its size; it stands out like a monstrous brass doorknob, visible for miles around. But on this occasion it seemed a doorknob in need of a good polish. It reminded me of a baddie's HQ in a low budget sci-fi movie rather than one of Islam's great pilgrimage sites. On the first anniversary of the Ayatollah's death, thousands of mourners had converged on the shrine, but now the whole area seemed neglected.

While the Ayatollah's shrine was struggling to lure mourners the nearby Behesht-é Zahra cemetery, a massive expanse of flat graves many of which are identified by photographs of young soldiers, had no such trouble. The cemetery is a sobering reminder of the thousands of lives lost in the Iran–Iraq war. Between 1980, when Saddam Hussein invaded Iran, and 1988 when the conflict petered out, the cemetery almost doubled in size. Apart from its tragic dimensions – it is now believed to be the largest cemetery in the world – Behesht-é Zahra has become renowned for its macabre fountain of fake blood, built in honour of the fallen.

'One of my uncles was killed in the war,' said Davood as we surveyed the endless ranks of the dead. Several of the graves were decorated with flowers or pot plants and a few flags were flying. 'Such a waste. But he was a fanatic, first into any battle. He was crazy on Allah.'

'Can we find his grave?' I asked.

'Not now,' said Davood. 'It was just to let you see the numbers.' Like so many on my trip, the visit had been hopelessly brief but was still a valuable eye-opener.

On the way back, Davood explained that while Iraq had banked on hi-tech weaponry and American back-up during the war, Iran had relied on greater numbers and the religious zeal of their soldiers. In 1978 the population of Iran was a little over thirty million. By 1988 it was thought to have shot up to nudging sixty million; a population explosion deemed necessary when boys as young as fifteen were being sent by the lorry load to the front line.

Despite the appalling suffering during the war – trench fighting, gas attacks, infantry charges – the Iranian army rarely showed signs of mutiny or battle fatigue. They were consistently heroic. Indeed, by the end of the war Iran was thought to have sustained six times the number of casualties suffered by Iraq. I wondered whether the sacrifices of the Iranian soldiers had been inspired by faith, patriotism or a combination of the two. Faith seemed the more likely motivation. After all, over 92 per cent of Iranians are Shia Muslims, who, unlike the Sunnis, are followers of Ali, the Prophet Mohammed's son-in-law. Shias have always put special emphasis on sacrifice and martyrdom ever since Ali's successor, Hosain, fought to the death against a vastly superior Sunni army at the battle of Kerbala in AD 680. Today, Shias are still the underdogs. Of the world's 800 million Muslims, more than 90 per cent are Sunnis. Iran, Bahrain and to a lesser extent Iraq are the bastions of the Shia faith.

'Were Iranian soldiers more willing to die because they were Shias?' I asked Davood.

'Not at all,' he replied, a hint of anger in his voice. 'It was the Ayatollah. He turned the whole country crazy, full of hate. It's only now that Iranian people realize how crazy he was. But we are still careful what we say; the *Komiteh* (religious police) are big Ayatollah supporters.'

Davood drummed the Paykan dashboard with his fingers. 'To be fair to the Ayatollah,' he continued begrudgingly, 'he did believe absolutely in what he taught. He was not, how you say, a hypocrisy. He died a few months after the war finished, you know. Not winning probably kill the old fool.'

'The old fool!' shouted Hammid, angry with his friend's

acquiescence. 'OLD FOOL! The man was monster, Davood. We are lost people because of him. Half of us dead, filling up that terrible cemetery, the other half longing to leave the country.' He slapped his forehead hard with his palm. 'Wake up, Davood. What future does that give us? Huh, Davood. Where do we go?'

The car became uncomfortably quiet. I caught Davood's eye in the wing mirror. He looked a little worried.

'So where do we go, Davood?' probed Hammid again, calmer this time.

'Home,' replied Davood, looking tenderly across at his friend. 'It's the Prophet's birthday and I want to see my family. Let's go home.'

The following morning was a bit of a disaster. I headed over to the British Embassy in the hope of cadging some decent maps and finding out about visa extensions. Apparently, if you played your cards right, it was possible to secure visas for up to a month.

I showed my passport to the armed guard who stood outside the front gate. He nodded and I walked inside the office which was large and gloomy, brightened only by small patches of sunlight. A woman sporting octagonal glasses and a walnut-whip hairstyle was hectoring an Iranian family. She spoke Farsi with the crisp authority of a Women's Institute matriarch. Once she had made her point, the dejected Iranians slunk away and I stepped into their place. A smiling print of the Royal Family was on display above the counter.

'I'm hoping to bicycle through Iran,' I explained.

'You're not the first,' the woman replied tartly. 'I'm afraid we can't keep tabs on you. It's your own risk.'

'Of course,' I replied. 'I just thought it might be sensible to let you know.'

She handed me a form. I scribbled down my details while she prattled on about visas and heatstroke and ungrateful Iranians. She clearly considered Tehran a dud posting. Eventually I escaped from her cool office back out into the stifling humidity.

The next stop was the visa extension office, which provided a frazzled contrast to the quiet, briskly efficient British Embassy. Snaking outside the office was a long ill-tempered queue at whose head a scrum of frustrated Arabs was berating two officials at a desk. The desk was piled high with leaning towers of passports. Photos and application forms were spread out in a collage. No way was I letting my passport loose in that lot. I decided to find an alternative.

Back at the Iran-No, I bumped into Simon, who had fared better at the Canadian Embassy. They had told him to get his visa in one of the smaller towns – Esfahan, Tabriz or Shiraz – as Tehran was notoriously chaotic. I thanked my lucky stars I had trusted my instincts and walked away, but I was angry that the frump at the British Embassy had told me Tehran was the only place to have my visa extended.

Simon and I sorted out bus tickets for the following day. I realized I would now have to put in my visa renewal application only hours before it was due to expire.

That evening we splashed out and dined at the nearby Fars Hotel. We shared a table with Sadik, a melancholy Iraqi refugee who had endured prison and torture in Baghdad for his anti-Saddam views. He had escaped to Iran in 1982 and settled in Ahvaz, a grim industrial city in the south-west. There he had met his Iranian wife and they now had three children. Sadik was a sculptor and was in Tehran showing some of his work at a state-funded exhibition.

Sadik's story was relentlessly bleak. Once he had escaped from Iraq, he told us, he had thought he would be home and dry. But Ahvaz had proved an artistic wasteland and Sadik had struggled desperately to make ends meet. Iran was also a miserable place for an Iraqi emigré, even one who had been beaten by Saddam's secret police. Sadik had spent the last fourteen years battling for a visa, any visa, just to get away. He had tried every consulate possible – Australia, France, Uzbekistan – but he was always turned down.

Sadik did not possess a passport, his only proof of identity was a dog-eared UN document with his haunted mugshot stapled to the left corner. The photo had clearly been taken many years earlier, before his hair had receded along with his hopes. He also carried a heartbreaking letter, embossed with roses, which explained his life story. It began, 'Dear Honest Ambassador . . .' in looping childish writing.

Simon had been hanging on Sadik's every word. 'I can help you,' he told him. Canada was willing to take immigrants. He would go to the embassy the next day and Sadik could accompany him. Sadik's face was a study in rapture.

When Sadik left the room to telephone his family I turned on Simon. I told him he was giving Sadik false hopes. Would he be prepared to be Sadik's financial guarantor? To be responsible for him and his family for up to ten years? Cope with all their problems? Simon said he was not sure, but it was worth a try.

'Worth a try!' I fumed. 'The man already thinks he's a Mountie. Buy one of his sculptures, that will help him more. This is just giving him false hope.'

'False hope is better than no hope,' countered Simon. 'At least I can get that handwritten letter typed for him. That will make it look more professional. Little things count too. Put yourself in his shoes. I'm not a fool you know; I know I can't just take him home.'

Simon's counter-attack surprised me. I was really beginning to admire him. He was only twenty years old and he really did believe that he could make a difference, whether with Sadik's visa or the whales in Quebec. I felt old and mean and cynical next to him. At first Simon had riled me because I thought he was all hot air – saving this, saving that – without any intention of doing anything. But I had got him wrong.

Tomorrow, Simon really would stay behind. He would take Sadik to the Canadian Embassy, get his letter typed out and, if nothing else, show that he cared. I would simply hop on a bus to Esfahan and forget about the pair of them; and I was the one with the gall to moralize.

Poor Sadik. We left him dreaming of Beluga whales, jazz cafés and maple syrup. A place where his work would be respected and his family safe. An impossible place. A place called home.

As planned, I rose early and caught the 8 a.m. bus to Esfahan, once again passing the Ayatollah's holy doorknob but this time continuing south down to Qom.

Qom has a reputation as a dry joyless city and is the place where the Ayatollah first delivered his sermons against the Shah. It is a major centre of Shia learning and provides an ascetic environment in which Muslim clerics and pilgrims ponder the meaning of the Koran and the Hadith, the traditions of the Prophet.

The sanctity of Qom is not respected by everyone. In the same way irreligious Italians make fun of the Vatican and non-devout Jews crack jokes about Jerusalem, some Shias like to quote the popular proverb, 'A dog of Kashan is better than the nobles of Qom.' I was glad I was not stopping there; from the bus window it did not look the place to welcome a bicyclist in auburn hippy trousers.

But I was determined to do some pedalling in Iran, preferably from Esfahan down to King Darius' ancient capital at

Persepolis. However, it daunted me that so far the road south of Tehran had been nothing but a desolate bone-dry waste. After Syria, Jordan and Sinai I was beginning to pine for the lushness of Swanbourne, the hedgerows and brambles, the dandelions and cow-parsley: the reassuring patchwork of green.

To take my mind off the unvarying sea of sand outside, I opened up my copy of the previous day's *Tehran Times*. Sunday edition, 4 August.

It was good eye-popping stuff. The headline immediately gave away the editorial thrust of the paper: 'Man's Salvation Possible Through Islamic Ideology.' Some of the editorial was spectacularly anti-American. Although 'USA is Satan' placards were a thing of the past in Iran and soldiers were now banned from burning the Stars and Stripes, *rapprochement* still had a long way to go if the press was anything to go by.

Take, for example, this passionate excerpt justifying Iran's right to deploy nuclear weapons. 'President Rafsanjani pointed out that the United States . . . has the world's biggest atomic arsenal . . . holds a notorious criminal record of genocide through the use of nuclear power . . . has fully equipped Israel, its illegitimate entity, with atomic bombs . . . has no right whatsoever to dictate its will . . . from giving Iran nuclear technology for the peaceful purposes.'

Even the Atlanta Olympics coverage was a little jingoistic: 'The Islamic Republic of Iran finally won its first wrestling gold in the freestyle competition which ended here Friday.

Rasoul Khadem beat two-time Olympic champion Makharbek Khadartsev of Russia 3–0.

"I just wanted to avenge for my teammate and watch the Iranian flag go up and see the Americans get on their feet and listen to our national anthem," Khadem said.'

Other parts were just incomprehensible: 'The Ayatollah added that what today man is suffering in the era of industry and under the shadow of dazzling and enticing materialism is more painful than what he suffered in the yonder days in the abyss of ignorance.'

The newspapers made for very different reading when Paul Theroux travelled through the Shah's Iran in the mid 1970s. In his book *The Great Railway Bazaar* he noted during a stop-off in the capital that there were two daily papers in English, a French daily and a German weekly, and the sports page of the *Tehran Times* concentrated mainly on US baseball results. How things change in twenty years. The only international news in my *Tehran Times* was a little slot on the back page. Even the children's section on page four, with its recipes and join-the-dot puzzles, had been allocated more space.

I had heard so many good things about Esfahan – its gardens, its architecture, its tranquillity – that it upset me to discover its suburbs were almost as vile as Tehran's. Opposite the bus stop was a huge Ayatollah portrait dominating the façade of a derelict tower block and, far from being tranquil, all I could hear was the clank and clamour of factory machinery.

I loaded up the bike and pedalled off in search of the 'cool as Seattle' part of town that David had spoken of. It did not take long to find. I have never been anywhere near Seattle but, if Esfahan is anything to go by, it must be a very cool place indeed.

It was mid-afternoon, too late for me to attempt to deal with my visa, so I headed straight for Emam Khomeini Square, the site of Shah Abbas's beautiful mosque which has won over visitors for three centuries or more. Unlike Tehran, orientation in Esfahan is straightforward and the wide tree-lined main street, Chahar Bagh, cuts through the city down to the meandering River Zaindeh.

On arrival at the square I propped my bike against an ice

cream vendor's trolley which, apart from ices, offered a kind of frozen vermicelli marinated in lemon juice. It was an Esfahan speciality and tasted splendid. I ate two bowls and asked the friendly, gap-toothed vendor to watch my bike while I looked around the square, promising I would be back for more.

The square or *maidan*, the second biggest in the world after Tiananmen in Beijing, is a dreamscape of breathtaking symmetry and elegance, flanked at every compass point by architectural show-stoppers.

To the south is the turquoise-domed Masjed-é-Emam. This gorgeous, mosque took twenty-six years to build, and has a cavernous double-layered interior that echoes like a Snowdonia valley. While I was inside, a young girl sang a single shrill note which soughed its way up the curving walls and rebounded like a choir of angels. The mosque's twin minarets complete the perfection and, like divine lighthouses, they taper up to the heavens in a flourish of white and blue arabesques.

On the east is the less extrovert Masjed-é Sheikh Lotfollah. It is considerably smaller but more accessible for that. As it has no minarets I found my eyes drawn to its blue kaleidoscopic dome which is like an exquisite and delicately shaped shallot.

Completing the majestic rectangle are Shah Abbas's seven-storey palace on the west and, to the north, the city's labyrinthine bazaar – crowded alleys of merchants and mountebanks, some selling wares of the highest quality, others tawdry pap. Its cobbled passages are thought to stretch for more than three miles. Impressive as they looked I'd had enough of Middle Eastern bazaars and so I sauntered back out into the square for another frozen vermicelli.

It really was a perfect spot: relaxed without being lonely, beautiful without being swamped by tourists. I lay back and pictured the polo matches, the concerts and the scandalous soirées that would have taken place here over 300 years ago.

For me, the chief attraction was watching the little horse-drawn *doroshkehs* rattle around the *maidan*. This was a not a place that had faded with history. It was still wonderful to experience and very quiet. I hadn't felt so at peace with the world since my sojourn with the Jurdis in Beirut.

The only thing that marred the splendour was the knowledge that the genius who masterminded it all, Shah Abbas, had been a rampant megalomaniac whose sophisticated exterior belied a ferocious heart. As John Simpson noted in his book *Lifting the Veil*, Shah Abbas 'kept a troupe of forty cannibals who followed him everywhere he went, and . . . from time to time he would feed his victims to them . . . sometimes he killed them simply because he was bored.'

Like the slave-driving pharaohs who whipped the pyramids into existence and the Moguls who created India's finest palaces Shah Abbas, for all his sadistic excesses, built something his people will continue to cherish for generations to come.

The following day passed like a dream. I had been terrified that if I did not secure my visa extension before Friday (the Islamic Sabbath) I would be stuffed; I need not have worried. Within an hour I was brandishing a passport safe with a two-week stay of expulsion. I rode my bike back under the shady chestnut trees fringing the university.

At the River Zaindeh I braked to photograph one of the honey-stoned bridges straddling the water. It was an animated scene: children dangled multi-hooked fish lines from the bridge while the odd canoe came drifting by. A coffee house was positioned underneath the bridge's end arch. I leaned the bike against a table, ordered a coffee and began scribbling my diary.

'Can I sit here?' A girl shrouded in a black chador was pointing to the seat next to me.

'Of course,' I replied. Then, as an afterthought, I whispered. 'Is it safe for you?'

'It's fine, don't look so worried,' said the girl and sat down. She looked at my diary. 'What are you writing?'

'Nothing much.' For some reason I put my hands protectively over the pages.

She told me her name was Faranak and that she was an English teacher at the university. She was twenty-three years old with dark nervous eyes, an aquiline nose and an infectious laugh. Beneath her chador I could see she was wearing blue jeans. I was glad about this; it helped demystify the chador and reveal an individual rather than a clone.

Faranak told me that when she went out with her girlfriends in the evening she sometimes defied tradition and wore a blue, green or even yellow veil. She made it sound like a very rebellious thing to do, the equivalent of a London teenager sporting a see-through blouse or a tongue stud.

'Do you wear these coloured veils to rebel against religion?' I asked.

'No, it's only for a bit of fun,' she replied. 'I am a Muslim. I believe in Mohammed, peace be upon him, and in Allah. Islam gives me strength. I like it.'

Despite her faith Faranak's life had not been without sadness. Her elder sister had secretly dated a man her pious father disapproved of. The couple eloped to America and her father had disowned them. Faranak said she and her sister had been very close, but she now accepted that she might never see her again.

'Do you want to leave too?'

'Not really. My father can be hard, but he is a good man. It is my duty to stay with him. I am an Iranian and a Muslim, the West is not so good for me. I like Esfahan.'

'It's a beautiful place,' I agreed. It was nice to meet a young open-minded Iranian not hankering to get away; a Muslim at one with her God and her home. To my astonishment Faranak volunteered to be my tour guide. Was it really safe for her? I was worried. Very safe she repeated impatiently and the next thing I knew she was hailing a taxi.

One of the quirks about Esfahan cabs is that they pick up punters like buses, sometimes cramming four or five people on to the back seat. I thought it would be very embarrassing for Faranak to be seen with a foreigner, especially a scruffy bum like me. To make things worse the driver kept cracking jokes about Faranak and me being an item. Everyone laughed including Faranak, and as she was clearly not embarrassed, so did I. The driver was making harmless fun, the way a Venetian boatman might tease a young couple on a gondola or an Agra rickshaw wallah might show off to honeymooners *en route* to the Taj. It was nice, momentarily, to feel we could have been anywhere.

Faranak wanted to show me as much of Esfahan as possible. She led me up the Manar Jomban, alias the Shaking Minarets, which sway gently if you give the walls a Samson-like shove. She bought me *gaz*, a nougat and pistachio delicacy which melts in the mouth like liquid honey. She guided me past acres of the most beautiful carpets but when I expressed my admiration she said sharply, 'Children break fingers making these. Carpet men are bad men.'

Our longest stop-off was at Jolfa, the Armenian quarter. Shah Abbas had set up this isolated enclave for the Christian Armenians in 1606, during his wars with Turkey. In return, the Armenians helped the Shah construct some of Esfahan's greatest buildings. I took a photo of Faranak outside the attractive sand-coloured All Saviour's Cathedral. I felt a bit like Gregory Peck's paparazzo character in *Roman Holiday* snapping an unsuspecting Audrey Hepburn. Jolfa had a slightly Italian air, with its classical churches and stone piazzas. All that was missing was Rome's bustle – with only 5,000 Armenians now living in Jolfa, it felt more than a little abandoned.

Faranak gaped at the cathedral's interior walls in horror. They showed scenes of hell and of Christian martyrs being tortured: victims on racks, hung upside down by chains or lowered into vats of boiling oil. Fortunately, heaven was represented too, the good and the holy with beatific smiles of salvation. 'I don't understand Christians,' Faranak concluded as we walked back out into the sunlight.

Later, our 'nudge nudge, wink wink' cab driver dropped us back at the bridge. Faranak paid the fare; she had paid for everything all afternoon. I had tried to contribute but she took umbrage whenever I reached for my wallet. The same thing had happened with Davood and Hammid. None of them had asked for anything in return except company. I felt ashamed of my preconceived one-dimensional view of Iran as a place of manic mullahs and socially invisible women.

Faranak said she would like to meet again the following day. I said I would love to but that I had to pedal on south to Persepolis. I had become so relaxed in her company that I almost gave her a peck on the cheek, a spectacular breach of Islamic etiquette. Instead I shook her hand. Faranak looked me in the eye very gravely, then walked off down the street, hunched up in a paroxysm of giggles.

I woke at 4 a.m. the next day. The owner of the guest house was at the bottom of the stairs, white cap on his skull, crouching towards Mecca. I was glad I had already paid and did not have to disturb him. He appeared to be in some sort of pleasurable trance.

I rode over the River Zaindeh, its will-o'-the-wisp waters illuminated by the crescent moon, then under the silhouetted plane trees, past a military compound and out into the boulder-strewn desert. I began to miss Esfahan almost immediately. Of all the cities I had cycled through so far it was, without doubt, the one I most hoped to revisit.

From Esfahan it took me three days to reach Persepolis. Despite the harshness of the scorched land the roads were smooth and straight, some of the best I'd seen on the trip to date. Villages were tiny and up to thirty miles apart but I always received a warm welcome. People were friendly without being intrusive, helpful without being hassley, and many spoke rudimentary English.

In Abadeh, like every foreign cyclist who has ever passed through the town, I met Sasan. I had been fast asleep in the *mosaferkhune* (dormitory) when he burst in on me. 'Bicycle good!' he said repeatedly, shaking me into reluctant consciousness. Before I had time to tell him to bugger off, he had dragged my bike outside and was steering it towards his house around the corner. I tailed him, protesting sleepily.

Sasan's home was a simple place with no furniture but beautiful carpets. His wife was there with one of her friends. They sat cross-legged on the floor in their blue jeans and silk blouses, gossiping and laughing.

Sasan showed me an album of other travellers who had dropped in on Abadeh. He had pictures of them all, pinned in place like rare butterflies. 'This John, he Land Rover Australia. This Paul, he motorbike China. If they Abadeh, I find them.' There were many cyclists too, including a pair of flute-playing London missionaries who had ridden a tandem through Iran and Pakistan in the late seventies.

The following morning I pedalled over to Sasan's father's farm. On the way, I saw boys in sombreros harvesting grapes and others digging irrigation ditches using spades with handles almost as long as vaulting poles. At the farmstead I breakfasted with the family on honey, pitta bread and fresh nectarines. The kitchen window looked out over a headland of blossoming sunflowers and life could not have been sweeter.

The good thing about travelling is that it keeps you on your toes. Just as you start to get complacent, something pulls you back into line. About thirty miles out of Abadeh, I was flying along when a battered Toyota Landcruiser drew up beside me. Three men were inside, all resembling baddies from an *Indiana Jones* movie. The driver was shouting at me. At first I thought he was just having some fun, so I waved at him and pedalled on. In retrospect, it was a very stupid thing to do. The vehicle overtook me and stopped again, this time blocking my path.

I had no choice. I pulled over, laid down the bike and approached the driver's window. He was still shouting. When I was near enough he grabbed my money belt and pulled me towards him. 'Police. Passport.' I pulled out my passport and gave it to him. While the driver scanned my stamps, the two loutish passengers alighted and started ripping clothes out of my back panniers.

'What the hell are you doing?' I shouted at them, grabbing back my passport from the driver. They were giving the bike a thorough mauling. My mind was racing. I had heard reports of thieves masquerading as *Komiteh* and these three fitted the description perfectly. They looked as bogus as could be.

Think, Tom. What to do? Number plate! That was it! Take down their number plate! I squatted down and grabbed a pen from my money belt. The plate was in Arabic and splattered with squashed insects. I didn't understand a bit of it, but began to write it on to my forearm all the same. My hands were shaking terribly.

In a flash the driver was behind me. He was shouting again. I stood up and he shoved me against the bonnet. I was furious. 'GET YOUR HANDS OFF ME!' I shouted. 'POLICE!

POLICE!' he shouted back. He pushed me against the bonnet again, taunting me. I tried to calm down. I really didn't want to end my days here. Not here, not now.

'No problem,' I said, raising my hand to placate him. The man softened his grip on my shoulder and said firmly, 'Police. Me police. OK.' We both relaxed a little. Suddenly he started to laugh; a hollow humourless sound, not a laugh at all really. He shoved me away from the Landcruiser. My legs were shaking uncontrollably and I was ashamed my fear was so apparent. He looked at me long and hard, deciding what to do next. Then he murmured, 'OK, OK,' and signalled to his lackeys to get back in the vehicle. He jumped in last, fired the engine and raised his eyebrows at me, maybe in apology maybe as an insult.

As the vehicle skidded off in a whorl of dust another Landcruiser pulled over. My heart was pumping so hard I could practically see it through my T-shirt. I had lived such a charmed existence until this moment but it suddenly dawned on me how vulnerable I was, stuck out here in the desert like a flea on a camel's back. Inside this new vehicle was a German couple, Wolfgang and Anna. Both were fair-haired, he with a ponytail, she with dreadlocks. They too had been pulled over by the same rough-looking trio. The driver had kicked up a fuss about the fact Anna's passport photo was illegal as she was showing too much hair. Anna had paid a small fine, which appeased him. Wolfgang said the men were definitely *Komiteh* as he had asked to see their ID cards. Why hadn't I thought of that?

Anna gave me an ice-cold litre of water. I glugged down half of it and poured the other half over my head. She told me they were driving down to Bandar Abbas on Iran's south coast and eventually hoped to reach Australia. She asked if I would like a lift. I looked inside at the empty back seat, at the gourd of chilled water and the bag of mints on the dashboard. Classical music was playing on the stereo. 'No thanks,' I said. 'Once I'm in there you'll never get me out.'

The *Komiteh* incident had shaken me up. But nothing had been stolen, no bones had been broken and I tried to look on it as a minor glitch in a country that had otherwise offered incomparable hospitality. Putting it to the back of my mind, I carried on pedalling past the ancient Achaemenian capital of Pasagardae, home to King Cyrus's crumbling tomb, and down to Persepolis.

One thing about travelling on your own is that sometimes you have a place of exceptional historical and architectural significance all to yourself. Persepolis may have been levelled by Alexander the Great in 331 BC and eroded by the passing centuries, but only a little leap of imagination is required to recall its former glory.

I climbed a monumental staircase to the ancient metropolis and there I was, king of a lost city, albeit a king who needed to flash his student card to gain a discount entry.

Persepolis was conceived by Darius the Great in 512 BC and completed by a succession of kings – including his son Xerxes – over a period of 150 years. The finest artists from the Persian empire were conscripted to work on the city. It was an exercise in ego, as with many of these epic monuments, and both Darius and Xerxes made sure they were boldly immortalized in stone. One bas-relief depictes Xerxes sitting at the top of a stairway guarded by ranks of identical soldiers. Coming up the stairs to pay Xerxes tribute are representatives from all corners of the empire – Parthians, Scythians, Indian Brahmins, Ethiopians and Armenians – some bringing gifts, others simply their fealty. Not all the bas-reliefs are so decorous: I saw one which showed a unicorn being graphically savaged by a lion and another devoted to a troupe of Persian lancers skewering enemy infantry. The figures of the horses, a much-respected animal in Persian mythology, were especially beautiful. In its mouldering splendour, Persepolis glorifies much of what was great about the Persian empire but it also hints at the vanity of its rulers and their capacity for self-destruction.

After Darius III had been trounced by Alexander at the battles of Issus and Gaugamela, the Achaemenian empire crumbled. Rather like Petra, Persepolis then disappeared to be dug from the dust only in 1930. Subsequently the last Shah used Persepolis as the setting for a ludicrously extravagant pageant to celebrate the 2,500th anniversary of the founding of Persia. Guests included Imelda Marcos, King Constantine of Greece and Haile Selassie of Ethiopia who brought with him dozens of servants and a chihuahua with a diamond collar.

Rumour has it that when the Ayatollah seized power in 1979 he ordered a fleet of bulldozers to knock down the ancient capital once and for all. The machines set off from Shiraz but apparently when they reached the gates a group of sweet-talking watchmen at the site persuaded them to turn back. How heartening that a few well-chosen words succeeded in saving the wonders of Persepolis where whole armies had once failed.

My visa time was running low again. Rather than recharging it, I decided to make for Pakistan before it expired. In Islamabad, Pakistan's capital, I could secure my Indian visa and then resume my original route via Delhi across to Kathmandu.

I decided the cheapest and most interesting way to reach Bam, an Iranian town towards the Pakistani border, would be to hitch-hike. Hugh the priest was right about it being a form of transport based completely on trust – and I had come to trust the Iranians. Apart from the isolated incident with the *Komiteh*, I had been shown nothing but goodwill.

The only problem with hitch-hiking in Iran is that you are never alone. Ideally, hitch-hiking is a solitary sport; you do not want to be surrounded by a crowd of friendly hangers-on when cars drive past. Securing a lift is hard enough without a driver thinking he will have to take on board two shepherds, the local mechanic and a group of schoolgirls. To beat the crowds, sometimes I would have to ride several miles out of town before sticking out my thumb.

The success rate was good. My first lift was in a pick-up truck. I sat in the back soaking up the views of the Zagros mountains, before being deposited near the city of Sirjan.

My next chauffeur was a simian lorry driver called Hussein. He spoke little English but what little he could say he liked to use. Every ten minutes he would turn to me and shout, 'You, England. Me, Iran,' usually just as I was nodding off. To keep the dialogue going I would shout back, 'Iran, you. England, me.' We did this repeatedly until we reached a camping ground on the other side of Kerman. Hussein and I made a fire and slept under the stars. We were woken by a dawn chorus of donkeys and long-eared goats.

Later, Hussein dropped me back at the roadside; I offered money but, as always, it was refused.

After three more lifts, including one on a local bus, I was deposited at Bam's central clock tower. I pedalled to a nearby guest house which, after two days of pick-up trucks and sleeping rough, was a paradise out of the pages of *Omar Khayyam*. There was a dormitory swept by a breeze and a little courtyard with a pool of cool water. Date trees sprouting sticky red bunches of fruit arched over from the garden opposite.

I found out from a Japanese boy in the neighbouring dorm that my train to Pakistan was due to depart in two days. That meant I would have to reach Zahedan, the Iranian border town, sometime the following day. The train only departed once a week, first thing in the morning and to miss it would be a huge hassle as my visa would once again be hanging by a thread.

I arranged to hitch a lift with Philip and Julia, a London couple who were driving their Land Rover to Kathmandu. They were so much the typical Brits as to verge on parody. Both were tall, friendly, no-nonsense types, flushed with sun. They kindly agreed to clear a space to fit me in.

Their Land Rover was called Penelope Pitstop and a map of their route had been painted on her flank. A fishing rod was tied to the roof-rack, a packet of Frosties stood next to the jerrycans, the BBC World Service ruled the airwaves and books by Wilfred Thesiger jammed the glovebox. Philip was a disillusioned solicitor and Julia an artist in need of inspiration. They were off to run a lodge on the Annapurna Circuit for six months. We arranged to meet at dawn the following morning.

I did a lightning tour of Bam's magnificent citadel – part of which dated back to the twelfth century – and that evening, after tidying the contents of my panniers, spent some time reading the guest house comment book. Most books of this type tend to be a little hackneyed but this one was a gem. I had heard reports about it from as far afield as Damascus and Cairo.

Many of the contributors were travellers who had reached Bam under their own steam – hitch-hikers, motorbikers and cyclists. Their comments ranged from the sacred to the profane, from purple prose to bawdy doggerel.

A Singaporean called Ho had drawn three or four pages of immaculate diagrams explaining how to fix motorbike engines, especially those choked by sand. Tony Brooks, a British naval officer, was cycling to the Bering Strait in aid of the Salvation Army. (The Bering Strait! Didn't that mean Siberia in winter?) Tony had written some advice on keeping up morale while on the road. Next to it a man who called himself Rob Roy had written a terrific piss-take of endurance travellers: 'POGO STICKING PERSIA!! That's me. Generally I manage to cover 20–30 km a day. ALWAYS remember to oil the widget left of the release spring, it has a tendency to overheat. If any problems there's a good pogo parts shop in Shiraz. NEXT YEAR – UNICYCLE YUGOSLAVIA!!'

There were poems about the plight of the Kurds and the Chinese invasion of Tibet. There were rants about the French nuclear tests in the Pacific. There was information on Bhutan, Iraq and Manchester and one or two excellent cartoons.

Nick Green, UK, won the prize for the least politically correct entry: 'TOP TIPS FOR CUSSING THE NATIVES. In Iran why not try your luck with 'Pedar Sakhte' – Your papa's burnt up in hell, or if you are heading to Pakistan the ubiquitous 'Panchodh' – Sister bonker, works a treat. When in Indonesia don't forget 'Nochok' – Chicken willy. The latter is especially poignant when holding up the little finger and waving it very slowly.'

But for hard-hitting comments on Iran itself, as usual Captain Charles's diary took some beating. In August 1830 Charles visited Bushire, at the time Persia's chief port, to assess its trading possibilities. He found the town, and the country, in a mess and considered Bushire's governor, Shaik Abdul Rassool, a despicable poltroon. Charles wrote:

> The Country appears to be in a most unsettled state . . . [Shaik Abdul Rassool] called on me and sent a present of Bullocks Sheep and Sweetmeat . . . I understood that he was a most cruel and despotic Wretch constantly putting his Subjects to death and making them suffer the most barbarous torments . . . his appearance is not prepossessing as he has only one eye and his expression of countenance very disagreeable . . . I was quite disgusted with him.

A more temperate footnote mentions that Bushire's exports at the time included 'Silk, Medicines, Rose Water, Arsenick, Pickles, Horses, and Tobacco, Gum, Almond, Raisins and Treasure'.

The following morning, Philip hoisted my bike on to the Land Rover's roof and Penelope Pitstop set off across the sandy moonscape. I lay in the back, using a watermelon as a pillow, listening to Julia's tapes of chanting Gregorian monks. We arrived at Zahedan at midday. Philip let me out, said 'Bloody good luck' and drove off towards Pakistan, fishing rod jiggling above the bonnet.

After a night at Zahedan's grubbiest doss-house, I caught my slow train to Pakistan. It chuffed along at walking pace before speeding up into a light jog and then away. Away from the land of Darius and Xerxes, of Faranak and Davood. Away from the land of Reza Vazifekhah.

CHAPTER THIRTEEN

JUMPING INTO OBLIVION

The train was packed. Two pretty Australian girls, Katie and Kim, with rucksacks the size of hay bales sat opposite me. Now we were heading out of Iran they had rolled up the sleeves of their shirts, exposing slender tanned arms. Next to them was a fidgety Pakistani swamped in a cement-grey *shalwar qamiz*. He was sitting on a hessian sack full of plastic coat-hangers. Another sack was perched on his lap, two more were at his side and one balanced on top of my bicycle; all of them chock-full of hangers.

The carriage was as shambolic as Camden market. The luggage racks were crammed with electronic gadgets, the aisles were blocked with piles of T-shirts and polystyrene Thermos flasks. The goods were as varied as their owners. In the neighbouring compartment a red-shawled Afghan woman with a pale dignified face sat next to a nose-picking smuggler in a crumpled jacket laced with gold chevrons. He was slicing up a melon with his penknife, its juice dripping down on to his leg.

The heat hung in the air as the train was not moving fast enough to work up much of a breeze. Outside, some wild camels cantered past kicking up dirty clouds of sand. Inside, our carriage was noisy with the clank of pistons, the burr of flies and the strangled cries of overheating babies.

Before long, the train sighed to a halt. We had reached Taftan, the Pakistani border post. The sun had reached a furnace-like intensity and even the leather-skinned old men touting biscuits and bananas were wilting in its glare.

During the stop-off, Mr Coat Hangers was interrogated by a couple of heavies in dark uniforms. They shouted at him in enraged Urdu. Mr Coat Hangers stayed silent until one of them began to prod him with a truncheon, as if to test that he was still alive. Mr Coat Hangers didn't like this teasing and grabbed the truncheon from his tormentor's hand, firing off a stream of hysterical insults. After a short-lived but desperate tussle he was frogmarched off and pushed into the back of a rusty pick-up, his sacks thrown in on top of him.

Considering we were now in Pakistan, a country which reputedly smuggles out over 80 per cent of Britain's heroin, it seemed rough justice to be dragged away for dealing in a few sackfuls of useful plastic triangles. Over the previous four months I had become accustomed to the polite oppression of the Middle East and I suddenly felt thrown headlong into somewhere altogether wilder, far less predictable.

As we pulled away into the dry plains of Baluchistan, the desertscape livened up. Mud huts with corrugated tin roofs came into view. The colours of the villagers' clothes were dazzlingly bright after the neutral greys and blacks of Iran. Suddenly, here were nomads in bright-green and azure shawls; they looked as dramatic as the brightly cloaked Tuareg tribes-men of the Sahara.

The villages *en route* to Quetta had the most evocative names: Nok Kundi, Yakmach, Nushki, Kishingi. They sounded as if they were straight from the pages of Kipling or perhaps even an Edward Lear poem. Kim had fallen asleep on Katie's shoulder and a cool breeze now brushed the carriage. Further down the train a man was singing a mournful ballad. I felt happy and lethargic.

When I awoke it was dark and the train was stationary. Children with baskets full of samosas were shouting through the windows. I stretched my legs, climbed over a couple of wooden chests and jumped down on to the platform. The humidity had vanished and it was noticeably cooler. An excited crowd surrounded a balding man holding up a book, his sallow face lit by the dull glow of the hurricane lamps. I went to see what the fuss was about.

The man was Kuno Kruse, a German journalist. The book was *Around The World In Eighty Days*. Kuno's newspaper, *Die Zeit*, had commissioned him to follow in Phileas Fogg's footsteps. He was accompanied by a po-faced twitchy photographer called Axel.

'Ve start in Cairo,' explained Kuno. 'Ve go to Amman, ve go to Dubai, ve get boat to Bandar Abbas, now bloody train to Lahore, then Delhi. Then, sank God, another journalist take over and ve go home. Thees bloody Fogg is too fast; next time I vant a slower explorer.'

He stopped to blow his nose and then carried on with his catalogue of distress.

'And thees bloody Fogg is a bore. All he does is spend every evening playing vist. Passpartout at least gets drunk, gets lost. Pays some attention to vat is going on. Thees bloody Fogg is the vorst traveller. I vould much rather be at home vith my vife and three sons in Hamburg.' He took out a grubby photo of his family from his money belt. 'But I am here, eating spicy potato and drinking milky tea. Following thees explorer who has been followed a million times before.'

I liked Kuno. His whingeing was very tongue-in-cheek and he had a winning way with the locals. They swarmed around him as he displayed a passport photo of his wife. Occasionally, he would hold it to his chest and grimace like a clown, delighting the crowd.

'I'm too old for thees,' he lamented. 'I used to love it, thees travel. But I vant to be home now.'

Back in the carriage, Kuno and Axel joined me and the two girls, who had just woken up. Kuno kept asking what made us travel. He was eating from a tin of corned beef with his fingers. He truly was missing home.

'Well,' said Katie. 'In this carriage we have Kim, she's an insect expert; we have a German journalist who dreams of home and his photographer who dreams of being Passportoo, whatever his name is, and we have a pom on a push-bike. Plus a wonderful cast of locals. Where would I find that back home?'

'In most cafés in Melbourne,' replied Kim glibly.

I was peeling an apple with my penknife, listening carefully. The apple suddenly slipped out of my hand and the blade sliced into my left forefinger. A fountain of blood jetted on to the floor. Little droplets sprayed on to my shoes, some on to Katie's shirt. I stared down at my pumping wound, surprisingly calm. The cut had been so clean it hadn't hurt at all. Kim ripped open her money belt, pulled out a strip of white lint and pressed it on to my pulsing digit. The lint turned red within seconds. She wrapped another thicker strip of gauze around then tightened it with a Band-Aid.

'That'll do for now,' she said. 'When you pull it off it will hurt like hell.'

It was not until late afternoon on the following day that we approached Quetta. The journey had been uneventful: lots of reading, sleeping and looking at pictures of Kuno's wife, but in the final fifteen minutes all hell broke lose. Our placid Pakistani co-travellers who had been so amiable until then, quietly chatting and puffing on hubble-bubbles, ceased to be sanguine Jekylls and became raging Hydes.

The wispy-bearded man opposite, who had done nothing more antisocial all journey than snore, picked up a steel jemmy from under his seat and began smashing loose the bars on the window, like Jack Nicholson in *The Shining*. The bewitching Afghan woman likewise morphed into a shrieking harpy, barking high-pitched orders to all around her.

Outside the train a line of pick-up trucks and horse-drawn carts was waiting to take away the smuggled merchandise. Lugubrious water buffalo stood lowing while they were loaded with bags of flip-flops and calculators. Then they lumbered off across the maze of irrigation ditches into the surrounding paddy fields. It was a smugglers' paradise.

Axel was snapping roll after roll, Kim and Katie were falling around in hysterics and Kuno just looked completely non-plussed. Our wispy-bearded Mr Hyde had finished hacking at the bars of the window, thrown his cardboard boxes into the arms of a waiting friend and made off at a run. Within a few minutes Kuno, Axel, Katie, Kim and I were the only people left in our carriage, other than an elderly local couple who, judging by their composure, had seen this all before.

The train pulled into Quetta, an oasis town, about twenty minutes later. My wound had started to seep blood and hauling my bike on to the platform was agony. Perhaps this was a message from Johnny Ginger that I should stop dossing about on trains and start pedalling again. Quetta had the feel of a frontier town. Despite the pall of dust and undistinguished architecture it was a charismatic place. The surrounding hills could just be made out in the darkness.

The five of us threaded our way through the psychedelic motor rickshaws. I had never seen anything like them; each one was ablaze with colour and weighed down with hanging trumpery. They made even the *tuk-tuks* of Thailand and the *jeepneys* of Manila seem sober. Their bumpers shone like burnished silver and the external paintwork had something for everyone: fighter jets, butterflies, Benazir Bhutto, crescent moons, love hearts and smiling prophets. Even the bullocks harnessed to rickety carts were decorated, their horns painted in blue and green and orange.

Katie, Kim and I shared a room in a downtown hotel. They took the two beds and I unfurled my sleeping mat in the gap between them. Kuno and Axel made a beeline for a more upmarket place across the road. That evening, Kim re-dressed my wounded finger and applied a stinging Tiger balm poultice.

After a bucket shower, I joined the girls for something to eat. We found a street hawker surrounded by several sizzling braziers who was carving fatty slivers from a haunch of lamb. It smelt wonderful. The lamb was served skewered on to bicycle spokes. It was the tastiest food I had eaten since the Jordanian wedding. We ate ravenously, washing down the meat with cups of strong gritty coffee.

In the morning, Quetta looked even more zany. The sunshine revealed an eclectic population: Pathans in woollen rollmop caps, swarthy Baluchis and turbaned Afghan refugees. This really was the Wild East. Youths toting shotguns sped around on Russian motorbikes, children played cricket in the dust, groups of brightly robed women twittered like starlings, rickshaws crashed and dogs scavenged. I wanted so much to stay but knew I could not spare the time.

I paid 150 rupees (about two pounds sterling) for my train ticket on to Rawalpindi and secured the help of a man called Altaf, who usually drove a cab in Bradford. He was visiting his country for the first time. He wore a red cardinal's tunic and said 'wicked' every other word. Together, we threw my bike on board. He ran down the length of the platform waving goodbye with his green Pakistan cricketer's cap.

*

I sat myself on the floor next to a posse of white-cloaked Punjabi tourists. The scene outside was surprisingly lush, the rice paddies the colour of dairy pasture. I lay under a wooden propeller fan shaped like a machete which swished down a cool steady breeze. It was too good to be true: a few minutes after departure the fan juddered and clunked to a halt. The heat enveloped us like a malign wraith.

An old woman with earrings the size of compact discs offered me a sponge cake. I took it and nodded thanks. After one mouthful I realized what a mistake I had made. It stuck to my mouth like putty. I swigged down some lukewarm water which left a pungent iodine aftertaste. As I put the cap back on the water bottle my dressing slipped and the tip of my finger, still sticky as a date, began to bleed again.

We arrived at Rawalpindi at midnight. I could not face riding the remaining nine miles to Islamabad. I blew up my mat and dozed on the station floor.

The following morning I set off at dawn. The town was still sleeping apart from the odd foraging dog. The road north was initially rough and puddled but then it linked up with the smooth Islamabad highway. I followed a blue-turbaned cyclist with a milk churn tied to the back of his bike. He rode with great poise, his back as stiff as a ramrod. He reminded me of a Swanbourne farmer called Tommy Vickers who, at the age of eighty, would still pedal through the village with a pitchfork of straw over his shoulder.

But Islamabad could not have been less like Swanbourne. The streets were wide, the buildings smart and plain. This was a functional capital, like Tel Aviv or Canberra, rather than a historical or charismatic one.

I headed for the Tourist Campsite in some parkland to the south of the city. It was perhaps the cheapest camping ground in the world as it cost only eight rupees (four pence) to pitch a tent. It looked like a croquet lawn gone to seed with the luxuriant grass being harvested by women in crimson saris wielding scythes. A catatonic Pathan who smoked roll-ups the size of dynamite sticks was living in the camp office.

The washrooms were a war zone. The urinal was blocked with turbid slime and the showers, which at best managed a lacklustre dribble, were full of acrobatic red and black bugs in their death throes. The basins looked like tureens of oxtail soup.

Apart from these minor details the place was perfect. I was exhausted and simply wanted to spend a few days cleaning the bike, writing my diary and psyching myself up for the punishing ride from Lahore to Kathmandu. I also had to secure a visa for India, an irritating and expensive procedure which involved paying twenty pounds at the British Embassy for a letter of recommendation.

The campsite had very few tents, most of the other residents being in trucks, mobile homes or camper vans. I was pitched next to a retired Scottish electrician called Jack who had driven his jalopy from Dumbarton to Delhi and was now on his way back. He was grey-haired, blue-eyed and looked the picture of health. A nomadic lifestyle evidently suited him. The same could not be said of his neighbours, a frighteningly skinny student called Paul and his even slimmer Belgian girlfriend Hilda, who was three months pregnant and suffering from dysentery. The pair of them had motored through India, hated it, and were longing to secure an Iranian visa to enable them to drive home. They had already been waiting more than a month and Hilda's health was deteriorating fast. If the visa fell through, their only other option would be to head down to Karachi and spend US$6,000 shipping their battered Mercedes truck back to England.

But if Paul and Hilda were in dire straits it was nothing

compared with Omar, an Iraqi refugee who had lived at the Tourist Campsite for over a year. Omar told me he had been a pilot in the Iraqi Air Force but had left the military in protest against Saddam Hussein. After a brief spell of imprisonment, he had fled from Baghdad to Iran and then on to Pakistan.

One could not help but feel sorry for Omar. He was a proud intelligent man who had retained his dignity despite appalling luck. He longed to find work again. At the campsite he lived in the dormitory – a place hellish enough to break anyone's spirit. When he showed me the inside I realized why he preferred, when possible, to sleep under the stars. The dormitory was nothing more than a concrete shed with straw mats. Two of the residents were heroin addicts. One of them was a hollow-eyed Iranian who had supposedly lived in the dorm for seven years. A syringe rested on a sheet of toilet paper by his bed. Despite the open window, the place reeked of urine.

'They are hopeless people,' Omar whispered. 'I hate them. There is another man, Steve, who shoots up all day. Sometimes he shits himself in the night. They have no respect. I hate these European addicts the most. They have all this money and spend it on drugs. Me, I have no chance, I have no money. I was a pilot before, a professional man. I have been beaten, put in prison. But I have more self-respect than any of them.'

I started to spend more time away from the campsite. I breakfasted at the local bazaar on nan bread and fried eggs washed down with cups of cool thick *lassi*. Omar loved cricket and we would watch the local matches on the withered pitch near the Holiday Inn. He also kept me up to date on all the test matches. At the time of my visit, England was in the process of being whitewashed by Pakistan.

Cricket is Pakistan's passion. While the Turks and Jordanians prefer Alan Shearer and Jurgen Klinsmann, the Pakistanis idolize Imran Khan and Ian Botham. When Pakistan beat India in the 1986–7 series, the whole country indulged in an orgy of celebration the like of which has never been witnessed. A ten-mile avenue of fans welcomed back the triumphant squad as they drove from the airport.

After several days of hanging around I secured my Indian visa and was ready to go. But by then my plans had changed radically. While with Omar one day he had told me the story of an Italian man who had made it from Pakistan into Afghanistan. The Italian had travelled up to Chitral in North West Frontier Province, then trekked to the end of the Bumburet Valley, found a guide and walked over to Nuristan, the area of Afghanistan fringing north-west Pakistan. He had made it to Kabul and then come back the same way.

Since reading Eric Newby's *A Short Walk In The Hindu Kush* as a teenager I had dreamed of visiting Nuristan. The chance of doing so was too good to miss. I decided to hotfoot it up to Chitral and, if possible, spend a week in Afghanistan. My schedule was already skewed and if I made it into Nuristan it might impress my sponsors anyway, bicycle or not. I arranged to catch a bus to Peshawar and into the tribal hills of North West Frontier Province.

One day Katie and Kim turned up. They had been in Lahore but had left due to the flooding there. Cycling along the Grand Trunk Road in flood water would have been misery, Katie told me. Perhaps it was just as well I had decided to delay cycling for a week or so; maybe it was a sign that my jaunt to Afghanistan was meant to be.

On my final evening I enjoyed a leaving party with Katie, Kim and Omar in a local *kebabji*. Afterwards we returned to the campsite and played cards in the long damp grass. Around us the toads croaked and the cicadas clicked while the stars glittered above like jewels.

At about 10 p.m. a Bedford van screeched to a halt at the campsite gates. A man with tousled hair tied in a pigtail like a Spanish pirate fell from the back. He was naked. A mob of angry Pakistanis surrounded him. He lashed out with his arms which were then bound with thick cord. Another rope was noosed around his neck. One of the Pakistanis pulled him along as if he was an obstinate calf on a halter.

Omar and I walked over to investigate.

'Mister,' said one of the mob. 'You know this man?'

'No,' I replied. 'Is he OK?'

'He is crazy. He jumping in the street. Jumping!'

'Jumping?'

From what I could gather the jumping criminal had walked into the local market and calmly stripped naked. He had poured a flask of petrol over his clothes and his money belt and ignited the lot. He then began jumping up and down shouting his head off. As most of Islamabad's travellers hung out at the Tourist Campsite, it had been presumed that he did too. They had come to bring him back.

The jumping criminal was speaking in manic French. At times he struggled with his ropes and spat at his tormentors, at other times he stood quietly rocking and dribbling. He was clearly in the throes of a devastating trip. I could make no sense of his ramblings. When I started speaking my hopeless French, it seemed to make him even more angry. Neither Katie, Kim, Omar nor I had ever seen him before.

'Let him spend the night here,' I said. 'I'm sure he'll be all right in the morning.'

'He go polis. He crazy. He jumping. Polis, only polis.' The mob dragged him back into the van and sped off, skidding on the damp verge.

'Good,' said Omar. 'Another stupid hippie.'

What would happen to the man, I wondered. Did he have

any family or friends who would help him? Would the French Embassy bail him out? Perhaps he would end up in the dormitory tripping himself into oblivion like Steve. What became of all these lost souls?

'The problem is drugs are so cheap,' fumed Omar, biting his thumbnail.

'How come?' I asked.

He explained that opium poppies were mainly grown in Afghanistan, then processed into heroin in laboratories and illegally smuggled over the Khyber Pass and across to Peshawar. From there they filtered down to Karachi and were freighted off to the West. The heroin that remained in Pakistan was ludicrously cheap.

'Bastard hippies,' Omar cursed again.

'Why do you hate hippies so much?' asked Katie, surprised by Omar's aggression. 'Surely it's the dealers? The drug barons.'

'I hate the hippies because I might become one,' he shouted. 'Before Steve came to Pakistan he told me he never used heavy drugs. Now look at him. Fucked. Totally fucked.' He threw a stone hard towards the dormitory.

'Please, God,' he whispered, but with great violence. 'Please God, get me out of here.'

Two days later, after a brief stop in Peshawar and an uncomfortable but exhilarating ride over some high serpentine passes, I was in Chitral. Chitral was wonderful in every way. Any city surrounded by snow-capped mountains has an edge but what made Chitral so terrific was the rogues' gallery of locals, mostly Pathans. Wrapped in Kashmiri shawls and extravagant turbans or *shalwar qamiz* and rollmop caps, they varied from Nordic types with sandy hair and blue eyes to dark steely-faced elder statesmen with unruly grey beards.

For all its charm, Chitral is not a wealthy town. Many houses are little more than wood and mud shelters and there is an 80 per cent illiteracy rate. Guns are a common sight – there are thought to be over a million Kalashnikovs in North West Frontier Province alone – most of which are used in internecine fighting in Pakistan's tribal belt. Some of the weapons are still sold to Afghanistan but not nearly as many now that the Mujahedin have long sent the Russians packing.

I checked into a room in the YZ Hotel with a view over Tirich Mir, a stunning mountain with several overlapping peaks. The hotel owners were a charming pair of brothers who agreed to let me keep my bike in their house while I tried for Nuristan. They were devout Muslims and five times a day would appear on the hotel's balding lawn and prostrate themselves towards Mecca.

I planned to head off first thing the following morning for the Bumburet Valley, beyond which lie the passes to Nuristan. It was almost September and I was well behind time. Six months on the road and only 5,000 miles to show for it. But when you are about to illegally trek into somewhere like Afghanistan time ceases to matter.

Before I left I had to experience one of the things with which Chitral had become synonymous: a game of polo. By good fortune, there were some chukkas that afternoon and I walked down to the field beyond the bus station. Before the game could get going various ruminants had to be ushered from the field.

I had always imagined polo to be rather a dull sport, but not so the Chitrali variety. The stocky ponies with their richly coloured saddle-cloths charged about, nostrils aflare, as if attached to Ben Hur's chariot. There seemed to be no tactics, both teams just went hell for leather after the ball. There were no team colours, no referee and no team allegiances and the crowd roared whenever anything vaguely exciting happened.

The best bit was after a goal had been scored. Not only would the fans reach new levels of hysteria, but a three-piece band on a podium would joyfully blow pipes and beat tabla drums. The highlight of the final chukka was when a raffish player in an open shirt windmilled his mallet and hit the ball straight between the opposition's posts from the halfway line. It was polo perfection, a goal in one.

At the end of the match, the players ripped off their helmets, fell from their horses and lay spreadeagled on the ground like corpses on a battlefield. Having seen such aggression on the polo field, I tried to envisage what the Afghan game of *buzkashi*, which involves forty riders tearing around after a dead calf, would look like. The game is played in North West Frontier Province too but was sadly off-season in August.

Later that evening while wandering along the bustling main street, I heard cheering near the city mosque. When I went to investigate, it seemed an even bigger crowd than had been at the polo had assembled. Predictably, it was a football match.

I stood on tiptoe to get a better view. From the little I could see, it would be a long time before Pakistan qualified for the World Cup. The players hoofed the ball from one end to another with determined but inaccurate aplomb. Dribbling was a rarity. Fighting was not. On several occasions shirts were torn and one unfortunate player was grabbed by the shorts, twirled around and propelled into the crowd. It was as entertaining as watching the Keystone Cops.

I didn't stay for the whole match and traipsed back to the YZ Hotel, past the ranks of old men spitting green oysters of *naswat* (spiced tobacco) into the dust. One of them fiddled with a machine-gun magazine.

I watched the dark scarf of cloud above Tirich Mir and wondered what the following day would bring.

The next morning, I hitch-hiked out of Chitral over the

Japanese-funded bridge that spans the River Kunar. An hour later I was walking through deodars and poplars on to a zigzagging dirt track that marks the start of the Bumburet Valley.

I had left all my belongings at the YZ apart from a daypack which contained my tent, thermals and a water bottle. My objective was to reach Krakal, the village where Omar told me the Italian had found a Nuristani guide. I would have to tread very carefully. It was illegal to trek into Afghanistan and asking the wrong person could prove dangerous. I did not want to get myself into trouble, or for that matter, anyone else.

I spent a glorious day walking past fields of luminous maize and varied mountains; some were as bleak as the slate hills of the Lake District, others resembled fertile pyramids mottled with snow. This is the land of the Kalash people. They live along the Bumburet and the two neighbouring valleys, the Rumbur to the north and the Birir to the south. The Bumburet is the most touristy of the valleys. I found it was not so much western backpackers who flocked here, but air-conditioned four-wheel drives filled with Punjabis or Baluchis, out in search of the wilderness experience. With their pantheon of oddly named gods and penchant for sacrificing goats, the Kalash are a tourism goldmine. Fortunately, the spectacular valleys are inaccessible enough – at least for now – to ensure they're not transformed into living museums.

The most striking aspect of the Kalash is their dress. The difference between a Kalash man and a Kalash woman is as startling as that between a cock and hen pheasant – except that with the Kalash, the female has the vibrant plumage. The men dress in drab *shalwar qamiz* while the women sport gowns decorated with spangled yellow and orange ornaments made from cowrie shells and beads.

At a village called Anish, a group of these brightly clad

women were collecting kindling. Their faces were dotted with mulberry juice and they were singing. They were not singing songs but stories, in beautiful soft soprano voices. Sitting in the long grass, cooled by the wind and looking out at the achingly beautiful landscape was all a bit much. I could have stopped and listened for ever.

But, of course, moments like this are only so special because they are transient. I had to move on. The Kalash were another of my picture-postcard encounters. They were people I would later read about in colour supplements, see on documentaries, promise myself I would visit again but who, in all likelihood, would be forever represented in my imagination by that one blissful encounter.

I arrived in the tiny village of Krakal at dusk and checked into the local guest house, a lovely wooden lodge by a fast-flowing brook. I hoped to make some discreet enquiries here about finding a guide so I sat down in the lodge's tearoom.

My enquiries did not take long. I clearly had I WANT TO GO TO NURISTAN tattooed on my forehead. I drank a bottle of warm Sprite in the company of a bewhiskered, wall-eyed man called Abdul. After a couple of minutes spent exchanging pleasantries – 'Sir, you are from Germany?' – he leaned towards me conspiratorially.

'You want to go to Nuristan? Yes?' he whispered.

'Yes,' I said. 'But I will need a guide.'

'Of course,' he said, flashing a best-price-for you-my-friend grin. 'I know only one. His name is Ghafor.'

CHAPTER FOURTEEN

GHAFOR THE KING

The first thing I noticed about Ghafor was his green lips. He appeared young, too, perhaps seventeen. Then there was the gun, slung casually over his left shoulder. A Kalashnikov. He looked like Huckleberry Finn toting a fishing pole, but I had been assured he was a professional, a killer, and that I would need somebody like him in Afghanistan.

'I can shoot butterfly off cow's tail, Mr Tom,' he had promised me when we met.

But, even accompanied by dead-eye Ghafor, the journey still seemed reckless. 'Eleven foreigners and two local climbers have disappeared in the Himalayas and the Hindu Kush this year,' proclaimed a story in the *Pakistan News* on the day of our departure. I wondered what 'disappeared' meant – buried in an avalanche, slain by bandits or just hopelessly lost.

I pointed out the article to Ghafor. 'Don't worry, Mr Tom. Hindu Kush very big but it is my home. You must not have weak spirit. We will travel like kings.'

This all sounded a bit rich. The only rations Ghafor had mustered so far were a chicken which when plucked resembled a consumptive pigeon and a bag of biscuits which smelt of creosote. Considering we would reach heights of 5,000 metres, it also worried me that his map had no contours.

But Ghafor was insistent. 'Mr Tom, don't worry. I am warrior and you are very danger man. I have guided many people, even man from Denmark television. We will not die.'

And so, following a prophetic Sundance Kid with green lips and weighed down by a rucksack of dubious survival gear, I walked out of the village of Krakal and through the maize fields of the Bumburet Valley. The low-lying meadows were teeming with life: frogs, field mice and crickets with silver wings. Hereford-like cattle and black goats were grazing amid the clover and buttercups. The occasional squawk of what sounded like a magpie echoed around the mountains which filled the horizon like a row of broken teeth.

After a couple of hours we stopped off in an isolated mud-brick house inhabited by an Italian called Marco. I had already heard about him, as rumours of a druggy hermit singing dirges at night had filtered down the valley. With his tousled hair and cornflower-blue eyes Marco looked like one of the local Pathans. He was crouched on his hams puffing on a chillum of hashish.

'My wife has left me,' he told us. 'Now I am in retreat. All the valley thinks I am crazy.' He exhaled a plume of blue smoke. 'Gossip is always so cruel to the lonely.'

Marco did not sound crazy, just bored. I noticed that his forearm, sinewy as celery, was pock-marked with punctures. Another of Pakistan's lost souls. Another Westerner reliant on the country's bargain heroin; rootless, friendless, his mind pickled by hallucination and no one to show him the way home. After a mug of coffee we pushed on, leaving Marco primping his goatee and staring out at the mountains. Somewhere out there, he seemed to be thinking, is a better place. I hoped he was right.

The air was cold and fresh, spiced occasionally with the sweet resinous smell of burning pine wood. The gangs of grubby urchins shouting 'give me pen' or 'one dollar, mister' who had been tailing us earlier had vanished. We were on our own now. I felt more alive than I had at any point on the whole trip. The anticipation of Afghanistan had sparked the sort of excitement I had so often felt as a child, so rarely as an adult – the strongest and most simple of highs.

We walked steadily for hours. Eagles circled above and bees buzzed among the tiny alpine flowers. As we climbed higher, the clumps of tough grass gave way to scree, the goat tracks tapered and the slope steepened so dramatically we were forced to scramble up the rock on all fours. Ghafor remained sure-footed while I was as clumsy and weak as something freshly hatched. The thin air made my heart pump furiously and my head feel light. I had to stop, catch my breath and let my blood decompress. As far as the eye could see was now an expanse of icy shale broken only by outcrops of granite, some intricately fissured, some smooth enough to have been squeezed from a giant tube. There were no other signs of life at this altitude, no plants or wildlife just rock, snow and ice stretching up to the jagged lip of the pass.

'I can smell my country,' Ghafor shouted, firing off his rifle one-handed like an Apache. 'My country is free, Mr Tom. America rules Iran and Pakistan but nobody rules Afghanistan. Not Russia, not Englistan. Nobody.' He had a point. But freedom clearly has its price when a teenager could handle a Kalashnikov with such casual competence.

In a final surge of energy we scrambled upwards, the shale giving way beneath our frenzied steps, our breath rasping; and suddenly there it was – Nuristan, Afghanistan's north-east corner – a desolate wilderness beneath a halo of brindled cloud. Arm in arm Ghafor and I charged down towards the forbidden turf, glissading across the snow and whooping with excitement like tropical birds. This is it, I thought, this is why I came here.

We stopped beside a lake and ate some potatoes and raisins. The wind had picked up but we were sheltered behind an isolated crag. I took a good look around. Crows wheeled above us in the bruised sky while grey snow stretched out beneath us. Ghafor pointed out the sharp silhouettes of the distant Bushgal Mountains. It was a scene from the pages of Tolkien; alive with mystery, a landscape of infinite severity.

Later that evening we met up with some shepherds. 'They are my uncles,' said Ghafor. Every Afghan we met was either Ghafor's uncle or brother. We were exhausted and decided to spend the night with them in their bothy, a rough shelter made from dark fist-sized stones.

Ghafor's uncles were a comical wild-bearded bunch. One had sandals made of old car tyres, another wore a 'Townsville – Queensland's Pride' T-shirt and carried a carbine with a tele-scopic site. We hunkered down by the fire and drank tea in silence.

The following morning I woke to a rhythmic splashing sound. I crawled out from my sleeping bag. One of the shepherds held aloft a goat carcass, skinned and inflated, which he shook like a huge maraca, slooshing around the milk inside.

'Soon that will be butter, Mr Tom,' said Ghafor. 'My uncles will carry to Pakistan to sell. After they sell they drink much wine. They dance, they sing. Then they walk home.'

'When they are in Pakistan do they ever speak to the tourists?'

'Oh, yes, all the time. One uncle have German girlfriend. She help with Afghan refugees in Peshawar. She beautiful, so tall, with nipples like melons.'

'Not nipples like melons, Ghafor. You mean breasts.'

'Yes, yes. Mr Tom. Nipples like breasts.'

The shepherds took it in turns to give Ghafor and me farewell embraces. I could not believe it. Here I was in the heart of the Hindu Kush being bear-hugged by a group of Rasputin lookalikes. At home my English prudery would have made a male embrace an embarrassment but here it felt right, a natural display of camaraderie.

'Mr Tom, they ask me if you believe in God.'

'Not really, Ghafor. Only when it suits me.'

He paused to translate this to one of the shepherds.

'He very sad for you, Mr Tom. Very sad. He say look at these great mountains; then you will believe.'

'Only if they move, Ghafor. Then I might.'

But I was not the only infidel to have visited Nuristan; previously the country had been known as Kafiristan or the Land of Unbelievers. The Kafirs had practised a form of pagan animism, drunk gallons of wine, kept slaves and fornicated with great frequency and imagination. Such debauchery had declined over the centuries and fidelity became increasingly respected but in 1895 the Afghan leader Abdul Rahman still deemed it necessary to conduct the conversion of the Kafirs to Islam with considerable brutality. His jihad involved blowing the most troublesome unbelievers from the mouths of cannons or freezing them solid in mountain lakes. Now Kafiristan was known as Nuristan, the Land of Light.

We were bathed in light that morning. Sunbeams lanced through the conifers flanking our path. A hoopoe, with its elaborate pink headdress, flew past. Ghafor ran along, dribbling a pine cone the size of a coconut.

'Me football man, Mr Tom,' he said, punting the cone into the air. 'Me Manchester United.' The fact Ghafor had heard of Manchester United depressed me mightily. I thought I had finally found a land devoid of western influence. Manchester bloody United. Run them through with scimitars, the poncy red-shirted lot of them.

But my sour mood did not last. How could it? This land had no other evidence of humanity. No cairns of rock like the Scottish Highlands. No prayer flags and painted eyes like the Himalayas. No litter or the other human detritus that spoils the tamer ranges.

Up here there was only the simple rhythm of nature, the scrunch of Ghafor's leather boots, the purling brook that slalomed through the cedars, the tonk, tonk, tonk of my stave hitting the rocks as I forged ahead, the sun and the clouds. It was a landscape without any past or future. It was here and now, an instance never to be repeated, both temporary and timeless.

That afternoon we reached Barg-e-Matal, Ghafor's village. It was such a fine place, so alien, like the Land where the Jumblies live. Honey-skinned women in scarlet robes winnowed grain in the sunshine while children shinned up trees to pick walnuts. Ghafor and I wandered along the river bank, bright-winged butterflies in our wake.

The following day, a French doctor arrived on a mule. His name was Gerard and he worked for *Médecins sans Frontières*. He dismounted and embraced us.

'Who are you?' he asked, clearly astonished.

'Travellers,' I said.

'I haven't seen any travellers here for twenty years. How the hell did you make it? The Khyber Pass is closed.'

'Over the pass at the head of the Bumburet valley.'

'Why? Why on earth come here?'

'Well, it's Nuristan, I suppose.'

He laughed. 'That was enough for me too. And many before us.'

This was true. Through the centuries a determined trickle of pilgrims, explorers, empire builders, spies, hippies, communists and Danish TV crews had all been lured by Nuristan's potent sirens.

The earliest visitor is thought to have been Alexander the Great. His army skirted the area before 300 BC and the Mediterranean appearance of many of the Afghans we had seen was probably a legacy of this visit. Another high-profile visitor was Genghis Khan. In the thirteenth century he tore through with his Mongol hordes *en route* to Persia, followed by Tamerlane over a hundred years later, who is reputed to have married a Kafir.

Of all the stories of the adventurers, my favourite tells of a Christian missionary, Fazl Huz, who visited Kafiristan in 1864. At huge personal risk he spent two months among the Kafirs, much of the time disguised as a woman, using lime juice to write invisible diary entries. He only left Nuristan when the snow became too thick and he was finally forced to pilot a raft back to Pakistan along the Kabul River.

Gerard's exploits were equally remarkable. He had been visiting Nuristan for over twenty years. During the Russian war he masqueraded as a Mujahedin in order to distribute his precious medicines. Recently, a colleague of his had been arrested at the Khyber Pass, manacled and pelted with stones. Gerard, after much pleading, had managed to secure his friend's release. The incident did not seem to have put Gerard off his work; indeed he said nothing would stop him visiting Afghanistan, whatever the politics, although he admitted the country was heading towards the most oppressive regime he had ever witnessed.

'The Taleban will soon start bombing Kabul,' he said, fingering his grey beard. 'They are religious hardliners, very serious. They are also the best guerrilla fighters in the world.'

The Taleban had already taken the historic city of Herat in west Afghanistan. 'Here, at last, is Asia without an inferiority complex,' Robert Byron, author of *The Road To Oxiana*, wrote of the city in 1934. But many of Herat's architectural treasures had been turned to dust and the Taleban were already dropping their bombs on fresh targets.

The word Taleban, literally, means student of Islam, explained Gerard, but these students were not academically inclined. Their leader, Mullah Mohammed Omar, was about as zealous as they came. A one-eyed recluse, he refused to ever hold audience with non-Muslims and only spoke to women, all of whom he regarded as unclean, if they were out of his sight. Armed with MIG fighters and missile launchers Omar's ultra-conservative Taleban were well trained, and received covert backing from Pakistan. His 'students' did not resent the fact that they were earning less than £2.50 a month. They believed they were in possession of an all-powerful holy truth. This, like Tibetan troops wearing Dalai Lama amulets, made them fearless fighters.

'Many of the Taleban are the same people who fought so bravely against the Russians,' added Gerard. 'Their ancestors probably fought against the British during the Afghan Wars. Perhaps even Alexander the Great. Sadly, when the warlords have no outside enemy to fight, they turn on each other.'

One of the English-speaking villagers surrounding Gerard recited a chilling list of Taleban policies. 'All men must wear beards, thieves will have their hands cut off, radios will be destroyed, dancing, picnics and kite-flying will be banned, women will not be allowed to go to work or stand close to their husbands in public . . .' The rules were endless.

Women clearly had the worst deal. The only women I had seen in Nuristan so far had been a far cry from the apparently sluttish Kafirs of Alexander's day. They were rangy and elegant, swathed in muslin and very shy. It was unthinkable that their tenuous foothold in society could become shakier still.

Gerard and I were shown around the local school which comprised a ramshackle assembly of sagging shacks. Shaven-headed children sat on the floor and watched, with grown-up eyes, as their teacher chalked Pashto on a slate. An old poster on how to recognize Russian landmines had been stuck to the wall. Outside, a skeletal pony was lying in the shade. Two young boys were playing tag by the river. I wondered whether the Taleban would add tag to their un-Islamic hit list for being too frivolous. What with the abolition of kite-flying and dancing perhaps childhood itself would soon be in jeopardy.

'This is one of the most remote areas on earth,' said Gerard. 'Apart from Tibet, Afghanistan is the only country in the world with no operating railway. In this village there are no vehicles either and only the rich own mules.

'I love the seclusion but it is bad for education and healthcare too. Afghans are hardy people but often suffer from malnutrition due to lack of milk. TB is another big problem. As for your chapped lips, Ghafor, stop smearing on that ointment. You look like a monster.' He threw Ghafor a cream-coloured salve. 'Use this.'

We ate a farewell breakfast – eggs, nuts and grapes – in a sun-dappled room dominated by a huge picture of Mecca. Inexplicably, there was also a Salvador Dali print and a poster of Zurich city centre which stated 'Progress is Persistence'. If progress was best defined by Zurich, I prayed, please God, do not bother the Afghans with it.

'I love the peace here,' said Gerard, finally breaking the silence. 'There is a proverb: A bad pumpkin has many seeds and a bad man talks too much. Afghans like proverbs, they talk little but wisely.'

Gerard waved us off as the muezzin yodelled from the mosque in the centre of the village. We retraced our steps past the carrion dogs and dishevelled chickens and over the shaky bridges flanked by Corsican pines. We sang and picked sunflowers, stopping briefly to chat to a one-legged boy leaning on a crutch; he had a dragonfly perched on his cap.

Ghafor and I moved fast. We were both strong, having fed on mutton stew and melon the previous night. We reached the shepherds' shelter by afternoon but they had left. A long plaintive howl came from the valley behind us. In his invisible lime-juice diary entries Fazl Huz had mentioned leopards, wolves and even bears living in the area but that had been over a hundred years ago. It was probably only a dog or a fox. Soon we were near the top of the pass again.

Then something awful happened: my guts suddenly liquefied. I dashed for cover. As we walked on this happened repeatedly, about every ten minutes. After an hour I felt as though a syringe had been plunged into my navel and had sucked out my insides, save for a cluster of highly virulent, kick-boxing parasites. I started to rant and accused Ghafor of losing his way. Any trace of dignity vanished; I had become as loose-bowelled as a calf. My tissue paper was finished and I resorted to tearing pages from my novel. (*East of Eden* by John Steinbeck, fortunately 643 sheets long plus a Kipling short story as back-up.) It was either this or resorting to the Afghan method: a handful of sand.

Slowly we struggled back towards the pass. I had started to throw up. 'Come on Mr Tom, you are Englistan man. Very strong man. Very danger man. No stop.'

Once we were back on the Pakistan side, my spirits fleetingly lifted. But we were still very high up; it was freezing and the light was fading fast. Ghafor and I slid down a moraine of loose shale. As the slope levelled, I began to walk again – a clockwork soldier running out of power; no longer thinking, just enduring.

'Keep up, Mr Tom. Remember you are danger man. Very danger man.'

'Ghafor, if you call me danger man one more time, I'll shoot you.'

We found a sheltered spot beside a stone wall and pitched the tent. I lay in my sleeping bag while Ghafor made a fire. He brewed me a cup of sweet tea which, even after a couple of sips, filtered through my system like poison. I dashed out, my bare feet crunching on the snow. When I returned I was in a bad way, caked in vomit, crazed and febrile.

Ghafor was sympathetic but I could see the panic in his tired eyes. What a mess. It had all been so smooth up until this point. No robbers to fend off. No blizzards or storms. I knew what had caused my sickness – that river near Barg-e-Matal, ice-cold, clear as glass, tantalizing. I should have just washed in it but I had drunk from it too. My mouth had been parched and the water had looked so clean, so fresh. No need to boil it. Fool.

I was shaking crazily now. My head was swirling. What was I doing? Who would find me? My bicycle, which had been left in the hostel dormitory in Chitral, would be my only legacy. MY BICYCLE. That was it. I was supposed to be bicycling to Australia. My Afghan experience had been so overwhelming I had almost forgotten. Now this was it, the end of the line. I had let down my family, my friends, my sponsors, because of an impetuous whim to trek into Nuristan. I had already pedalled 5,000 miles. That would count for nothing now.

'You are a good man Ghafor,' I whispered. 'I'm sorry I shouted at you.'

'In Hindu Kush every man is good, Mr Tom. Just look

around. These mountains. Every man is a king here.' There was something great in what he said. Someone so young, so rough, so poor but who recognized his luck, the simple beauty of his life, without the need to make comparisons.

You have got it right, Ghafor, I thought. You are a king. You are seventeen, ugly as sin and cook the worst chicken chasseur this side of Kabul but you are truly a king. A king of simple riches.

I vomited in my mess tin. There was nothing left inside me and my body convulsed violently. After I had finished groaning and spitting we both laughed but there were tears welling too. I had never felt so weak.

Later, Ghafor curled up in his thin nylon sleeping bag. He tossed and turned like Houdini in an escape stunt; he was obviously very cold. If I had not delayed him, he would have been at the bottom of the mountain, safe and warm. Meanwhile, I was snug, cocooned in goose down. How unfair. He had guided me though the mountains, nursed and encouraged me, without complaining once. I suddenly felt enormously grateful to him.

'Just think when we get back to the valley, Ghafor. Chicken stew, wine, mulberries, German girls with . . .' But Ghafor was asleep.

I sat up and looked out at the night sky. The kick-boxing parasites in my gut were finally still, locked in a clinch. A single star, bright and distant, flickered beyond the blue penumbra of the mountains. Perhaps there is a God, I thought. I began to pray but realized it was too late for that.

Instead, I opened Kipling's haunting story *The Man Who Would Be King* which is set in Nuristan. I shone my torch along the faded print. Daniel, the vagabond hero who the Kafirs crown their king, gets bitten by a native girl he tries to seduce. The enraged crowd now realize Daniel is human and not a god, because his wound bleeds. They march him to a high bridge and cut away the ropes. He crashes down on to the rocks followed by his golden crown. Yet another Hindu Kush statistic.

Of course, I did not become another Hindu Kush statistic. In my weak-limbed state Ghafor led me back down to Krakal, then escorted me in a crowded jeep to the hospital at Chitral. Here I was administered two dozen white antibiotic capsules called Zolen DS, a bottle of chewable carbon tablets to settle my stomach and a fistful of Imodium.

I gave Ghafor a handsome tip, a green and yellow Pakistani cricket cap and *The Man Who Would be King*. He gave me a bear hug – not the best thing with dysentery-gripped guts – and told me that next time I was in the Kalash valleys we would reach Kabul. 'Mr Tom, you are very danger man,' he teased, before turning on his heel and setting off at his usual brisk pace. The man who had saved my life did not look back. He was off, off back to the mountains which he ruled, and which in turn, ruled over him.

I spent several languorous days in bed reading the unsoiled remains of *East Of Eden*. At regular intervals, I would have to make semi-house-trained dashes to the communal thunderbox. It was a grim time. Since the start of the trip, I had shrunk from ten and a half stone to just over eight. I looked like a consumptive bushbaby. The staff at the YZ Hotel were attentive and generous, bringing me unleavened bread and bananas, or cups of sweet tea. I even had trouble keeping this insipid diet from being instantly expelled. I began to wonder whether I would have to call it quits.

But no. Right now this trip was all I had. My only friend. My only focus. I had to go on. I ferreted out the necessary pills from my medical kit, swallowed enough to turn my belly to porridge for a couple of days and caught a relay of buses down to Lahore. It was a terrible journey. Even the colon-clogging Imodium was struggling to cope with whatever bacteria were surfing through my gassy entrails.

I got to Lahore and pitched my tent in the Young Women's Christian Association under a palm tree and very near the washroom. I had never stayed in a YMCA before, let alone a YWCA. It had been recommended to me by a Brazilian traveller on the bus from Peshawar. He told me he had fallen victim to one of Lahore's notorious rip-off hotels. His money belt had been snaffled in the night by a thief who popped up through a trap door. In his state of despair, the YWCA had let him stay for free until he secured some fresh funds.

The YWCA could not have been safer. A security gate was permanently manned and the tranquil grounds provided the perfect antidote to Lahore's anarchic streets. In the state I was in I had no energy to peruse the city's Moghul masterpieces, I could just about manage to walk down the road to the local bakery.

As the days went by my condition improved. I started to eat yoghurt, boiled eggs and even the odd vegetable *roti*. My lank flesh began to tighten again and I rejoiced that I would soon be able to tackle my upcoming Indian leg. The only embarrassment was my tendency to fire off volcanic farts at the most inopportune moments. A YWCA was no place for such indecorous behaviour.

Dysentery had been bound to strike me down somewhere and I was just glad it was over. The simple joy of being a healthy human being again was a source of perpetual rapture. No more midnight sprints across the grass, no more three-loo-roll afternoons or spontaneous bowel combustion. Best of all, no trace of pre-trip beer belly. I was now as svelte as a greyhound. The antibiotics had run their course. I was one hundred per cent. Tip top. Ready to face everything and anything.

Considering I was just about to confront India that was probably just as well.

CHAPTER FIFTEEN

SPINNING THE WHEELS
OF LIFE AND DEATH

The book that tops many an Indian traveller's reading list is
Kim. The eponymous hero of Kipling's classic is a streetwise
orphan who joins forces with an elderly lama in search of 'The
Truth'. The unlikely couple become embroiled in many adven-
tures as they cadge lifts on steam trains and bullock carts along
the Grand Trunk Road before finally reaching the Himalayas
for their showdown with immortality.

It is a masterpiece because, unlike so many books written by
colonialists, it respects India. For all Kipling's imperial swagger
he respects the holy man's quest for the truth as much as he
respects Kim's pro-Empire contribution towards the 'Great
Game' of espionage between Russia and Britain. The two work
together. Kim protects the lama with his youthful pluck and
energy, while the lama teaches Kim through his patience and
spirituality.

The two of them first meet at the Zam-Zammah gun in
central Lahore, opposite the museum where Kipling's father
was once the curator. It seemed the perfect place to begin my
journey into India too. I propped my bike against the cannon's
wheel, re-balanced the panniers and kicked off down towards
the Grand Trunk Road which, like Kim, I would follow as far
as the holy city of Varanasi.

Getting out of Lahore was tricky. Much of the road looked like it had been bombed and there was strong evidence of the recent floods. Craters filled with scummy water impeded the dense crawling traffic. As I zigzagged through the queues of motor rickshaws and Tata trucks I felt my lungs tighten with the traffic fumes.

But soon the Indian border, less than twenty miles from Lahore, was within reach. Despite the initial bedlam, once out in the country I almost had the road to myself. Flocks of sheep with drooppy ears wandered along the verge, marshalled by boys in clumsily tied rollmops. A cloud of bees hovered above a woman holding a basket of cakes.

At Customs was a sign: WELCOME TO THE LARGEST DEMOCRACY IN THE WORLD. With India's population nudging a billion, there was no disputing this fact but democracy had come at a price. It was now nearly fifty years since partition, and it amazed me that this border had been responsible for the largest and perhaps most violent two-way exodus the world has ever known. Droves of Muslims had fled across to newly formed Pakistan while Hindus and Sikhs had struck out in the opposite direction. There were appalling acts of carnage on both sides, villages razed, trainloads of migrants massacred, corpses lining the tracks from Lahore to Amritsar. Within a few weeks, over a quarter of a million people were dead.

Although tensions between India and Pakistan are still palpable, my border crossing could not have been easier. It was hard to imagine those scenes of devastation that afternoon; other than the squawk of parakeets and the clip-clop of buffalo hoofs, the road beyond the border was as quiet as the clouds scudding along the horizon.

Things began to liven up near Amritsar. I passed an elephant with a blue trunk being ridden by a half-naked mahout; rickshaws brimming with brightly turbaned Sikh schoolchildren; the crumbling façade of a palace; a man with a spear; a troop of silver monkeys; barefoot girls in dazzling saris and a beggar playing a flute with his nose. I thought everywhere would seem tame after Afghanistan, but India was something altogether different.

In Amritsar there was really only one place to stay: the Golden Temple, the Sikhs' holiest shrine. Like all Sikh *gurdwaras* it offered free accommodation – a spartan but homely dormitory with a few mattresses on a stone floor. I leaned my bike against the wall next to a meditating backpacker who stank of incense and ripe feet. Levering off my cycle pumps, I walked out into the sunlight.

The Golden Temple itself looks a little like a copper-gilded cricket pavilion, although this is a pavilion that sends shivers down the spine. Like Jerusalem's Western Wall, it is the atmosphere, the urgent pulse of faith that is overwhelming, not the decorated marble or the burnished gold of the shrine itself.

The temple sits in a large square pool and its walls are reflected in the shimmering water. Some of the pilgrims were whispering chants as they circled the shrine, others were chattering and laughing. Venerable priests were sitting reading excerpts from the Granth Sahib, the holy book of Sikhism.

Compared with the immaculately uniformed Sikh men and the elegantly shawled Sikh women, the travellers resembled lesser mortals, shuffling along in their baggy slacks and stone-washed T-shirts. I felt disrespectfully underdressed. I was wearing a lumberjack shirt, threadbare through repeated hand washings, a pair of tracksuit bottoms and a baseball cap. I suddenly felt the urge to scrub myself down and put on a jacket or a waistcoat, but there was nothing even remotely dapper in my panniers. There was no denying that I was a fully fledged bum.

An old man in a blue turban and a necklace of marigolds

walked past me blowing an instrument like a hunting horn. A band of acolytes followed in his wake, eyes closed in devotion, one of them beating a tabla drum. It was 7.30 p.m. – time for dinner. I followed the crowds into a long cavernous room, where hundreds of people were sitting in cross-legged lines facing each other. I sat opposite a Sikh girl with a saffron shawl whose dark eyes were enhanced by kohl and candlelight.

At first, the meal could have been straight out of *Oliver Twist*. There was an interminable reading of grace, during which all the diners solemnly looked at the floor. This was followed by a terrible clanking as tin trays and water bowls were distributed. Dhal was ladled out while a man with a bronze watering can filled our bowls. Last of all, a tower of chapattis was handed around.

The food was indigestible, the water brackish and the floor uncomfortable, but none of this mattered. It was the spirit of the occasion that left such a wonderful aftertaste. Where else in the world could you sit with hundreds of others, eating and drinking free of charge, a mass of different creeds and colours all high on each other's company? There are few occasions in life when one feels intensely proud to be a human being. For me, dining at the Golden Temple canteen was one of them.

But Amritsar has not always been so tranquil. In April 1919, one of the least distinguished episodes of British rule occurred when up to 2,000 Indian men, women and children were gunned down in Jallianwala Bagh, a stone's throw from the Golden Temple.

I found it a sad experience to walk around the memorial site the following morning. I perused the martyrs' gallery of the slain, the stone well where dozens of protestors had jumped to escape death and the large sign which read, 'This ground was hallowed by the blood of innocent Hindus, Sikhs and Mussulmans who were shot by British bullets . . .' With butterflies skitting about and wild flowers in bloom Jallianwala Bagh was now peaceful. One could only try and imagine the terrible consequences of General Dyer's repeated orders to fire at the nationalist crowds.

In 1984 violence flared up in Amritsar again. Sikh militants championing the formation of Khalistan – an independent Sikh homeland – occupied and fortified the Golden Temple. In a hawkish initiative, known as Operation Blue Star, Indira Gandhi ordered the Indian Army to flush them out. The militants eventually surrendered but only after much bloodshed. In retaliation, Mrs Gandhi was assassinated by her Sikh bodyguard later that year.

I had found Amritsar friendly and dynamic, and I was sorry to leave. However, I was to enjoy regular contact with the Sikhs over the ensuing week as I cycled through the Punjab and the tiny neighbouring state of Haryana.

Cycling here was fun. There was always something going on and the road signs were eye-catching. MILK – THE SECRET OF PUNJAB'S VIGOUR stood next to a billboard advertising GODFATHER – INDIA'S STRONGEST BEVERAGE which depicted a Walter Raleigh lookalike supping from a frothy tankard. The messages on the trucks were just as good: USE DIPPER AT NIGHT, TATA and BLOW HORN NOW! along with my favourite, DON'T BE RASH, LESS YOU CRASH!

The Sikhs were unfailingly generous. I was always welcomed into *gurdwaras* and spent the nights dining on lentils and sleeping on *charpoys* (rope-strung beds). During my week in the Punjab, I spent no more than ten pounds sterling and that was through making small donations, rather than paying fees. It was the cheapest week of the trip, if not my entire life.

My favourite place was Patiala, which had once been the Sikh capital and was still an important pilgrimage site. It was here that I met the splendid Kuldeep Singh, a retired telephone engineer and devout *Khalsa*. He sported a mauve turban and a toothless grin. Kuldeep was most enthusiastic about the bicycle ride. 'I am coming with you Mr Som,' he kept telling me as he steered his Hero bicycle alongside mine, the ferrule of his umbrella sticking out from under his bike saddle like a pointer's tail.

He referred to my bike ride as the 'great struggle', which was more than a little flattering. The 'great escape' or the 'great indulgence' would have been more accurate. 'This is your great struggle Mr Som,' stressed Kuldeep, grabbing my arm. 'Remember this. If you lose money, you lose nothing. If you lose health, you lose something. But if you lose character – you lose *everything*!'

Kuldeep seemed half bonkers, but in a vigorous, life-embracing sort of way. He wanted to show me everything at once. He began by leading me around the town's impressive *gurdwara*, which featured an identical pool of water to the Golden Temple, but this time with fat brown carp bobbing on the surface. There were the usual circulating pilgrims, carpets of flowers and offerings of *langoor* (free food); this time not lentils but a semolina-type stodge wrapped in a palm leaf.

Kuldeep led me into a museum at the edge of the *gurdwara* which displayed some of the most gruesome art I have ever seen. There were pictures of Sikhs tied to a railway track in front of an oncoming train, Sikhs strung up on torture wheels for not converting to Islam, Sikhs massacred at Amritsar, Sikhs garrotted and disembowelled.

'Oh dear,' said Kuldeep, grasping his *kirpan* scabbard. 'Now you know why I carry this, Mr Som. We Sikhs are warriors; we must defend ourselves.'

The Sikh religion was founded by Guru Nanak late in the fifteenth century and was created as an independent third way, crystallizing the best aspects of Hinduism and Islam. Nanak believed in devotion to one God, in moral vitality and tolerance towards other religions. But by the time of Guru Gobind Singh, the tenth and final guru, the Sikhs had suffered much persecution and in 1699 a military aspect was introduced to the faith, known as the *Khalsa*.

The *Khalsa* – the Pure – are a casteless fraternity, all given the name Singh (lion) which most Sikhs are called to this day. Devout *Khalsa* still wear five specific symbols: unshorn hair, a sword, knee-length drawers, a small comb and a steel bangle. With these accessories they tend to stand out from the crowd. Indeed, after riding through the Punjab I thought the highly distinctive Sikhs comprised most of India's population but actually there are a mere eighteen million of them, a tiny number in a country of nearly one billion.

Kuldeep rambled on about the brilliance of Guru Nanak, including the fact the great man had travelled all the way from Mecca to Kabul to spread his message. 'You see, Mr Som,' said Kuldeep wobbling his head, 'Sikhism is a combination of the best parts of many religions. We learn from other faiths, but we are also very individual.'

One Sikh on display at the museum who was certainly very individual was Ranjit Singh. Ranjit, born in 1780, was surely the most extraordinary of the Sikhs' post-guru leaders. With only one eye (he lost the other through smallpox) he was even more dramatic-looking than most of his fellow *Khalsa*. He reputedly married twenty times and sired seven children, each with a different spouse.

Above all, Ranjit Singh was a skilful soldier who considerably expanded his empire and was revered as 'The Lion of the Punjab'. He was also a legendary drinker with a penchant for slugging down cocktails spiced with opium, musk and animal meat. When he dropped dead a year short of his seventieth birthday thousands of mourners attended his funeral. So emotional was the occasion that four of the great leader's wives and seven of his handmaids threw themselves on to his burning pyre, accompanying him to the afterlife.

However, Ranjit Singh's sexual predilections were nothing compared with some of Patiala's other maharajahs, who seemed to have had a freehold on decadence. The sauciest of the dynasty, Maharajah Bhupinder Singh, supposedly boasted a harem of 365 wives, one for each night of the year. What was it with these Sikhs?

I read this out to Kuldeep and asked if he knew whether Bhupinder had left any legacy of his bad behaviour. Kuldeep told me that one of the old maharajahs' palaces had been turned into a museum but that he could show me where Patiala's current maharajah lived. Within minutes he had ushered me out of the *gurdwara* and jumped back on his bicycle. I followed him through the chaotic streets.

The incumbent maharajah (the title is largely defunct these days) lives in a white mansion on the edge of Patiala. The house looks out over a manicured lawn which on the day of my visit was being cut by a *mali* in a grey pyjama suit. The entrance door is guarded by two stone lions and several miniature cannon that fire out towards the rose beds.

It is not normally open to tourists but as the maharajah and his family were away Kuldeep managed to get one of the staff to give us a reluctant and very brief tour. We had about thirty seconds in each room; enough time for a quick gawp at a tiger skin hanging in the billiard room, a miniature model of the Golden Temple, an epic chandelier and a sepia photo of Viceroy Wavell. The house was beautiful but in an austere and predictable way; to me it felt more like a museum than an active family home.

The only hint of carnal excess was in the library. Amid all

the spiritual texts, the leather-bound classics and thick encyclopedias, I noticed a book called *Madame Sex* by Isaac Goldberg. 'Only 2,000 editions printed,' read the dust jacket. 'For collectors of distinguished erotica only.'

Maharajah Bhupinder would have been proud.

Before I left Patiala, Kuldeep gave me a swift embrace.

'Mr Som, I will not join you on your struggle,' he said firmly.

'Why not Kuldeep?' I asked. 'You were so keen before. Is it because of your family?'

'No, no, Mr Som,' replied Kuldeep.

'Are you too old?' I joked. 'Too fat?'

'No, no,' he repeated, pointing up and grinning like a Halloween pumpkin. 'It is because soon it will be raining.'

Kuldeep was not wrong, but thankfully that afternoon the monsoon was only light. Three days later however, just as I was penetrating Delhi's suburbs, the bloated sky really let rip. I had never experienced anything like it. Rain pelted down in apocalyptic sheets, drenching everything it touched within seconds.

But there was no reason for it to stop me. The rain might have been strong but it was short-lived and beautifully warm, nothing like the chilling rains of a Swanbourne winter. After a while I began to enjoy it and the water felt wonderfully cleansing.

By the time I had weaved through the treacherous innards of Old Delhi to the home of Mr and Mrs Anand, I was once again dry.

The Anands lived in a wood-framed colonial-style house to the west of the capital. Mr Anand was in the courtyard beating a carpet with a broom handle. When he heard the creaky front gate open, he backed away from the cloud of carpet dust that engulfed him and squinted towards me. 'Acha,' he said. 'You must be the boy on the bicycle.'

The Anands were the parents of my Indian friend, Virendra, who I had known when I worked in Asia. Virendra had left India for Hong Kong in his early twenties. He loved it and has stayed there ever since selling air fresheners to the Chinese. I hoped to meet up with him in three months' time and celebrate Christmas in his Happy Valley apartment.

The home of Virendra's parents, however, was quite ascetic. They were evidently spiritual people too. There were tapestries of scenes from the Hindu scriptures draped across the walls: the monkey chief Hanuman defending Lord Rama and another of Prince Arjuna steering a chariot into battle. Scanning the collage of divine characters on the Anands' tapestries was like reuniting with a group of old friends.

'Let us help you with the bike, Tom,' said Mr Anand. He was a quiet kind-faced man dressed in a blue donkey jacket who had recently retired from his job as a railway engineer. Mrs Anand was plump and jolly with a mop of hennaed hair which she kept swiping from her eyes. Together they showed me to my air-conditioned bedroom while fussing around me with slices of melon. What bliss. Even though I had never met them before, I instantly felt at home.

That afternoon I dealt with practical needs. I put in my application for a Nepalese visa, washed my dust-caked bicycle and sent some postcards. This still gave me just enough time to pedal to Birla Ham, the elegant house, now a museum, where Mahatma Gandhi spent his final weeks.

As Gandhi had been such a frugal soul, the museum curators had clearly struggled to find belongings of his to put on display. Hanging on one wall was a touching exhibit, a glass cabinet entitled 'Bapu's Wordly Remains'. Inside it were two spoons, two forks, two knives, a walking stick, a pair of round glasses and a pocket watch. In a room to the side was a spinning wheel. And that was it. For a man of Gandhi's immense international stature, it was an impressively simple legacy.

Making up for Gandhi's lack of worldly remains were tributes from world leaders: printed eulogies from Nehru, Albert Einstein, Martin Luther King and Chiang Kai-shek were all on show. The one major leader of the time who shunned him was Winston Churchill who, vehemently resenting Gandhi's push for Indian independence, described him as 'a half naked fakir'.

Walking back out of Birla Ham I noticed a rock on the lawn near the exit gates. I walked over to get a closer look. Fixed to it was a plinth inscribed with a parting message from The Great Soul.

'I will give you a talisman,' it read. 'Whenever you are in doubt or the self becomes too much with you, apply the following test: Recall the face of the poorest and the weakest man whom you have seen and ask yourself if the step you contemplate is going to be of any use to him – will he gain anything by it? ... Then you will find your doubts about yourself melting away.'

They were certainly words to prick the conscience. However, given that the next step I contemplated was stuffing my face with several of Mrs Anand's home-made cakes, it would be some time before I experienced that melting away of doubt. Like so many others, I fully agreed with what Gandhi preached but knew I would rarely have the moral strength to put it into practice.

The next day I picked up my Nepalese visa and dropped off my passport at the nearby Chinese Embassy. I then booked a train ticket to Bombay so that I could pick up my bicycle spares: fresh tyres, brake pads, inner tubes and WD40 oil. Phil the mechanic had sent this mercy package off to Bombay before I had a chance to tell him about my change of route. The box needed to be signed in at Bombay's Customs.

I would leave for Bombay that evening, grab the spares and come straight back. It was an irritating detour but new tyres were essential, especially as I was about to cycle through Nepal and Tibet.

The rest of the day I devoted to pedalling around Delhi. I began my ride in the alleyways of the old city and glided down towards the wide shady avenues of Sir Edwin Lutyens's New Delhi.

The contrast between the two Delhis is extraordinary. In Old Delhi are scrums of people: hawkers with trays of coconut chunks, beggars picking through the rubbish berms, rickshaw wallahs, hotel touts; there are sharp stinks and a heavy heat. But looking down the Rajpath, New Delhi's graceful verdant main street, is a different world. I wandered along beneath the shade of neem trees, admiring the white colonial bungalows and Lutyens's masterpiece, the old Viceroy's house, made from rhubarb-tinted sandstone and topped with a beautiful hemispherical dome. The whole Rajpath area is a perfect blend of style and symmetry, of sub-continental serenity and imperial swank.

I ended the day by cycling through the once-majestic Coronation Park. The park is now little more than a dull waterlogged plain but I visited it to pay my respects to another member of my family, this time on my mother's side. Colonel Osmond Barnes, my great, great grandfather, had been here when Queen Victoria was honoured with the title Empress of India.

During his eventful career, Colonel Barnes fought in campaigns as diverse as Abyssinia and Afghanistan but most of his life was spent in India. Barnes was decorated for his bravery both at the seige of Kotah during the Indian Mutiny and for his command of the 10th Bengal Lancers (Hodson's Horse) in the 1884 Zhob Valley conflict in present day Pakistan.

But as his obituary in *The Times* (21 May 1930) noted, 'The most picturesque event in the career of Colonel Barnes . . . was his service as Chief Herald at the great Durbar held at Delhi on January 1st, 1877, for Queen Victoria as Empress of India . . . One reason for selecting him for it was his great height – 6ft, 6 inches in his stockings. (Barnes's) voice was heard over the whole arena . . . from the moment he opened his lips until the time he closed them with a wonderfully emphatic . . . "God Save the Queen."'

The obituary added that when the artist, Prinsep, was commissioned to paint a picture of the scene, he depicted Colonel Barnes standing on the steps instead of on the dais as his formidable physique would have made the others, especially the Viceroy, look ridiculously small.

I leaned on my bicycle looking out over the dreary parkland. What would great, great grandfather Osmond make of this now I wondered. His days of snipe shooting before breakfast and tiffin on the banks of the River Jumna were long gone. But I like to think he was an honourable man who typified the best aspects of the Raj: not through pomposity or profiteering, but pride in his adoptive country.

That evening, I caught my sleeper to Bombay and two days later, armed with my box of spare parts, chuffed back to Delhi. It was the most fleeting of visits to India's largest city but it left me with several unforgettable impressions.

I spent my nights in Bombay's Salvation Army hostel, a friendly doss-house near the Gateway of India, the huge archway that had been erected to commemorate the landing of

King George V and Queen Mary in 1911. For years the gateway had been an imperial landmark for incoming British ships. Now it looked little more than a decaying gravestone, its watery foundations licked by floating cigarette butts and plastic bags, the flotsam of a restless new tide.

Despite Bombay's many colonial splendours and shining skyscrapers, what struck me most about the city was its squalor. This was highlighted by two separate incidents. The first was on Falkland Street, the red light district.

'BABA, BABA, sucky sucky,' shouted one of the whores, an Indian girl with a face paled by powder. 'Hey boy, white boy,' hollered another, perhaps a Chinese or Korean girl, with her hair tied in a double ponytail. 'Jiggy jig. Jiggy jig.' There were Thai and Burmese faces too, with wide eyes and ruddy lips, taunting and blowing kisses.

These were Bombay's cage girls, so called because many of them live in interlinking hutches with grilles like prison bars. Those girls not behind grilles were peeking out from accordion blinds or crouching on their hams on the pavement. Many were lined up in twos and threes, shouting and clicking their tongues at the men on the street. They all looked very young and many were gorgeous in a coltish devil-may-care way. I wanted to go and talk to them to see what was life was like behind those bars, behind the mascara and the ribald gestures, but, intimidated by their laughter, I shied away.

Falkland Street was a war zone. A shrew-faced crone offered me hashish and when I refused she suggested a blow job instead. The whole area – the balconies, the corrugated roofs, the billboards – was decaying before my eyes. But there were cures on offer. MEDICAL POWER – LIFT YOUR BREAST read one sign. PUDIN HARA – THE ONLY REMEDY FOR GRIPING AND GAS! promised another.

The girls sensed my confusion and baited me with a chorus

of whistles and come-ons. I felt myself turning bright red, but I admired the way they kept their morale up in such squalid circumstances. They might have been poor but they never came across as victims; in fact they scared the life out of me.

The second Bombay incident which left its mark was my visit to the tomb of Haji Ali, a drowned Muslim saint. The tomb itself is unremarkable although it sits offshore and can only be reached by crossing a long causeway at low tide. Due to its restricted visiting hours, beggars wisely take the opportunity of lining the causeway during pilgrim rush hour.

The ranks of beggars make a heart-rending spectacle. I saw groups of amputees lying in circles and wailing. There was a blind man with arms extended and a starving child with a withered foot. Some of the mendicants reached out to touch the passing pilgrims, others sat in prayer. One little boy lay on his back shaking violently and shouting to himself. He was covered in sores and had an illegible sign balanced on his stomach.

Money changers at the tomb's exit swapped rupee notes for handfuls of tiny coins. Some pilgrims carefully inspected the beggars for maximum sympathy value and salved their consciences accordingly, making a show of doling out their loose change.

On my way back to the Salvation Army hostel the pavement was blocked at one point by a long queue waiting silently outside a kiosk selling candles and kindling wood. When I asked what was going on, I was told I was outside the Anjuman Ateshbehram, a famous Zoroastrian temple, which was celebrating the fact its flame had been burning for one hundred years.

I knew very little about Zoroastrians, only that they originated from Persia, worshipped fire and that their dead were left on towers of silence and picked clean by vultures. I expected them to wear a distinctive uniform but they all looked very ordinary, dressed in neutral shirts and trousers. Although my train was due to leave in a couple of hours I decided to wait and catch a glimpse of the flame.

'When you see the flame all your worries fly away,' said an old man in a blue tarboosh next to me. 'The flame explains everything. It explains God. In some Zoroastrian temples the flame has been alight for one thousand years.'

'I can't wait,' I enthused. 'My faith is getting more confused every minute. Perhaps seeing the flame will enlighten me.'

'But *you* cannot see the flame,' rasped the old man in horror. 'It is forbidden. Only Zoroastrians can look at it.'

'Oh, I'm terribly sorry,' I said, retreating swiftly into the crowds. Minutes later I was hotfooting it back to the station, just as spiritually perplexed as ever.

Back in Delhi I collected my Chinese visa and fitted my bicycle with its spanking new tyres. Finally I was set for the next long drag to Varanasi. It was nearly October and even if I was to ride non-stop for the next few weeks, I would still be cutting it fine to scale the Himalayas before the snow.

On the plus side, I was as fit as I had ever been in my life. The dysentery had successfully deflated my spare tyre of flesh, my legs were tanned and hard and in India I had stuck to a strict vegetarian diet and drunk not so much as a thimble of alcohol. Even my double chin had disappeared. I had never in my life boasted such an athletic physique. At this rate, I would be modelling Calvin Klein underwear in no time, as long as I didn't freeze my balls off on the way to Lhasa.

The morning I was due to leave Delhi, Mr Anand woke me at 5 a.m. Ever since Paris I had made a concerted effort to leave big cities before dawn. With typical generosity Mr Anand had brought me in some tea on a tray decorated with pink and white rose petals. I showered and dressed and tiptoed out into the forecourt.

Mrs Anand and several other members of the family were waiting beside my bicycle. I squinted at them in the dull light. This must be a dream, I thought. My bicycle, which was normally blue, was bright orange with luminous white handlebars. As I walked closer I saw that the whole frame of the bike had been garlanded with marigolds and the handlebars draped with nosegays of jasmine.

Mrs Anand approached me with a little bowl of red paste. She stuck her thumb in it and marked a tika dot in the middle of my forehead. She then strung a necklace of wild flowers around my neck. I pressed my palms together in thanks. Mr Anand ferreted around in a sack by his side and pulled out a coconut. He held it high above his head and brought it crashing down on the bike's crossbar. It broke into three or four pieces sending the milk showering all over us. 'This is a sign of good luck,' he said proudly.

I instinctively dashed over to inspect the damage to the bike. There was a noticeable dent beneath the marigolds but nothing terminal. The family laughed at my concern. 'Good luck, it's for good luck,' repeated Mr Anand.

'Yes, good luck,' I agreed. 'Absolutely.'

Mrs Anand had laid on an epic breakfast, bowls of ghee and yoghurt, toast and chapattis, a mass of fruit – mangoes, star fruit, bananas – a jug of orange juice and a pot of sweet tea. I was so touched I was speechless.

'Soon you will be a stranger again, Tom,' said Mr Anand. 'I know the feeling. My family used to live in Lahore but were forced out during partition. Delhi is not my real home, but I'm stuck with it now. I have grown fond of it, but in some ways I'm like you.' He slapped my back. 'I'm always a stranger.'

By the time we finished breakfast it was light. Mr and Mrs Anand led me across to the main road and waved me off. And so, with a tika dot on my forehead and garlands of marigolds around my neck, I pedalled out of the Indian capital looking like a throwback to the 1960s in search of peace, love and answers blowing in the wind.

I bowled through India at full speed. What struck me most about the country was the sheer number of people. I never once had a moment's privacy while cycling. Everywhere I stopped, whether a major city or a tiny farming hamlet, I would be swamped by crowds of curious onlookers. But for a lone cyclist this non-stop camaraderie, although at times exhausting, was a boon rather than a bind.

India was the perfect place to bicycle. Not only was my route consistently flat but there was always somewhere to pull over for a cup of reviving *chai*; always something going on to cheer me up, catch my eye or make me think. It might be a brown bear on a lead, a kingfisher or a pied wagtail flitting past, maybe a gang of road builders sledge-hammering at boulders, a buffalo pulling a lawnmower, a multicoloured sunset or a sadhu covered in ashes and bits of mango skin trudging his way to enlightenment.

The Grand Trunk Road was one long carnival, but a dangerous one. Kipling had been right when he described it as 'the river of life'. Tata trucks or ancient buses would come steaming along at top speed, indulging in some daring overtaking. I regularly came across overturned, badly crunched vehicles, their load of logs or cabbages or tinned meat capsized across the bitumen.

In Vrindavan, the Hare Krishna headquarters 130 miles south of Delhi, I slept the night in a crowded ashram. Vrindavan is famous for being the site where Krishna flirted with some *gopis* (shepherdesses) and stole their clothes while they bathed in the river. This made it sound rather fun but Vrindavan was not much fun at all. The Hare Krishnas – many were Westerners on retreat – wandered around with shaven heads and pink robes mumbling mantras. They all looked utterly miserable, as did the tragic white-robed Hindi widows who had travelled to Vrindavan to live out their remaining solitary years as ascetics and beggars.

After the tolerance and generosity of the Sikhs, I found the Krishnas heavy going. I tried talking to some of the Westerners in the ashram but they were withdrawn and stiff. None of them laughed or smiled or volunteered any information about themselves or their faith. They had clearly risen to some sort of higher plane. From the layman's perspective the ashram seemed the most selfish of set-ups; nobody appeared to give a damn about anything except their own salvation. Hare Krishnas believe there is nowhere more holy in all India than Vrindavan and it is easy to see why many Indians look upon it as the perfect place to prepare for death. To me, it also seemed a place where many foreign visitors had already given up on life.

Like everyone who visits India, I stopped off at Agra and rose at dawn to goggle at Shah Jehan's splendid Taj Mahal which he built as a tomb for his wife, Mumtaz Mahal, who died giving birth to their fourteenth child. Despite the twin threats of pollution and countless tourists this seventeenth-century masterpiece is still one of the world's great architectural show-stoppers. Shah Jehan, however, was no soppy romantic; he killed both his elder brothers and their two children in order to gain power. He also had a voracious sexual appetite which he often directed towards the wives of his generals and, according to some accounts, even towards his own exquisitely beautiful daughter, Jaharana. But Shah Jehan, for all his cruelty and promiscuity, is remembered principally for the Taj Mahal.

Perhaps it goes to show a work of great beauty can eclipse its creator's darkest vices: just one look at the Taj Mahal and it is easy to see why.

The extravagant grandeur of the Taj Mahal was in sharp contrast to my night at the International Guesthouse in the village of Karampur, some 120 miles east of Agra.

I had pedalled into Karampur exhausted and soaked to the skin, expecting to spend the night on a charpoy in one of the *chai* houses, the equivalent of a Grand Trunk Road's Little Chefs, but to my delight I saw a sign for THE INTERNATIONAL GUESTHOUSE with a white placard displaying a host of different flags, including a Union Jack painted in red, white and . . . green.

The guest house lawn was abloom with hollyhocks and wild roses, a waterlogged mango tree in the centre. The rooms were simple: mine had a mattress, a bucket shower and a trail of black ants walking along the window sill. Other than a silent heavily wrinkled receptionist I was the only inhabitant. I sat down and read the guest house's comment book by candlelight.

The hostel had been set up in 1980 by a man named S. N. Tripathe in honour of his parents. It was free of charge but, due to its obscure location, less than twenty foreign guests had stopped off since it opened. Those who had stayed tended to be independent travellers, many of them cyclists.

The guest whose comments took up the most space was a man named Steven M. Newman who had spent four years walking around the world, a total of 16,000 miles. He subsequently sent the hostel some excerpts from his book, *World Walk*. His adventure clearly knocked the socks off mine and his book proved 'what a great and beautiful planet we live on'. But after reading a few pages, I got rather fed up with his relentless jollity. Surely all travellers get jaded or grouchy sometimes? Besides, without a few really bad times, you cannot appreciate the really good times. Steven M. Newman's book was like listening to the most uplifting track on an LP again and again, without ever airing any of the bluer numbers. I think I was just jealous though. I consider myself an optimist, but compared with Steven M. Newman I am clearly one of the Horsemen of the Apocalypse.

The following week I cycled deeper into India's most populated state, Uttar Pradesh, (over 150 million people) like a man possessed. I was fit, focused and enjoyed looking at my map at the end of each day, knowing I had sometimes clocked up a hundred miles – a thumb's width closer to Nepal, Hong Kong and Swanbourne. The fitter I became the more I wanted to cycle; exercise had become a drug. I was on a high: the wind on my side; mind, body and soul fused in a rush of energy. Or perhaps I'd just overdosed on the dextrose tablets Phil had sent me. Whatever it was, I did not want to let it go. I decided to speed on until I reached Bodh Gaya, the place where Buddha found enlightenment under a bo tree. That would be a perfect spot to chill out for a day or two.

I blazed down to Kanpur, or Cawnpore as it was once known, the place where in 1857 the first sparks of the Indian Mutiny had ignited. There I spent an hour at All Souls' Memorial Church, in the midst of the town's quiet grassy cantonment, wandering the tombstones.

IN MEMORY OF AN EXCELLENT SON
erected by his parents Admiral and Mrs Martin
JOHN NICKLESON MARTIN

who whilst gallantly fulfilling his duties was treacherously killed by the mutineers on the boats at Cawnpore on 27th June 1857 in his 18th year. The Lord Giveth and the Lord Taketh away. Blessed be the name of the Lord.

Not all of the memorials were so personal, some were simple slabs of stone covered with the names of the dead. IN THE GLORY OF GOD and the Memory of more than a 1,000 Christian people who met there deaths hard by between 6th June – 15th July 1857: Lady Wheeler and daughters, Lieutenant F. G. Jellicoe, wife and children, 10 musicians, women and children . . . Vengeance is mine and I will repay saith the Lord, Romans 12.

I noticed several of the tombstones were in honour of Hodson's Horse, great, great Grandfather Osmond's regiment. One such stone, after a long roll-call of the deceased, simply had the epitaph THY WILL BE DONE.

Thousands of British soldiers and civil servants had dedicated their lives to India. 'How could such an uprising be possible?' must have been the reaction of many an old India hand at the time. Certainly, much of what the British East India Company had achieved in the sub-continent was constructive and well meaning – but, perhaps until the mutiny, had never been questioned as exploitative. This dam-burst of violence from the generally gentle and compliant Indians had shaken the very foundations of the Empire and sparked the need for a far stronger military strategy.

Naturally, the mutiny was eventually put down by the British troops and with brutality. In the capital alone, over 3,000 Delhi wallahs were executed, some shot, some hung and others blown apart when tied to the mouths of cannons. I realized that it was in Kanpur, with all its surfeit of 1857 tombstones, that British colonial supremacy would never again be taken for granted.

From Kanpur I followed the road south. I stopped in Allahabad, the meeting point of three sacred rivers (the Ganges, the Jumna and the mythical Saraswah) and home to the Kumbh

Mela, the biggest religious festival in the world, which attracts up to ten million people. (The next one is in 2001.) I visited sacred Varanasi and took the inevitable sunrise boat trip down Mother Ganga. I did not get to see the city's famous burning ghats though. Apparently electric cremations were now the norm and only one third the price of wood fires. Grey vultures perched on the bank, adding to the funereal ambience. Drifting along with my fellow tourists, I decided there was something magnificently humbling about the Hindu devotion to the Ganges; they could ignore the river's filth, and see only a place of purity and cleansing, a place to drink and wash and swim, to rejoice and be reborn.

At Sasaram, seventy miles on from Varanasi, I camped in a field near the tomb of Sher Shah Suri, the Afghan emperor of India who masterminded construction of the Grand Trunk Road. The beautiful tomb is a domed sandstone building, flecked with blue inlay, in the middle of a lake. I was the only visitor and there was a spectacular sunset that evening, making the experience all the more special.

Finally, I reached Bodh Gaya in Bihar, one of India's poorest states. I had blazed quite a trail to get there. Other than a single day in Varanasi to do my washing, clean the bike and eat some banana pancakes, I had pedalled just about non-stop; 700 miles in ten days and the fastest stretch of the trip. It was now 15 October and at this rate I would reach the Tibet border by 1 November, having covered almost 7,000 miles. I could not have been in better shape to slog up the Himalayas. But nevertheless I wanted a couple of days off.

Bodh Gaya is a tiny place but probably the most important Buddhist pilgrimage site in the world. I stayed at the Burmese monastery, a haven of peace behind a pair of hefty wrought-iron gates. I set myself up in the dormitory opposite the prayer hall where each bed was shielded by a mosquito net. Two pet cows, Lakshmi and Vishnu, wandered around outside grubbing for food. They were the healthiest cattle I had seen for months.

Opposite the monastery was a tent restaurant called the Lotus Pole Pole. Of course meat was off the menu but I was delighted to find the Pole Pole served curd, a rich, sour yoghurt, mixed with honey and nuts. There was also a variety of *thali* dishes and, best of all, banana porridge for breakfast. I knew I was going to like it here.

On my first evening, the Pole Pole was full of Westerners; few were travellers as most had come to Bodh Gaya specifically to study Buddhism. Unlike the Vrindavan ashram where many of the Hare Krishnas had eaten in silence, the trainee Buddhists were a lively bunch, keen to share their experiences.

There was Elisabeth, a buxom Australian who had already spent six months studying Hinduism and was now giving Buddhism a go. There was Chuck, a quiet American with eyes like saucers. He had been intrigued by Buddhism since reading the *Tibetan Book of the Dead*. There was a gawky hippie, who everyone referred to as the Dude, twiddling a string of beads, and finally there was Lotta, a very pretty Swedish girl who didn't really know what she was doing there.

'This meditation is killing me,' said Lotta petulantly. 'I thought it would be so relaxing but it is *so* tough. Sitting there with your legs crossed for hour after hour.'

'Buddhism *is* tough,' replied Elisabeth. 'It's a discipline, not some airy-fairy mystic thing. Buddhism is about extinguishing your cravings, your desires, because only then can you find happiness. Craving leads to greed and sorrow. Good meditation should strip away your cravings.'

'The only thing I crave when I meditate is to swat the bloody mosquitoes landing on my arm,' huffed Lotta.

'You're not supposed to want to kill anything,' said Chuck, laughing. 'The Jains are even more strict than Buddhists. Some of them wander around with mouth guards on so that they don't kill any bugs by swallowing them.'

'Jesus, this country,' sighed Lotta. 'It's so confusing.'

'Listen my darling,' said the Dude, drawling like a spaced-out oracle. 'That's what's so great about India — nobody understands it. It's like religion itself. Yes, siree!'

'Now you've confused me even more,' said Lotta. 'What's your religion, anyway?'

The Dude rubbed his hands on his face and pulled his mane of receding grey hair away from his cheeks. I noticed he had a yin and yang sign tattooed on his forearm.

'My religion, eh,' he said, yawning so hard that his eyes shut. 'Well, I've looked at religions all over the world and Buddhism is the one for me. It's the only faith where you take responsibility for yourself, your own spiritual path, without being reliant on any god. Buddha was a teacher not a deity, as you all know.'

'Sure,' said Lotta, hanging on to his every word.

'Now look at this diagram here.' The Dude pointed to a circle he had drawn which was filled with odd-looking doodles. 'This is the wheel of life. All of life on earth is in this wheel somewhere, whether an animal or a god, a human or a hungry ghost. The only way out of the wheel is to attain an enlightened state, to achieve nirvana.'

'So what's the best way to nirvana?'

'By keeping your faith simple,' replied the Dude solemnly. 'Try to live a good life, help others, be happy, then at least if you don't attain nirvana this lifetime, you might in the next. There's no need to freak out your family by walking around in a yellow robe or anything like that.' He stretched out his arm, once again revealing his tattoo. 'And remember, too much soul searching, whatever the faith, can make you crazy. Just look at me, I'm loopy as an owl.'

'I thought owls were clever!' challenged Lotta.

'In Europe, yes, but not in India,' said the Dude. 'They are considered the silliest bird in the wood. And believe me, I am silly sometimes. Like everyone else, I often forget the most important thing about life: to keep it simple.'

The next day I poked around Bodh Gaya. It might have been little more than a dusty market town but it was rich in good-natured charm and contained representative monasteries of the different Buddhist countries. I spotted a Japanese temple with an immense stern Buddha standing sentinel. There were Bhutanese, Vietnamese and Tibetan temples too, and a Thai temple, reminiscent of a Bangkok wat, where a group of monks in burgundy robes crouched beneath a large parasol.

My final visit was to the Mahabodhi temple, originally built by Ashoka in 3 BC, with its impressive pyramidal spire. To my mind its finest feature was the frieze of different Buddhas running around its lower walls. There were Buddhas with blue hair, Buddhas with four arms, Buddhas with one leg pointing down and one leg up and black Buddhas defaced with graffiti. My favourite was a fat smug Bodhisattva – a divine being who stays within the wheel of life to help mankind attain salvation – who looked like a Sumo wrestler on Valium.

When I went to inspect Buddha's famous bo tree, who should I see underneath it but the Dude. He was wrapped in a white robe and deep in meditation so I did not disturb him. Beside him was an angelic, shaven-headed girl wearing black bell-bottoms. She lay face down on the grass, stretched out, got up and repeated the prostration gracefully, again and again. She looked so peaceful and innocent, I could have watched her for hours. The bo tree, said to be a cutting from the original, was hemmed in by a railing draped with multicoloured prayer flags. The tree's grey bark was ravaged but its trunk remained sturdy.

According to the story Prince Sakyamuni, alias Buddha, arrived at the bo tree after a long journey. The prince had been born near Lumbini in Nepal and, as a child, had been sequestered from suffering by his loving father. As he grew older, however, the young prince witnessed human poverty and sickness first hand and, realizing his privileged life was a sham, shunned it for the pursuit of truth.

After living as an ascetic for six years, supposedly surviving on one grain of rice a day, Sakyamuni was on the verge of death. He finally decided that this was not the best path to take and instead revived himself with a meal and began meditating beneath the bo tree. It was here that he attained nirvana, a state of perfect bliss beyond suffering, free from the cycle of birth and death. Sukyamuni had turned his back on desire, but also on radical asceticism. He had discovered a happy compromise known as the Middle Way, only achievable by following a moral code known as the Four Noble Truths.

It looked as though the Dude had temporarily given up on the Four Noble Truths. His hands were slumped on his lap and his head was lolling from side to side. Either he had attained nirvana or he was fast asleep.

Early the following morning, it was time to hit the road again. I wheeled the bike past Lakshmi and Vishnu who were nuzzling a trellis of honeysuckle on the monastery wall, and then I was off, trying to revive the fierce energy I had felt on the way to Bodh Gaya. But it would not return. It had not helped that my Buddhist friends had urged me to stay, warning me how dangerous the next stage of my journey would be. Their gloomy advice was still ringing in my ears as I pedalled.

'There are bandits everywhere,' Chuck had stressed. 'They will steal from you, beat you up. Whatever you do, don't cycle after dark.'

'Some people say the caste system is dead,' the Dude had told me. 'Not in Bihar. The Untouchables are being killed by the Brahmins and vice versa. It's a hellish situation. The caste system only worked when people respected religion. In Bihar nobody respects anything. The place is run by criminals, including half the police. It's anarchy out there.'

It was a grim picture: the state witnessed over a dozen murders a day and a kidnapping every few hours.

My apprehension took much of the fun out of riding and it became something of a chore clocking up the miles. I tried to be calm and open-minded but Bihar really was grim. The landscape was flat and bleak. There was no energy in the place and even the cattle looked more lacklustre than usual, their bones clearly visible beneath their sagging hides. There was little fresh food and often all that was available at the *chai* shops was the sticky fly-infested local confectionery.

In the slums of Delhi or Bombay I had expected desperate poverty, but until now India's rural poverty had not been so noticeable; the villages had been lively, the people healthy and busy. As I rode north towards Nelanda, the site of the world's oldest Buddhist university, rural India's vitality seemed to dissipate. The children no longer chased my bike, the old men squatting in the *chai* houses no longer waved. The bike was viewed with suspicion or apathy, rather than excitement.

It is easy to romanticize poverty as a traveller. It is easy to reassure yourself that the poor are happy despite having so little. Goodness knows how many times I have soothed my conscience in this way. And in some places this is surely the case. Some villages are self-sufficient, happy with their fruit trees and chickens and buffalo. But many Bihar villages did not even possess these bare essentials: life was clearly tough, anguished, boring and inconsolable. But for all that no one ever tried to rob or hurt me and many people displayed a lazy kindness. After all, in India there is always hope, if not this time around, then possibly on the next spin of the wheel of life.

The most surprising incident I faced in Bihar was on arrival in Patna, the state's run-down capital, at the height of the Dusshera festival. Dusshera celebrates the victory of Lord Ram over the army of Ravanna, the demon king. Patna's army of revellers was certainly out in force when I reached the centre of town after a long weary pedal through the city's slums, dodging open drains, dogs and stone-throwing children.

I have never in my life seen such a throng of people as there was that night. To get to my hotel in Exhibition Road from the town centre would have taken five minutes on a normal evening. That night it took me over an hour. The crowd was running against me and there was nothing I could do about it.

Buffalo with painted horns trotted by pulling cartfuls of Hindu Gods: Durga riding on a tiger, multi-armed Kali the destroyer with her necklace of skulls, and popular Ganesh, Siva and Parvati's son, with his elephant head. A group of boys was standing on the back of one of the tumbrils throwing red and green powder over everyone.

I could not believe the numbers of tiny children amid the mayhem, some in makeshift papooses, others clasped to their mothers like baby bears, one or two held high on shoulders. Everybody seemed impervious to the racket, the incense, the heat. They were all having a great time but I just wanted to crash; it had been a long day. I was the only white face in the crowd, something I normally relished, but tonight it gave me no thrill. Perhaps it was a sign I was ready to leave India, or at least Bihar. I was going slowly mad.

Eventually, I made it to the Shyma Hotel on Exhibition Road. I checked into a grungy room with mouse droppings under the bed and then went to fetch my panniers. The two Bihari receptionists watched as I dragged my bike up the stairs, pausing at every step. When I asked for help they laughed and I shouted at them like a maniac. They shrugged their shoulders, one of them spitting a gob of betel juice on the floor. I finally made it to my room and collapsed on to the unforgiving mattress.

Indians live like this all the time, I told myself, stop being such a prima donna. But I was a Westerner and I was sick of the poverty. Unlike the Biharis, I had the option to get out; I had no need to live like this. Soon I would be tucking into chocolate cake in Kathmandu. Stop feeling sorry for yourself, Fremantle. And why had I shouted at the receptionists like that? Who the hell did I think I was? What was I turning into?

Outside, the noise of the crowd was reaching a crescendo. I glugged down a litre of boiled water from my bottle and curled into a ball. For the first time on the trip I was stung by an unbearable sense of loneliness.

Three days later – 26 October – I made it to Raxaul, the deadbeat border town which would lead me into Nepal. I sat down on a stool in one of the canteen shacks and ordered a slice of treacle tart – a celebratory indulgence for completing India. The tart was wrapped in newspaper which I unfolded as the *chai* wallah, a friendly man in a grubby dhoti, poured me tea from a saucepan. I needed the tea to warm me up; for the first time in months I was wearing a jumper.

Unlike the lama in *Kim* who found enlightenment at the end of his journey down the Grand Trunk Road, in many ways India had simply baffled me. I had cycled over 1,200 miles through this maddening landscape, mingled with people from every age, every faith and caste, but still understood so little. I liked India for its refusal to be pigeonholed and for the generosity of spirit that rises above its myriad woes. Of all the countries I had traversed, it was the one where people most wanted to see my trip succeed. They had egged me on, complimented me, told me I would make it as if their own lives depended on it. Although I did not appreciate it at the time, India was a tremendous inspiration.

The India I had seen had been a land of dreamers, some simple like Lattan Baba with his dream of rolling to salvation and others more ambitious like Mahatma Gandhi with his dream of uniting the country; but dreamers all the same.

In many ways Kipling's lama was reflective of Indians everywhere, dreaming of their next spin on the wheel of life, and no doubt wondering about it made even the starkest of lives seem all the more bearable.

CHAPTER SIXTEEN

KATHMANDU

The Himalayas were always going to be the Becher's Brook of my journey – the obstacle that would send me either charging towards the finishing line like Red Rum or bruised and limping back to my stable. This metaphor struck me as I sat in Birganj, the Nepali border town, armed with a mug of Iceberg beer, writing up my diary. As it was my first alcoholic drink in months it took hold in no time at all. My diary became less and less legible and its final profound entry for that evening (25 October) read, 'BECHER'S BROOK! PUSHBIKE! Sod that!'

But this was no time to be defeatist. I had always known that the Himalayas could easily destroy my trip, just as they had the potential to provide its finest hour. Besides it would be good to be off the flat, to push myself again. For most of the time in India I had been on auto-pedal, clocking up the miles with long easy sprints.

On the second evening, after a straightforward ride from Birganj over some preliminary hills, I stopped off at the village of Hitauda which is only about eighty miles from Kathmandu. An easy day's ride; or so I thought. I certainly hadn't counted on my toughest cycling to date.

In Hitauda I camped in the grounds of a ski-chalet-type

lodge called the Avocado Motel, a homely place festooned with pine and eucalyptus. There were also, predictably, several avocado trees, the fruit of which provided the motel's speciality, 'Avocado Milky Shake', without doubt the most execrable drink known to human lips; although to be fair, I had not yet sampled Tibet's yak butter tea, a beverage in a league of horror of its own.

At the Avocado I found the customary comment book: it did not make for inspiring reading. Not only did I discover that hundreds of cyclists had braved this road before me, (always disappointing) but that they had, without exception, found the ride to be everything from 'gruelling' to 'ball breaking'. One wag had added that 'the only downhill bits are the pot holes'. A Japanese cyclist called Hideo who had pedalled up mountains all over the world – the Andes, the Atlas, the Karakoram Highway – claimed the steep pass to Daman was 'a monster'.

It was hard to disagree with him, even from the comfort of the motel sofa. Analysing the contours on my map, I realized I would have to ride over several high passes, one of them, the Symbhanjang, at almost 2,500 metres. In one day I would have more of an uphill climb than I had faced at any time over the previous two months. It was at times like this that I wished I had been blessed with an ancestor who had done something less ambitious than Captain Charles; sailed to St-Tropez perhaps, or circumnavigated Belgium in a sedan chair with a case of Krug and an entourage of comely masseusses.

I rose the next morning at dawn. After eating a bowl of porridge and a couple of boiled eggs, I carried out a number of stretching exercises. I then drank two cups of coffee, brushed my teeth and drank another cup of coffee. And then a cup of tea. I was doing anything to postpone the agony of those first hills. I remembered the pain of Passo Bracco and the tortuous ride into Jerusalem and multiplied it several times. Look on the bright side, I told myself; at least I'm not Lattan Baba wrapped in a dhoti and rolling over the high passes.

Eventually I could procrastinate no longer. I attached my panniers and pushed off towards the mountains. Surprisingly, the first three miles turned out to be downhill. I freewheeled beneath the palms, admiring the riot of yellow and blue flowers along the verges. Just before the first incline a soldier waved me down. He was wearing a wide-brimmed hat with a red madras band. He did not want to check anything, just to say hello and admire the bike. He smiled a kind embarrassed smile and wished me, 'Namas-te,' a Sanskrit word that all Nepalis use meaning, I salute you.

And then I was off again, inching my way up the rugged switchbacks towards the village of Kalitar, 300 metres up. The road was steep and badly pitted, with a hard shoulder that had disintegrated into a shaly crumble. The surface made for uncomfortable cycling, jarring my tyres and even on one occasion dislodging my handlebar pannier. For the first time on the trip I had to concede that a mountain bike would have been better, at least for this stretch.

On the plus side I felt strong and motivated. I had forgotten how much I loved mountains: the shifting mists, the damp intimacy, the shriek and chatter of wildlife and even the serpentine roads.

I was off to a good start.

At Kalitar, a village of crudely thatched huts, I stopped for a break. A young girl poured me tea from a sooty kettle suspended above a fire. Unlike India, where whole villages would inspect the bike, here only a little cluster of people assembled and even then kept a safe distance. The other villagers gave me a cursory glance and continued with their work lugging water buckets or harvesting reeds.

Two barefoot Sherpas struggled by, one with a blue gas cylinder which he carried by means of a strap around his forehead, the other with a hessian sack full of cabbages. The girl poured me some more tea. She looked no more than sixteen with wide pretty eyes and a tika dot made from grains of dyed rice.

The sky had turned the bluey grey of a pigeon's wing, unsure whether to rain or not. I remounted the bike and plugged on up the rough bitumen. I was coping with 200–300 metres at a time, then collapsing and admiring the wonderful views: buffalo submerged in a muddy quagmire, the moonscape of a craggy neighbouring peak and, best of all, the sight of swirling loops of conquered road.

Apart from the odd motorbike or jam-packed bus, vehicles were scarce. It was wonderfully peaceful. Progress was slow and steady but, by mid-afternoon, I had climbed to over 1,800 metres and reached the village of Mahaveer. I was physically drained and punch drunk from the vibrations of the rattling bike. I sat down beside a stack of maize, drank some water, ate some biscuits and dozed off.

I was woken by a child running past spinning a large hoop. Standing up, still slightly dazed, I limbered up my stiffened limbs. I suddenly realized I was very cold; my sweat had chilled and a heavy fog had descended on the village. Visibility was so poor I could only just make out the silhouettes of the surrounding mountains. At the local *chai* house a group of men in dark fezzes surrounded a *carom* match. *Carom* is a very popular game, in which counters are flicked along a smooth small board. It's like a cross between snooker and Subbuteo, but rowdier than both. I watched for a few minutes before pushing on.

I had been on the road for about seven hours now and, apart from the odd tea break, had pedalled relentlessly. In less than 600 metres I would reach the Symbhanjang Pass, the highest point, but I was flagging badly. The fog had turned into a real pea-souper, as if the clouds had fallen to earth. My precious horizon had gone, which always disorientated me; I could only try to imagine it now.

After another 200 metres up a zigzagging hill I reached Aghor, the last village before the pass. I had not planned to stop but it was just too tempting. I leant the bike against the sagging shack of a *chai* shop and dashed into its dark smoky interior. A rosy-cheeked woman with a nose ring and a necklace of glass baubles ladled out a bowl of rice pudding while her snot-nosed son pointed a pistol at my head and fired off a round of caps. On the wall was a Bollywood film poster and a picture of the goddess Kali with her countless arms. I ate the warm pudding like a Neanderthal, shovelling it into my mouth with my fingers. It tasted magnificent.

I had only 400 metres to go before the pass but the invisible sky was spitting cold hard rain. I zipped up my Gore-Tex jacket and flicked the bike up a couple of gears. I was getting very wet now and needed to push myself harder. It was important to reach Daman before dark, to keep myself moving.

The final stretch cut through the woods in a series of jackknife turns. There was nobody else around, just me and the fog and the dull outlines of the surrounding trees. My legs were wobbly with fatigue and soon I was back in the lowest gear. I tried the old trick of shouting at myself to keep going. I howled and cursed and whistled and sang and somehow managed to keep my legs turning. The thin mountain air was making my pulse race but my pace remained miserably slow. I almost resorted to Brambilla's tactics, whacking my thighs with a bicycle pump to speed up. But before I had the chance, I struck an awkward rut and fell off. The fall grazed my knee but not badly, just a spot of blood. I could not face getting back on the bike though, and anyway, in this state, I decided it would be quicker to walk. I suddenly felt wretched: weak, tired and rather scared. But I need not have worried.

Two minutes after beginning to push, I found myself at the top of the Symbhanjang Pass. If the fog had not been so thick, I would have been able to see the Daman sign some way back and kept riding, clearing Becher's Brook in triumph. As it was, after a day of Herculean athleticism (at least by my standards) I had fallen at the last, two minutes from victory, and was now limping home like a drunken muleteer.

Still, who cared? I had made it. In fact I felt terrific. Here I was 2,478 metres, above the world, the fog swirling, the rain spitting and safe in the knowledge it was mostly downhill to Kathmandu from here. I'd pedalled forty miles uphill on a loaded bicycle. I was entitled to be shattered.

'I've done it,' I whispered to myself, punching the air. 'I've cleared Becher's bloody Brook.' I freewheeled down through the fog towards Daman. The village was less than a hundred metres below me but still completely invisible, shrouded in a ghostly haze.

The cycle down to Kathmandu was a doddle. Down, down, down. Down past the terraced paddies, down past the gravel diggers, the bulldozers and the flocks of white doves, down through the puddles and potholes, beneath the arches of frangipani and banana palms. Up briefly over the Naam Dungha Pass and then down, down, down into the splendid pandemonium of Barkhor Square, among the tiered pagodas and the temple spires of Nepal's ancient capital.

To arrive at Kathmandu on a bicycle is an overwhelming experience, especially at rush hour. The first things you notice are the eyes: bright painted eyes peering from the sides of the stupas (small temples), the cake shop windows and the T-shirts of the travellers. Wherever you go Buddha is watching you with a calm meditative gaze. But fighting for your attention are the hawkers with their *kukri* knives and Tibetan prayer wheels, their Javanese masks and Indian carpets. 'Anything you want, gentleman,' they shout. 'Anything.' And somehow, here you believe it.

I was pushing against the tide, dodging the children with painted faces, the half-naked holy man holding up a candle. The blood of a slaughtered animal seeped through the cobbles, holy cows slumped in the dust, one of Freak Street's few remaining hippies busked in his Jesus sandals and baggy trousers but everywhere there were eyes, Buddha eyes, watching.

I did the rounds of Freak Street's guest houses, many of which were full but I finally found a terrific place, tucked in at the end of an alley overrun with flowering creepers. The room was £1.50 a night with a view over a garden dominated by a grapefruit tree.

This was all too good to be true. I could spend two or three days here and still make it to the Tibetan border by 1 November. That meant tonight I could go out, have a drink, meet a few fellow travellers, perhaps go dancing and have some fun. I had been dreaming of a night like this for ages. The last couple of weeks had been very isolated, highlighted by that lonely evening in Patna.

I put on my only clean T-shirt and began to trawl the capital for a likely nightspot. Kathmandu had long been a travellers' oasis: a place to relish western comforts — videos, chocolate cake, crisp sheets — to recharge after the frustrations of India, the restrictions of Tibet, and the rigours of a trek to Everest Base Camp. Freak Street freaks had long since moved on to Phnom Penh and Dali. Kathmandu's new army of travellers comprised freaks of the fitness variety. In Gore-Tex boots and fleece jackets they marched the cobbles, lungs free of hash, pockets full of cash.

I looked around at the signs: THE REALLY CUTE LITTLE SHOP, KUMARI LODGE, MONA LISA, NAMAS-TE VEGETARIAN FOODS, MOVIES TONIGHT, BOOK SWAP, E-MAIL. I eventually plumped for a pseudo Italian restaurant and ate a clammy lasagne. The atmosphere in the place was not conducive to conversation as everyone was watching a film called *12 Monkeys*, a strange affair with Brad Pitt speaking gobbledegook and not a monkey in sight. After this lonely episode, I was lured into a nearby bar called Carpe Diem, which had a *Betty Blue* film poster on the wall and Ian Dury on the jukebox. I felt at odds with the place. It had been so long since I had spoken to anyone properly that I had lost all social confidence. Besides, unlike many travellers' bars, the drinkers were in close-knit groups that were hard to infiltrate. I sat at the bar eating chocolate cake and listening to snippets of conversation.

'You know the Gurkhas can only be selected from the mountains, not from Kathmandu?' shouted a hearty English voice over 'Hit me with your Rhythm Stick'. 'They breed them tough in the hills. Terrifying little guys. Over twenty VCs between them. They still use them as the enemy at Sandhurst, you know.'

'What is this music?' whined an American girl. 'Haven't they got any Alanis Morissette or anything?'

'I'm working on a permaculture project near Pokhara,' said another voice, perhaps Dutch or German. 'No, I'm not quite sure what permaculture is, either.'

'Have you visited any prisoners yet?' I suddenly realized this question was directed at me. 'Hey, you there, I said have you been to the prison?'

'The prison, er, no,' I stammered. 'Why should I?'

'I'll tell you.' The voice belonged to a very earnest girl who spoke like she had just swallowed a balloon full of helium. Her name was Jacqueline. She explained that Kathmandu prison was home to several Western prisoners serving long sentences, most of them for smuggling or possessing drugs. She quickly wrote me a list of European and American inmates desperate for company and told me the best times to visit.

'Take along some food or a book,' she said, and after noticing my apprehension added, 'They don't bite, you know.'

And then she was off, cornering Carpe Diem's other customers, her helium voice battling to be heard above the strains of 'Reasons to be Cheerful (PT.3)'.

My wild night in Kathmandu had not materialized, but it did not bother me. I'd enjoyed the lasagne and chocolate cake and hearing a few old Ian Dury songs. At home that would have constituted a very dreary night out but here, up in the mountains, my body weary, my soul at peace, it was all I wanted. I went back to my room and slumped down on my bed. It was 8.30 p.m.

The following day I had a number of chores to do. Kathmandu, as the hawkers promised, did have anything I could possibly want. This was especially true of Tamel, the principal travellers' hang out, a mass of winding streets filled with every commodity imaginable: bootleg CDs, jazzy waistcoats and even such luxuries as Dextrose tablets and Kendal Mintcake. Some of the shops could have been in Oxford or Cheltenham – glass-fronted with fancy window displays – but others were wonderfully ramshackle with wooden eaves and musty interiors.

What surprised me more than anything was the amount of bicycle gear on offer. I was able to purchase new bungees and screws for my rack, a bulb for my front light, a can of WD40 and some fresh puncture-repair glue. The staff at the shop even provided a tub of petrol to clean up the bike chain, which had been peppered with grit.

While I was fiddling with the chain, one of the mechanics

began tampering with my rear wheel hub. By the time I turned around, my worst fear had been realized. All the tiny ball-bearings from the hub assembly had tumbled out on to the shop's grubby floor and the springs holding them had also pinged off. The mechanic, who was a Nepali version of Phil (without the Lord Kitchener moustache) looked down and tut-tutted. I glared at him in anger and despair. Did he realize this was a highly specialized bit of kit he had dismantled? He looked at me and smiled, the way Nepalis do. He then calmly picked up the bearings and springs one by one and, with podgy but dextrous fingers, greased the bearings and jammed back all the tiny springs holding them in place with a strip of cotton. They slotted in perfectly and he gave the wheel a vigorous spin to prove that it was a job well done.

'The bearings need grease very bad,' he said.

'Where did you learn to do that?'

'Many cyclist pass here,' he said. 'My family help broken foreigners for many years!' He made it sound as if his family had fixed Alexander the Great's chariot.

'*Namas-te*,' I said, handing over some cash, which he calmly handed straight back.

The practicalities dealt with, I still had plenty of time to visit one of Jacqueline's prisoners. I pedalled off into Tamel's madding crowds. Twenty minutes later I reached the city jail, a grim tangle of cells near the main post office. The prisoner I had come to see was a man called Stuart. I filled out various forms, showed my passport and was led by a lethargic warder to a row of chairs opposite a set of latticed peepholes.

Jacqueline had already given me the lowdown on Stuart at Carpe Diem. He was twenty-three and halfway through a five-year sentence for drug smuggling.

'Hi,' Stuart said from behind the grille. 'Good of you to see me.' He had cropped fair hair and earrings hanging from both lobes. His conversation was animated but edgy, unable to focus on one subject for more than a few seconds. He began by telling me about his crime, which had been to smuggle a bag of hash from Kathmandu airport.

'It was pretty minor really,' said Stuart. 'Nepal is known as a soft drugs sort of place, it's Burma and Pakistan where the big heroin and opium boys operate. I was just unlucky. A small fry in the wrong place at the wrong time. I suppose I was bound to get nicked eventually.'

He was speaking very frankly and I was concerned the prison guards might pick up on the conversation.

'Don't worry about them,' replied Stuart, gesturing to the row of warders. 'Half the guards are prisoners anyway. After two years, if a prisoner has shown good behaviour, he can work here as a guard himself. Only Nepalis mind you; the foreigners don't get that privilege.'

'So why did you smuggle the drugs?'

'Long story, mate. I've been an orphan since the age of three, used to live at this home in Kilburn. I was offered my first job aged sixteen by one of the older boys, smuggling a little bag of charlie from Amsterdam. It earned me a few hundred quid. I didn't look back.

'I've done a lot of runs, see. I've got a house in Milton Keynes, a Harley-Davidson, used to have plenty of girls. I'm owed a bit of money too. I'll be all right when I get out, but I won't deal in drugs again. Five years is a long time to be sitting around in a cell. Do you know I've been in Nepal for over two years now and not even seen the mountains. Crazy. It makes me sad to think that I've wasted so much time.'

Stuart told me his cellmate was a Polish man who had overstayed his visa in Nepal by two years. He had been sentenced to ten years.

'The guy is depressed as hell,' explained Stuart. 'All he needs is someone to pay ten thousand dollars and he's out, but none of his family can afford to, or are prepared to. Poor bugger. He's pretty close to the edge.'

'You seem fairly upbeat though.'

'I guess I am. You might as well be philosophical about it. Besides it's giving me masses of time to read. Trash mainly but I've had a go at a couple of books on Buddhism.'

I thought this would be a good opportunity to present my book: *Gulliver's Travels*, which I had just finished. I handed the book to a guard who took it round to him.

'I thought it might help you travel out of your cell.'

'It's a nice idea,' he said, looking at the cover. 'But I think I'll have to wait three more years for that.' The guard hinted that it was time for him to go back. 'Know what the first thing I'll do when I get out of here, when I get back home?' Stuart mused. 'I'll eat a full cooked breakfast then take my Harley for a spin in the country. That's what I call freedom.'

He smiled at the thought of it and nodded farewell. Together, he and the guard walked quickly away.

The following morning I headed off for Kodari, the town nearest the Tibetan border. Only another sixty-odd miles. I was sad to be leaving this little kingdom in the hills. Nepal is something of an oddity as it is very much its own place, being one of the few Asian countries – China and Thailand being the other notable exceptions – that was never fully colonized. That said, many believe the flood of tourists and trekkers to Nepal over the last decade is just a different form of colonization.

Indeed the effects of modernization are starting to permeate beyond Tamel. I became most aware of this on my way north out of the capital, heading towards Tibet. Although the road has some of the most beautiful scenery in the world, cycling through it I felt that something was wrong: unlike on my relaxed ride up through Birganj and Hitauda, the children here automatically shouted 'one rupee' or 'one pen' as soon as I came into view. Their begging was aggressive and they would sometimes throw stones at the bike.

In the hills beyond Bhaktapur, billboards began to appear. EVEREST VIEW and HIMALAYA PARADISE they advertised, irritatingly blocking off any glimpse of a view or paradise. These developments would no doubt provide a few jobs for well-educated Nepalis, but could also upset the rural equilibrium for ever. Small guest houses and hotels are fine, but surely concrete pleasure domes have no place here.

FOR THE BEST VIEW IN NEPAL blazed the biggest of the billboards, JUST RELAX. WE BRING THE MOUNTAINS TO YOU. But it was heartening to know that beyond these shallow messages towered an infinity of brilliant peaks stretching east and west, north and south, far from the clutches of mankind, as immutable as Buddha's many eyes.

CHAPTER SEVENTEEN

BUDDHAS AND WALNUTS

Crossing the Friendship Bridge on the way to the Tibetan border, was nerve-racking. Butterflies fluttered in my new slimline belly and my left hand, the one holding the passport, was gently shaking.

The Chinese border guard was wearing a pair of red slippers and a uniform the colour of spinach. He looked about thirteen years old and spat into the air with casual insouciance. None of this would have bothered me much were it not for the fact that the future of my trip rested on his decision. If this gobbing oik turned me down, I would have to retreat along the Friendship Highway to Kathmandu and fly into China. The only overland alternative would be to backtrack through Nepal and India, re-enter Pakistan and slog up the Karakoram Highway and into China via Kashgar – a near-impossible detour.

I knew groups of tourists were allowed into Tibet but that arrangements were strictly supervised by the CITS, the Chinese Travel Service. These arrangements could also prove very expensive, anything up to £350 to be escorted to Lhasa in a four-wheel drive. It was an outrageous rip-off. Anyone who had purchased a Chinese visa in Kathmandu had to follow this option, but the fact I had secured mine in Delhi meant I might slip through the net. My only other hope was that I would be taken for a madman, cycling to Lhasa in November, a time even the yaks consider off-season.

'This OK,' said the teenage soldier, smiling politely and stubbing out his cigarette. 'You go.'

'Thank you,' I said, the butterflies in my belly turning to dust. I snatched back my documents before he changed his mind. 'Thank you very much.'

'No problem,' he said, gobbing at his feet this time. I suddenly felt pity for him, stuck out here in an alien land, probably through no choice of his own. No wonder he spent the day hawking bile and smoking Lucky Strikes; apart from scanning the odd passport, there was little else for him to do. Home for him was a distant memory, just as it was for the thousands of exiled Tibetans living in Dharmsala and Kathmandu. My pity did not last long though as my mood was one of jubilation: after all I was now in the Land of the Snows, a place some still referred to as Shangri-La.

What made me doubly happy about my border triumph was the fact I had proven the doom-mongers wrong. So many of the travellers I'd met over the last few months had told me I had no chance of infiltrating Tibet. Of course they had not been to Tibet themselves, but they had been assured by so-and-so or a friend of so-and-so that it was a no-go area. And on a bicycle! Forget it. To be fair, most of them were only trying to help, to prevent me wasting my time. But when travelling one has to be very selective when it comes to advice, to take on board the valuable and ignore the hyperbole.

Problems of a more physical nature began to present themselves. The three-mile road leading up to Zhangmu, Tibet's first pitstop, was not only fantastically steep but about as comfortable to ride as a bobsleigh going over a cattle grid. It was also waterlogged. After the first mile, the bike was all but shaken to pieces. I resorted to pushing, slipping and sliding up the wretched road, and my tracksuit bottoms were soon spattered with mud.

When I arrived at Zhangmu, dripping with sweat despite the morning chill, there was another border crossing and I realized that this was the true entrance to Tibet. A Chinese soldier in a tunic with brass buttons and an oversized Mao cap ushered me towards the checkpoint. Oh God. Please no, not again. I thought my passport had already been stamped. I opened it up. Bugger, not a trace.

There were three desks, each manned by an official with red chevrons on the shoulders of his uniform. The last desk had a misspelt cardboard sign hanging from it: HELTH CHECK. I pictured a vigorous examination involving stethoscopes, coughing and urine samples. But it was all very straightforward. My passport was passed quickly along the sour-faced trio and stamped twice before being handed back, no questions asked.

Home and dry.

Well not quite. It was Sunday and I had no local currency. I knew I needed to pay a ten-yuan fee at the CITS office (payment in dollars unacceptable) before I could move on. I would have to wait until the bank opened on Monday before I headed off. There was also a two-and-a-half-hour time difference between Nepal and Tibet, which meant it was already early afternoon. Oh well, I had seen worse places than Zhangmu.

Zhangmu was ramshackle, with the atmosphere of a Wild West frontier town. A seedy bar with a karaoke machine was sandwiched between a number of lopsided huts. An electrical store with a satellite dish sticking from its door was beside a Tibetan butcher's shop with goats' legs hanging from its awnings.

What struck me most was that there were as many Chinese as Tibetans. I had expected this in the big towns like Lhasa and Shigatse, but not out here, a stone's throw from Nepal.

Apart from the soldiers, the majority of the Han Chinese seemed to be shopkeepers eager to milk the flourishing trading links with Kathmandu. They sold sleeping bags and radios, cans of Fanta and bottles of Head and Shoulders shampoo.

But the Chinese did not really look at home here in Zhangmu. The men wore light suits and cheap brogues, their hair slick with gel, whereas their wives favoured silk shirts and anoraks. They sat around, rubbing themselves to stave off the cold, babbling on telephones and slurping noodles.

In contrast the Tibetans strolled around like highwaymen, their plaited hair wrapped in scarlet rope, their faces burnished by the sun and wind to a russet-brown, their clothes a lucky dip of donkey jackets, felt trousers, yak-skin ponchos and broken plimsolls. Many of them were covered in dirt. 'Tashi dele,' they said as they marched by, laughing amongst themselves. Many of them were Kham-pas, the wild warrior race from eastern Tibet.

I spent the night as the only guest in the town's sole hotel. The 'Zhangmu' was a Chinese-run labyrinth of long drab corridors, cold draughts and anarchic plumbing. I almost expected a sinister oriental version of Daphne du Maurier's Mrs Danvers to appear with a mug of poisoned Horlicks. But the hotel's one saving grace was its staff, a group of chubby Chinese girls in blue uniforms who kept sneaking into the dormitory, ostensibly to fill my hot-water thermos but really to gawp at my bicycle. The most confident of the group, a bob-haired tomboy with high ruddy cheekbones, gestured that she would like to take it for a pedal.

I unhooked the panniers, stuck the bike in low gear and wheeled it over to her. With a look of delight she pushed it into the foyer and, for the next hour, the girls took it in turns to pedal up and down the hotel's gloomy corridors. The excitement it stirred in them – simply pedalling a bicycle

Arrival at Lhasa, which at 3,606 metres is the highest capital city in the world. In the background is the imposing Potala Palace, the Dalai Lama's principal home before he was forced to flee to India after the Chinese invaded in 1950.

The loneliest bicycle in Tibet. One of the more remote stretches of
the Friendship Highway, the road which links Kathmandu and Lhasa.

Two fashionably hatted Tibetans outside the Tashilhunpo Monastery in Shigatse.
They are laughing at my diary – even though it is being held upside down!

The magnificent seven – my ever-hospitable Chinese
bunk-mates during the ferry ride down the Yangtze River.

Teacher Zhao Xiong performing a spirited version of
'Jingle Bells' at the Christmas party in Changsha.

The bicycle posing by a milestone in Vietnam.

Vietnamese children in Hanoi's Old Quarter.

Vietnamese newly-weds, with the groom sporting almost as much make-up as the bride.

Right: Vietnamese cyclists on the road to Saigon.

Below: One of the Bayon's many faces, just part of the beautiful Khmer ruins at Angkor in north-west Cambodia.

Above: Cambodian girl outside the Bayon temple.

Left: Some of the 8,000 skulls in the Memorial Stupa at Choeung Ek in Cambodia's Killing Fields.

Claire in Kuala Lumpur, respectfully
enshrouded in pink muslin.

One of Malaysia's morale-crushing
gradient signs.

Electioneering by the mob – chanting Golkar supporters ride through
the streets of Dili, East Timor, in the build-up to the Indonesian elections.

Sashi, an indefatigable Japanese walker, who was pushing an overloaded wheelbarrow 2,600 miles between Perth and Darwin. When asked why on earth she was doing it, she told me: 'I like walking.'

My parents at Cable Beach, Broome.

My bicycle was my home – or at least contained my home, a versatile North Face tent, which throughout the journey was pitched everywhere from the lawn of the Young Women's Christian Association in Pakistan to the forecourt of a petrol station in the Jordanian desert.

After 12,763 miles, fifty-six punctures and a severely jeopardised sperm count, I finally make it to the signpost I have been dreaming about for over a year.

along a grubby floor – was quite wonderful to witness. Watching them made me appreciate my own luck, my own spectacular freedom.

The following morning was overcast with grey cloud. I walked up the main street to the bank, which was no bigger than Swanbourne Post Office. There I changed US$100 into yuan and paid off the CITS. A soldier in camouflage combat fatigues with a snub-nosed pistol hanging from his belt stamped the necessary wad of papers. If I stayed in Tibet much longer I would need a new pannier to cope with all the filing.

'Lansly,' the soldier shouted after me. 'Lansly, ten kilometre. OK, mister.'

Lansly? What the hell was he talking about? And then I remembered a sign I had seen on the way up to Kodari: LANDSLIDE FALLING AREA Just my luck, a bloody landslide in ten kilometres. Or maybe camouflage pants was just joking, trying to wind me up. I'd find out soon enough.

The road north was less steep than the Zhangmu hill but equally rugged. I remained in the very lowest gear and within five minutes my breathing had become heavy and my heart was beating faster than Keith Moon's drumsticks. But I felt terrific; the air was so fresh it was almost drinkable. I was thankful I had not suffered any headaches due to the altitude yet. The fact that I had inched my way up the gradients on a bicycle, rather than by speedier transport, must have helped.

Soon Zhangmu was out of sight and the horizon had turned into a dreamscape. The sun had burnt off even the faintest wisps of cloud leaving a brilliant blue sky. The dark ridge of pines on the horizon was topped by a single snow-capped peak, all the more magnificent for its isolation.

Soon my thoughts were focused on less ethereal matters. As the camouflaged soldier had warned me, after about seven miles

I came across a queue of trucks, delayed by the landslide. It was easy to see how these avalanches of rock could occur, with the surrounding mossy scree so friable and loose.

Various makeshift tents had been erected at the edge of the road, beyond the snake of delayed traffic. In one of them was a brightly dressed Tibetan selling boiled eggs and cans of Jin Li Bau, a popular Chinese drink that tasted of fizzy tangerine. Others sold tea and packets of instant noodles or chewing gum and lollipops. Having stopped pedalling, I soon became cold and hitched up with a Tibetan family in one of the larger canvas shelters. The whole tent was blanketed in smoke from a yak dung fire burning on the earth floor. Through the haze I could make out a woman with jewels in her hair and a baby in a papoose. The woman smiled, revealing a gold tooth. Her baby's face looked filthy. When she lifted it from the papoose, I noticed that the child's jumpsuit had a vent in the backside, obviating the need for nappies.

'Dalai Lama picture,' said the mother. It was to become a familiar request throughout Tibet. I had no Dalai Lama pictures but showed her the pictures of Tibetan scenes in my guidebook, which she seemed to enjoy, pointing delightedly if she recognized one of the monasteries: 'Potala, Jokhang, Dreprung.' She reeled off the names as if they were old friends.

Over a bowl of noodles I read my book, *Danziger's Travels*, which I had bought in a Kathmandu second-hand store. With each page I became increasingly envious of the intrepid Danziger, who made an extraordinary solo journey along the Silk Road in the mid eighties. Not only had he travelled right through the Ayatollah's Iran and war-torn Afghanistan (where he teamed up with the Mujahedin) but he was the first traveller ever to officially be stamped over the Khunjerab Pass between Pakistan and China. What's more he had still found the time to make love to several beautiful and exotic women. Some guys have all the luck; my most amorous encounter to date was a bear-hug from a shaggy Afghan shepherd. Oh well, at least Alexandra would be waiting in Hong Kong.

But in many ways I could not have been happier. I had made it into the heart of the Himalayas, after all. The stars had never looked brighter. That night they were luminous spangles of light spread out like a shattered chandelier. Orion was clearly visible as were many other constellations and I was sorry I did not know their names. I sat out, entranced, until I began shivering with cold and then returned to my smoky shelter to sleep a night filled with hopeful dreams.

The following morning I was startled awake by a series of blasts which echoed across the valley, detonations from way up the road. The noise hung in the air for some time, like the humming of a wineglass tapped by cutlery. The Tibetan lady laughed at my surprise and poured me a cup of tea. I took a grateful slurp and winced. Oh God, I had been warned about this stuff, yak butter tea.

I sipped some more. It was true; it really was the most appalling drink on earth. Liquefied rancid butter for breakfast just does not go down well with a palate accustomed to years of Honey Nut Cornflakes. But I also knew that to refuse this greasy beverage would be offensive to my hostess. As I sipped, I mastered a technique of shutting down my sense of smell in order to make the taste less lip-curling. I also sipped slowly to prevent the need for refills. Despite tasting like a mixture of sour milk and antifreeze, yak butter tea is actually an excellent source of body insulation. That morning, my warmth was further increased by thermal underwear, gloves, bobble hat and Gore-Tex jacket. It felt good to be wearing all my kit for the first time since France; it justified lugging it through thousands of miles of sunshine.

After breakfast, I was all set to tackle the road to Nyalam.

My Tibetan hostess, baby still strapped to her back, came over to see me off. She wrapped a white *kathak* scarf around my neck to bring good luck. It was a touching and totally unexpected gesture. The scarf was the equivalent of a prayer flag, tied tight under the chin.

And then I was off, pedalling up the freshly cleared track. Apart from one livestock truck with a dead battery and another with a lopsided load of logs, most of yesterday's traffic jam had dispersed. The only vehicle that overtook me was a Toyota Landcruiser full of tourists, the pennant on its bonnet snapping in the wind. 'Keep going mate,' an Australian voice shouted out as it roared past.

It was a beautiful morning. I traversed gently flowing brooks, passed beneath thundering waterfalls and rode through dark forests with the distant white peaks always providing a tempting horizon. But it was hard work. Nyalam was 3,750 metres high and my breathing became increasingly erratic. I pushed the bike up the steeper sections and rode only once the switchbacks became less severe.

The road was little more than a dirt track and I often had to pull over and clean off my mudguards. My only companions were Tibetan road workers. They wore white face masks and rode around on strange three-wheeled tractors – Robin Reliant meets Mad Max – with a single huge headlight sticking out like a Gorgon's eye. Much of the work seemed to involve breaking up boulders to create chipping to surface the track, but the workers were cheerful, often pulling me over for cups of yak butter tea.

As I neared Nyalam, the road began to flatten out and the peaks on the horizon became more clearly defined. But there was one remaining problem: as the gradient reduced the wind ripped into my side with increasing severity, slowing the bike down to near stalling point. It seemed rough justice having slogged up the hill, to be rewarded with this on the flat.

Anyone who has ridden a tour bike against a strong side- or head-wind will know the levels of frustration it can induce. It drives you crazy. Not just mutter-under-your-breath crazy but bellow-till-the-veins-in-your-forehead-pop crazy. You hate everybody who is travelling with the wind, you hate the trucks coming in the opposite direction, you hate the tourists in their four-wheel drives returning to Kathmandu and you even hate the donkey carts with their jingling bells and flapping multi-coloured prayer flags. You cannot understand why God is favouring them and against you. You imagine how sweet it would be to ride with the wind bowling you along in the opposite direction. You bellow blasphemies and prayers rolled into one. Jesus Christ, you rant, even Lattan Baba rolled faster than this. Anger is the one thing that sustains you in the wind. No gentle pleas or whispered curses will do. You have to throw body and soul at it, rage against the elements and clock up the kilometres in small concentrated bursts, pretending that every hundred metres is the final leg of the Tour de France. But if you go faster, too proud to ever stop, faster, your dead muscles powered by the fury in your heart, faster, till the tears of imminent failure fall, faster, faster, faster, then you might just make it.

By the time I reached Nyalam, I was a wreck, but I also felt a huge sense of triumph. My victory was all the more pleasing given the setting.

From the town of Nyalam, perched on the edge of the Bhut Kosi Valley, there is an imposing panorama. Most impressive is the view of Shishapangma, a snowy peak of over 8,000 metres to the west. Nyalam is situated at the beginning of the Tibetan plateaux and, although I still had the 5,750-metre

Pang La Pass to battle with, I hoped the climb from here on would be more gradual.

Nyalam, like Zhangmu, is a combination of Tibetan and Chinese. There are wonderful wood-framed houses with brightly engraved eaves and fat lintels painted in red and blue. But, inevitably, glass offices have started to appear on the fringes of town, courtesy of the People's Army. I noticed that most of the main street restaurants were Chinese and the gorgeous smells of dumplings and frying meat were wafting from their drab interiors.

The choice of hotels was interesting. I had to plump for either The Power Station Trade Union Hotel or the Road Worker's Hotel. I chose the latter which was at the end of town near the river. I had a draughty four-bed dormitory to myself. As with almost all hotels outside Lhasa the only hot water on offer was inside a couple of thermoses. I did not particularly care about washing any more. It was becoming too cold to take my clothes off for even a few minutes; I couldn't give a damn how I smelt and more importantly, nobody else could either. In the extreme cold, unlike the extreme heat, hygiene was not a big concern.

I ate a bowl of scrambled egg and tomato at a local restaurant, brushed my teeth down by the river and eventually tumbled into the soft drooping bed. Bliss.

At least, initially, it was bliss. Then I heard a sound I had been dreading. A sound that I prayed I would not hear on this trip, although I knew I was bound to at some point. A wheeze. A very faint wheeze, certainly, but a wheeze all the same. A wheeze that would turn to a rasp and then a desperate fight for breath. As always when asthma strikes, I tried to stay calm, to tell myself it would go away.

I tried to loosen my breath, taking in deep long gusts of air and listening carefully to the exhalations. At first they sounded all right but then gradually became more husky, before finally turning wild and panicky. Just bloody great, I thought, my first asthma attack of the trip happens in the most remote place imaginable. There was only one thing for it – my inhaler.

Holding my pocket torch between my teeth I made my way over to the bike, ripped open the Velcro strap of my handlebar bag and groped around. My fingers made contact with the L-shaped plastic. I pulled out the inhaler, stuffed it in my mouth and pushed down the canister, poised to inhale its cold fumes. Nothing. *Shit*. I tried again. Nothing. *Bollocks*. I could hear my breath rasping like a dying animal. The inhaler seemed to have no pressure. I shook it. It sounded as if it still had some liquid in it. Come on. I tried again. Still no pressure. *Fuck it*. I threw it against the bike. OK, Tom, calm down, mate, just calm down. I knew I had a back-up inhaler in my medical kit. I unstrapped my rucksack, pulled out the plastic bag and fumbled around like a bomb disposal expert who has five seconds to save the world. Where are you, you bastard? Come on. OK, got you. I stuffed the inhaler in my mouth and fired. The icy moisture hit the back of my throat and I hoovered it down. Already the rasping was fading. I pushed in another dose and my breathing was restored to a fast pant. I lay on the floor, my body heaving with a relief that was almost carnal. I slept the rest of the night clutching my inhaler like a lover's locket.

The following morning after some green tea and a couple of boiled eggs I pedalled off, puffed up like a spaceman in all my layers of clothing. The road was not too bad, although the sandy parts made for heavy going. I was fine on the flat but when the track veered up towards the La Lung-la Pass it all became too much. My breath once again began to rasp so I jumped off, rested a while, took a puff of Ventolin and began pushing the bike instead.

It was a painfully slow process and winter was really starting to take hold. It had been bitterly cold before the sun had risen and even in the middle of the day it remained chilly. My progress so far along the Friendship Highway had been markedly slower than on any other stretch of the trip. I was struggling to clock up thirty miles on a good day which was half the distance I usually aimed to cycle.

I had told Stoke Mandeville that I would cover at least 12,000 miles between the two Swanbournes. This I was determined to achieve, and even if I hitched the odd ride I would still have clocked up 7,000 miles by the time I reached Lhasa, and many more by Hong Kong. But if I carried on walking like this I would end up dead. It was time to swallow my pride.

When the next vehicle approached I gratefully flagged it down. It was a spluttering blue-bonneted Dong Feng truck, transporting drums of oil. Sitting on top of the drums were three Kham-pas who had also cadged a ride. They were swarthy and sun-wrinkled, wrapped up in the usual hodgepodge of clothing. One of them wore a deerstalker-type hat with extendable ear muffs, another had a long knife sheathed in a richly decorated scabbard. All three held wooden buckets full of butter.

As the cab was already full I jumped in the back with the Kham-pas. The driver, a short stocky man, passed up the bike and then we were off, rumbling up the dusty track. The truck seemed to stop for as many breathers as I did. On the steeper sections, the driver would pull over every twenty minutes or so and pour water on to the radiator, causing it to spit and sizzle like a scalded pan. The three Kham-pas sat in the back singing ballads, occasionally bursting into an ebullient chorus. When they pressed me to sing all I could manage was a short version of 'Jerusalem' before running out of breath. It was good diverting entertainment though and before long we had sung our way up the La Lung-la Pass and were at a height of 5,200 metres.

The pass was a beautiful spot with multicoloured prayer flags that flapped in the breeze. There were cairns of loose stone and everywhere I looked layers of snow were cemented to the rocks by the icy wind. I was glad I had some company because apart from the odd herd of yaks, it was a scene of breathtaking desolation. I remembered Gerard telling me that Tibet and Afghanistan were the only two countries without functioning railway systems and, looking down the valley, it was easy to imagine that we were the last people on earth.

The truck carried on down towards Tingri, the next little town, the day becoming increasingly cold and restless as the afternoon sun drained away and a chalky twilight closed in on us. The mercury was falling fast and so I pulled my bobble hat over my ears and tucked my hands into my jumper. Once we were back on the flat, the truck pulled over and the trio of butter-carrying Kham-pas jumped out. We said our goodbyes and off they walked into the middle distance still singing. I could hear them for some time before they were drowned out by the roar of the truck engine.

It was freezing. I tried to sleep but now the truck was on level ground, it had picked up speed and was jouncing around uncontrollably. The night continued to close in and so I huddled up, using my panniers as a windbreak until eventually I could take no more.

'Stop!' I bellowed, leaning towards the driver's cabin. 'Please, I'm freezing. Stop. STOP!'

It was hopeless, the truck and the wind were making far too much noise for me to be heard. I fell back. Come on, Fremantle. Pull yourself together. I finally managed to haul myself up, using the truck's rails as leverage, and began banging on the cab roof.

'For Christ's sake stop, you're going to kill me,' I screamed. 'It's too cold. You've got to let me in the cab. STOP. STOP. STOOOOOOOOP!'

I smashed on the roof like a lunatic. I knew the driver would have stopped for me, but the noise in the cab was probably almost as bad as it was out here. I looked at the black silhouette of the mountains but there was no sign of light. Bugger it. I slumped down and huddled up again. I sang 'Jerusalem' repeatedly, it seemed a good thing to do. Perhaps not what the SAS would have recommended but it was the only survival technique I could muster.

It was 8.30 p.m. when we finally pulled into Tingri. I was frozen stiff, but not so stiff that I could not stand up and shout at the driver. A crowd of Tibetans formed around the truck and began hooting with laughter. I shouted wild abuse at all of them. I was shaking so much that I could hardly stand and my voice sounded like that of a robot.

A couple of Tibetans jumped up on to the truck's tailboard and took down my bike. I lowered myself gently on to the ground from the back of the truck, afraid my icicled legs would snap if I landed too hard. The truck driver led me into a wooden hut which contained a rug and some cushions beside a wood stove. I sat down, allowing the heat to defrost my palsied limbs. A heavily built Tibetan lady with blue beads in her hair and a gold-coloured girdle around her waist appeared with a kettle. She poured me a cup of yak butter tea. I drank it down in long gulps and, rancid or not, I think it was the finest cup of tea I've ever tasted. I held out my cup for more, my hand still shaky.

A little later some men joined us around the fire and a meal of noodles and mutton was served. Throughout the evening the Tibetans impersonated my shivering fit and burst into fits of uproarious laughter. After a pompous attempt at reprimanding them, I found I was unable to keep a straight face and we all laughed till tears ran down our faces. Laughter like that is something precious, and something with which the Tibetans, despite the harshness of much of their lives, are clearly very familiar.

Over the following week, I took it in turns to ride and hitch. My breathing was still far from perfect and it was so cold in the mornings that my gloved hands stuck to the handlebars like glue. The other problem I faced was diet. All of the high-energy foods I had bought in Kathmandu had been eaten and I was surviving on yak meat, yak butter tea and noodles. Occasionally I would eat *tsampa*, a roasted barley flour which the Tibetans love. I felt my stamina was badly flagging and the fact that my fat reserves had been lost as a result of the dysentery did not help.

But although physically I was deteriorating, mentally I was firing on all cylinders – when you are on the Tibetan plateaux it is impossible not to be. The landscape is always dramatic, with jagged, rust-coloured rocks and swathes of stony desert.

I took photos of donkeys ploughing fields and Chinese squaddies on parade. I passed long-horned *dzu*, their bellies strapped with red cummerbunds like prizewinners in a Home Counties show. And all around were the mountains with their proud Tibetan names: Xixapangma, Cho Oyu and of course Chomolungma, the Mother of the Earth, otherwise known as Mount Everest. To reach Everest Base Camp, I would have been forced to make a forty-five-mile detour and I decided it was not worth it. I was no longer after the biggest or the best and the mountains, whatever their size and shape, had all become friends.

Ten days after leaving Kathmandu, I parked the bike on a high ridge, ripped off my sunglasses and looked down over Shigatse, Tibet's second-largest town. I was in a good mood. I knew that from here on the road to Lhasa was only a little over 150 miles and that it would be bitumen all the way.

My first impressions of Shigatse were not great; it seemed to be populated exclusively by Chinese soldiers and undernourished dogs. The streets were filled with loud hailers blasting out Mandarin pop songs or People's Army propaganda. Finally I tracked down the Tibetan area, using as a guide the ramparts of Shigatse's ruined *dzong* (fort) on a high ridge hundreds of feet above the city. Within minutes I was in the lively swirl of a market.

It was a demented but good-natured affair. Much of the merchandise was horse-related with stacks of leather saddles and tack, stockman's boots and felt riding breeches. One of the most impressive and surprising displays though was the fine millinery selection: Cossack hats, fur-lined fezzes, pork-pie trilbies, stetsons and tea cosies. I treated myself to a can of coconut milk and a banana – individually wrapped and imported from Ecuador – reopened my map and headed for the Tenzin Hotel.

The Tenzin was a terrific hideaway. It was located in a shady alley at the top of a flight of narrow wooden steps. In its forecourt was a red prayer wheel brocaded with a gold lint the size of an oil drum which an old man with a shaven head cranked round every now and then. Washing was hanging from lines and travellers were sitting in deck chairs reading and drinking beer. I was ushered up to a dormitory on the roof by a Tibetan girl wearing a Sergeant Pepper-style jacket and with yak grease in her hair.

The dormitory was homely and clean and at twenty yuan a night (about two pounds sterling) it was a good deal. But the most luxurious aspect of the Tenzin accommodation was its hot shower, powered by a solar panel.

I caught a glimpse of myself in a shard of mirror in the shower room and did a double take. My hair was shaggy and sun-bleached, my face gaunt and grimy and my beard a tangle of fluff. My body was swarthy, with a navel full of grit, my toenails long and crooked. I smelt like sweat and bonfires. It was time for a scrub. The shower only produced a trickle of hot water but that was just fine with me. I lathered my entire body and scrubbed it until my skin felt as fresh as it had after the hammam in Damascus.

Later in the evening I joined the other travellers sitting out on the roof. I cracked open a bottle of Blue Ribbon beer and stretched myself out on a pile of cushions. This was the life.

Tales were being exchanged with enthusiasm. Gus, a tiny puckish Malaysian, had been knocked half-unconscious by a stone-throwing farmer while cycling around Yamdrock Lake. Julie, a Californian, talked a lot about the wicked Chinese and the fact she had just completed a pilgrimage to remote Mount Kailas. But it was quietly spoken Joe, a heavily bearded Scot, who stole the show. Joe had done it all: acted as a film extra in Bombay, crashed into a river in a bus near Darjeeling and, of course, hitch-hiked Route 66. None of the stories ever began, 'I had such a comfortable bus ride from Samye,' or, 'Isn't the food superb at the Hard Yak Café?' We seemed only to thrive on tales of suffering, bad luck and rum behaviour.

Joe's most shocking story did not involve travel at all. We had got on to the subject of Tibet's colonization by the Chinese. Julie was talking of the horrors of the 1959 invasion and the fact that over one million Tibetans were now dead and thousands of refugees unable to return to their country.

'Yeah, everybody knows that side of the story,' said an

American man in a ponytail, who had been listening in. 'But what about the fact that thousands of Tibetans helped the Red Guards smash up the monasteries? What about the fact that many of the Tibetans hated all the monkish oppression? Tibet was a theocracy. Know the only other place that was recently a theocracy? Iran.'

'I don't think the Ayatollah can be compared with the Dalai Lama,' replied Julie, upset that anyone could criticize her beloved Tibet. 'Anyway you're exaggerating. Very few Tibetans joined the Chinese.'

'Listen,' said the drawling man. 'I like Tibet. OK. I like the Dalai Lama. And I agree nobody can excuse what the Chinese did here. But I don't like all these hypocritical Richard Gere types telling everybody it's Shangri-La up here. The monks often lead a very tough life that doesn't suit everyone. That's all I'm saying.'

'But at least it's a noble life, a peaceful life,' trilled Julie. 'It doesn't have to suit everyone.'

'Listen, just listen. Tibet is too often portrayed as perfect. It dilutes its cause. Nowhere is perfect.'

'And I've just bought this great album,' chipped in Joe, clearly wanting to change the subject. 'It's by a singer called Dadawa. It's not so well-known but its the most incredible thing I've ever heard. Really beautiful, really haunting. Dadawa is Chinese but she loves Tibet and knows a lot of its mythology. The album is called *Sister Drum*. It's got this incredible story surrounding it.' Everyone was listening to Joe now.

'Tell us,' said the drawling man.

'OK,' he said. 'But I warn you this is not for the squeamish.' He smiled and took a swig of beer. 'It goes something like this. Once upon a time there were these identical twin sisters who lived in a little town in the Tibetan mountains. They were inseparable; they slept in the same room, ate together, played together, went to school together. Then, one day, one of the sisters woke up and found the other had gone. Completely vanished. She searched high and low for her, she asked everyone in the village if they'd seen her but to no avail. She was nowhere to be found.' Joe stopped for another swig.

'Go on, go on,' urged Julie.

'One day, many years later, the single sister was at a festival in a neighbouring village; the candles were lit, the gongs were bonging, the dancers were performing. Suddenly, amid the confusion, the sister heard a drum beat, a very loud distinctive drum beat. DUM DUM DUM DUM. She was mesmerized by it and tried to locate the drum. DUM DUM DUM DUM. She pushed through the crowds, the masked faces, the dancers. DUM DUM DUM DUM. And then she found herself in front of this enormous drum being beaten by a man in a white mask.'

Joe's voice was becoming more urgent. 'She knew the drum beat was a signal from her sister but could not understand why. DUM DUM DUM. It was definitely her sister speaking to her. DUM DUM DUM. She could even understand what the drum was saying. DUM DUM DUM. It was telling her that her sister was inside the drum. DUM DUM DUM. That the drum was made of her sister's skin. DUM DUM DUM. That the drum *was* her sister. DUM DUM DUM.' He stopped suddenly. Everyone was silent.

'So that's why it's called *Sister Drum*,' Joe added nonchalantly, as if he had just explained the meaning of the latest Fleetwood Mac album. 'Spooky, hey?'

The following morning I made for the Tashilhunpo monastery. On the way I passed an old woman in rags prostrating herself on the pavement, a most humbling sight. Every few yards, she would kneel down, fall on her face and extend her arms. She was very grubby, her knees and hands protected by cardboard pads. In one hand she held some beads and she was chanting a mantra over and over again.

I paid to enter the monastery which is spread over a wide area and comprises a steeply rising series of prayer halls, some brick-coloured, some ochre; the principal buildings are topped with gold. Far behind, peeking above a line of pale cloud, I could see the mountains.

The Tashilhunpo was founded in 1445 by Genden Drup, who was posthumously given the title of Dalai Lama or Ocean of Wisdom. The title has been inherited by subsequent lamas to this day, the current Dalai Lama being the fourteenth in the line. He now lives in Dharmsala, having escaped from Lhasa to India when the Chinese first invaded Tibet in 1950.

The Tashilhunpo monastery, however, is famed for being the seat of the Panchen Lama, the Dalai Lama's spiritual second in command. Panchen, meaning great scholar, was a title given by the fifth Dalai Lama, probably the most revered of all Tibet's leaders, to the abbot of the Tashilhunpo back in the seventeenth century. There have been Panchen Lamas ever since. Sadly, the child chosen by the present Dalai Lama as the eleventh Panchen Lama mysteriously disappeared in 1995, replaced by a Chinese-sponsored substitute.

The four winds had been painted on one of the walls near the entrance. They were a fierce quartet of sentinels: a blue-faced warrior with saucer eyes brandishing a scimitar, a red-faced man, perhaps a wizard, holding a snake, a white-faced musician playing a lyre and a yellow-faced character cuddling a mongoose which was spewing a fountain of jewels from its mouth. I had no idea which of them was east, west, north or south, but between them they made an excellent gang of spiritual bouncers.

Caught up in a swirl of Tibetan pilgrims rotating hand-held

prayer wheels and mumbling devotions, I moved from room to room, past the tomb of the fourth Panchen Lama and all sorts of Buddhas, some with huge ears and wide eyes, others sleepy and serene. In the softly lit, uncluttered assembly hall, one of the oldest buildings in the Tashilhunpo, lay the centrepiece – the Panchen Lama's throne. Below this sat a group of monks, mostly teenagers, chattering and laughing away like any group of schoolboys.

The great thing about the Tashilhunpo is that, unlike so many of Tibet's monasteries, it escaped unscathed during the Cultural Revolution. Seeing the beauty of some of the Buddhas, the intricate *thangkas* (religious paintings) and the rooms of prayer wheels and ancient scrolls, it was sad to think of the destruction Chairman Mao's Red Guards must have caused to other monasteries in that period.

The *pièce de résistance* of the Tashilhunpo is the Maitreya Chapel at the west end of the complex where the huge statue of Maitreya, the Future Buddha, sits. He is destined to return to earth 4,000 years after the death of Sakyamuni. All around the statue were tangles of prayer flags and the flicker of hundreds of butter candles.

Outside, the sun was shining but the wind was sharp. Some red robes were swaying on a washing line and an old monk bashed a cymbal suspended from a willow tree. On the way back to the Tenzin I passed the same old woman I had seen on my way in. She was lying face down on the pavement, body extended in devotion. She reminded me of a diver in mid plunge, uncertain whether the water was deep enough.

I arrived in Lhasa (at 3,606 metres the highest capital city in the world) on the afternoon of 15 November after an easy three-day ride through a landscape of ice and silver birch trees. For much of the way my route ran parallel to the holy

Brahmaputra River. Lhasa was once called the Forbidden City because until the beginning of the twentieth century it was closed to foreigners. Things have changed more than a little since then for now there is a Holiday Inn, a Hard Yak Café and several nightclubs. Although Beijing statisticians deny it, substantially more Han Chinese than Tibetans now live in Lhasa.

The first thing I did, like a good tourist, was to take about a dozen pictures of my bicycle outside the Potala palace. The Potala is Lhasa's equivalent of the Taj Mahal, perhaps not as romantic or symmetrical but every bit as eye-popping, rising sheer and massive out of the hills, a serried mass of white and tan and gold. I could not stop smiling. The highest capital in the world. It really was all downhill from here!

I billeted myself in the Banak Shol, a charming hotel with brightly painted dormitories and a breezy courtyard. The only other guest in my dorm was a scruffy Canadian dope-head called Scooter. He was from a place called Jasper in the Albertan backwoods and spent his time smoking grass and raving on about Allen Ginsberg and 'Quent' Tarantino. He also played long games of chess against himself on a handmade board he had bought in Kathmandu.

'Why the hell do you want to break your balls on a bicycle, dude?' asked Scooter, eyeing my panniers. 'You should buy a snowmobile. Ha, ha.'

'Ha, ha.'

I used Lhasa as a place to rest up. I had been travelling practically non-stop since Delhi and it had caught up with me. Lhasa was a good place to put on weight: lots of half-empty travellers cafés serving everything from yak burgers to chocolate cake. I drank too much tea, wrote postcards and idled around the sights.

Despite the evidence of Chinese intrusion – the tacky new nightclubs, the ubiquitous security cameras at the Potala, the absence of Dalai Lama pictures – there were still wholly Tibetan enclaves in the capital including the markets at Barkhor Square, where one could buy everything from tin-openers and antique coins to lacquered jewellery boxes and children's kites. The monasteries provided the strongest reminder of Tibetan culture, above all the overwhelming presence of the Jokhang, Tibet's oldest monastery, with its stinks and chants and clanging gongs, its knots of eternity, jolly monks and immutable holiness.

I never asked the Tibetans about the Dalai Lama or their attitude towards the Chinese but on two occasions I was made aware of continuing resistance to rule from Beijing.

A monk led me into his room and, because he spoke little English, we sat for a while exchanging embarrassed smiles over our yak butter tea. Then he reached under his bed and pulled out a furled parchment. He snapped back the rubber band, unrolled it and pointed excitedly at a colourful picture. It showed a yellow sun with red and blue rays flanked by two rampant snow lions. It suddenly dawned on me that I was looking at the Tibetan flag. The old man put his hands together in prayer and looked at me, nervously seeking approval. I put my hands together too and we stood smiling at the illegal pennant, proud of our peaceful defiance, however impotent.

On a separate occasion, while wandering around yet another dark room flickering with candles, I was beckoned over by a group of young monks. They pushed me eagerly towards one of the monastery's shrines which was bedecked with some sepia photographs of dead lamas. 'Dalai Lama,' said one of them. I thought he was after a photograph. I apologized and told him I had none.

'No, no,' he said firmly. He pointed at one of the photographs. 'This Dalai Lama.'

I looked harder at the photo. It showed a smiling moon-faced woman standing next to a young boy. The monk pointed at the child in the photograph. The Dalai Lama can have been no more than ten, but once I had been told it was him I could recognize his face immediately.

'We no allow Dalai Lama picture here,' said the monk. 'But Chinese no think this Dalai Lama! We too smart!' They all burst into giggles.

'Very brave,' I said.

'His Holiness the Dalai Lama come home,' said one. 'His Holiness come back. Ten years he come back for sure.'

The Chinese are not the only people to have invaded Tibet; Britain too had stuck her imperial ice axe into the Land of the Snows. The 1903–1904 invasion, led by Sir Francis Young-husband, was provoked by exaggerated rumours of Russian influence in Lhasa.

I am ashamed to say I hadn't even heard of Sir Francis Younghusband, one of the Great Game's key players, prior to visiting Tibet. A Swiss man called Luke, Lhasa's resident Tibetaholic, put me right by lending me a biography of the man entitled *Younghusband, The Last Great Imperial Adventurer*, by Patrick French. I assumed the British invasion had been rather a benign affair. Compared to the Chinese suppression of the 1959 uprising it was, but even so it was not without brutality of its own.

The bloodiest incident occurred when over 600 Tibetans were killed at the battle of Chumi Shengo having been fooled into extinguishing their matchlock fuses. The Tibetans fought heroically with spears and knives but were eventually cut down. Hundreds of Tibetan soldiers were later killed by British troops at Gyangtse and there is now a 'Museum of the Anti-British' (no doubt Chinese prompted) at the town's *dzong*.

The British invasion was largely a vainglorious waste of

time. The thirteenth Dalai Lama had fled north to Mongolia by the time troops arrived in Lhasa in the summer of 1904, and a convention had to be signed by a regent from Ganden monastery in his absence. Other than the beauty of the major palaces, the British saw little to impress them. The capital's deserted streets were for the most part full of rubbish and scummy water and, perhaps most distressing for Younghusband's men, there was not a Russian in sight. It seemed the occupying forces spent most of their time in Lhasa organizing gymkhanas, playing football, fishing and hanging the odd subversive lama.

I found it fascinating that Younghusband had similarities with Captain Charles; they spoke the same dialect, a sort of imperial cant mixed with occasional compassion. Younghusband was a man who considered the Tibetans unfit 'to be left to themselves' and even referred to a group of terrified monks as a 'cringing lot . . . not worth powder and shot'. And yet he was deeply moved when presented with a tiny bronze Buddha on his last day in Lhasa. Handing it over, the regent asked that whenever Younghusband looked at the little Buddha he should think kindly of Tibet. The following day, gazing out over the Himalayas with the Buddha in his pocket, Younghusband cast his Edwardian stuffiness aside and was overwhelmed with joy. It was clearly one of the most significant experiences of his life.

On my penultimate day in Tibet I hitched a ride with a Czech couple who had hired a Landcruiser for the day. We visited Yumbulagang, a quirky white and ochre lighthouse-shaped monastery that overlooks the Yarlung Valley, the stamping ground of Tibet's ancient kings. Although much of Yumbulagang's architecture is contemporary its foundations reputedly make it the oldest building in Tibet.

I sat myself at a vantage point near the top of the monastery that took in the panoramic sweep of craggy mountains above the flat grassland. An elderly monk in a maroon cloak appeared behind me. From a fold in his garment he took out a handful of walnuts and offered them to me. I took one and nodded my thanks. A wave of quiet euphoria swept over me; it was as if I was back on Cemetery Hill with Johnny Ginger. I had harboured so many doubts about this journey but now I knew I could see it through. For the first time, high on Yumbulagang's ancient ramparts, holding on to that walnut, the bike ride made perfect sense.

CHAPTER EIGHTEEN

CHRISTMAS IN CHANGSHA

What with all the sightseeing and a healthy bout of indolence, it was ten days before I left Lhasa. But I felt much better for having rested up, better than I had for weeks. There was only one problem: it was 25 November, only thirty-one cycling days until Christmas. Tibet could be chilly at the best of times, but during the festive season it would be madness to cycle.

My options were limited. I could hibernate in Lhasa over winter, meditating and eating *tsampa*. I could hitch an illegal ride on an eastbound truck and risk death either from exposure or, more likely, from crashing over a ravine. Or I could take an eighty-hour bus journey, on an almighty northbound detour via Golmud to Chengdu. The latter was the only practical solution and I was well prepared, having bought *Great Expectations* from Scooter to stave off the tedium of lying in a sleeper bus with frosty windows for over three days.

The bus was a warhorse, its roof rack straining under the weight of a mountain of luggage on top of which was roped my lonely bicycle. By the time I boarded there were only a couple of bed spaces left at the rear of the vehicle, next to a Chinese family. I threw my panniers up to them and bedded down.

Throughout the journey my companions – two young couples,

an old woman and a toddler – munched sackloads of peanuts, watermelon seeds, dried broad beans and mandarins. By the end of the first night, we were lying on a mattress of sweet-smelling snack detritus. The days turned into nights, the nights to days. It was one of those journeys where time becomes meaningless. Over the course of the eighty hours we only stopped for a total of about seven, most of them in Golmud, a charmless transport depot of a town deep in the heart of Qinghai province. The other stops were roadside halts, when the women would scuttle off to find whatever cover they could and the men would form a urinating firing squad.

These calls of nature and brisk tea breaks were the only chance we got to properly see our surroundings. The best view of the journey was supplied when the bus wheezed to a halt on a high pass south of Lanzhou. We all spilled out on to the icy tarmac. The sky was a soft bird's-egg blue above the peaks. We waited, huddled in our thick jumpers, as the driver looped chains over the tyres, but soon we were all back in the darkened bus as it inched gingerly down the serpentine switchbacks to link up with the main road into Chengdu, the capital of Sichuan, the most populated of China's provinces.

My companions on the journey were a friendly bunch and they never once moaned about the discomfort; they were too busy enjoying themselves. Travelling seems to bring out the best in the Chinese. On previous visits to China, while I was working in Hong Kong, I had found it easy to make friends on trains or buses, with people on the move.

We reached Chengdu on 27 November at 11 p.m., astonishingly the expected time of arrival. I was sorry to say farewell to my companions; days spent sharing a bed of fruit rind and peanut husks facilitate a certain unhygienic bonding. But once we had alighted the cameraderie soon disappeared and my bunk mates skittered off fast into the night with only the old lady stopping to give me a hand with my panniers. I opened up my map of Chengdu which, considering it depicted a city of nine million people, showed a worrying lack of detail.

I wavered off into the darkness, crossed a bridge over a wide river and carried on south. There was no traffic and I sped along through the bitterly cold night, dodging the puddles. After a fifteen-minute ride I pinpointed the Traffic Hotel and wheeled my bike inside. A pretty but morose girl dressed in red livery took my passport and presented me with a key.

I shoved my bike into the lift and rattled up to the empty second floor dormitory. I enjoyed a long very hot shower and tumbled into the fresh linen of my bed. There was even a television. I turned it on. It was *Top of the Pops* from the early eighties – the theme music from *Fame* followed by lots of men in trilbies dancing around singing about Arthur Daley.

Home suddenly seemed a million miles away.

On my first day in Chengdu my most pressing need was to obtain a visa extension at the Public Security Bureau. It was a piece of cake: the office was an easy walk from the hotel, there was no queue, no hassle and the stamp allowed me to stay in China until 30 December. I had hoped I would be in Hong Kong for Christmas but that was beginning to seem highly unlikely.

Chengdu was a city in a state of flux. There was a Holiday Inn, a Hong Kong department store and a chain of restaurants called American Dine-In Country Chicken. There were Chinese girls dressed in denim riding mopeds and men in blue boiler suits returning from the factories on bicycles, while at the fully computerized bank I saw an abacus on the cashier's desk. It was an enthralling city; steeped in tradition but undergoing rapid modernization.

One place I was especially keen to visit was the Chengdu

University of Traditional Chinese Medicine because I had always wondered whether there might be an alternative cure for my asthma. On arrival at the campus, a mass of dowdy symmetrical blocks, I was told the main museum was closed but that I could be shown around one of the laboratories. I was escorted by a secretary called Angel who wore high-heeled boots and had her hair in a Snoopy clip. She led me to a door with a sign: The Room for Receiving Foreign Guests. Despite its designation, there was a conspicuous absence of foreign notes and labels. The only English phrases I could spot were on a poster: 'In this hall there are such precious and rare specimens as musk, bezoar, wild ginseng, portions of poria and such foreign specimens as rhizome of Japanese coptis. They help with many illness. These include simple obesity, sterility (or disadvantage with sexual function), pernicious vomiting and rough stool.'

But the good news was that every cure imaginable was on display. A tiger skeleton was the opening exhibit and revoltingly the flesh still hung from its bones; there were stuffed sea lions, hedgehogs, pangolins, alligators and even a panther. There were snakes in acid and tiny beetles in test tubes, lizards in ethanol and tortoises in salt water. Hundreds of eggs sat on clouds of cotton wool, there was a jar filled with large unidentified testes and another stuffed with deer antler shavings.

I could not understand the Chinese characters but Angel told me that beetles were good for the blood, snakes helped generate body heat, goose eggs kept you regular and lizards were essential for 'man problem' (obviously a sort of reptilian Viagra). Sea horses, too, add vim to the libido, she confided.

The stuffed and bottled wildlife, some no doubt extremely rare, was gruesome – but it was reassuring too. The scope for experimentation was staggering. Somewhere in this university, in a lab one night, you could imagine something sensational occurring: a young student stumbling on to a miracle cure for asthma made from tangerine peel, deer antlers and rhizome of Japanese coptis. Medical research thrives on luck and luck thrives on possibility; at the Chengdu University of Traditional Chinese Medicine the possibilities seemed infinite.

The following day I set off for Chongqing, roughly 200 miles south-east of Chengdu. On my way out of the hotel I bought some mandarins from an old man who weighed the fruit on a pair of antique scales.

Once on the streets I found myself caught up in the tide of bicycle commuters. It was nice to be among so many fellow pedallers, like the boy with a box of white rabbits strapped to his back rack or the old woman with a sheath of spring onions balanced on her handlebars. We were as close as soldiers on parade but never touched one another. Some of the cyclists laughed at my overladen bike while others eyed it with deep suspicion, as if it might suddenly sprout wings and take off. But on my bicycle – for all its twenty-four gears and fancy colouring – I was part of the street scene, using a form of transport that has been synonymous with China for over a century. I felt like one of the team.

After I had branched off the main roads and skirted the shanties south of the city, I was back in low gear, climbing into the hills. The monotonous grey sky began to drizzle and a faint mist blurred visibility. Rather than depress the landscape – the thatched tea houses, the poplar trees, the waddling ducks – the mist rather suited it.

Sichuan province is referred to by the Chinese as the Heavenly Kingdom. From my saddle it was easy to see why; the landscape was stunning. Every square inch of land was put to use, from tiny allotments of radishes to large fields of potatoes or maize. There were mandarin trees growing among the cabbages and strips of teased wool hanging like grubby clouds from the bulrushes. Men in lampshade hats herded buffalo and at times the bamboo was so lush it overarched the road.

The villagers were exceptionally friendly; many beckoned me into their homes for a meal and a snifter of blood-warming rice wine. I had never been granted this type of invitation during previous visits to China, so perhaps it was the natural geniality of the Sichuan people or perhaps it was the bicycle. The food was always delicious, crispy green *choi sum*, black chilli chicken or fried tofu in garlic. Sichuan is known for its spicy food and the meals would often leave me sweating with a warm glow in the belly.

The highlight of the ride to Chongqing was my sojourn in Neijiang. The town itself was nothing special, just more drab suburbs, but it was home to the impressive Normal School where I was to spend the night. I had been told about the school by one of the receptionists at the Traffic Hotel, who had drawn me a map of how to get there.

It was not the easiest place to find. Once in Neijiang I had to take a banana boat across a choppy stretch of river and ride up a steep slippery track before reaching the correct address. The school itself comprised a number of squat tower blocks bustling with Chinese teenagers carrying books and rulers. The Traffic receptionist had told me that a group of Westerners taught English at the school, and I had come to track them down.

The first fellow foreigner – *weigworan* – I met was Lisa. She looked stunned when I called out to her. 'God, you're not Chinese,' she whispered, approaching me. 'What are you doing here?' I must have made a pretty odd sight; a pale bearded man sitting on a bicycle with a tea cosy on his head. 'Oh well,' she said. 'I guess we should try to find the others.' She was a willowy Canadian who spoke in a gentle drawl. She let me dump my bike in her room and we went off to track down some of her colleagues.

We drew a blank. As it was Saturday, Lisa explained, they would either be in town, teaching private lessons or perhaps playing some sport. She volunteered to show me around Neijiang. As we walked we babbled away at each other as if we had just discovered the power of speech. She was on a two-year contract for the Peace Corps of which she had worked nine months. She was earning 900 yuan a month (about £100) and at the end of two years would receive a US$5,000 bonus.

'It's not much,' she admitted, 'but I like the life. Before this I taught English in Austria for two years and now I'm fluent in German. After two years here I hope my Mandarin will be pretty good. Four years with the Peace Corps and fluent in two languages, that must be worth something.'

'Absolutely,' I said. 'But do you like it here?'

'It's OK. The Chinese kids are great, very polite and hard working, but I'm quite lonely. I don't really mix with the other teachers. I keep myself to myself.' We were walking through a market. Some of the buildings were hideous – cream-tiled blocks with blue glass windows – but there were traditional houses too, with wooden eaves and wrought-iron balconies. She pointed to one of the market stalls which had a pig's skinned face stretched out on a slab like a grotesque Hallowe'en mask.

'Ugh,' I said. 'That looks grim.'

'God that's nothing,' she remarked, casually tossing back her hair. 'You should see some of the other stuff we eat.'

'And here I was thinking the tinned spam in my panniers was a culinary low point. Pig face is in a whole new league.'

Minutes later a man on a bicycle rode past with a live pig strapped to his back rack. The pig was squealing horribly, straining against its bamboo ligatures.

'The Chinese for animal is *dong wu*,' explained Lisa. 'It means moving thing. That's what an animal is to the Chinese: a thing that moves and then you eat it. There's no compassion.'

'Some people say you can judge a country by the way it treats its animals,' I said.

'That's unfair,' countered Lisa. 'China is a very poor country, made up largely of peasants who often have to eat anything they can. Only rich countries can afford to be fussy about diet. The Chinese eat every part of every animal. No waste.'

The next stall along was lined with crates of live frogs. Long strands of kelp hung from the awning, exuding a faint smell of the sea.

'So what do you do for fun here?' I asked Lisa.

'I read and write a lot. Occasionally I'll spend a weekend in Chengdu, but the workload is pretty full-on. The village has two little cinemas which show English language films every night. That helps me keep my sanity. I think it's *The Untouchables* this evening.'

We caught the little ferry back over to the school and joined the other teachers in one of the canteen shacks. Meyer was a friendly but boastful American and Rebecca a dreamy girl with prematurely grey hair. They were both Peace Corps members like Lisa, whereas Tai, a clean-cut Hong Kong Chinese, and Dave, a nineteen-year-old from near London, were on one-year gap schemes.

We chatted for a couple of hours. All five of them were deeply proud of Neijiang and the school. They all spoke of their terrific students, of basketball games and trips to Chengdu. They seemed to have a genuine love for the place and not one of them spoke of poor wages or isolation. They were not bitchy about each other; in fact there was a terrific rapport between them all. If anyone was the odd one out it was Lisa, but she seemed a loner by nature and happy that way.

'Man, we found this great Buddha today,' Meyer was telling us, slurping on his noodles. 'It's in this wooden house by the river. It's completely ruined and possibly pre-dates Christ. Amazing. It was just so exciting to find it. Just wild, man. It beats the Great Wall any day.'

'It all sounds great, but surely some people can't hack it here. Does anyone ever drop out before the end of two years?' I asked.

'There was one Peace Corps guy who hated it here so he got sent to Chengdu,' replied Meyer. 'He didn't like Neijiang's isolation, found it too boring. But to me Chengdu is just another big city; this is China.'

'He was a tourist,' said Rebecca. 'We are more like locals.'

'Yeah.' Meyer nodded. 'When I get home I'm gonna find it real hard to eat Western food, to sleep under a duvet, sit around on a beach, that kinda stuff. I like it rough now.'

I liked roughing it too, but only because I knew I could go back to a land of hot baths and home cooking, of dinner parties and bug-free beds. If it wasn't for that knowledge, I would hate it. There would be nothing to look forward to. The reason they all liked it here, I suspected, was because it was only for two years. They could pace themselves. A great experience, followed by the comfort of home and if not home, then a posting to a softer environment. If there was no end to it, that would be different.

'You might be a fat businessman one day, Meyer,' teased Dave. 'Making million-dollar deals before breakfast. Noodle and green tea breakfast, of course.' Everybody laughed, even Meyer.

'But you've got to admit we're still at the cutting edge here,' interjected Rebecca sleepily. 'It's great.'

There was no denying her this fact. These five teachers were at the cutting edge of China. They were surrounded exclusively by Chinese in a town with virtually no Western influences, mingling with the locals, speaking Mandarin at every opportunity. There is often a distinction made between travellers and tourists. On my bike-ride I was really only a tourist. I stopped off in unusual destinations, sure, but I always moved on after a few days. A nomadic tourist, perhaps, but a tourist all the same. These five teachers were the travellers; they were giving something back.

That night I watched *The Untouchables* with Lisa in one of the cinema tents. The film was, of course, subtitled and the Chinese loved it. I had not seen a film for ages and was spellbound by the whole experience: the ancient whirring projector and flitting insects, the shrieks and claps from the audience. Sadly, the projector conked out shortly after the slow-motion shoot-out at Chicago station. We went across to the opposite tent and watched *The Empire Strikes Back* instead. The last thing I had expected in the middle of rural Sichuan was to be listening to the zap of light sabres and Darth Vader's gravelly truisms, but it was all the more enjoyable for the unexpected novelty.

The next morning I got up early to track down the Buddha Meyer had been talking of. He had drawn me a map which pinpointed the ruined riverside house where the ancient statue was located. Going inside, I took a candle from my front pannier, lit it and held it up to the dark Buddha. The figure was about forty feet high and squatted like a sumo wrestler. It reminded me of a picture I had seen of Xian's terracotta warriors, the same calm but stern features. The face was damaged, with broken mouth and eyes, but it was still very impressive and probably dated back over two thousand years. I could understand Meyer's excitement as he was almost certainly one of the first Westerners ever to clap eyes on it. It thrilled me too but I was too late. Meyer had been the traveller and I, as usual, was just the tourist.

I arrived in Chongqing five days after leaving Chengdu. The journey by train would have taken me less than five hours!

Chongqing is a chaotic smoggy city which was the headquarters of Chiang Kai-shek's Kuomintang government until he fled from the communists to Taiwan in 1949. It really did seem a grey and grubby place, and I could appreciate the saying, 'When the sun comes out in Chongqing, the dogs bark.'

After slogging up and down the city's hills, something seemed to be missing and finally I realized what it was – I was the *only* cyclist. Whereas in Chengdu I had been swept along with shoals of other bicycles, here I was the lone fish, struggling upstream. Chongqing is a city of steep streets and polluted air; no one rides bikes.

Chongqing lies at the intersection of two great rivers, the Yangtze and its less celebrated tributary the Jalian. The Yangtze is the third-longest river in the world, after the Nile and the Amazon; its 3,900-mile course runs from the fringes of Tibet to the East China Sea. The dreamers christened it the River of Heaven and it is where China's favourite poet, Li Bai, drowned in the eighth century, while attempting to make love to the moon. Of greater importance to me was the fact that this river would transport me all the way to Wuhan in Hubei province, through the meandering, picturesque and treacherous Three Gorges.

At the port I booked my ticket on the following day's slow boat. There were four classes and I plumped for third class, which meant an eight-bed dormitory somewhere in the bowels of the ferry.

Next day, I wheeled my bike over to the pier where a wiry man in singlet and flip-flops gave me a hand to lift it on deck. The gangways were swarming with passengers and I waited until the aisles had emptied before dragging my bike below.

The ferry reeked of diesel oil combined with the cabbagy pong of a kitchen catering for hundreds. I soon noticed that there were not four classes, but five. The cheapest tickets belonged to those with no bed who lay in the gangways with Dick Whittington-type bundles at their feet. But they seemed happy enough and, within an hour of our creaky vessel setting sail, had formed little groups, chatting, playing cards and drinking the first of many cups of green tea from their Thermoses.

I rejoined my room-mates among whom were the owlish Mr Chow and his stern but sexy wife. Mr Chow was a civil servant based in Nanjing and spoke English well enough for me to understand about one word in every ten. From what I could decipher of his lispy whispers the other guests were an elderly couple from Shanghai enjoying their first-ever holiday, an electrician from Hunan, a soldier from Urumqi and a man whose job I did not understand who spent most of the trip sleeping, belching and picking his toes.

Apart from the toe-picker with no name, they took an almost parental interest in me. Mr Chow brought me polystyrene containers of soup from the kitchen, the elderly couple loaned me an extra blanket and the soldier brewed me cups of coffee. Within a few hours we were all on intimate terms. When it was time for bed we said protracted goodnights to each other with the wholesome geniality of the Swiss Family Robinson.

The steamer took three days to reach Wuhan. It stopped in Feng Du, the city of ghosts and demon sculptures, and Fengjie, capital of the ancient warrior state of Kui. Beyond Fengjie were the splendid Three Gorges: the Qutang, the Wu and the Xiling. Sadly, all the gorges, even the fifty-mile-long Xiling, were shrouded in impenetrable mist, reducing them to little more than a few spectral pinnacles. The surrounding rocks had the most wonderful names: Peak of the Immortals, Bellows Gorge, Tear Drop Number One, Horse Lung Gorge and Rhinoceros Looking at the Moon, but all of them were lost in the haze too.

Despite the disappointments of the Three Gorges, the trip was mostly a joy and my greatest pleasure was the early morning t'ai chi. I used to wake early and find a corner in the communal lounge, which would still be carpeted with the previous night's sunflower seeds and cigarette butts, to watch the elderly Chinese perform their morning workouts. The physical grace of these venerable athletes – including an eighty-year-old woman who stood on one leg while whirling her arms – was impressive.

On the penultimate morning of the voyage, I awoke before dawn and as usual sat writing in the lounge. I was alone. A short while later an old man came in holding a sword. He was wearing a green overcoat with a rabbit fur collar which he took off together with his black jumper. He was probably about seventy but his bare chest was that of a man half his age. He was so absorbed in his swordplay that I was not sure whether he had seen me or not. He began with gentle slow motion moves before picking up speed with some thrusts and parries, finally whipping the blade around like Zorro. Like a fool I clapped at the end of his performance. He turned and looked at me in mild surprise, then bowed, wrapped his sword in his coat and walked away.

On the final night, as we were nearing Yichang, we were raised to a different water level in a gigantic lock. As the steamer gently elevated, I was reminded of the fact that we were travelling along the river at a contentious time: the Three Gorges hydroelectric project was under way.

The statistics are impressive: the project will cost at least US$20 billion and not be completed until 2008 at the earliest; its centrepiece will be a two-kilometre-long dam, over 600 feet high, behind which will be created a lake stretching over 350 miles. The project is not without its critics. The chief concern is that by the time it has been completed at least one million riverside dwellers will have been displaced and will need to be relocated. Over a hundred towns and countless farms are due to be submerged. On the plus side it is hoped the dam will help prevent the Yangtze's terrible annual floods and also, thanks to the hydroelectric turbines, reduce China's coal usage by fifty million tonnes per year. Whatever the pros and cons, the Yangtze will never be the same again.

We docked in Wuhan on 16 December, bang on time. There was no chance of making it to Hong Kong by Christmas, but I still had to pedal my way there for New Year before my Chinese visa expired. I wheeled the bike down the gangplank and stopped off in the one of the riverside restaurants. I wanted anything, anything, but noodles. I ate a tasty bowl of pumpkin and pork fat, a bag of pineapple chunks and a packet of biscuits called Fancy Smell Crispies, which weren't fancy, smelly or crispy, but which went down a treat all the same.

With a freshly filled belly I pedalled off to find a bed for the night. Wuhan was another vast city under a grey sky. Unlike Chongqing, it lies on both sides of the Yangtze and Wuhan's 1,100-metre Yangtze River Bridge was one of the Communist Party's first great engineering triumphs.

I checked into the Shengli Hotel, a revamped British-built guest house in Hankou, the central area of the city. I managed to get a bed for fifty yuan in a room at the back of the hotel in a charming courtyard of ornamental trees.

Wuhan, I discovered, had once been a city of the future, a trailblazer. In the early nineties it had all looked rosy: major investment had been planned, Hong Kong developers were sniffing around, the extensive textiles industry sensed a revival and private enterprise had begun to blossom. But it was not to be. Investors soon discovered that Wuhan was a spent force. Polluted, exhausted, its buildings crumbling, its infrastructure medieval, it could not rise to the challenge. Peasants flooded in hoping the streets would be paved with gold, but unemployment spiralled and more modern cities like nearby Shashi attracted the investment instead.

But Wuhan's pioneering spirit was not entirely dead and buried. There was a Kentucky Fried Chicken for heaven's sake. Surely the fact that the city would be at the heart of the Three Gorges project would put it back on the map? I sat in the KFC, Wuhan's pride and joy judging by the myriad signs pinpointing its whereabouts. I hoped Colonel Sanders would reveal to me a more upbeat Wuhan, a place where the city's beautiful young things congregated.

As I looked like Willie Nelson with a hangover Wuhan's beautiful young things gave my table a wide berth, although I did meet Melvin, a Filipino singer. He had worked in Hong Kong for years and saved no money at all, he told me. Since he had been living in Wuhan and singing at a place called the Rodeo Café, his wages had spiralled while his rent was a fraction of what he had paid for his Hong Kong shoebox. He told me he knew of only seven other Filipinos living in Wuhan whereas in Hong Kong there had been thousands.

'Do you like Wuhan?' I asked.

'Ah no, my friend,' said Melvin. 'It's a terrible place but it makes me rich. I loved Hong Kong but never saved any cash. If I can stick it out here for a few years I can go home to the Philippines a wealthy man.'

Later we were joined by a Chinese girl called Linda, who told us she was a swimming instructor. 'In China many people no swim,' she explained. 'And Wuhan is very far from sea, no one able to swim at all. Very good place for swim teacher.' She told me I should teach Chinese people how to ride bicycles. 'Everybody think all Chinese can bicycle, no true. I never even try. I have scooter.'

That night I had a strange experience on my way back to the Shengli. I had stopped by the river to blow my nose, but after a prolonged sneezing fit my head began to swim. I had to sit down on the pavement for a while, trying not to be sick. Unable to walk in a straight line, I nevertheless made it back to the hotel. I asked the girls at reception if there was a doctor I could see. They told me I should try the Union Hospital, but that it would be best to wait until the morning.

That night I could not sleep. My sense of balance was distorted and my breathing was wheezier than ever. My head and lungs were full of phlegm and my inner ear was humming. At 8 a.m. sharp I hailed a taxi and was dropped off at the Union, an enormous building somewhere in the suburbs.

'Er dwor, er dwor,' I told the white-coated nurse at reception, while pointing at my ear. She led me to a counter where I was presented with a yellow chit. She then led me down several corridors, past a girl in pigtails inhaling on a nebulizer and a groaning man on a stretcher. The nurse guided me up several flights of stairs to a doctor who reminded me of Mole in *The Wind In The Willows*: plump, fidgety and with a permanent squint. After feeling my pulse he opened a briefcase and extracted a tuning fork. After tapping it on his knee he thrust it into my ear. It made a dull hum. He then took out a small rod about the size of a finger with a cone-shaped probe on top. He stuffed this up my right nostril, hard. I yelped with anxiety and he extracted it and shoved it up my left nostril. By this time I was frazzled, my head spinning. The doctor extracted the probe again and opened up a dusty book. Among the Chinese characters I saw an English phrase: Secretory Exudative Otitis Media. He pointed at it proudly, apparently delighted at having diagnosed my illness. I smiled politely, as if I knew exactly what it meant.

I was directed into another room. A white screen was put up to segregate me and I was told to lie down. My nurse, a grey-haired, kind-faced woman, smiled and told me, 'Never mind.' She then stuck another probe up my nostril but this time much deeper. The instrument acted like a little Hoover and I could feel the contents of my inner nose being sucked up like fluff from behind the sofa. After this my head was so far gone I didn't really care what happened to me, barring a lobotomy. Yet another probe was inserted in my two nostrils. This time it delved far, far deeper, mining its way into the corners of my brain. Instead of vacuuming, this time the probe actually exhaled air and I could feel the pressure on my eardrum. I started to whimper. The nurse tut-tutted at my cowardice. 'Never mind, never mind,' she said sympathetically. By the time she had finished both eardrums felt clear and my equilibrium was partially restored. I was given two nose-squirters, some antibiotics and a bottle of cod liver oil to melt my ear wax. The whole operation had been completed in less than an hour and cost only four yuan. For all Wuhan's faults, I had to concede that the healthcare was outstanding; myopic doctors, tuning forks, nostril vacuums and all.

The next day I headed south. After the friendly atmospheric Sichuan landscape, Hubei was a let-down. I had begun to imagine that all rural China would be an agricultural idyll of rice terraces, buffaloes and farmers in lampshade hats. What confronted me instead was one of the most tedious stretches of the trip, a bland plain punctuated by industrial sites where the people were not openly hostile, but rarely friendly either.

The days in Hubei and then Hunan passed slowly and I often spent the nights in truckers' dormitories. They cost only ten yuan a night but were usually empty and soulless, with grimy linen. Often, I would be propositioned by sour-looking prostitutes and I longed for the friendly banter and spicy food of Sichuan. In Hunan, it was a struggle to make any sort of human contact at all. Perhaps it was a hangover from the Cultural Revolution, a time when friends betrayed friends and families denounced families to Mao's violent Red Guards. Perhaps it was just the weather or the bleakness, but something was wrong.

It was probably just me. My sinuses were blocked, my head fuzzed by the antibiotics and I was desperate to be among friends: not the friends I had known for a couple of days in a campsite in Pakistan or a youth hostel in Marseilles, but friends I had known – worked with, studied with, lived with, loved – for years. I had not had a proper conversation with anyone since my night with the Peace Corps in Neijiang, almost three weeks before.

My worst day, perhaps the nadir of the entire journey, was Christmas Eve. It began badly when I slashed my front tyre on a shard of glass just outside the little town of Miluo. I sat beside the busy road and threaded on my emergency spare; a thinner weaker one but it would have to do. An hour after putting on the fresh tyre, I had suffered four more punctures. It was only while fixing the fourth that I realized a piece of sharp gravel had become embedded in the rubber and was inflicting the same wound each time. When the puncture patch failed to stick I flew into a rage and, for the first time on the trip, kicked the bike.

Finally I reached Changsha, a town so ugly it was enough to take your breath away. It almost made me homesick for Milton Keynes.

What a place to spend Christmas.

Things did not improve. For some bizarre reason the budget hotels were not prepared to accommodate foreigners. I went from one guest house to the next dragging my bike through the rain, hawking phlegm and muttering curses under my breath. The Binhua Hotel, *meiyou* (no); the Lotus Hotel, *meiyou*; the Xiangjiang, *meiyou*. With pathetic irrationality I told them: 'But it's Christmas.'

I poked my head longingly into the reception of the Furama Hotel. It looked so tempting: plastic reindeer, a puppet Santa with a cotton wool beard, Mariah Carey singing festive muzak. All that for seventy quid a night. Should I treat myself? *No*. I reminded myself that the trip was about simplicity and endurance. *Wow*, look at that waitress. *Stop that*. Remember, Captain Charles never stayed in a Furama. *Stuff Captain Charles*. See that buffet, the drumstick on that turkey? Get on with your quest. Christmas is just another day. Seventy quid is a huge chunk of your budget. But look at that tree, the fairy lights, the presents, the mistletoe.

With a heavy heart I wrenched myself away before I heard any champagne corks pop and eventually bedded down in a miserable room somewhere behind the railway station. At midnight I opened a bottle of beer, prising off the top with the door handle. The bottle slipped out of my hands and smashed on the concrete floor. I began to laugh then slumped down on to the bed and looked out at the jaundiced moon. Happy

Christmas, everybody. Outside, some of Changsha's road drills were still at work, pulsating through the night.

I woke late. It's Christmas Day, I thought. CHRISTMAS DAY. Sod it, I WILL treat myself, if only to breakfast. I left the bike in my room, fought my way through the washing and bird cages hanging on the guest house balcony and walked up the main road to the Furama. Pushing open the glass swing doors I sashayed past the reindeer and plastic Santas and made a beeline for the restaurant. My grey tracksuit bottoms and cycling shoes were filthy and I had not shaved for over a month. The sharp-suited receptionist eyed me warily.

I sat by myself and studied the menu. 'For 45 yuan eat as much as you like from our breakfast buffet.' Oh yes! I piled my tray with every breakfast ingredient imaginable: scrambled egg, bacon, sausage, tomatoes, toast, Rice Krispies, watermelon, yoghurt, honey, fruit salad, cups of coffee, orange juice, grapefruit juice and milk. The temptation was too much and I ate most of it with my fingers, shoving in mouthful after mouthful.

I finished the lot within about fifteen minutes and leant back, looking about the room while the waitresses fussed around me. This is the life, I thought. An American family was at the far end of the restaurant; they were all wearing paper hats. The rest of the diners were Chinese businessmen, eating conservative portions of congee (rice porridge) or boiled eggs. They sat reading papers or chatting quietly on mobile phones. A girl in a blue skirt was playing 'Jingle Bells' on the piano. This is just great, I told myself, but it wasn't really great at all. I had forgotten how boring smart hotels could be: no lovers' tiffs, no travellers' yarns, no guitars, no cockroaches. It was safe, comfortable, everybody looked the same, none of the waitresses scowled; there was no bustle, no dodgy plumbing, no despair, no comedy, no life. Luxurious yes, but very dull.

The one good thing about the Furama was that I could send a fax home. I was horrified at how sentimental I was becoming about an occasion that usually only prompted cynicism. The thought of my nieces and nephews surrounding the Christmas tree at Swanbourne left me misty-eyed and nostalgic. The carol singers on the silage trailer, the candles at midnight, *Only Fools and Horses – that* was Christmas – not eating Rice Krispies at the bloody Furama.

The fax operator was a helpful soul with a droopy Charlie Chan moustache who, sensing my homesickness, told me that I should contact the Changsha School of English. He was sure they would be having a Christmas party. He wrote down the telephone number of a man called Zhao Xiong, the headmaster. Why not? I thought. Sure enough, two hours later the exuberant Zhao came to pick me up in a taxi.

Zhao was a tubby man with a lank mop of hair wearing black jeans and a check shirt. As we drove through Changsha he described the city as if it was the eighth wonder of the world, pointing at the hideous tower blocks with enormous pride and reciting population statistics or the price of real estate. It was not as if Zhao was unable to make comparisons. He had lived in America for over a year, teaching at a school in Iowa; he had seen New York and the Grand Canyon. He had also travelled around many of the more salubrious parts of China; but Changsha was his home, his Swanbourne, and neither hell nor high water would drag him away.

The school of English was unusual, he told me, because part of it was a boarding school, one of the first in China. It was an experiment that had only been running for six months but he was confident it would be a success.

'A boarding school,' I said. 'Surely it is against your country's politics?'

'Not really,' replied Zhao as we drove past a rank of rickshaw drivers. 'China is changing fast. I admit that ten years ago it would have been impossible but now the private sector is booming and accounts for about a quarter of the economy.'

'So how much do the pupils pay?'

'About 2,400 yuan for two months. In pounds that's about two hundred and fifty. I know it's high but we get excellent results and if pupils leave speaking good English, their job prospects seriously improve. All the teachers are highly qualified too.'

'Do any of the pupils come from Beijing or Shanghai?'

'Oh no. Only from Hunan Province,' he replied. 'Quite local. They have all finished state education and just want to try living away from home, to have a go at learning English intensively.'

We reached the school at lunchtime. It was located high in one of Changsha's central tower blocks and was much smaller than I had expected, only catering for fifty boarders, almost half of whom were girls. The students were mainly in their late teens and early twenties.

Zhao gave me a quick tour. The classrooms were drab but seemed to be well equipped, with slide projectors, videos and computers scattered about. Further up the corridor were the dormitories. The girls' room was very neat and there were several posters of Andy Lau, the current darling of Chinese teeny-boppers. The boys' dormitory was reassuringly messy, with Stallone and Pamela Anderson clearly favoured as pin-ups.

I had lunch with Zhao in a café up the street and then we returned for the afternoon Christmas party. All of the students had turned up and were very excited. One of the classrooms had been cleared and a karaoke machine set up; streamers garlanded the windows and there was a plastic tree with several presents beneath it. Zhao vanished for a few minutes and then reappeared in a red anorak with a white cotton wool beard stuck on his chin with Sellotape, much to the delight of the students.

The party had been organized as a talent contest, in which everybody had to speak English. We sat on plastic chairs around the room. The first performer was a prim girl in a black dress who nervously recited 'The Crow and The Fox', one of Aesop's fables. It was received with generous applause. She was followed by Henry, an effusive boy, who talked of his love of the school, of learning English, of how China needed to open up and integrate globally. He finished by shouting, 'I love you all, I really love you all.' In normal circumstances, it would have made me wince, but here in the middle of grey industrial Hunan, it almost made me want to cry.

Henry was succeeded by a girl in a flowing blue robe who performed a slow dance, elegantly swinging her body and head while her hands fluttered like little moths. It was a performance of unexpected sensuality. This was followed by a girl playing a Chinese harp the size of a small coffin. She plucked at the strings, of which there were at least twenty, her pale face contorted with concentration.

Then it was my slot. I felt utterly embarrassed by my lack of talent: I could play no instrument, barring a poor rendition of 'Greensleeves' on the trumpet; I could not sing, dance or remember any suitable poetry. So I spoke about my bicycle ride. I talked of the incident in Turkey when I had shouted at the bus and when I had frozen in the truck with the Kham-pas in Tibet. I talked of the women in Iran, the sunsets over the Ganges; I talked of the Anands and of Ghafor. At the end I told them, 'Until this afternoon, I had been having a really tough time in Hunan. I thought I would be spending Christmas alone. But now I have enjoyed a Christmas I will never forget. As Henry would say, I love you all.'

Talking about my trip to this animated audience made me

appreciate how lucky I was. Here I was with a passport which now had seventeen stamps; half of these students would probably never have the chance to leave Hunan and might never see Beijing, let alone the places I had mentioned. Things were back in perspective; it was time for me to stop whingeing and crack on.

'Thank you for a great evening,' I told Zhao, when he dropped me back outside my guest house.

'Will we see you tomorrow?'

'No, I have to move on.'

'You mean you are not going to Shaoshan, Chairman Mao's birthplace? It is very near here.'

'I heard there wasn't much to look at now.'

'Some days, no, but tomorrow is special,' said Zhao. 'Tomorrow is Chairman Mao's birthday!'

Zhao's tip-off was just too tempting. And so, on Boxing Day, I caught the sluggish train to Shaoshan, the village where Mao Zedong was born. The distance was only sixty-odd miles but it took four hours, during which patriotic anthems blasted out in the carriages. In a courtyard near Shaoshan station, I queued with the other pilgrims to catch one of the shuttle buses into the lush valley where Mao spent his childhood. We sped down a series of twisting roads and the landscape looked as appealing as the hills I had cycled through in Sichuan several weeks before.

The first attraction pointed out to us was Mao's house beside a small lake. Like the other peasant houses, it was mud walled with a thatched roof but Mao's father had been an ambitious land-owning peasant and his family home was bigger than most, with enough space for Mao, his two brothers and his sister to have a room each.

I spent the day wandering the area. There were thousands of Chinese milling about – stooped old men in blue Mao suits, smartly dressed party cadres and their manicured wives and flocks of excited youngsters. The centrepiece is a bronze statue of Mao, ten metres high, which was unveiled by Jiang Zemin in 1993 before he became China's president. The statue towers over the tourist market. In celebration of Mao's birthday a large area alongside the statue was carpeted with red firecrackers and they crackled and flipped in the air throughout the day.

One of the museums contained a mass of photos and cuttings, capturing Mao at every stage of his life from schoolboy to teacher, from dashing communist soldier to Long March hero, from poet to dictator, right up to the bloated and paranoid monster of his dotage. There were pictures of him with his sour-looking wife, Jian Qing, and his long-suffering sidekick, Zhou Enlai. Perhaps the most poignant was of Mao's son, Anying, shortly before he was killed in the Korean War.

Mao only returned to Shaoshan twice during his time in power: first in 1959 and then in 1966. But it still became the most sacred pilgrimage site in China during the Cultural Revolution. After Mao's death in 1976 the number of visitors tailed right off until the resurgence following the Tiananmen Square massacre in 1989. In 1991, over a million visitors flocked to the village but interest is once again on the wane.

Internationally, Chairman Mao is the one name (excluding Confucius) people most associate with China. Yet according to the writer John Gittings, a year after the fiftieth anniversary of the People's Republic of China, 'a survey showed that two-thirds of a sample of primary school pupils in Beijing had not even heard of Chairman Mao (and only one could recite the national anthem)'.

I suspected there would be no more firecrackers in Shaoshan until the following Boxing Day. In fifty years' time there may well be none at all.

*

Over the next few days I covered a vast distance. I cycled furiously through Hunan's grey towns and villages hoping to get within striking distance of Hong Kong before my visa expired. By 29 December I had reached the cheerless town of Leiyang, roughly 150 miles south of Changsha. There I jumped on to a southbound train, sharing a hard seat with a man cradling a wicker box full of cats. The following afternoon I caught a swanky hovercraft, known as a Jetcat, from Guangzhou to Hong Kong. I had cut it fine, leaving China with less than half a day to run on my visa.

Three hours later, the Jetcat docked at Tsimshatsui. 'Welcome to Hong Kong,' said the captain. My heart pounded. Thank God, I thought, finally a place where I know my way around; a place of fond memories and old friends. Hong Kong was an important stopover in the trip. I would mark the occasion with a celebratory bottle of Tsing Tao, but not before doing something I had been looking forward to for over a year. It was time to call Alexandra.

CHAPTER NINETEEN

1997 AND ALL THAT

Alexandra was not in her office. She had left a message explaining she was spending New Year's Eve with her father in Thailand. 'Nobody knew where you were,' her secretary told me. It was a fair comment; I had not called for months. Virendra was not in his office either, off on a business trip somewhere. Ali Kwan had left Hong Kong, so had Yvonne and Andrew, Marcus and Irena and half a dozen other people I had once known.

I had forgotten that this was Hong Kong, the human funfair where few visitors stayed on the merry-go-round for long. But there was one person I knew would still be there: Les Charlton, an old journalist friend who lived across Victoria Harbour in one of Wanchai's tower blocks.

The Star Ferry, the famous fleet of green and white boats that have plied between Kowloon and Hong Kong island for over a century, refused to allow my bike on board. I remounted and pedalled instead to the bicycle-friendly pier at Hong Hum. Signs advertising CUP NOODLES, NIKON and CROCODILE blazed from Central district's skyscrapers, their red and gold and purple lights motionless and strangely beautiful. By law, Hong Kong's neon never flashes or flickers – to avoid confusing the pilots landing at Kai Tak airport or the navigators of passing ships.

Les's flat was on Queen's Road East in the boisterous heart of Wanchai. From the ferry terminus I wheeled my bike past a hawker frying octopus and a boy spinning a luminous yo-yo. Victoria Harbour looked as lovely as ever with the junks and sampans and the distant tankers and warships. It also smelt as vile as I remembered, its water so toxic that, a photographer friend had once told me, it was possible to develop negatives in it. Far ahead was the dark distinctive pinnacle of Victoria Peak.

I dodged the trams and the red taxis and barged my way along pavements full of early-evening revellers; the young *taipans* in their sharp suits, the strip-show touts and the wide-eyed tourists. Wanchai was just as dynamic as I remembered it.

Les was not at his flat so I asked the staff in the nearby tea house if they had seen him. They shrugged their shoulders. Surely Les had not deserted his beloved Hong Kong? He was probably out late, working on a story or an editing job; so to kill some time I decided to take a walk down memory lane.

When I first arrived in Hong Kong to look for work in the spring of 1992, I hated the place. I had come fresh from a Cotswold cottage flanked by a field of ancient oak trees and a job on a weekly paper so rustic the locals knew it as The Hedger and Ditcher. After three happy years writing about prize-winning sheep and crop circles, I needed a change. I bought a one-way Aeroflot ticket and decided to try my luck in the Pearl of the Orient, one of the most densely populated few acres on earth.

My first home had been a noisy fleapit on Lockhart Road between a tailor's and a strip club but only HK$2,200 (about £200) a month. I shared it with Grace Chan, a mainland Chinese woman who owned a wildly disorganized clothing business, and Tony Chow, a morose chef who worked all hours to pay off the Triads. We never saw much of each other as Grace was often in China and Tony was always cooking. So I spent my time, having failed to land any journalism work, pulling pints at a bar called the Wanch in the evenings and teaching English in the afternoons.

I went down to the Wanch which was as lively as ever; inside, a band called Miss Venezuela was blasting out old Blondie numbers. I fought my way through the throng and ordered a beer at the bar. The oriental parasols were still hanging from the ceiling, I was happy to see, and the Bogart film posters were in place, along with the yard of ale and jars of pickled eggs.

But I knew nobody now. The two British bar girls I had worked with were long gone. There was no sign of 'Ice Baby' Frances, or any of the Filipino crew, no sign either of Roland or Howard, the maverick Scottish engineers who owned the bar. My head was filled with bitter-sweet memories, and I regretted that Teddy, the old Filipino bar manager was not there.

Teddy had been the boss during my three-month stint at the Wanch. The night I started work back in March 1992 was the night of the International Rugby Sevens, Hong Kong's most delirious social weekend. I pulled pints, shook cocktails and microwaved steak and kidney pies non-stop from 6 p.m. to the early hours. It was great. I was on a high, operating the optics with Tom Cruise-like dexterity.

Just as I was leaving that night Teddy called me over. He squinted at me through his heavy-framed glasses and nervously ran a hand through his hair. He told me that HK$500 was missing from the till. Nothing like this had ever happened while he had been in charge, he said. As I was the new boy, the finger of blame was pointed my way. My pockets were searched and, although no money was found, I was fired. I slunk back to my noisy den at 4 a.m., wondering why on earth I had not stayed in the Cotswolds.

The following morning I seriously contemplated jacking in the whole idea of life in the Orient. But before I could head for the travel agent, the telephone rang. It was Teddy. He had found the missing money underneath the till tray. He apologized and asked me back. I accepted grudgingly. Within a few days I was glad I had stayed. Gradually, I came to love Hong Kong and its furious pace.

Teddy and I became friends. Unlike the other Filipinos at the bar who were all delightfully unambitious, Teddy was very much the manager: he took his job seriously and wanted to earn money to travel. He talked of visiting China and America and Europe. In the mornings I taught him to play tennis and in the evenings, after work, he taught me to play mah-jong with his Filipino friends. They were happy times but Teddy was restless. He talked of Los Angeles and Beijing, of the Grand Canyon and the Great Wall.

After three months at the Wanch I found work with a publishing company and, fed up with living in my Wanchai shoebox, moved to Mui Wo, a fishing village on Lantau Island some twenty miles away. I began commuting back and forth from Central by ferry and visited the bar less and less. Teddy and I slowly drifted out of touch. After an absence of many months I returned to the Wanch and was surprised to see a new manager, a softly spoken Scot called Hamish.

'What's happened to Teddy?' I asked him.

'Teddy?' he replied. 'Haven't you heard? He's dead.'

'Dead! My God. What happened?'

'Apparently he took a suitcase of Hong Kong dollars over to Manila,' explained Hamish. 'He changed the money into US dollars in a back street. Having completed the deal, he jumped into the back of a taxi. Two gangsters jumped in on either side of him; they drew guns and told Teddy to hand over the case. He refused and they shot him. Terrible business. We had flowers on the bar here for a week or so.'

I could just see Teddy refusing to hand over the money. He had been so proud. That suitcase of cash had represented his dreams, his Great Wall, his Grand Canyon. He had been unable to let it go, even with guns in his side. Now he was six foot under in the family graveyard, his hard-earned savings in the hands of Manila gangsters. Of all people, he did not deserve that. Life made no sense sometimes.

For old times' sake I ate a steak and kidney pie before returning to the flat. Les was still not back. I fell asleep on a chair leaning against a pillow lent to me by the concierge. Les eventually turned up at 2.30 a.m. after a long stint putting a magazine to bed. It was great to see him. Good old Les.

We dragged my bike into Les's sixteenth-floor flat before I slumped down on his sofa. Les cracked me a beer and retired to the kitchen to fry up some chips. Les is one of Hong Kong's survivors, one of life's survivors. His rollercoaster career has included work as a plumber, a bantamweight boxer, a corporal in the RAF and a Fleet Street feature writer. He has written two novels, both set in Zambia, and a biography of the controversial preacher, Colin Morris. He is now an established Hong Kong freelance writer.

Now in his sixties, Les shows no sign of slowing down. The fact he is in such excellent shape is miraculous. He lives on eggs, chips and beans, consumes about twenty mugs of milky tea a day, each with five sugars, and smokes enough cigarettes to dent the ozone layer. Indeed, he inhales so aggressively that the smoke never reappears, not from his mouth, his nose or even his ears. Somehow it becomes absorbed in his system, yet he never coughs or wheezes and thinks nothing of walking up dozens of stairs.

Only Les's closest friends know that his left leg has been amputated below the knee. I had known him for two weeks before someone mentioned the fact to me, and only then did I notice he had a slight limp. In all the time I have known him, I've never once heard him complain about his dummy leg, unless to crack a joke about it. He is a friend who commands the utmost respect.

Les and I first met at the Foreign Correspondents' Club in Hong Kong. At the time I had just secured a two-week job – the regular columnist being on holiday – with the *South China Morning Post*, writing a dreadful social column called 'People'. It was the cushiest of jobs. I had to turn up at any parties or promos, snap a few pictures and write sycophantic dross about the assembled glitterati. Les was at one of the parties I covered and started taking the piss out of my instamatic camera. We became friends soon after.

Les and I stayed up until the early hours, eating chips and watching *Hancock's Half Hour* videos. We were on the verge of 1997, a date synonymous with Hong Kong's destiny. One thing was certain about the colony's future: Les Charlton would be part of it. He was one of the few expats who had every right to call Hong Kong home.

I ended up staying a fortnight in Hong Kong. I made endless enquiries about hitching a ride on a boat to Singapore, but came across the same hurdles – insurance, red tape, lack of seafaring certificates – as I had done at the Suez Canal. Securing lifts on cargo boats was clearly a problem the world over. The only other way south, as planes were not an option, was to pedal down through Vietnam and Cambodia into Thailand.

After obtaining a Vietnamese visa I spent much of my time

visiting former students; sweet-faced Jenny Tin, who ate bees' wings to stave off flu, nervous Alan Kwok, whose father rapped him on the knuckles with a bamboo wand if his spelling was poor, then there were Francis and Ada, cousins who were having a discreet love affair when I first met them but were now happily married. I had taught them both in Ada's tiny family flat in Happy Valley surrounded by her brothers, her hundred-year-old grandmother, a plastic Buddha embedded with incense sticks, a tank of fat goldfish and a cage of quails. I begged Ada to ask her grandmother what she thought now that the handover to China was imminent. 'Never mind,' the old woman had replied. 'Never mind.' Ada told me her granny was far more concerned that the 2000 Olympics were to be held in Sydney, not Beijing where she had been born in 1897, while the Dowager Empress Ci-Xi still ruled from the Summer Palace.

I met up with cheeky Albert Cheung, who lived in one of Tai Koo Shing's many Meccano-style tower blocks. He was, as with so many Chinese of his generation, an only child. His parents adored him and invested all they had in his future. They wanted him to be the best at everything. Not only did I teach him English every day after school, but he also attended lessons in piano, karate and chess. As was often the case in Hong Kong, his parents both worked long hours and the boy's closest friend was Ophie, the Filipina maid.

When I visited Albert this time, three years after I had first met him, the change was extraordinary. The wiry, bright-eyed lad I had known had become fat and haughty. I hardly recognized him. He wore a red and white school uniform and carried a leather satchel. Albert had been transformed into one of Hong Kong's Little Emperors. When I had asked him what he wanted to be three years ago, at the age of seven, he had replied, 'A fireman.' Now he told me, without a trace of humour, that he wanted to be 'a rich man, teacher, a very rich man'.

The change in Albert could not be applied to Hong Kong as a whole. It looked much the same. Of course there had been more land reclamation, the new airport near Lantau, Chek Lap Kok, was nearing completion and some of the traditional roadside hawkers and barbers had packed up. But Hong Kong was essentially the place I remembered. It still pulsed with entrepreneurial fervour, from the cobblers and fortune tellers in the back streets off Queen's Road to the glistening elegance of the China Bank. From the seedy warrens of Chungking Mansions in Kowloon to the designer malls of Pacific Place, Hong Kong ran on money, and now more than ever, everyone was after their cut.

Unlike most other British colonies where the local population had been eager for independence, Hong Kongers seemed strangely ambivalent. Like Ada's grandmother, 'Never mind, let's wait and see,' was the prevalent view. During my visit the papers were filled with 30 June handover build-up stories. An anarchist had emptied a huge pot of red paint over a statue of Queen Victoria and been sentenced to twenty-eight days in prison. Shan-Shan, the young Hong Kong woman who had recently won a gold medal in Atlanta for windsurfing, had become the colony's first and last Olympic heroine. There were articles by pro-democracy politicians on how unemployment would spiral under Chinese rule, and other pieces championing the 'One Country, Two Systems' model. There were features on the fate of the colony's Vietnamese refugees, who were being sent home in droves now that their crowded camps were closing down, and others expressing concern over the rare Chinese White Dolphins, as Hong Kong's last few pairs were threatened with extinction by work on the new airport.

'Within a year or two of the handover little will change in

Hong Kong,' Les told me. 'But within twenty years it will be as if the British were never here.'

On my second-last day in Hong Kong, Alexandra returned. We had a nervous reunion in Times Square, the most recent shopping complex to be constructed in Causeway Bay. It turned out to be the briefest of meetings.

Alexandra was at the time, quite simply, the love of my life. In Hong Kong it had always been Alexandra and Tom, Tom and Alexandra; we did everything together. I would make a move, she would reject me; I would ignore her, we would re-unite; I would make another move, she would ignore me, then we would make up, and so it went on. It was a relationship founded on expectation. Only when I left Hong Kong late in 1995 did I start to shrug off Alexandra's influence on my heart. When she was close at hand she always cast a siren-like spell over me. I had no idea how we would feel about each other now, after more than a year apart.

She looked as beautiful as ever, like a Botticelli angel smoking a Silk Cut. She wore black jeans, a suede cowboy belt and a black polo neck jumper. Her long fair hair framed her lightly freckled face. Oh God, I thought immediately, I'm still in love with her. We sat in an Italian restaurant and looked at each other for a long time, as if scanning favourite photographs. For an hour or so we talked about old times, the walks on the MacLehose Trail, the junk trips, the friends who had moved on.

'So your father is still working you hard?' I finally asked. Alexandra helped manage her father's company, which distributes leather goods — handbags, wallets, belts — over much of Asia.

'Yes, of course,' she replied, in her soft German accent. 'I've always told you I'm married to my work.'

379

'So there's no one else?'

'No. What about you?'

'No. But I'm starting to find my bicycle strangely attractive.'

'You must have met lots of beautiful girls on the trip?'

'But none of them as beautiful as you.' Oh God. Corny, Tom, seriously corny. 'What I want to know is why you haven't been swept off your feet by some debonair entrepreneur, Alexandra. Your father would love that.'

'Stop being so cynical, Tom. You always have to bring my father into it. He's a great boss. Besides, you've never even met him.'

'You never wanted me to. Anyway heaven forbid, he'd probably challenge me to a duel.'

'God you're boring. You're always telling me that being a businesswoman doesn't suit me, that it's draining me of my youth. It's always your same nonsense. You only get one shot at the dream, blah, blah, blah. Come on, Tom, forget it. Let's talk about something else. You never grow up, do you? Cycling around with your head in the clouds.'

'It beats being in your boots, baby.' *Baby*? Where did that come from? I must have been hanging around with too many Americans.

'Don't call me, baby!'

'OK, crackle pants.'

'Stop it. Just stop it. No wonder we can never be together. We always end up fighting.' After a long pause, the silence creeping over us like the roots of an invisible plant, she said in a shaky voice, 'I'm sorry, Tom, but the truth is you always loved me far more than I loved you.'

Her words hit me like a fist in the face.

'Now *you* are talking nonsense,' I countered aggressively, even though I knew what she said was true. 'Why on earth did you spend so much time with me? Why? What was the point of that? Why didn't you find another boyfriend?' I banged my fist down on the table and the glasses trembled.

'Stop it Tom. Jesus. Look at you, you are crying.'

'So are you.'

'No, I'm not.' She wasn't, but at least her eyes looked bloodshot and wounded. 'And I'm not going to cry either.' She banged her fist down on the table and the glasses trembled again. A few diners from surrounding tables had started to look at us. We looked at each other again and burst out laughing. It was a nice moment, and helped me to better disguise my waterlogged eyes.

'So you won't marry me then, Your Majesty.' I moved to hold her hand.

'I have thought about it sometimes,' she said, brushing her fingers through my hair. 'Living in the country somewhere, far away from all this. But not in this lifetime.'

'Oh well, there's always my bicycle.' I looked away from her. 'I'm sorry I mentioned your father.'

'Yes, the two of you would actually get on well,' she said softly. She stopped picking her beer mat and looked up at me. 'We've certainly had a weird and wonderful time together, Tom.'

'Don't tell me. You're vonderful and I'm veird.'

She laughed at my hammy German accent. I enjoyed making her laugh, she always looked so lovely.

But this was the end of the road for Alexandra and me. I ordered the bill and shepherded her through the rain to the nearest taxi rank where we held each other, very hard, for a long time. We no longer cared about the rain or the looks of others in the queue. A taxi pulled in at the rank.

'See you,' said Alexandra. 'Good luck.'

'You too,' I replied.

She jumped into the back seat and slammed the door shut.

As the taxi pulled away, I could see her slump down with her hands to her face. Her unhappiness soothed my pride, but swelled my heart with an unbearable sense of loss. I knew we would never see each other again.

Two days later I returned to Guangzhou having caught a return Jetcat. It was already 14 January and I wanted to reach Vietnam as quickly as possible. Hong Kong had buoyed me in some ways – seeing Les and some of my old students – but I was glad to be on the move again. Travel is the best palliative for a damaged heart.

I booked into the Guangzhou Youth Hostel on Shamian Island in the Pearl River. The hostel had changed since I last stayed there in 1992. Then, I had slept in a huge open-plan barracks with over forty beds. Now I was billeted in a neat three-bed dormitory with an *en suite* bathroom. The room even had a tree decorated with little red envelopes in readiness for Chinese New Year.

Other things about Guangzhou had changed too. Five years earlier I remembered it taking several minutes to cross the main road due to the constant torrent of cyclists, but now that torrent had dwindled to a thin easily-dodgeable trickle. Modern Guangzhou, the capital of Guangdong, China's wealthiest province, was now a city of cars and motorbikes, of mobile phones and foreign investment. In many ways it seemed Hong Kong was influencing Guangzhou rather than the other way round. But along with the rich, as always, came the poor, the dowdy refugees from the countryside, dreaming of a slice of Guangzhou's fortune while huddled in blankets outside the city's railway station.

Guangzhou was certainly a very different place when Captain Charles visited in 1831. At that time the East India Company conducted a lucrative trade in tea, silks and porcelain through

Canton (the city's old name) despite strong resistance from the Chinese authorities. The tea was principally paid for by opium from India which was smuggled by the British into south China. This opium dealing – the Chinese referred to the drug as 'foreign mud' – infuriated the Chinese authorities and, in 1831, the trade was temporarily suspended. Captain Charles was sent in the *Challenger* to deliver a letter of protest to the Viceroy of Canton. At the time there were no other British warships in Chinese waters.

This is what Captain Charles wrote to his brother, Sir Thomas Fremantle, back at Swanbourne, on 23 December 1831.

> It is impossible to tell you the sensation that has been created by my arrival in Canton, the Chinese are greatly alarmed ... It is truly absurd their fears, the style of their letters, their little knowledge of the art of War and their general blustering manner. I am ordered away and told that I am not to come here making disturbances of which I of course take no notice ... it would be great amusement to bring the Chinese to a sense of our power, until we do that we shall never be able to trade with them on a respectable or firm footing.

Writing of the opium trade in a later letter, Captain Charles revealed that he was not unaware of the immorality of the traffic. 'It is perhaps the most extraordinary trade carried on in any part of the World, immense fortunes are made by the English ... the injury that is done throughout China by it is terrible as it is spreading everywhere and is smoaked (sic) from the Emperors Palace to the lowest person who can afford to purchase it.'

After delivering the letter of protest Captain Charles stayed in Canton for another couple of months, until trading between the East India Company and China resumed and, on his return to England, made some recommendations to the Admiralty.

He identified Kowloon as a good base for any future attack on Canton. 'From my Knowledge of the different Islands . . . I am of the opinion that the Town of Cowloon situated on the Main Land is well adapted for all the purposes that would be required, it is rather a large Town possessing a beautiful Harbour formed by the port of Hong Kong opposite.' These were prescient words. Hong Kong was ceded to Britain in 1842 after the first Opium War. Captain Charles had arrived in Hong Kong a decade before it became a colony, and I was leaving six months before the Chinese claimed it back.

Five days later I was in Pingxiang, a little town a few miles from the Vietnamese border. It was time for the final leg.

CHAPTER TWENTY

THE ROAD TO SAIGON

My first few days in Vietnam got the trip back on course. Not since India had first impressions of a country been so positive. It was just what I needed: a landscape to fire up my imagination and quicken my pulse; it seemed that for the last few weeks I had been doing little more than tread water.

It was easy to say goodbye to China, a country that had charmed and infuriated me in equal measure. At first I had relished its many challenges, enjoyed scratching at its intriguing surface, but after a while its vastness had begun to wear me down. I hoped to be back one day, but for now it was time to move on.

What thrilled me most over those first few days was rural Vietnam's exuberance. Only minutes after crossing the border, approaching the little town of Dong Dang, a group of child cyclists swooped in alongside me. One of them was a young girl pedalling a bicycle far too large for her, pumping at the pedals as if her life depended on it. 'I love Russia,' she shouted at me. She was following two boys on BMX-style bikes, who wanted to race.

At first they shot ahead of me. Then I clicked through my gears and pulled ahead. And so it went on for at least half a mile with each of us jockeying for position along the deserted road. Eventually we fell into an acrobatic routine: I would raise my right arm and swerve over, and they would follow, then we would stick our legs out in unison. After they got the hang of it, the boys took the lead and I started aping their moves. Sometimes they would raise both arms from the handlebars for thirty seconds at a time – I could manage ten seconds tops – and we would take flight; except for the little girl who pedalled furiously behind us, hands glued to her handlebars. After the oppressiveness of biking in Hunan, I appreciated the spontaneity.

What I remember most about Vietnam are the skies. Within a few hours they could vary from smoky-grey to brilliant blue, while the sunsets would evolve from translucent orange to blood red as the light died. Always in the foreground would be the intense green of the rice paddies and banana palms, the women in black pyjamas stooped over the seedlings, the fishermen in waders casting their nets, the Minsk motorbikes with piglets strapped either side of the engine, the mud-spattered buffalo and the white geese. Then the sky, sometimes bruised, sometimes clear, but always dramatic.

The Old Quarter in Hanoi, north of Hoan Kiem Lake, is one of the most boisterous spots on earth. A jigsaw of ancient trading streets spill over with life and it is a place where you can, give or take the odd bootleg CD, transport yourself back to the turn of the century.

As I rode alongside the lake, enchanting girls in white *ao dai* wavered past on bicycles, flower sellers offered garlands of jasmine and mah-jong tiles could be heard all around, as Graham Greene wrote, 'like shingle turning after a big wave on a beach'. The fruit sellers, with their betel-nut smiles, had the best-stocked stalls I have ever seen, with piles of papaya, avocado, custard apples, jackfruit, green bananas and knobbly sugar cane.

Barefoot *cyclo* riders, their passengers seated in front of them, trundled through the cobbled alleys and at St Joseph's Cathedral children were playing tag around a statue of the Virgin Mary smothered in pink blossom. Men in soup-tureen helmets offered to ferry tourists to Ho Chi Minh's mausoleum on the back of their Vespas, while all around the smell of lemon grass and diesel fumes filled the air. I fired off three rolls of film in a single morning, as much as I had used during a month in China.

During my three days in Hanoi I stayed with Hoi Trinh, a Vietnamese friend I had known in Hong Kong, where he had worked briefly as a volunteer in a refugee camp. Hoi is one of the most infuriatingly gifted people I know. Not only is he fantastically clever and morally upright, but he's also irresistible to women. If he weren't so damned charming, I would hate him.

Like so many Vietnamese, in the late seventies Hoi's family escaped on a boat to Australia. Hoi, who was only eight years old at the time and spoke no English, arrived in Melbourne, disorientated and hungry. His father odd-jobbed his way through the lean years in order to give his children a start in life. Hoi won a scholarship to school and later secured a law degree and a job as a trainee solicitor. Six months before my arrival in Hanoi he had been posted to the city by his company – his first time back in Vietnam in over twenty years.

When I cycled into Hanoi the evening of 20 January, Hoi was waiting for me outside St Joseph's, sitting on a bicycle which was far too small for his lanky frame. Together we pedalled back to his home, a stuccoed apartment with green worm-eaten shutters in a narrow alley south of the French

Quarter. Hoi was convinced the apartment was under surveillance. He told me the police were interested in him because he mixed with Vietnamese refugees who had recently returned from Hong Kong.

'This city is a madhouse, mate,' said Hoi, in his thick Australian accent. He pulled down my sofa bed, pushing away a pile of magazines to make room for it. 'You realize I had to get permission from the police to let you stay here?'

'You're kidding?'

'Not at all,' replied Hoi, amused by my surprise. 'I know this is Vietnam, the new darling of the backpacker brigade and all that, but it has its sinister side too. For all the tourism and foreign investment Hanoi is a communist city. Remember this is the place where Ho Chi Minh sleeps.'

'I'd like to visit the old boy's tomb.'

'Don't bother,' advised Hoi. 'He's embalmed in an expensive mausoleum, surrounded by armed guards and gawped at by thousands of gormless tourists all day. Poor bastard, all he really wanted was a simple funeral, for his ashes to be scattered across different parts of the country.' Hoi threw his arm in the air to demonstrate, accidentally whacking a set of wind chimes. He waited for the jangles to subside before continuing.

'Uncle Ho seems to have stood the test of time better than many leaders. Want to know why?' asked Hoi, pacing his little sitting room, dodging the pot plants and empty coffee cups. 'Because he was secretive, that's why. He never married and never wrote dairies; and that is the key to his sustained popularity. I just read a book on Chairman Mao that talked about his acute constipation. How can you revere a man when you know stuff like that about him?'

The following morning I was startled out of bed by the loud crackle of a street tannoy. An avuncular sing-song voice, which sounded like a Vietnamese Ronald Reagan, echoed through the neighbourhood.

'Shut up, you patronizing shithead!' Hoi shouted out of the window. He was dressed in a suit and tie ready for work.

'What's he lecturing about?' I asked.

'This morning it's about the evils of prostitution,' replied Hoi, sipping from a glass of soya milk. 'Tomorrow it will probably be about respecting politicians or something. Sometimes I wonder if Vietnam has changed at all since I last lived here.'

'Do you remember much about that time?'

'All I remember is that I was a hungry kid selling candies on street corners in Saigon,' said Hoi. 'Twenty years later I have come back wearing a business suit. I've been lucky, kids on the street corners come up and ask me for money now.

'I feel a little strange mixing with other expats sometimes,' he admitted. 'A lot of my work colleagues are fine but there's a certain superiority too. That's why in my spare time I like to teach, so I can try to remember who I once was, remember the Veitnamese Hoi as well as the Australian lawyer Hoi. I guess I've got two sides to me, just like Hanoi.'

That night I experienced the full blast of Hanoi's dual personality. Early in the evening Hoi took me and some of his students to a flashy new nightclub called the Queen Bee. A friend of his had cadged some free tickets to the launch of a new brand of cigarettes. It was an extraordinary event. Girls dressed as bumble-bees stood on top of giant cigarette boxes and writhed to rave music. Video screens pulsed with kaleidoscopic colours, lasers zapped, neon flashed and Hanoi's smart set danced the night away in leather jackets and short skirts.

'Welcome to communist Vietnam,' shouted Hoi, above the strains of deafening techno music. The half-dozen students who had accompanied us to the club had clearly never seen anything like it. They were nervous and far too embarrassed to dance. It was as glitzy as anything I had seen in Hong Kong and drinks were priced accordingly.

After half an hour we departed, heads numbed by the din, lungs full of low-tar 555. Hoi and I said farewell to his students but, before heading home he suggested there was one more place to visit. We cycled several miles into the north-east of town along the bank of the Red River. Hoi finally pulled over outside a decrepit riverside building. He told me some of his students lived there, a group of orphan boys.

The orphans' home was little more than a dimly lit warehouse with corrugated walls and mattresses spread over the floor. The boys dashed over to greet Hoi who distributed the complimentary cigarettes from the Queen Bee.

'Most of the young smoke in Hanoi. It's America's new way of killing us,' Hoi said, laughing. 'These boys were in a home but it got closed down. There are ten of them, all in their late teens.' For a while Hoi stopped speaking in English and chattered away in Vietnamese to his students. As he talked he imitated the extravagant gyrations of the dancers at the nightclub, reducing the boys to hysterics.

'If I teach them English twice a week, they have a much better chance of finding work,' explained Hoi, turning towards me. The boys surrounded us, dragging on their cigarettes. 'At the moment they are all working in factories for about five US dollars a day. Peanuts. The same price as a single drink at that nightclub. Such are the contradictions of brave new Hanoi.'

From Hanoi it took me roughly three weeks to reach Saigon. What I found curious about this stage of the trip was the number of other cyclists I met. On the stretch from Hanoi to Quang Ngai, I joined forces with five fellow pedallers, four Dutch and one Canadian, more than I had met at any time on my entire journey to date. Vietnam was clearly the new hot spot for the Lycra-panted.

The first two Dutch cyclists cruised alongside me soon after leaving Hanoi. Jan and Jorgen were stolid balding types, with identical panniers, who clocked up their miles with military determination. Both were in their early sixties and recently retired. Jan had been a businessman of some sort and Jorgen a school's inspector. They had met only weeks before the trip through a cycling club.

They were very game and pedalled at a fair lick, but after a day their fastidiousness became irritating. 'Excuse me, this salad is not crisp,' or, 'We must stop, my back right pannier is a little dirty,' and other such prissy observations. In body they were in Vietnam, but in attitude still somewhere in the Netherlands commuter belt. Perhaps in time they would succumb to Indo-China's exotic unpredictability, but I did not want to wait and find out.

The other Dutch cyclists overtook me on the road to Hue. They were a couple about my age, called Vicker and Ann Marie. Vicker was a country boy from Friesland, whereas Ann Marie was an urbane Rotterdam media student. They made a fine-looking pair: Vicker was tall and blond with a pointed Van Dyck beard and Ann Marie was moon-faced and athletic, her short hair in a bandanna. They had been joined by Jim, a quiet Canadian in his late thirties, who was pedalling, like me, down into Cambodia.

Throughout the following week the four of us cycled as a group. I teamed up with Jim as we were steady cyclists who liked to rise before dawn and pace out the day. Vicker and Ann Marie were late birds but super-fast and usually caught up with us around lunchtime. After this we would all ride together, sometimes racing, sometimes plodding along in leisurely formations.

Vicker and Ann Marie had started their cycling trip in Ulan Bator in Outer Mongolia and had zigzagged their way south into China hoping to end their adventure in Saigon. Miraculously, neither of them had suffered a single puncture yet.

On the way down to Saigon Vietnam continued to cast its spell – especially in Hue, the old capital, with its breezy canals and tombs of the ancient kings and on the glorious high passes leading into Da Nang.

One day we passed a wedding procession, a huge crowd cheering off the bride and groom. The young couple was riding on the back of a motorbike, the bride's skirt flapping in the wind, the coiffured groom wiping off his lipstick with the back of his hand. (It's not unusual for Vietnamese grooms to wear make-up.) Later the same day, near Quang Ngai, Jim and I came across a funeral party. At first I thought it might be another wedding as it all appeared very jolly, with vodka and betel-nuts being distributed to the elaborately dressed guests. There were women in baggy red shirts, men sporting yellow tabards and elders in blue smoking jackets and jaunty hats. There was also a band, dressed entirely in black, playing trumpets, cornets and lyres. A lone drummer thumped a melancholy rhythm as the coffin, suspended like a sedan chair, was lowered into the earth.

At the side of the grave was a little shrine to the dead man garlanded with sprigs of jasmine, bougainvillaea and hibiscus. A framed photo of the deceased was leaning against the flowers; he was smiling and had a crew-cut. A trio of middle-aged women in white robes shrieked with sorrow, clawing at the grass, as the band reached an ear-splitting crescendo. Apart from the women, everyone seemed to be in a remarkably sanguine mood. Jim and I stayed for a while, unsure what etiquette demanded, then made a small donation and headed on south.

The saddest place on the road to Saigon is the cemetery at My Lai. The massacre in this village on 16 March 1968 was one of the most notorious events of the Vietnam war. A platoon of American GIs went on a rampage, killing as many as 400 South Vietnamese civilians, many of them women and children. Not one shot was fired at the Americans and the only US casualty was a private who shot himself in the foot to avoid taking part in the killings.

Today, My Lai is a moving memorial, a graveyard and a museum in a garden of manicured box hedges, fruit trees and dragonflies. One headstone in particular stuck in my mind; the names of seven family members are engraved on the stone, from a seventy-year-old man down to a baby. It reminded me of the graves at Kanpur – the same savagery and waste.

The museum contained a simple display of photos and cuttings, 'to make people understand that this must never happen again'. There was a photo of Lieutenant William Calley, the portly officer who had ordered the killings. Calley, the only soldier found guilty of murder at My Lai, was subsequently sentenced to hard labour for life. President Nixon protested and the sentence was commuted to house arrest. After three years Calley was paroled. Among the other pictures was one showing the huddled corpses of the slain villagers. The most disturbing photographs were of those about to be killed: an old woman with a gun pointed at her temple, a family group cowering by a tree, a child in tears.

That evening we met up with Vicker and Ann Marie as usual. They were heading inland with Jim, up into the hills, while I was carrying on down the quicker coastal route. This would be our last meal together and I realized how much I would miss them. Ann Marie and Vicker were nearing the end of their trip and in two weeks would be back home in Holland. Jim was leaving for Vancouver a week later, after visiting Angkor in Cambodia.

Parting with my friends reminded me that the sand in my traveller's hourglass was running out. In less than 4,000 miles my adventure would be over.

I arrived in Ho Chi Minh City, still widely known as Saigon, on 8 February, just as Tet (Vietnamese new year) was kicking off. Tet is a family time and Hoi had flown down from Hanoi to see his aunt and uncle, carrying armfuls of peach blossom to bring good fortune to all who smelt it.

I pedalled to their home in a leafy suburb to the north of the city, following Hoi on his uncle's moped. It was a simple house, full of children and rangy dogs. I slept in a hammock downstairs in the kitchen and Hoi's relatives force-fed me with iced custard apples and pancakes stuffed with suckling pig. His aunt was so concerned by the wretched state of my tracksuit bottoms she took a needle and thread to them. I was never allowed to pay for anything and the more I protested, the more hospitable they became.

There were areas of the city that were still charming, especially Lam Song Square, where it was still possible to imagine the lost Saigon of Graham Greene's *The Quiet American*, with Fowler and Pyle sinking a beer in a shady alcove of the Continental. But generally it was no longer a city of opium dens and mellow afternoons; it was alive with the sound of cash tills, of people on the make.

Saigon certainly lacked Hanoi's superannuated charm and the Tet weekend seemed to bring out the worst in its citizens. Gangs of youths on mopeds roared around, terrorizing the other traffic. There were numerous fights and violent arguments on the streets, including one between a backpacker and a Vietnamese lorry driver who was transporting a cargo of dogs. The dogs whimpered and yelped, squashed tight in wooden crates, their limbs sticking out at impossible angles. One had hung itself trying to escape. The backpacker shouted at the driver and banged on his door. The driver made an insulting gesture and sped off.

On my last day in Saigon, Hoi took me to visit the War Crimes Museum, the city's top tourist attraction. Outside the museum was a mass of military equipment including Huey helicopters, F-5A jets and 'land shakers', enormous seven-ton bombs which, a notice claimed, could destroy everything within a 100-metre radius. These outdated armaments looked strangely harmless, like playground equipment that had gone to rust over a long winter.

In the museum itself the most shocking photographs were those that depicted the devastation caused by Agent Orange. One photograph showed a lush stretch of the River Mekong, lined with rows of stilted houses. After a single spraying of the defoliant, the whole area was so blackened it was impossible to make out even the outline of the river. A caption below stated that more than two million Vietnamese had been physically harmed by the after-effects of Agent Orange.

There were several apologies from American soldiers. Sergeant William Brown had sent the museum his seven combat medals. Beneath the display case was the message: 'To the people of a united Vietnam – I was wrong.' Private Richard Cavendish simply wrote to say that he was sorry. Beside these messages was a quote from Ho Chi Minh: 'To reap a return in ten years, plant trees. To reap a return in 100 years, cultivate the people.'

On the pavement outside the museum, hawkers were selling GI dog tags, each listing the soldier's name, number and religion. There were other tacky items such as cartridge-case necklaces and Zippo lighters inscribed 'God made Grass, Man made Alcohol. Who are you going to trust?'

'So what did you think?' asked Hoi.

'Most of it was enlightening,' I replied. 'A little one-sided though.'

'Why shouldn't it be?' exploded Hoi. 'The Americans have made countless films about Vietnam, written books about it. What about all the South Vietnamese who helped the Americans fight the Viet Cong? The ones who were left behind to suffer at the hands of the communists when Saigon fell in 1975? The ones the Americans deserted? When is Oliver Stone going to make a film about them?'

'Cool it, Hoi. Point taken.'

'Sorry mate, but it gets to me. Now that it's safe the Americans are filtering back to Saigon again. Here to make a quick buck. Ho Chi Minh might have beaten the US Army but sadly he'll never fight off the dollar and MTV.'

The Cambodian border is only sixty miles from Saigon but I planned to make a short detour via Tay Ninh, the headquarters of Cao Daism, an intriguing faith that incorporates aspects of Buddhism, Taoism, Confucianism, Islam and Christianity.

En route to Tay Ninh I also visited the famous Cu Chi tunnels, the remarkable underground network started by the anti-French Viet Minh in the 1940s. After France's devastating defeat at Dien Bien Phu in 1954 and subsequent withdrawal from Vietnam, the tunnels were expanded by the Viet Cong. By 1965, a 150-mile labyrinth had been dug. Despite appalling living conditions – scorpions, heat, disease and lack of space – the tunnels (some of them are only 80cm wide) provided vital secret roads to the edge of Saigon. American attempts to flush out the tunnels proved largely ineffective and the Viet Cong used the complex as a headquarters during the Tet offensive of 1968. Some months later American B52 bombers seriously damaged the Cu Chi network, but by then it had largely served its purpose.

The tunnel network is without doubt a hugely impressive feat of human engineering, but after an hour of dodging the souvenir touts and studying the educational videos and Cu Chi guerrilla mannequins, I had had enough of this strange subterranean theme park.

That night I slept at the house of a local family, putting up my tent on their verandah to shelter from the warm tropical rain. The man of the house was named Tam; he spoke broken English and had a moustache no bigger than an eyebrow. At the age of twenty Tam had lost his right leg fighting near the Cambodian border. Like Les he was extraordinarily stoical about his disability – swinging himself around on a wooden crutch, climbing ladders, riding a bike, playing with his baby son. Tam was one of many amputees I saw in Vietnam, especially Saigon; in Cambodia I was to see many more.

The following day, after a pleasant ride through a dusty red landscape dotted with eucalyptus trees, I made it to Tay Ninh. It was beginning to get dark so I made straight for the outrageous Cao Daist cathedral with its funky pagoda-style towers. It seemed I had arrived on an important day. Hundreds of people in white robes were filtering into the building while outside a group of dancers in colourful masks was performing. Founded in the 1920s by a civil servant, Ngo Van Chieu, Cao Daism is an eclectic collection of beliefs quirkily numbering Joan of Arc, Louis Pasteur, William Shakespeare and Winston Churchill among its significant luminaries.

I pushed my way through the excited crowd to try and get a seat in the cathedral. There were no other tourists and my presence seemed to be causing something of a stir. At the entrance a small walnut-faced woman told me I could only watch from the door. A man in an orange robe and a white fez was conducting the prayers for a congregation dressed exclusively in white, women to the left, men to the right, all of them kneeling.

The cathedral's interior was a riot of symbols. The most noticeable feature was a series of pink pillars threaded with snakes and dragons. The pillars soared to the sky-blue roof which was speckled with gold like sequins on a dress. The centrepiece was a huge blue orb, representative of the Divine Eye, the Cao Daists' principal symbol. To me it resembled a cross between a Salvador Dali creation and a Pink Floyd album cover. Lots of smaller eyes, each generating blue rays, peeked out from other parts of the building. But for all the cathedral's Day-Glo kitsch, there was something intensely moving about its atmosphere. Unlike the Church of the Holy Sepulchre in Jerusalem, where the atmosphere seemed divisive, at the Tay Ninh cathedral it felt genuinely harmonious, perhaps because the Cao Daists were not looking for converts.

I watched the white-robed masses as the priest said prayers. Outside, hundreds of candles were flickering in the dark. I felt a shiver go down my spine and knew that this day, 14 February 1997 was a special day. A day when I realized there was a spark of faith inside me after all.

It seemed to me that if a cyclist with stumpy legs, limited language skills and a bad sense of direction could pedal, unscathed, halfway across the world, then surely there must be some sort of God. Christ had steered me through the tangled streets of Rome and Jerusalem; Allah had guided me through Beirut and the desolation of the Sinai Desert; Brahma, Shiva and Vishnu had provided a spiritual convoy across the Punjab and the plains of Uttar Pradesh; and Buddha had inspired me up to Lhasa and then on through the hills of Sichuan.

The Cao Daists believe that Buddha is just as credible as Jesus Christ, that Confucius is just as valid as the Prophet Mohammed. Ultimately it is really just geography that determines which faith an individual belongs to. Why is it not possible to respect all faiths? All prophets?

That night I prayed for everyone I could remember, for my family and friends back home and the myriad faces I had met on the road. For the Jurdis and the Anands, for Les and Alexandra and Hoi. I gave thanks for the trip's many wonders and tried to make sense of its occasional sorrows. Finally, I prayed for a successful conclusion to my journey. The following day I would be crossing the Cambodian border and I would need every benign spirit available to watch over me.

CHAPTER TWENTY-ONE

INTO CAMBODIA

Before the writer Norman Lewis visited Cambodia in 1950, he imagined it as a country accompanied by 'tinkling, percussive music'. Sadly, it has become a place associated less with gentle drumbeats and rather more with the crackle of gunfire or the blast of a landmine. Cambodia, like Lebanon or Afghanistan, is a country with an unshakable stigma but I had often found the places I had feared the most to be hospitable and rewarding. I was confident that Cambodia would be the same.

Hoi had assured me that the hundred miles from the Vietnamese border to Phnom Penh would be fine: 'You might see the odd soldier, mate, but they aren't going to be interested in a pom on a bicycle.' It was the stretch beyond Cambodia's capital that worried him. I was hoping to reach the port of Sihanoukville on the south coast. It was near here that three foreigners, a British couple and an Australian girl, had been kidnapped and murdered by the Khmer Rouge three years prior to my visit. The risk would not be over at Sihanoukville either as from there I would have to catch a boat, illegally, into Thailand, a route already tested by determined travellers with varying degrees of success. I decided to reach Phnom Penh and then make my mind up whether to continue. I always like to keep my risks calculated, never suicidal.

Cambodia's opening miles were dramatically bleak. Vietnam's lushness disappeared as though a plague of locusts had descended leaving only a scorched and barren plain studded with skeletal trees. But within ten miles Indo-China's jungly abundance was back with eucalyptus and coconut palms by the roadside in a variegated, thickly scented hedgerow alive with the squawk of parakeets.

The landscape had a fairy-tale quality, a mixture of the grotesque and the beautiful. Roadside hawkers sold dried frogs impaled on sticks and green coconuts full of cool translucent milk. A young soldier in combat fatigues and a floppy hat wandered past with a rocket launcher slung over his shoulder while a saffron-robed monk cooled himself with a fan. At Svay Rieng I was served coffee by a long-haired man in a black T-shirt which simply read: CAMBODIA = BOMBS. The coffee tasted like nothing I had sampled before – treacle with the tang of minerals. A young girl steered her buffalo along an irrigation canal. She rode in such a relaxed manner it looked as if she was lolling on a sofa, her silhouette framed against a backdrop of unworldly blue.

The Cambodian people seemed much more laid-back than the Vietnamese. The pale, stern Chinese features of Saigon were replaced by a swarthier gentler look. Most of the Cambodians wore big lazy smiles on their moon faces. Considering the twenty years of war and repression their country had endured they displayed a remarkable lack of hostility towards outsiders.

The natural friendliness of the Cambodians, their whistles and casual waves of encouragement, bolstered my confidence as I rode through the villages, along the flat potholed roads fringed with huts of wood and corrugated tin. On my first night, I stopped near the village of Phumi Prek Toch on the banks of the Mekong River, where I knew I would have to wait for a ferry the following morning. I was unsure where to spend the night, but as usual serendipity played its part.

'Hey bro. Hey you with the bike.' A short podgy man in a grey singlet was waving at me. 'Hey bro, pull over.' I wondered what someone dressed like a Thai beach bum was doing out in this wilderness.

'Hi,' I replied. 'Do you know somewhere where I can spend the night around here?'

'Sure I do. You can spend it with us.' He slapped me hard on the back. 'Me and the boys. What the hell are you pedalling around here for any hows?'

My new friend was called Bob, and he and the boys were part of the US Army. They lived in a wooden house on the edge of the village where they lent me a small dark room plagued by diaphanous geckos skittering up and down the walls. The saving grace was the rickety air conditioning. It may have sounded like a blender full of walnut shells, but after a day's cycling in the raging sun, there was nothing more luxurious than a blast of frosty air.

Bob and his boys were part of a Missing In Action (MIA) team. It sounded very Chuck Norris but was actually much more sedate. The team consisted of Bob the translator, Matt the clean-cut team leader, Ken the laconic bomb disposal expert, medic John, and Snapper the team's photographer. Occasionally they were joined by an anthropologist, the only civilian in the group, currently in Phnom Penh. The rest of the team were all diggers, one of whom was a cheerful heavy-set West Indian called Ruggins. He wore an American football shirt with a number eight on the back.

'What you doing here on a goddam bicycle?' Ruggins demanded. 'You come to look at that Angkor rock, whatever it's called? Holy jumping Jesus, you crazier than hell, guy.' He grabbed my arm. 'Now my man, look at you, you gotta eat. You skinny as a damn cheerleader. You go and get some of that meat on a stick they're selling opposite.' He pointed at one of the street hawkers. 'You get one for your friend Ruggins, too. None of us soldier boys are allowed out after nine thirty.'

'You're joking?' I said.

'I ain't joking, boy,' growled Ruggins. 'We ain't allowed out after nine thirty, we ain't allowed into any nightclubs, not that there are any out in this chickenshit village, and we sure as hell ain't allowed to sleep with no Cambodian girls, nor Vietnamese for that matter. Only Thais. What we live for is our visits to good old Pattaya. Oh yes, sir, the land of silk and honeys.'

When I returned with two skewers of sizzling flesh, Ruggins and Bob popped open some cans of beer. We were joined by Matt. As the alcohol took hold they began to talk more freely about their work. They told me their MIA unit was based in Hawaii, but posted throughout the world. Their job was to track down the remains of missing American soldiers. They did this by examining and identifying bones, dog tags and whatever other human detritus was available. Matt said he only needed two teeth to be able to identify a body.

'What's the point in hunting for bodies?' I asked. 'Surely if somebody has not returned from Vietnam by now they must be dead.'

'Probably, yes,' agreed Matt. 'But many relatives want to know where their loved ones died, however far back. They want that reassurance.'

'This never happened after other wars, did it?' I asked. 'It sounds like a bit of a waste of money.'

'It does cost thousands of dollars to keep us operational,' admitted Matt. 'I think America is the only country that has MIA units. They are not purely for Vietnam though. We can be posted anywhere from Korea to the Middle East. Often we have to visit World War One and Two battle sites or even those from the American Civil War.'

'Nobody is waiting for loved ones to return from Gettysburg, are they?'

'No, no,' said Matt. 'Much of our work is purely for historical records, factual stuff.'

'So how are you getting on?' I asked.

'We've got our problems here,' mused Ruggins, shooing a fly off his kebab. 'One of them is body looters. Locals tell us they've found a body, but will only show it to us if we pay them. They give you the grid reference of the corpse and it turns out to be the bones of someone dug up from a graveyard, or even the bones of a dog or a buffalo. Damned nuisance. But that's nothing; the main problem is the landmines.'

'Tell me about it,' interrupted Ken the sapper, who had been silent for most of the evening. He had recently worked on the minefields in Bosnia. 'There are six million landmines in Cambodia. Only Angola, Afghanistan and Iraq have more. My work here is purely with this MIA team but there are several big internationally funded squads of de-miners in Cambodia too.'

'How do they locate the mines?'

'They use underground probes. Once they've found a live one they usually detonate it in a cordoned area. It seems unfair really. Most of the wars here were not the Cambodians' fault yet they are often the ones putting their lives at risk working in the minefields. They get paid about one hundred-fifty US dollars a month, much higher than the average income here. That's why they are prepared to take the risk. Quite a few of the de-miners are women.'

'Is it very dangerous?'

'It can be,' he said. 'Landmines are getting more sophisticated all the time which makes it harder for them to be deactivated. But the people who are most at risk are not the de-miners but the farmers. There are many injuries. Only last week a nine-year-old girl jumped down from a coconut tree and landed on a mine. She lost a leg. Another amputee to add to Cambodia's 30,000 or so. It breaks your heart. There are warning signs up to warn of landmines but often the villagers can't read them.

'The most tragic thing is that landmines are still available on the black market in Phnom Penh. Apparently, wealthy landowners buy them and plant them on the borders of their properties to ward off intruders. Poachers also buy them to blow up tigers in the jungles to the north of Cambodia. Tigers are very rare and their parts have high medicinal value. Its all pretty sickening.'

'How long do you think it will take to clear the mines across the country?'

'At least ten years. There are some competent Cambodian officers being trained up by Western de-miners, but the political situation here is so volatile, you never know how long the foreign presence will be tolerated. I just hope to God the de-mining continues – at the moment dozens of people are still being injured every month.'

'How much longer are you all here for?' I asked.

'Five more weeks, thank God,' shouted Ruggins with a whoop. 'I like my work and I feel sorry for Cambodia and all that, but to be honest with you I am just here to dig up some bones and get out. Then I'm down to Pattaya, baby. The land of silk and honeys.'

The following day I reached Phnom Penh. I threaded through the tangled streets to the banks of the Mekong and headed straight for Bert's Books, the guest house recommended to me by the MIA boys. Bert's Books was a narrow multi-storey building, the ground floor acting as a cluttered bookshop and the first and second floors divided into sleeping cubicles. When I arrived the only space left was a mattress on the roof, with a view over the Mekong for about one pound sterling a night.

Bert was a burly forty-something American who resembled a bookish Henry VIII. He was married to a lovely Cambodian girl, who everyone called Mrs Bert. Like many of the older expats including Hurricane Bob, a loud but likeable American who ran a nearby doss-house called The Last Home, Bert had been in Cambodia for years.

I spent much of my time in Phnom Penh simply hanging out at Bert's Books and The Last Home as they were lively and good places for picking up gossip. I really just wanted to take it easy, drink coffee, write my diary and breeze around town.

At Bert's Books I met Brooks, a Californian carpenter, and his half-Chinese, half-German girlfriend, who handed me a name card that read 'Brenda May Dunkleberger: Sentient Being'. We spent a fair bit of time together wandering the city, walking past the ancient *wats* and the colonial façades; past the skinny kids playing games of fling the flip-flop – a faster, rubberized version of bowls. We sipped coffee at the elegant propeller-fanned Foreign Correspondents' Club and shot pool at a grungy bar with black and red walls called The Heart Of Darkness. Brenda spoke French to some of the old *cyclo* riders who remembered the colonial days.

In the evening we sat out on the roof of Bert's Books. It was a perfect spot. We would lie there drinking melon juice as a cool breeze swept over us, a respite from the February heat. There was only one problem: the gunfire. On the first night we all woke simultaneously as a nearby machine-gun fired off into the night.

'Bugger me,' I said, looking out over the balcony.

'Can't help there, darling,' said Brenda. 'Nor will that blanket you're holding over your head do much good, Brooks, unless it's bulletproof. We may as well get used to it, guys. This is Cambodia.'

'You're right, honey,' replied Brooks, ripping away the blanket in a gesture of mock heroism. 'As they say, you gotta die of something.'

Death was something many of Cambodia's visitors seemed actively to seek, especially residents of The Last Home. Hurricane Bob said that Bert sent him all the freaks and psychos that he didn't want at Bert's Books.

'The Last Home should be called the last fucking resort,' said Bob. 'The sort of people who stay here are the ones who find out where the Khmer Rouge are, and buy a one-way ticket to go and see them.'

'I thought the Khmer Rouge were a spent force,' I said.

'Oh no. There are certainly fewer of them and they are much more fragmented than before, but they will still be with us for a while. And if you are kidnapped by them, heaven help you.'

'Do you think it's safe to cycle to Sihanoukville?'

'Should be. The KR are mainly up in the Battambang region in the north. One of my guests headed up there this morning. A crazy German with a death wish.'

'He actually wanted to get kidnapped?'

'Who knows?' said Bob, sticking up a map of Phnom Penh in the reception area. 'Some people are genuine thrill seekers, others are just braggers. They go around dressed in combats, pretending the war is still on, but they don't usually go anywhere near the fighting. We call them the Phnom Penh SEALS – The South East Asia Liars Society. But not all our guests are fools, we get some quality characters too. Take this guy.' He pointed to a yellowing newspaper cutting stuck to the noticeboard.

The article from the *Phnom Penh Post* concerned Tom Stone, a former US Army sergeant, who had walked over 12,000 miles around the world. He had been on the road for three years at the time of the piece. Part of the reason for the walk was to honour the memory of his brother Dana Stone, a CBS News journalist who had disappeared with his colleague Sean Flynn (son of the actor Errol Flynn) during the Vietnam War. The pair were last seen ten miles from Svay Rieng near the Vietnam–Cambodian border. Tom Stone said he liked Cambodia best of all the countries he had visited even though it had claimed his brother's life. I especially liked the closing quote of the article: 'Travel is like going to the theatre,' Stone had concluded. 'There's always something going on, something to watch out for. If I'm bored it means I haven't been paying proper attention.'

I decided Stone's theatre analogy could also be applied to the history of Cambodia.

The stage was dramatically set in medieval times by the Khmer rulers. Never would Cambodia surpass the magnificence of that inaugural performance, the splendid vanity of Angkor, the innovative irrigation systems, the kingdom that stretched all the way from east of Saigon to west of Bangkok and up towards the mountains of Luang Prabang. It was a masterpiece of an opening season, an impresario's dream.

Trends changed, egos deflated and Cambodia's stage shrank dramatically to a low-budget, smaller scale set-up. Through the years the actors were heckled by the Thais from the west wings and the Vietnamese from the east, but it was a flamboyant, if cavalier, appearance by the French in 1863 that came to dominate, despite attracting some fiercely negative reviews.

The curtain closed on the increasingly farcical French performance in 1954 and, once again, a jumble of different players fought aggressively for the leading roles. A confused cast of Vietnamese communists, King Sihanouk nationalists and the Khmer Rouge auditioned. In 1975 the military leader Lon Nol put on a brief one-man show, but relied too much on strong prompting from America. He disappeared while on a US tour and master villain Pol Pot brought the house down with a monstrous four-year tragedy, from which Cambodia is still trying to recover. Early on in his run, Britain and France gave him rave reviews but the applause died when the horror hit home and his performance ended in a denouement of destruction and death. Everyone in Cambodia is now praying there will never be an encore.

One of the principal reasons I had decided to travel south via Cambodia and not take the more conventional – and legal – route via Laos, was in order to catch a glimpse of the temples at Angkor, considered by many to be the pinnacle of human architectural achievement.

The problem was how to get there as Angkor sits at the head of Tonle Sap, an enormous lake north of Phnom Penh. At Bert's Books the noticeboard suggested the only safe way to reach Siem Reap, Angkor's nearest town, was to fly. The other options were to take a fast boat, a hovercraft, which would occasionally get shot at by angry fishermen fed up with their nets being snagged, or a slow boat, which might be hijacked by bandits or, if very unlucky, the Khmer Rouge. As for the roads, they were the most problematic of all due to potholes, military checkpoints and thieves. As time was an issue I plumped for the fast boat – it took a morning – and then the slow boat back.

The boat left at 6 a.m. and I sat with Brooks and Brenda on the top deck. They both puffed away on clove cheroots while I read Norman Lewis's *A Dragon Apparent*, which covers his travels through Indo-China almost fifty years ago, when it was still possible to make an appointment for tea with King Norodom in Phnom Penh.

As we neared Siem Reap, I looked up. We had steered into a channel hemmed in by lush vegetation and surrounded by huts of wicker, thatch and wood. There were fishing boats being steered with poles like Oxford punts and women in bright shirts selling coconuts and papaya fruitshakes from houseboats. A child somersaulted into the lake from the bank; the water was choppy and dirty, spotlit by beams of sunshine.

Once we had docked I untied my bicycle from the stern and wheeled it on to the crowded wharf. Brooks and Brenda jumped into a minibus leaving me to pedal alone to Siem Reap where we had arranged to meet up. Siem Reap is a sleepy market town near the temples, filled with budget hotels. I tracked down Brooks and Brenda at the Eclipse Guest House, a wood-framed building behind a mango tree under which a group of Cambodians were playing round-robin table tennis. I joined in for a game or two, then ate some sticky rice from a palm leaf, wrote some postcards and fell into a mighty slumber. Tomorrow would be a long day.

I woke at 5 a.m. as excited as a child on Christmas morning. Angkor is a group of dozens of beautiful temples, all built by the fabulously wealthy Khmer rulers between the ninth and thirteenth centuries. To do them all justice would take weeks, but the thought of a just glimpse of them was thrilling. I knocked on Brooks' and Brenda's door and while I waited for them to stir I decided to read Norman Lewis on the Khmers to whet my appetite further.

If it had not been for the spectacular arrogance of the first Khmer king, Lewis concluded, the temples at Angkor might never have been built. The king, whose name is uncertain, returned from an expedition to Java a hero, having freed Cambodia from the island's rule. In a fit of self-congratulation he declared himself a god, the Lord of the Universe. Thanks to his megalomania, the first temple at Angkor, the Baphuon, was built as a replica of Mount Meru, the mountain which, according to Hindu cosmology, supported the heavens. This extravagant building programme was continued by subsequent kings, sustained by the richness of the area which was abundant in fish and fertile farmland.

The Hindu influence at Angkor was obvious, even from the pictures in my guidebook. The temples looked more akin to those in Rajasthan than to any Chinese or Cham architecture. I was looking forward to inspecting them closely.

Once Brooks and Brenda were up I pedalled off through the dark, the cicadas chirruping all around. The heat was already powerful, the sort that glues your clothes to your body in seconds. Tourists zipped past me on motorbikes, including my friends, perched on the end of a saddle behind their corpulent guide.

Outside Angkor Wat, the first major temple, a large crowd was milling about. Some of them were aiming video cameras at the three giant fir-cone-like towers just becoming visible in the dawn light. Within a few minutes, the whole façade was lit up by the rising sun. Brenda, Brooks and I strode along the stone path, the wind soughing through the surrounding palms, before ascending the monumental and very steep stairway, past a meditating hippie in yellow trousers and an elderly man with half-moon glasses fingering the smooth grey brickwork. All around, people were concealed in the crannies of this titanic building, looking out over the dry flat plains lost in their individual reveries. We found a quiet corner and leaned against the cool stone. A small black bat fluttered by; it screeched once and then all was quiet. We sat in silence for some time.

'It's easy to see why the guy who built this believed he was a god,' said Brooks finally.

'Yeah,' agreed Brenda, blowing a smoke ring with her clove cheroot. 'Totally bitching.'

Later, we studied the intricate bas-reliefs which stretch for 800 metres along Angkor Wat's mammoth flanks. The most celebrated of these is the Churning Of The Ocean Of Milk which depicts gods and devils in a tug-of-war to win immortality, all of them pulling on an enormous serpent. Many characters from Hindu mythology are among the fray; Siva, the destroyer; Hanuman, the monkey god and Vishnu (whom Angkor Wat was built to honour) is represented as a turtle. Then there are the *apsaras*, the luscious dancing girls who appear in many of the other temples; always beautiful but never erotic.

My time was short and I spent the day pedalling madly through the jungle from one stunning temple to another. I passed the Bayon, with its dozens of vast impassive faces hewn from the rock. I passed the Terrace Of Elephants, a 350-metre-long row of life-size pachyderms, some jigsawed by fissures, others with ivy bursting through their bodies but many perfectly intact. The elephants lead on to the subtler Terrace of the Leper King. This impressive ensemble of bas-reliefs was built by Jayavarman VII who, although the most egotistical of Angkor's leaders, was by far the most prolific and inspired builder. He was also thought to be a leper, which may explain why he built more than a hundred hospitals. My favourite of the temples was Ta Prohm, Jayavarman VII's most outrageous creation, which, in its heyday, was covered with five tonnes of gold plate.

When the French explorer Henri Mahout came across the temples of Angkor in 1859 and they first caught the world's attention, most of them were cleaned up and made more accessible. But not Ta Prohm, which looks just the same today as it has for centuries. In fact, in some ways it probably looks far more impressive now than it did when its sandstone walls were pristine back in the tenth century.

At Ta Prohm nature has taken over and run rampant, ripping and strangling the stonework with its jungly tendrils. Walls are uprooted, masonry rent in two, flag stones pinned down by a fist of unbudgeable ligatures. Fig trees sprout from shattered corniches and hornets the size of peach stones buzz about; the eyes are never at peace alerted by the constantly shifting chiaroscuro of sunlight and shadow. Any minute you half expect Indiana Jones to leap out of a doorway pursued by a cascade of falling rocks.

I stayed at Ta Prohm until sundown, marvelling at its splendour. When I cycled back in the twilight, past the serene faces of the Bayon and the towers of Angkor Wat with the jungle hissing all around, I felt euphoric. I could fully under-stand how, in this atmosphere, surrounded by extraordinary architecture, the ancient Khmer rulers could believe they had created an earthly heaven.

The following day I caught the slow ferry back which spluttered to a halt midway down Tonle Sap. The passengers were herded on to a fleet of little boats, taken ashore and then driven at high speed along a dirt road back to Phnom Penh. We arrived late in the afternoon, dust-caked and sore-arsed.

From Phnom Penh it was 150 miles to Sihanoukville on the south coast. My guidebook advised me to avoid the area due to the Khmer Rouge murders back in 1994. But that was almost three years ago and most people, including Bob and Bert, said that I would probably be safe.

'Cambodia is one of those places where the dangers are always blown out of proportion,' said Bob. 'Having said that, for God's sake watch your back. There's some trigger-happy dudes out there.'

Before my ride south, I wanted to visit the killing fields of Choeung Ek. I pedalled out of Phnom Penh, past a cigarette billboard with an Alain Delon lookalike promising smokers THE TASTE OF FRANCE. I passed the high wall of the American Embassy and an Irish pub (is there any capital in the world without an Irish pub?) and then I was out in the rice paddies that less than twenty years ago had been part of Cambodia's killing fields.

The Khmer Rouge overran Cambodia in 1975 and, during their four years of power, the whole country was turned into a labour camp. The camp at Choeung Ek, where the infamous S-21 prison (now a museum) was located, was one of the most brutal: thousands of men, women and children were murdered there, most of them bludgeoned to death to save bullets. A memorial shrine erected in 1988, contains over 8,000 skulls retrieved from mass graves around the area. It is a haunting site. The skulls are arranged in layers according to age and sex but, without flesh, they all become one.

'Unbelievable isn't it?' said a voice behind me. It belonged to Chantal, a Cambodian girl in John Lennon glasses. She told me that she now lived in California, where she studied law. 'This is my first visit home for nearly twenty years. I was seven when I left Cambodia. I lived in a village called Pailin near the Thai border. When the Khmer Rouge took over in 1975, my family were able to escape easily over the border. We stayed in a Thai camp for six months and then flew to America.'

'How do you feel?'

'Seeing this sort of thing is unbearable,' she said, shaking her head. 'I could easily have been one of those skulls. But my life has been so distanced from all this. In America I have many Cambodian friends; there are over a million Cambodians in

California. I'm glad I've visited here though, I'm very proud of my home country and its capacity for survival. But I am an American now.'

That night, *en route* to Sihanoukville, I camped in the town of Angk Tasaom and by the second night had made it to Kampot, about eighty miles south of Phnom Penh. There I briefly met two de-miners at the local guest house: Lance, a hangdog Canadian and Bruce, a larky Australian. They both worked for CMAC (Cambodian Mines Action Centre) and together were in charge of three groups, each of 120 Cambodians. Their aim was to pass on as much information as possible so the local people could continue the job if Western aid was ever cut off. It was good to hear they were impressed by the bravery and skill of many of the Cambodians.

I arrived at Cambodia's only port, Sihanoukville (also known as Kompong Som), on the afternoon of 1 March. This time last year, I thought with some satisfaction, I was pedalling through the mists of the Loire Valley. Sihanoukville was a rather charming place, a sleepy port with white sand beaches fringed with shady trees beneath which girls sold pineapples and mangoes. But there was no time for extended hedonism as my boat for Koh Kong was leaving the following morning.

I had forged my visa in Syria, trekked clandestinely into Afghanistan and now I hoped to creep unnoticed through Thailand's back door. I wondered if I was pushing my luck. But the die was cast, there was no turning back now; the ticket was purchased and backtracking through Vietnam into Laos was out of the question. Besides, I had been reassured it was possible by a man named Vinnie. With his greying hair and restless gestures Vinnie reminded me of a Somerset Maugham character, a man in a hurry to make his mark on life before it was too late. Vinnie had worked in Bedford for many years as a construction worker and then, after he split up with his wife, headed for Cambodia as a UN volunteer. He met a Cambodian girl who lived in Sihanoukville and set up home there in 1994, the year the Khmer Rouge murdered the three foreigners. 'I knew all three of them, Dom, Kellie and Tina,' said Vinnie wistfully. 'Nice kids. They had set up a little restaurant near here. They loved Cambodia for all the right reasons but they were terribly naïve. The evening they were taken by the Khmer Rouge, they were driving after dark. You never do that in Cambodia. It was terribly sad; when the three of them died, for a while so did Sihanoukville.

'Kellie's dad stayed here for a while. He was a lovely man. Even after hearing that his daughter had been killed, he was still forgiving. His lack of rancour was extraordinary. He told me that as only one man had killed his daughter, you couldn't tarnish a whole country on the strength of it.

'Sihanoukville is beginning to be seen as safe again, thankfully,' added Vinnie. 'For a while the only people who turned up were nutters like you who wanted to get into Thailand.'

'So what are my chances?'

'Pretty good. We usually get about a dozen people a year who try it. Most get through, although the last guy didn't make it. He was a Belgian, a dickhead who sat smoking pot on top of the fishing boat that transported him. The police picked him up and he's in jail in Bangkok now. Apparently, the Thais are wising up to the scam, so be careful. Personally I wouldn't risk it.'

'What's your advice if I do try it?'

'Keep your head down, a real low profile,' said Vinnie, tapping his nose with a finger. 'Remember, once you've reached Koh Kong there will be no turning back. Make some subtle enquiries down at the harbour and one of the little boats should take you to the Thai coast. You might have to slip them twenty dollars or so. Your boat should drop you off at Ban Hat

Lek, which is a one-horse Thai village with no officials. If you encounter any awkward questions from the locals, all you can really do is smile and try to sweet talk your way out of it.'

Vinnie stopped to take a long slug of San Miguel.

'Once in Thailand you'll have to hightail it to Bangkok as fast as you can, in order to get a stamp in your passport. Go straight to the immigration authorities and own up that you have made a big mistake. Say that you thought Ban Hat Lek was a bona fide checkpoint. Look all doe eyed and goofy – shouldn't be difficult – and pray you get a lenient official.'

'What are my chances of getting caught?'

'If you're sensible they will be slim. If you do get caught, try to make it in Thailand, not Cambodia. The jails are much nicer.'

'Thanks, I'll send you a postcard.'

The next day I pedalled down to the port. A fat swarthy man with Khmer tribal tattoos on his forearms stamped my passport. He gave me a friendly wink which helped settle my nerves. I was going to miss Cambodia, I thought.

I pushed my way on to the boat, tied the bike to a railing and sat down next to a Cambodian family. The mother smiled and offered me a mango. This was going to be a breeze, I reassured myself, but I knew I could not afford to relax. After all, I had a passport that had been stamped out of Cambodia and had little hope of being stamped on arrival in Thailand. If ever I was in no man's land, that time was now.

Chapter Twenty-two

Running on empty

'Passport?'

Someone was nudging my arm. I rubbed my eyes and looked up at the Cambodian mother. I had fallen asleep on her shoulder. She smiled and pointed up at a thuggish official in a beige uniform.

'Passport?' he repeated. His breath smelt of alcohol, an unhealthy sign at 10 a.m. I pulled out my passport from my money belt. Although I had been stamped out at Sihanoukville I was not illegal yet as I was still within Cambodian territory. The official gave the passport a cursory scan and handed it back. 'You give two dollar,' he ordered.

'Why?' I said, immediately sensing I'd asked the wrong question.

'Two dollar,' he shouted.

'OK, OK.' I rummaged around and handed over the money. It was not worth arguing about, although I had not expected to start paying bribes quite so soon.

We pulled into Koh Kong about an hour later. The water was choppy, rocking the flotilla of little boats on the harbour front. I rolled my bike on to the quayside and pushed it towards the checkpoint shed. This was where things could get sticky.

'Are you going Thailand?' asked the torpid officer. He was an old man with dark irisless eyes which were impossible to gauge. 'Thailand?' he repeated. It was the last question I wanted to be confronted with. If I said yes, he might arrest me on the spot; if I said no, it would scupper my chances of reaching Bangkok later.

'No,' I replied uncertainly. 'No go Thailand. Is it possible from here?' That lobbed the ball gently back into his court.

'Why you come Koh Kong?'

'It's a beautiful place.'

'I think you want go Thailand,' he stated, still deadpan. 'Every foreigner come Koh Kong go Thailand.'

'Really?' I said with Oscar-winning astonishment. 'How much would it cost someone wanting to go there?'

'You give me ten dollars,' he replied eagerly. 'I help you. I find you boat.'

This was interesting. It could have been a trap but that was unlikely. Koh Kong was probably too remote to have a policy on travellers' scams. More likely he was a struggling official who wanted to earn a little on the side. I decided to bite the bullet.

'OK,' I replied. I ripped open the Velcro strap on my wallet and handed him a $10 note. It did not seem an unreasonable amount if he proved as good as his word.

The old man grabbed the money and stuck it into his jacket pocket as fast as a Newmarket bookie. He then walked out of the hut and straddled a motorbike leaning against the shed.

'Follow me,' he ordered, as he kick-started the bike. I pedalled after him along a muddy track leading to a secluded cove beyond the main harbour. Within a couple of minutes he was parked next to a series of large punt-like boats, some of which had outboard motors. A small crowd gathered around us. The old man waited until he had everyone's attention and then gabbled his instructions. Evidently he had done this before.

'They say no possible go Thailand,' he said, after a prolonged haggle. 'Too risky, too much problem. Trouble with Thai police.'

'But other people have done it,' I pleaded.

'Now too many people try. It dangerous.' Then, after a long silence, 'How much you pay?'

'I pay twenty dollars.'

The old man relayed the price to the boatmen.

'They want more,' he said. 'Maybe fifty dollar.'

I should have guessed. 'I'll give twenty-five dollars.'

'Forty,' demanded the old man.

'Thirty, absolute top. No more,' I said firmly. 'That's it. I've already paid you ten.'

'OK.' He was smiling; he had obviously done well from the deal. 'This man take you.' He pointed to a youth wearing dark glasses and a red baseball cap. He was standing in a long boat equipped with an outboard the size of an elephant's head.

Together we took the panniers off the bike and unhitched the front wheel. Once my equipment had been placed symmetrically around the little deck, the boatman untied the mooring line.

'Lie down,' the old man advised me, 'or police see you. Safe here but not out at sea.' I lay on top of my panniers, below the boat's stunted prow.

The boatman let out a loud wolf whistle and yanked the engine to life. He was obviously in a good mood about the deal too. I had probably been ripped-off but I did not mind too much; $30 seemed a fair price to me for an illegal voyage.

We headed out to sea. Occasionally, I peeked above the gunwales to catch a glimpse of a mangrove swamp or fishing boat. At times, especially when we bounced through the wake of another vessel, our boat would be severely rocked. Once or twice my prostrate body took off before thudding back down on the deck, my panniers acting as useful padding.

Sometimes in life you have to ask yourself certain questions. You have to ask yourself . . . what exactly is a thirty-year-old man from a good home and a loving family doing lying on his back in a boat so small that the owl and the pussy cat would have turned their noses up at it, steered by a wolf-whistling boatman who doesn't seem to give a toss whether he is spotted by the police or not?

You also have to ask yourself why you are doing this.

And your answer is that, although the situation is pretty desperate, all things considered, you have never felt more alive and more happy to be alive. You feel a rush of energy. You sense that this is a consummate moment in your journey, a life-affirming instant when you finally fear nothing, because you know it is unlikely things will ever get this thrilling again.

Thankfully, I splashed back down to earth as the boat approached the shore half an hour later. It was important to get my thoughts together fast because waiting at the harbour were two Thai policemen.

'Police,' pointed out my boatman, helpfully.

'If you are up there, God,' I whispered, 'this is the time to play a trump card.'

I pulled my bike on shore and dragged it towards the two uniformed men, one of whom wore a peaked cap. Vinnie had warned me that Thai officials were sharp and not to expect any Third World leniency. There was no way I could indulge in subtle obfuscation. I had disembarked from a boat in front of their noses. I could hardly pretend I was a shipwreck survivor or a trans-world windsurfer stopping off for a lunch break.

Sheepishly, I stood in front of the policemen. And then a

curious thing happened. It seemed to take a while for them to even notice me and once they did, they eyed me up for a long time before bursting into gales of laughter. They got so carried away, they put their arms around each other and had to fight for breath. I took out my passport and held it up but this only increased their mirth. Finally, I gave them both a thumbs up and briskly walked off, leaving them clutching their sides. I can only think they were either drunk, bogus or seriously inbred.

The rest of the journey to Bangkok was plain sailing. I caught a minibus through a succession of lush villages to the first major town, Trat, and from there was able to take a connecting night bus to the Thai capital. I arrived in Bangkok at 5 a.m. and pedalled swiftly through the busy streets, stopping off for the occasional puff on my asthma inhaler, the first time I had needed to use it since Tibet. With dawn approaching, I pulled into Khao San Road, the bustling backpackers' area.

Considering the hour, Khao San was surprisingly lively and all-night revellers wearing singlets and tropical knickerbockers were still prowling the bars. A Filipina girl with a honey voice was singing a cover of Patsy Cline's 'Crazy' at the Marco Polo café where a video screen showed a football match. TODAY VIDEOS: MISSION IMPOSSIBLE, ERASER AND FORREST GUMP, blazed a billboard. Others boasted WE MAKE HOLE — ear, eyebrow, stomach, breast. MONEY CHANGE, E-MAIL, SILK SUITS, TRIP TO CHIANG MAI, ELEPHANT SAFARI. A grossly fat tout with a crucifix hanging between his podgy breasts offered me a card which read, SEXY SHOW: PUSSY SHOOT PING PONG BALL, PUSSY BURST BALLOON, PUSSY WRITE LETTER, PUSSY EAT SNAKE, SEE PUSSY TONIGHT!

Khao San is one of those horrible but undeniably useful places where travellers tap into Western convenience, to buy gimcrack souvenirs and cash traveller's cheques, eat burgers and shoot pool. It is not representative of Thailand, or even Bangkok. There are places like it all over the world, places that, give or take the odd local ingredient, are almost exactly the same: functional tourist enclaves with desperate types in flip-flops flashing briefcases full of useless trinkets; squalid, sadly inevitable black holes in the backpacker firmament with Khao San Road being perhaps the blackest of them all.

I trudged around Khao San's guest houses, of which not one had a bed. Like an exhausted vampire, I became increasingly edgy as the cool night turned to bright sticky day. After a dozen or more refusals I began to wonder if there was a single free bed in Bangkok. I was tempted to put my tent up in a park.

'Hey buddy, what's cooking?' The voice belonged to Larry, an American bodybuilder. His singlet covered so little of his rippling physique that at first I thought he was bare chested. He told me he planned to cycle through Thailand and Laos with his friend, Bruce. When I told him where I had been he insisted that I sleep on the floor in his room. At first I was a little hesitant; after all this was a man who could knock me out with a flick of his forefinger or even a well-aimed sneeze. But I was so tired I no longer cared what happened to me, provided it didn't involve wandering around Khao San Road being handed cards advertising fortune-tellers or nipple rings.

Within a couple of minutes Larry had lifted my bicycle, panniers and all, up the Ploy Guest House's myriad stairs. He and Bruce turned out to be useful contacts as they had travelled extensively in South-East Asia and could offer all sorts of advice for the remaining stretch of my ride. They also insisted that I dress smartly for my appointment with the passport authorities.

'Thai officials don't like bums,' said Larry. 'No offence my friend, but you look pretty rough. I've only just arrived in

Bangkok so you can borrow a clean shirt and a sarong. They will like that, but piss them off and they will kick you out immediately.'

I turned up at the passport office clad in a white shirt and a purple sarong. Larry assured me that I looked sharp, but I felt like an exhausted drag queen, not having slept for over thirty hours. But I looked better than the haggard Canadian man queuing with me, who had lost his passport. He was as lugubrious as a basset in a vet's waiting room.

When the office opened, I shoved my passport through the grille towards a smart official in a white tunic.

'Why you go Ban Hat Lek?' he demanded in a clipped voice, after I explained my lack of a stamp. 'It no legal border.'

'Yes, I'm very sorry. I'm afraid I thought it was.'

'It no legal,' he repeated.

'Yes, it was very stupid of me, but you must understand I am not allowed to fly.'

'Not allowed to fly. Why?'

'I'm only allowed to bicycle. I am raising money for a hospital by riding my bicycle between England and Australia. One of the rules is that I cannot fly.' The official gave me a look of grave concern. 'Here, let me show you.' I pulled out a wodge of papers which included a *Bucks Herald* feature, a medical certificate and an introductory letter from Sir Ranulph Fiennes. He scrutinized them with calm precision.

'Who is Ranup Feens? He is doctor?'

'No, no. He is a great explorer. He walked across the Antarctic. He is very brave, but a little crazy.'

'Crazy! If he is crazy man why you have his letter? Why not letter from a doctor? A priest?'

'A priest!'

'Why you have letter from this crazy man?'

'Well, you see, Sir Ranulph is crazy in a good way, not in a crazy way.' This really was not going well. The official's look of grave concern shifted to one of deep suspicion.

'You wait here.' He whisked my passport off to another office. Oh shit, I thought, this either meant a spell in Bangkok Strangeways or a one-way ticket home. To help pass the time I rearranged my sarong knot. The official returned several minutes later and handed me my passport.

'You lucky man. You can stay for one month,' he said gravely. 'Now you go.'

'Thank you.' I hitched up my sarong and made for the exit before he could ask me any more questions about Sir Ranup Feens or the semantics of craziness.

That evening, after a long siesta, I watched a Thai kick-boxing match at a stadium near Khao San Road. There was none of the razzmatazz of a championship boxing match. If anything, its dinginess and sweaty odours brought to mind a Victorian cock fight. After buying a ticket, I was shepherded up some stone steps and squashed against a wire mesh barrier. Below me, spindly agitated men waved wads of baht notes at each other or else semaphored bets with their fingers. The place was packed.

The first two fighters were sizing each other up, stalking around like a couple of tomcats. They wore garlands of jasmine around their necks and both were dark and wiry with cropped hair, the only difference between them that one wore blue shorts, the other red. Red Shorts lifted his boxing gloves in a gesture of prayer and dropped to his knees, touching his forehead against the floor. After a bit more shadow-boxing, Blue Shorts joined him. It made for an unexpectedly dignified start.

The two men briefly held their gloves together then broke apart. There was a lot of half-hearted lurching and kicking before the fray began in earnest but suddenly all hell let loose.

Red Shorts whip-kicked Blue Shorts very hard in the stomach, while Blue Shorts countered with a barrage of fast but clumsy punches. Then the two men went into a clinch, trying to wrap their legs around each other's calves, like a couple of adolescent lovers. The crowd was hysterical.

The following ten minutes alternated between graceful athleticism and crude violence. Then, in the closing round, Red Shorts delivered a blistering kick to his opponent's face. Blue Shorts looked utterly shell-shocked, wavered slightly and then crashed to the canvas, blood oozing from his nose. The referee, who for some reason was wearing a pair of white snooker referee's gloves, gesticulated wildly.

Seconds later, a stretcher made from bamboo and palm leaves was dragged through the ropes. The comatose Blue Shorts was hauled on to it but just as the stretcher bearers were leaving the ring he sat up, lashed out at the referee and collapsed again. Red Shorts raised his gloves in victory and then quickly knelt down to pray. A gong sounded to herald two new fighters, but I'd had enough.

With the cheering crowds all around me, I should have felt elated, especially having pulled off my illegal entry into Thailand. In fact, I felt listless and deflated. I wondered what the hell was wrong with me.

I did not pinpoint the reason for my melancholia until I started cycling. Then it struck me: Cambodia had been the last big challenge of the trip. The remaining Asian stretch – Thailand, Malaysia, Singapore, Sumatra and Bali – would be relatively safe and straightforward. Access to these places was elementary, the food would be good, the roads solid. There would be campsites and dormitories with propeller fans, maybe even air-conditioning every now and then.

It worried me that I had begun to think like this: it was

arrogant and blasé. The remaining countries would be as idiosyncratic as all the others; friends back home would give their right arms to visit Penang or Ubud, and here I was writing them off as tame and undemanding.

Think back a year, Tom. Think back to that apprehensive cyclist setting off from Swanbourne. Think of the excitement of arriving in Calais, or Marseilles, let alone Damascus or Beirut. Try to recapture that thrill. Don't become like those feckless adrenalin junkies in Phnom Penh, only excited by the sniff of danger – understandable, perhaps even constructive for a war correspondent or a mercenary, but mildly absurd for a charity push-biker.

At times I was able to shake off this lethargy as I sped along Thailand's roads. One place that inspired me was Kanchana-buri, site of the bridge over the River Kwai. The museum, with its sepia pictures of the Death Railway, revealed that over 16,000 Allied POWs (plus thousands more conscripts from as far away as Burma and Indonesia) died during construction; roughly one for every sleeper on the track. The nearby grave-yards were wonderfully kept, many of the Allied soldiers' crosses covered with colourful blossom. Again I thought of my ancestor Halford, dead aged eighteen, having been in command of 200 men on the Western Front.

On all long journeys there is a stage when the traveller loses focus and becomes dangerously introspective. For me, this stage was the penultimate leg from Thailand down to the island of Timor. Until then, it had been fun, stopping off in a new place every night and packing up again the following morning. But suddenly I was fed up with this gypsy lifestyle, cycling all day then sleeping on a beach or in a dormitory, but always moving on. The thrill of being a perpetual stranger was waning. Some days I longed for a sense of routine; to wake up in the morning and breakfast on Weetabix and milky tea, to spend the day working – in an office, on a tractor, behind a bar, it did not matter – and to round it off with an evening drink with friends or a trip to the cinema. To live in a world where the weekend was not just another couple of days.

I also began to show less interest in the countries I pedalled through. Thailand, Malaysia and Singapore were all surprisingly Westernized. I no longer fired off my usual volleys of questions during evening noodles or took as many photos. But, strangely, during this period I wrote more in my diary than at any other stage on the trip, filling pages with relentless but often insipid detail.

I wrote about spending my thirty-first birthday at a retreat in Chaiya, where I camped by a lake surrounded by saffron-robed monks sworn to silence. I wrote about the pleasures of stopping off in air-conditioned garages and drinking cans of icy fizz. I wrote about the local birds, some of which had spectacular tail feathers, the length of a human arm. I wrote of the politeness of the Thai people and their intelligence, their devotion to King Rama and their ability to fend off invaders.

Further south, I expected the Third World to appear again but, if anything, Malaysia was even more Westernized than Thailand, at least along the route I cycled, a well-travelled road through the multicultural centres of Penang, Kuala Lumpur and Melaka, ending up at Singapore. It was worlds away from the Malaya of the early fifties, which my father had experienced when serving as a young naval officer during the 'War of the Running Dogs' against the communists. Much of the exotic wilderness he remembers has been tamed by agriculture or concrete.

But Malaysia was still a new experience for me as, for the first time on the journey, I was to be joined by a friend. Claire Sawbridge, a sweet-natured, startlingly tall nurse, had given up work for six months to cycle down to Australia with me. She had bought a mountain bike, given up smoking and set herself a brutal training regime. Her ex-boyfriend, Mark, a Malaysian Chinese, had kindly agreed to let us use his Penang flat as a rendezvous. We spent two or three days there resting up and finalizing our plans.

It astonished me that Claire had joined me at all. She had expressed a boozy wish to cycle from Penang to Perth at my leaving party but I had doubted she would follow it through. But here she was – I admired her sense of adventure.

Apart from a slew of initiation punctures, Claire's first week went well. Malaysia was a comfortable place for her to start as the roads were smooth, wide and uncongested. There were plenty of places to stop for iced juices and, even better, a benign tailwind propelled us along. Claire kept up well, one evening ploughing through an electric storm without batting an eyelid. That night, we stretched out our soaked belongings on the balcony rail of our Ipoh guest house and collapsed into easy chairs while above us clouds raced across an opal moon. It was great to share moments like this with somebody else and particularly a long-standing friend.

But fate started to work against us. Claire cricked her neck one afternoon and, by the time we reached Kuala Lumpur, it had become very painful. We spent a day waiting for her to see a doctor who, thankfully, remedied the problem with a vigorous massage. He warned Claire not to crick it again by looking up at KL's pride and joy, the Petronas Towers, the tallest buildings in the world.

For the next few days, we bowled along as usual, stopping for an occasional frozen soya milk or lime juice to combat the withering humidity. But, fifty miles from the historic port of Melaka, disaster struck. As we made our way up one of Malaysia's many hills, Claire's knee buckled. At first I thought it was just a minor problem, but soon realized she was in acute pain. Claire was desolate: she had cycled almost 300 miles with me and was determined to continue but there was no choice; she could barely stand up. I flagged down a bus for her, and we agreed to meet up that evening in Melaka.

Over the ensuing days Claire tried everything. She wrapped her knee in a high-tension bandage smeared with Deep Heat, but it kept rucking up her leg as she pedalled. She tried pain-killers, Chinese medicine and even cycling with one leg; but it was looking increasingly hopeless. She would doggedly join me at the beginning of the day and end up paralysed with pain after the first twenty miles, resorting to public transport to take her to the next major town. By the time we reached Singapore it was looking likely that she would have to head for home.

The reason I had included Singapore in my itinerary was to drum up money for Stoke Mandeville. My cousin, another Tom Fremantle and an ex-naval commander, was working for NSK/RHP, the company that had fitted the ball bearings into my bike. If I turned up in person in Singapore, they promised to double the substantial sum they had already donated. The company proved as good as its word. The British Embassy staff in Singapore also generously organized a fund-raising bash during our visit, taking the total amount raised to well over the initial target figure.

Singapore also gave Claire's knee some valuable recovery time. The only negative aspect to the visit was that we both loathed Singapore. At first I could not pinpoint why I hated the place. Singapore was full of lush and lovely parkland, the pavements were cleaner than Delia Smith's chopping board, the locals were paragons of politeness and the shops elegant and diverse. There was next to no unemployment, the economy was booming, there was no chance of invasion (although young Singaporean men still had to serve two and half years in the army just in case), there was no litter, no gum chewing and not a squashed monitor lizard in sight.

Lee Kuan Yew, Singapore's venerable elder statesman, is revered by his people, his popularity having just surged after publicly lambasting the Malaysian border town of Johor Bahru, as a 'place notorious for shootings, muggings and car-jackings'. Malaysia and Singapore are the bitchiest of rivals. Although Singapore is a fraction the size of Malaysia and relies on it for its water supply, it clearly considers itself far superior.

For me the problem with Singapore was its smugness. 'This is Utopia,' it shouted at you. 'Just try and find somewhere more civilized than this, sucker.' To be fair, it is unlikely that you ever would. The whole place smacked of repressed perfection, a place so anal that even the computerized public toilets flushed themselves; a self-congratulatory superstate that thrived on financial avarice and compulsory patriotism. Like one of Kublai Khan's eunuchs, I found it one hundred per cent obedient and immaculately built but devoid of any charisma or passion. Sadly, more than anywhere else I had pedalled through, Singapore offered a glimpse of Asia's future. It seemed a bad omen that Singapore's national flower is the rafflesia (named after its founding colonialist Sir Stamford Raffles), a huge fecund bloomer, whereas vibrant Hong Kong's flower is the bauhinia, a sterile hybrid that produces no seed. I wished it were the other way round.

Claire and I were becoming increasingly frustrated with one another. During our pedal through Malaysia, perhaps inevitably, a romance had developed. When things were running smoothly this was fine, but now that the chips were down the tension simmered between us. I had suggested she fly on to Darwin and that I would meet her there, but she did not want to be alone. Her lack of independence frustrated me, while she clearly found my dwindling reserves of sympathy selfish and difficult to understand.

By the time we reached Lake Toba in Sumatra, we could barely look at each another. Claire's rash of bad luck – her neck, her knee and the fact her grandmother had recently died – was making her pine for home. She began to talk about her friends and family constantly. It was time for her to call it quits but I just wanted to crack on with the trip.

We parted on miserable terms, both of us riddled with guilt at the way we had treated one another. If Claire's knee had not buckled I am confident she would have made it to Australia. It was a shame that fate had not smiled on us, but, that said, we were very different people. Fortunately, since my return from the trip, Claire and I have revived our friendship and are able to laugh about those calamitous three weeks. For all its tensions, in retrospect, the 350 miles we pedalled together were an experience neither of us regrets.

After Claire's departure, I pedalled off my loneliness like a man possessed. Claire was a valued friend and I felt wretched about the way things had worked out. All I wanted to do was reach Australia. I needed to see the light at the end of the tunnel, to stop feeling like a hamster on a wheel and to relish the inevitability of arrival.

As I headed further south, my main concern became how to make it to Australia without flying. It was already early May and I needed to secure a boat ride fast. I tried my luck in the Javanese port of Surabaya, where I was refused passage on a cattle boat heading for Western Australia on the grounds that I was a quarantine risk. I snooped around the port of Benoa in Bali, but was informed that the tourist tall ship that occasionally sailed to Darwin had been grounded somewhere off Kalimantan. Eventually, I arrived in Timor, the Indonesian island nearest to Australia's north coast – my last hope. If I could not find a boat there, then after over 10,000 miles of pedalling, hitching, sailing and walking, I would be forced to disappoint Captain Charles and submit to my first flight.

The island of Timor is tantalizingly close to Australia with just a one-hour flight between Kupang, its capital, and Darwin, Australia's northernmost port. A mere thumbnail of ocean separated me from my finishing line. Having failed to bicycle all the way from England to Australia, I badly needed the consolation of an exclusively earthbound journey. I simply *had* to find a boat.

Whereas the sea had been Captain Charles's highway in 1829, it had proved nothing but an obstacle to me. I had overcome it at Suez and Hong Kong with alternative overland routes and had survived the Sihanoukville run, but Timor was the end of the line. There was no land route to Australia and, as I did not trust my ability to make a raft out of oil drums and bamboo, flight seemed to be my only option, although I prayed that I would not have to resort to Merpati Airlines, Timor's local carrier.

At first it looked as though the gods were with me, for there at Kupang, anchored amid the fishing skiffs, was an elegant Australian warship, shimmering silvery blue in the morning sun. I pushed my bike to the edge of the wharf and shouted up to a couple of sailors swabbing the deck.

'Where are you heading?'

'Darwin,' hollered the taller of the two men, who was wearing a HOT TUNA baseball cap. 'We're leaving in half an hour.'

'That's perfect,' I said. 'Can you take me? I've got to reach Australia without flying. I'm on a sponsored bicycle ride.'

'Sorry, mate, this is a battleship. We can't just take civilians on board.'

'But four of my ancestors were admirals,' I protested, the desparation evident in my voice. 'The port of Fremantle was named after one of them.'

'Really,' shouted the second sailor, a stocky man with a black beard. 'And I'm Marilyn Monroe's half-sister.'

It suddenly dawned on me how pathetic my plea must have sounded. It was the first time I had attemped to cash in on the family connection and the sailor's riposte left me feeling suitably crushed. I had made my passage to Darwin sound like an issue of national importance when, actually, nobody gave a damn whether I crossed the Timor Sea by boat, plane or humpback whale.

I tried the shipping office. The staff were polite but produced the same excuses I had heard everywhere else. If I waited it was possible something might turn up, they told me – a round-the-world yacht, an easily bribed cargo ship, perhaps even a skiff carrying illegal immigrants – but from experience I knew this was unlikely. I could not face hanging around. I swallowed my pride and headed for Merpati Airlines.

Planes to Darwin left twice a week. I booked the Saturday morning flight, 24 May, which gave me three days to kill. Rather than waste time prowling the harbour front scanning the horizon like Robinson Crusoe, I decided to go to East Timor. I caught a night bus from the outskirts of Kupang which arrived in Dili, the sleepy East Timorese capital, early the following morning. During the journey, I sat next to a Javanese man called Koko, who had been sent by his company to sell educational books to East Timor's schools. Koko had the elegant manicured look of many urban Indonesians. He was clearly terrified by his assignment and took hungry drags on a cigarette.

'Dili is the city of death,' he whispered anxiously to me. 'I am from Jakarta. The people in East Timor will want to kill me.'

Koko's remarks did not surprise me. In Jakarta he was bound to have heard all sorts of hostile propaganda about FRETILIN, the East Timorese independence fighters.

East Timor has always been the odd man out, as it was the only part of the East Indies to be colonized by the Portuguese, rather than the Dutch, in the sixteenth century. After the Portuguese withdrew in 1975, the little country enjoyed only nine days of independence before Indonesia invaded. In the first two days of the offensive 2,000 East Timorese were slaughtered by Indonesian soldiers. Subsequently, despite some heroic resistance, the death toll has spiralled to over 200,000, roughly a third of the population.

I spent two days in Dili. I pedalled along the harbour front, past the crumbling Portuguese façades and up as far as the capital's Rio de Janeiro-style crucifix, where a church group was quietly strumming guitars. I had a puncture which was fixed by a friendly old man with a club foot. He plugged up the hole by sealing it with hot tar and squeezing it in a vice. On the first evening I lay on a straw palliasse on the beachfront eating octopus, drinking Bintang beer and taking occasional swims in the cool blue sea. Dili had a rather Caribbean feel; it was a city of waving children and scavenging poultry, of rusty cars and lush palms. The only thing to spoil this breezy atmosphere was the frequent sight of Indonesian troops in the streets.

The most disturbing part of my visit to Dili was an electoral rally in the centre of town. Hundreds of yellow-shirted Golkar Party supporters had come to see Ali Alatas, then Indonesia's Foreign Minister, make a rabble-rousing speech. Golkar was the party of Indonesia's President Suharto, who had been in power for almost thirty years. The other main contender in the election, Magawati Sukarnoputri, ex-President Sukarno's daughter, clearly lacked the intimidating influence of Suharto. In Indonesia it was still a case of electioneering by the mob.

The Golkar supporters in Dili that day – yellow uniforms, yellow flags, yellow bandannas – and the whoops of hysterical reverence were unnerving, especially as I seemed to be the only member of the crowd with a non-yellow wardrobe. I took a few photos and beat a hasty retreat. Later, I learned that many of the crowd were not Golkar supporters but had turned up to avoid attracting suspicion. Not showing allegiance to Suharto, especially in East Timor, could be interpreted as subversive behaviour.

'I hate Golkar,' one Dili man who attended the rally admitted. 'But I did not want to put my family at risk.'

As in Lhasa, I kept my eyes open for any signs of resistance within East Timor – perhaps a picture of Bishop Belo, Dili's Nobel Prize-winning patriarch, or some anti-Suharto graffiti. Sadly, the city seemed completely tamed; although to be fair, I had visited at a time when the Indonesian presence had been especially strong. I returned to Kupang on my third day to catch my plane, saddened by the oppression.

Chapter Twenty-three

Home run

Unloading my bike at Darwin was a cinch. Merpati Airlines had let me keep it in one piece, panniers and all, rather than going through the tiresome rigmarole of dismantling everything. They only insisted that I deflate the tyres, which apparently explode above a certain height. My bicycle was also the cleanest it had been since the day I left Swanbourne. I knew that Australian Customs could be fussy about dirt and dust being brought in from other countries so I had spent my final evening in Kupang scrubbing it from brakes to back rack with a toothbrush. I even doused my chain in petrol, which made its links gleam like tooth fillings.

The arrival at Darwin Airport was nevertheless a mildly disorientating experience. My fellow travellers were mostly loud cheerful Australians returning from holidays or business trips. It was the first time I had been among so many Westerners for months. 'How the hell can you ride that beast, mate? You don't look like you could wrestle the skin off a rice pudding.' I smiled. Here we go again, Tom, I thought. Another country. A whole new set of rules.

Darwin was the perfect place to break myself into the outback. Isolated enough not to be too comfortable but big enough to cash traveller's cheques and have a haircut. For a state capital, it appeared small but there were reasons for this. Over the last fifty years not only had Darwin suffered from extensive wartime bombing by the Japanese, but it had also been levelled by a devastating typhoon named Tracy on Christmas Eve 1974, leaving over sixty dead. Old Darwin was gone for ever and the new city was neat and functional but still boasted a certain lackadaisical charm. Modern Darwin has two main claims to fame: its consistently hot weather (rarely dipping below 30° C) and the spectacular beer consumption of the locals, not surprising when you consider the local brew can be bought in a bottle the size of an aqualung. The weather and the beer have combined over the years to send a number of Darwin's less resilient citizens 'troppo', a word that incorporates boredom, eccentricity and hysteria in equal measure. For this reason, only a fraction of the city's 70,000 population are permanent residents.

Dame Edna Everage may have branded Darwin 'a virus, not a city' but it was not a bad place to hang out for a day or two. I strolled along Mitchell Street and watched the crowds: the civil servants in their ironed shorts and long white socks; the Landcruisers full of young backpackers heading off to Kakadu; the clusters of barefoot Aboriginals sitting in the shade. I ate junk food and wallowed in the youth hostel swimming pool.

My strongest memory of Darwin is of an outrageous street performer. This man was no predictable magician or three-riff busker warbling 'Waltzing Matilda'. This was someone who would grab you by the lapels and shout, 'Watch me!' He looked like a savage; bare chested, Pilgrim Father beard, serpent-and-dagger tattoo on right bicep and huge dark eyes that rarely blinked. He also had a cruel and ready tongue.

'Hey, you two girls, stop and watch me now,' he shouted, pointing at a couple of giggly window-shoppers. 'You might get run over by a bus and die with *my* money in *your* pockets!'

Slowly a fascinated crowd gathered around him. I edged in to get a better look and once the performer was satisfied with the audience, he stopped his taunting. He picked up three fiercely blazing firebrands from the pavement and began to juggle them, starting with two and bringing in the third once he had found his rhythm. He threw them very high, singing 'Ob-La-Di, Ob-La-Da,' as they spun like Catherine wheels. At his side was a wooden table, on top of which sat a frying pan, an egg and an apple. First, he swiftly picked up the frying pan, smoothly adding it to the airborne firebrands. Next came the egg, then the apple. By this stage, he was throwing the firebrands as high as the surrounding palm trees. He looked comfortable enough, but he had stopped singing and his face was contorted in concentration, his forehead beaded with sweat. Firebrand, apple, firebrand, egg, firebrand, frying pan all swirled round and round in a freakish circle.

'Ready?' he suddenly shouted. 'I said are you ready, you jokers!' And then he let the firebrands crash to the ground. One, two, three. The egg and the apple were still high in the air, the frying pan was now clasped firmly in his right hand. The egg plummeted and smashed into the pan and the apple crash-landed in his mouth. He took a couple of bites, threw the core into the air and took a bow. It had been a mesmerizing performance.

'Last week I fried the apple and ate the egg,' he told the crowd after the clapping had died down. 'And other times I've set fire to my beard or been knocked out by the frying pan. This act takes dedication, people! Please help me out.'

Sure enough, when he passed around his Akubra, everyone paid up.

On my final afternoon, I bought a five-litre jerrycan, which I attached on top of the tool kit. With my three other water bottles, this made eleven litres in all. It was essential to carry this much water as, according to my map, there would be stretches of up to 180 miles between the outback roadhouses. It was winter in Australia at the time, but in the Northern Territory the heat could be fierce all year round.

I still had a further 1,400 miles to cycle before I clocked up my 12,500-mile target. It was 1 June and I had been on the road fifteen months. According to my map, all that lay between me and my odyssey's end was a finger's length of bright red dust. I could hardly believe it.

Australia was kind to me. Sometimes I was able to clock up one hundred miles per day along the flat empty roads. My surroundings were beautiful and moody, a stunning combination of burnt sienna desert and brilliant red rock, while up above were skies of cornflower blue. In the evenings, the landscape was bathed in shades of gold.

I loved the haunting quality of the outback, the parched soil, the white-stumped ghost gums, the silence. But for all its eerie, last-person-on-earth desolation, there were frequent surprises. After two hours of cycling along in a daydream, you might suddenly be startled by a couple of emus goose-stepping through the spinifex, or maybe a flock of white cockatoos in full cry or even a starburst of rainbow lorikeets, their plumage like fireworks. Then there were the kangaroos and wallabies bounding gracefully through the spinneys of sweet-smelling eucalyptus.

I was not starved of human company either. At least every half-hour a vehicle would pass – a caravan, a camper van or farmer's pick-up truck. More than often the vehicles would slow down. 'You right, mate?' the driver would ask. When I gave a thumbs up they would drive on. Sometimes, when I was resting at the roadside, they would pull over to give me a cold drink or a slice of watermelon. The majority of these Samaritans were retired Australian couples, travelling around their country for the first time.

'We never had a chance to travel when we were your age, young man,' they would tell me. 'So we're making up for lost time.'

These 'outback oldies', as the roadhouse staff dubbed them, were invariably well equipped, with barbecue tongs, video cameras and pictures of grandchildren in their wallets. It made a change to share a campfire with older people. They had less to prove than the younger backpackers and the conversation was more relaxed. It was good to escape from the 'we've been there, bet you haven't' brigade and the 'we were the first white people they had ever seen' types.

By the time I reached Katherine, a little town 200 miles south of Darwin, I had decided to cut my water supply from eleven litres to five. It was clear that if I ever found myself in dire straits, someone was bound to stop. The bush was clearly a place where people looked out for one another.

There was one vehicle in the outback that never pulled over – the road train. A road train is exactly what it says: a train on the road, an enormous truck hauling three or four trailers, but on tyres instead of rails. The reason these multi-wheeled bruisers failed to pull over was not churlish drivers, but a stopping distance the length of Ayers Rock. As a cyclist, it was vital to listen out for road trains. Their size and speed created a furious back draft of air when they overtook which could capsize a bicycle or, at worst, suck the cyclist under its wheels.

But road trains were just one of a litany of outback hazards that the Australians enjoyed winding me up about. Whenever I stopped in a roadhouse, one of the local bushmen, wise with outback truisms, would corner me.

'Jeez, matey, you riding around on a bicycle,' Crocodile Dundee would say, eyeing my panniers with amused disdain.

'You want to be careful. The outback is no place for pedal power. We've got fourteen deadly snakes out there and the red-back spiders leave you pretty crook too. Then there's the sea. We've got box jellyfish; one of them nips you and you'll be dead in two hours. No antidote either. Then there's crocodiles. The freshwater ones won't harm you, but the salties, ha, they'll snap a little fella like you in half.'

Although these warnings were often hammed up, they were not too far from the truth, especially regarding crocs. Saltwater crocodiles can reach seven metres in length and are responsible for several deaths each year in Australia, usually hapless tourists paddling where they shouldn't. But the misleading thing about the saltwater crocodile is that it lives in fresh water too, sometimes miles inland. When camping in the bush, I always kept an anxious eye out while washing in the rivers and billabongs.

My final month on the bicycle was a time of wonderment. I passed signs to such places as Rum Jungle, Snakepit Gorge and Skull Creek Minor, while other notices warned of flooding and giant wombats. One afternoon, in a kayak, I drifted down the Katherine Gorge hemmed in by towering red cliffs and iron-wood trees from which black bats were hanging like fruit ready to drop. At Litchfield National Park I photographed termite mounds, large and grey as tombstones. At Argyle Lake, the second largest man-made lake in the world, I was told of the golden weaver spider, which spins a web so tough and fibrous that the US Army were testing its suitability for bulletproof vests.

My favourite stop-off was Turkey Creek, a tiny settlement in the heart of the Kimberleys. It was nothing special, just a roadhouse, a café and a campsite, but opposite was an Aborigi-nal village. Warmun Community, as it is known, houses over two hundred Aborigines in prefab huts, some made of white brick, others corrugated tin. It was difficult to get access to such places and I had to ask permission to visit the community school from Sister Margaret, the tense kind-hearted head teacher. Fortunately she agreed, despite the short notice.

I was keen to meet some Aboriginal people, who, unlike white men, looked so at home in this parched landscape. Put a naked white man in the outback sun for too long without his factor 25 and he would burn to a crisp; after all he had had only two hundred years to acclimatize. An Aborigine, however, is as resilient and natural as the red dust, part of the scenery for over 2,500 years.

The Australians I met on my journey divided into two camps regarding the Aborigines. There were those who began their conversations, 'I've got nothing against blackfellas but . . .' Some of these were good people with strong opinions but others were downright malicious. One night, I had the misfortune to camp next to a group of charmless yahoos armed with a crate of Tooheys, a chainsaw and a hi-fi. They referred to Aborigines as 'smelly bungs' and the ringleader bragged, 'If one of them sits next to me on a bus, I always move. They're not the same as us.'

But many Australians are sympathetic towards the Aborigines, especially the fact that their ancient tribal culture is so at odds with the modern nine-to-five world. There is a sense of guilt over the treatment of them by the early colonists, and an appreciation of the need to put things right.

That said, even the most reasonable Australians I spoke to felt that positive discrimination in favour of the Aborigines was at times excessive and counterproductive. Some of the Aborigine claims to outback land are bona fide – for example at Uluru (Ayers Rock) and Kakadu where massive uranium extraction was planned – but demands for some other areas have been thought grasping and unjustified. An increasing number of Australians seemed to feel that many cash handouts to Aborigines were being squandered on alcohol or else being injected into housing or education projects that never reached fruition. Fortunately, Warmun Community did not seem to be a such a project. It was a dry community, alcohol being strictly forbidden, which had been running successfully for over a decade.

The school was the centre of the village, with over a hundred pupils. I spent a whole morning speaking about my ride to individual classes and was impressed by how animated the children were. They sat on the floor, listening with suspicious eyes and big smiles. 'What was your best day?' 'Did you ever cry?' 'How tall were you when you started the trip?' There were nine teachers at Warmun, all of whom seemed highly motivated. Sister Margaret said that the school used to have terrible problems with truancy, but that she had managed to largely remedy this by giving the pupils little prizes for class attendance at the end of every week. She stressed to me that many of the classes centred on Aboriginal culture.

During one such class, the children asked about my Dreaming. The Dreaming is an essential part of Aboriginal culture and refers to the animal or totem that every Aborigine believes he or she stems from. Whatever their Dreaming, whether it be a blue-tongued lizard or a honey ant, it becomes their brother. So, if an Aborigine has a kangaroo Dreaming, for instance, he would never be able to kill or eat a kangaroo. To do so would be cannibalism.

'What is your Dreaming, mister?' asked a wild-haired, very cocksure boy called Travis. He wore a grubby T-shirt that read 'Endless Summer II'.

'I don't have a Dreaming,' I said.

'Everyone has a Dreaming, mister.'

'Well, if I did have a Dreaming it would be, er, an orang utan,' I replied.

'Orang utan, mister?'

'A big monkey, quite like a human being. It eats bananas and swings through the trees.'

The idea seemed to tickle Travis and he suppressed a laugh. 'Do you like them or something, mister?'

'Very much,' I said, 'and I've certainly never eaten one.'

The Australian outback seemed to attract wacko travellers. Indeed, my cycle ride was the epitome of sobriety compared with some of the other pilgrims of the bush. These included Cliff Young, a seventy-five-year-old farmer who was jogging his way around the circumference of Australia. I met his support team early one morning while Cliff was taking a nap.

'What sort of distance does he cover in a day?' I asked a middle-aged lady in a track-suit, perhaps the venerable athlete's masseuse.

'Well, when he crossed the Nullarbor Plain he clocked up sixty-seven kilometres in one day. But he doesn't run, he shuffles. That way he can keep going for ever. He's what we call a little Aussie battler.'

But Cliff Young was not the only battler of the bitumen. Just as I was approaching Halls Creek, I met Sashi, a Japanese woman pushing a loaded wheelbarrow. She had already trundled it almost 2,000 miles up from Perth and was planning to finish in Darwin. Her progress was a painful fifteen miles a day and every night she camped alone in the bush with her little four-wheeled barrow, which was loaded with frugal supplies. She was thirty years old, with a weathered but calm face. Sporting a floppy hat and pink plimsolls she had rather an ethereal quality. She was the sort of person who, when I looked at her, seemed to expose everything that was greedy, shallow and mean about myself.

'Why are you pushing this wheelbarrow?' I asked.

'Why do you think?' she replied. 'Because I like walking, of course.' It was the best reason for a trip I think I have every heard. No apologies, no excuses, no worthy ambitions or need for escape.

I met another cyclist at Halls Creek campsite, a manic, off-road fanatic called Robin Rishworth who behaved as if he had just drunk a gallon of Red Bull. In 1989 he won a race up the stairs of the Empire State Building and ever since has been pushing himself to Olympian extremes of fitness. On this occasion he was hoping to cycle the length of the Canning Stock Route, the old livestock trail that stretches over 1,200 miles through the Gibson and Great Sandy deserts.

'My bike is loaded with sixty-five kilos of kit,' Robin told me. 'I expect that most of the time I'll have to drag it through the sand. I've arranged for food to be buried at intervals along the route, otherwise the wild dogs will eat it, and I pray that some of the artesian wells are functioning. If not, I may end up dead. Not much traffic comes along the Canning Stock Route these days and the sand will be hotter than a cobra's belly. I need to be clocking a hundred kilometres a day at least.'

'Why are you doing this?'

'I work as a cartographer in Melbourne,' he replied, fidgeting as if his fitness was a disease. 'I love maps, the more remote the area the better. I love cycling too. So cycling in the wilderness, I'm in heaven. Besides, if I make it, I will be the first person to cycle alone along the Canning Stock Route. It's worth the risk.'

The following day, I saw Robin off on his pack mule of a mountain bike. He pedalled furiously into the desert, kicking up red dust, and then he was gone, into his three-week battle with the sun, the sand and the solitude. Cycling along the bitumen that morning, waving at the passing caravans, I considered myself a very lucky man.

And then, after a month on the outback roads, I met up with my parents.

My father had recently retired as Lord Lieutenant of Buckinghamshire and as a leaving present his team and other well-wishers had got together to buy him and my mother tickets to Australia. The idea was that they would welcome me on my arrival in Swanbourne but, as I was so behind time, they turned up at Broome instead, a town in north-west Australia.

Broome was once a famous pearling centre but is now best known as a holiday spot. This is largely due to Cable Beach, a beautiful stretch of white sand lapped by the waves of the Indian Ocean. On the evening of my arrival, the view across the beach was gorgeous, with a train of camels lolloping through the surf silhouetted against the purply sunset. I pitched up at the local campsite and tracked down Mum and Dad in their hotel nearby.

I knocked on their door. Dad answered. He was dressed in a blue blazer and decrepit suede shoes while Mum was in a sort of Edwardian bathing costume and a wide-brimmed straw hat. She was also sporting a pair of seventies sunglasses with lenses the size of sports car wing mirrors.

I had thought the meeting might be awkward as they are such incurable home-birds and had not been abroad for almost twenty years. I had always sensed that they despaired of my wanderlust. But the meeting proved a great success. I only stayed with them for a day, but it was one of the best of the last sixteen months. Mum was not worrying about her dogs and chickens, Dad was not stressed out about his next county engagement and I was not traumatizing them with my next great plan for the future. We were at peace with each other and with our surroundings.

We swam in the sea and ate barramundi and chips. We drank too much wine and talked and laughed like we never had before. Dad and I are very different creatures: I had always been a little dismissive about his prominent role in the county and he had not been altogether happy with my dalliances with bar work, orange-picking, teaching, journalism and any other trade that was prepared to tolerate me.

But we had each come to better understand one another. Dad is a good man who believes strongly in duty and tradition. It often occurred to me that it can't have been easy for Mum and Dad when their friends told them their sons were army officers or barristers or married with a couple of kids and all they could say was, 'Our Tom is cycling to Australia.' But they never made a fuss, and I loved them for that.

'It's sometimes tricky trying to live up to two hundred years of brilliant ancestry,' I told Dad just before I set off south. 'And two such impeccably behaved parents.'

'We're very proud of what you've done, me and your mother,' Dad told me quietly. I nodded my thanks solemnly. His words meant the world to me but I wasn't going to show it too much.

'Absolutely,' chipped in Mum, peering over her epic specs.

'Thanks,' I said, pedalling my bike away towards the endless horizon. 'You never know, one of these days I might even settle down.'

'Where would that be?' Mum shouted after me. 'Papua New Guinea?'

Soon after the rendezvous with my parents I reached the Sandfire Roadhouse about 180 miles south of Broome. SAND FIRE FOR SAND GROPERS read a sign. (A sand groper is a nickname for a Western Australian.)

I ordered a cup of coffee and read a copy of *Truckin' Life*.

There was a column called 'Too Much Torque', about road-train drivers popping amphetamines to stay awake longer. When I finished reading, I ripped off my shirt and took a shower under one of the lawn sprinklers. Then I lay back on the lush grass, a peacock screeched in the distance and I was as happy as I could ever remember.

Sandfire was just like any other roadhouse, but it became special to me because it was the place where I finally clocked up my 12,500 miles. Well 12,516 to be exact. I had hit my target. And it was there that I decided enough was enough. Enough midday sun punctures, enough swallowed blowflies, enough treeless horizons, enough crocs and red-backs, enough singing old Harry Belafonte songs to myself, enough tinned sardines, enough spending all day perched on a small hard triangle dodging squashed wallabies. Enough! I would hitch-hike down the remaining stretch of coast to Geraldton, a town only 250 miles north of Perth. From there it would be three days' cycling – three trifling days! – to Swanbourne.

I hitched two rides, one with a British couple, Steve and Trish, in a spotless VW van, and another with a trucker called Bill, a jolly, stunningly foul-mouthed trucker, who delivered air-conditioning units all over the outback. Bill dumped me at Geraldton. 'See ya, ya push-biking Pommie prick!' Three days later, having ridden down through the wheat belt to a place called Gingin, I was poised for my final day.

July 11, 1997. I crawled out of my tent and pulled on a thick jumper. It was noticeably colder in the south. I remembered to put on my helmet too; in Australia it was illegal to cycle without one. I could get away with it in the outback but not in a big city. It reminded me that in a matter of hours my little odyssey would be over. I would once again have to conform to the laws of the real world.

I stopped more than usual that last day. I stopped to take

pictures of the roadside banksia trees with their grenade-shaped flowers, stopped to piss in the pine woods, stopped to drink lingering cups of tea. Anything to delay my arrival. This was not such a bad life, I told myself: cycling every day. Why not just keep on going?

I knew that the following day I was to have a welcoming ceremony at Swanbourne. The mayor was due to attend with several members of local cycling clubs, press and TV. My trip had suddenly provoked some eleventh-hour interest due to a case of mistaken identity.

A couple of weeks previously, a push-bike had been found near Turkey Creek. Although I had long since passed there, reports circulated that I was the missing cyclist. My photo appeared on the national news in Australia and even in the local press in Buckinghamshire as it was feared I might be dead. At the time, I was in the middle of nowhere and heard nothing about it until several days later. By then it had already been established that the unfortunate cyclist was a Victoria man who had drowned while swimming in a billabong. His body had become lodged under water and was not found for some time. So, partly because of this tragic accident, I was about to be thrust briefly into the limelight.

Perth is an easy city to pedal through with wide, clearly signposted streets, many of them lined with tropical vegetation. I drifted through the neat white-brick suburbs down towards the coastline. There, I finally reached a little wooden sign that read SWANBOURNE BEACH. I rested my bike against it. Several white-sailed yachts bobbed about in the distance while black-headed gulls mewed overhead. If, on 11 July 1997, at about 3 p.m., anyone saw a man in purple shorts and a blue jumper dancing around the Swanbourne seafront, yelling his head off like an Indian brave, it was only me.

I spent that night in the nearby suburb of Karrinyup with some great family friends, Ruth and Bill James. Ruth, an author, is an expert on Captain Charles. She and Bill had taken interest in my trip from the start and had helped co-ordinate my welcoming party with the flamboyant local mayor, Colin Barns.

The welcome party was a kind idea, but it was the last thing I wanted. At least, I thought it was the last thing I wanted but, when it actually happened, I loved every minute of it. I breasted the finishing line escorted by dozens of local cyclists. I swigged champagne, spoke to four different TV stations and was presented with a scroll from Stoke Mandeville Spinal Unit. I was heartened by the fact that none of my sponsors seemed to care I had hitch-hiked so much of the route.

'You still did a great thing, mate,' Bill told me. 'If a pom can make it across the world on a bike, there's hope for us all.'

To finish the event, I plunged into the sea with members of the local surf club. It was below 10°C, about the same as Swanage or Torquay in early summer. Compared with the bronzed hunks around me, I looked like an alien, my Mr Whippy-white chest goosepimpled in the breeze. But the worst was yet to come. As I dived into the surf, my baggy Caribbean shorts were whisked down to my knees and I hoisted them up just in time to avoid mooning the ABC News camera crew.

'I should keep your shorts on, Tom,' said one of the surfers. 'With skin that colour the sharks will mistake you for a jellyfish.'

The trip was over and my bike was packed up in a box ready to be shipped back home. I had met the Governor of Western Australia, the Mayors of Perth and Fremantle, I had planted a tree in a park, watched the Fremantle Dockers win at Aussie

Rules and read the lesson at St George's Cathedral. My fifteen minutes of fame was over and it had been fun, but suddenly I wanted out.

I did not miss the bicycle at all. In fact, every time the sports news showing the Tour de France came on the TV, I flinched, covered my eyes and changed channels. I did not miss my nomadic lifestyle too much either, although once or twice I had an urge to put my tent up in Ruth and Bill's garden.

Whenever I got restless, I reminded myself of Uncle Jo in Graham Greene's novel, *Travels With My Aunt*. Uncle Jo was an invalid who, in his twilight years, decided to buy a house with fifty-two rooms in it. He felt that if he lived in a different room each week, his life would become more enriched, less predictable. In a sense, Uncle Jo's story rang true. Whilst travelling, my time had never flown but never dragged either, as each week, however humdrum or sensational, always offered some fresh experience. But what Graham Greene meant, at least to my mind, was that fresh experience need not come from travel. It could derive from a number of sources: from work, or books, from faith or family. It was simply a state of mind.

Amid the official engagements, I was determined to fit in a visit to my old boss, Dan MacKinnon. Dan had employed me as a jackaroo on his sheep station, the Pinnacles, when I visited Western Australia as an eighteen-year-old backpacker. The Pinnacles was an impressive property, about forty square miles in size, with over 500 miles of fencing and 17,000 sheep. I had spent a wonderful time there revving around on motorbikes, tagging ewes, fibre-glassing water troughs and eating lamb for breakfast, lunch and tea. Shortly after I left the Pinnacles in 1985, Dan was forced to put the station on the market. This was partly due to poor wool prices but also because Dan and his wife, Helen, had three daughters and no son. The Pinnacles was a beautiful place but very isolated and Dan decided it would be kinder to bring up his three girls in the city.

Seeing the MacKinnons again after twelve years, now in their spotless Perth home, was a strange experience. Gone was the huge communal Pinnacles kitchen, the thrum of the generator, the pack of slumbering kelpies and the pet cockatoos. Helen was no longer wearing a lumberjack shirt and jeans but an elegant evening dress. Sue, the youngest daughter, who had been a tiny tomboy in overalls when I had last seen her, was now an attractive young woman far taller than me. And Dan, who I remember being permanently covered in dust and grease, was looking awkwardly dapper in a green blazer. It didn't suit him somehow; he reminded me of a farm terrier forced to scrub up and wear a rosette.

'Don't worry, Tom,' said Helen, sensing my confusion. 'Not everything's changed. We'll still be eating lamb tonight.'

It was the best meal I had tasted in months.

The selling of the Pinnacles was not the only thing to have changed since my last visit. Perth had run rampant, its suburbs extending for miles along the coast. Fortunately, Fremantle had undergone an ugly-duckling-style makeover. I remembered it as a dowdy backwater but, since hosting the America's Cup in 1986, it had been transformed into a bustling and attractive port. I like to think that Captain Charles would have been proud. During those last two weeks in Perth I thought a lot about Captain Charles. After all, it was largely due to him that I had set off on my cycling odyssey in the first place. Once again I pored over his diaries.

Captain Charles's voyage to Fremantle was the first significant feather in the young officer's cap and the one he would always be remembered for. He set sail from Madeira in January

1829, hoping to win his nautical spurs. 'My ship is so full of provisions that I have no room to stow anything away,' he wrote to his mother, Betsey, at Swanbourne, 'and now I am bound on such a Robinson Crusoe voyage that she is like a deep laden Collier full of everything in the world. I have my orders to proceed immediately to Swan River on the West Coast of New Holland and take possession in the name of His Majesty of the whole of that Coast . . .'

In another letter, the ambitious captain revealed that he did not take his responsibilities lightly. 'I get on very well in my Ship except that my own Servants are like yours always quarrelling, I believe I shall treat them in a different manner to you and give them a good flogging to make them agree . . . I am bored to death in my Ship sometimes in the Evening having nobody to talk to, as you are aware that a Captain is not very intimate with his Officers.'

After a hazardous passage from the Cape, Fremantle caught sight of the west coast of Australia on 25 April 1829. It took over a week to work the *Challenger* through a tricky stretch of water towards the mouth of the Swan River. At one point his ship struck a rock, but fortunately floated away without damage. Captain Charles recorded the incident in his log in typically bombastic prose.

> Never since I have been at Sea have I ever witnessed anything to equal the carelessness and stupidity of the Master; *he placed a buoy on a rock and then steered for the buoy and ran the ship immediately on it*. It was a thousand chances that we escaped being knocked to pieces, which must have been the case had it not been beautiful weather. *The master deserves to be hanged immediately* . . . Nothing has annoyed me so much since I entered the Service.

Having taken formal possession of the whole coast, Captain Charles set up a fortified camp on the mainland on the spot where the city of Fremantle now stands. His men busied themselves digging wells, growing vegetables and hunting for food, including fish, seals, penguins and 'a fine, large bird, very handsome but not good to eat, altho' my Steward turns everything into a pie'.

Captain Charles also described many encounters with the Aboriginals. He spotted the first group of 'natives' on the banks of the Swan the day after his arrival. He presented them with some clothes and fishing tackle. They, in turn, presented him with some skeins of string.

'They were perfectly naked,' wrote Captain Charles, 'with only a string tied about three turns (made I should think from the bark of trees) round the head and another round the lower part of the body ... They were very friendly ... They made a great noise and ... ran along the side in the water with astonishing agility ... They appeared to be in the greatest state of savage ignorance and had no idea of the use of a Musket.'

My ancestor left Australia on 28 August, four months after his arrival. By this time another captain, James Stirling, who later became Governor of Western Australia, had also dropped anchor at Fremantle. On his way into the Swan River, Stirling damaged his ship, the *Parmelia*, on the shoals and rocks that Captain Charles had skilfully (bar the incident with the Master) managed to chicane his way through.

After postings in China and India, Captain Charles returned to Fremantle in September 1832, almost three years exactly since he last docked. He noted that Perth had not 'kept pace with Fremantle'. While he was pleased with the thriving cultivation that had taken place in the colony, he was appalled at the general lack of provisions. He noted that mutton and kangaroo were very scarce and that many of the poorer settlers 'had not tasted a piece of even salt meat for many weeks'.

> I am of opinion that the best thing that can be done for the Colony is to make it a Penal Settlement . . . the labour of the Convicts would be most valuable as there is everything to do and no means of completing anything . . . I was sorry to find that there was a very bad understanding with the Natives, who were most troublesome and did much damage spearing the sheep, pigs etc in great abundance. Many deaths have also been occasioned by them and in return many of them have been killed.
>
> The Climate is most healthy and I found it enjoyable after India. The red cheeks and wholesome Countenances of the Settlers and their Children made it a pleasure to look on them . . .

Captain Charles left Fremantle for the last time only a few weeks later and sailed home via Hobart, Sydney, Tahiti and Pitcairn Island, where he visited the grave of the *Bounty* mutineer, Fletcher Christian.

For all his impatience and bluster Captain Charles at times showed a compassionate side behind his 'hang 'em flog 'em' fustiness. Take this closing appraisal of the Pitcairn islanders. 'Upon the whole I was much pleased with them, they are still a well disposed well behaved, kind hospitable people and if well advised and instructed would be led to anything, but I fear if left to themselves and are visited by many Ships what little simplicity they have left will soon vanish and they will be like the rest of the World.'

As mentioned earlier, Captain Charles went on to serve with distinction in the Crimean War. He died in London in 1869. A portrait commissioned in his dotage shows a jowly stern-looking man, his sideburns the size of guinea pigs, his coat ablaze with medals, his buttons straining against a spectacular paunch. He looks bored to death by the sedentary comforts of old age; a man whose true home is on the sea, on the move.

On my final day in Australia I met up with Lisa, the girl who had drawn a butterfly on my forearm in Athens the previous May. I recognized her immediately; she still had the butterfly amulet around her neck and the same psychedelic dockers on her feet. It was good to see someone who had been part of the trip. We drank a milk shake in one of the cafés on Fremantle's *cappuccino* strip and then took a walk along the harbour front.

'There used to a statue of your ancestor here somewhere,' said Lisa, pointing across the esplanade. 'But it got vandalized, I'm afraid. Thrown into the sea, I think.'

'An appropriate burial at least.'

'Shame, though. I'd love to have a statue of one of my rellies somewhere, especially one with a place named after him. That would be cool.'

We wandered along a thin finger of land that stretched out to sea. Neither of us spoke but that was fine, the silence felt right. Before long, the pavement petered out into boulders of slippery stone. A yacht with a red sail swooped by as we jumped from rock to rock, past a couple of boys fishing. The waves were now crashing around us, splashing us with a fine spray.

'We're going to get soaked,' shouted Lisa, above the wind. She turned away and started to slip and slide her way back.

'Wait,' I called after her, but she was already out of earshot.

I sat on a huge rock, most of which was now submerged beneath the sea. From the pocket of my jeans I pulled out a walnut. I threw it hard, the wind sending it spinning far out to sea. From the other pocket, I pulled a postcard of Captain

Charles at the age of twenty-nine, shortly after he had landed at Fremantle. He looked proud and dashing. I ripped the postcard into tiny pieces, tossed them gently into the water and watched them spiral, like skittish ghosts, into the depths.

'What the hell happened to you?' asked Lisa, as I stumbled back to the quayside a few minutes later.

'Sorry,' I replied. 'I was just saying goodbye to a couple of old friends.'

'You're troppo, Fremantle.' She smiled and hit me on the arm. 'Come on, I'll race you home.'

EPILOGUE

Swanbourne, Summer 1999

It's more than twenty years since my conversation with Johnny Ginger on Cemetery Hill and the world of Swanbourne has changed; like everywhere else, it had to.

For a start Johnny Ginger is dead. He suffered a stroke one evening and was rushed to Stoke Mandeville Hospital. Johnny regained consciousness briefly and wrote 'Thank you' on a scrap of paper before gliding up to the Swanbourne in the stars. His body is now buried with the other villagers in a plot on Cemetery Hill. He has no gravestone.

During his life Johnny always compared world events with those in Swanbourne. When Dutch elm disease struck the trees in the Old Park he likened it to global deforestation and when Swanbourne won a local football match he was convinced it would boost England's chances in the World Cup. He even compared the flood of commuters into Swanbourne as a rustic equivalent to the takeover of Hong Kong. To him the village was a microcosm of the outside world.

Both worlds are changing fast. When Johnny started work at Swanbourne House as a teenager, a legion of gardeners was employed, now there is only a tiny squad. Johnny's place has been taken by a man in a baseball cap who listens to a Sony Discman while raking the leaves. Johnny's sickle has been replaced with a mini-tractor from Japan, his bicycle with a Volkswagen Golf, some of his ideas with a computer. It is the same scenario everywhere. The Johnny Gingers of this world are on the very edge of extinction.

What I admired most about Johnny Ginger was his sense of wonderment. Nothing ever bored him. Like a fish in a pond he circled the same scenes all of his life but still remained so animated – excited by the sight of a fox on the run or the sound of jackdaws chuckling, by the smell of bonfire smoke or the piquant taste of blackberries plucked fresh from the bramble.

When Johnny's house was cleared after his death all that was found was a bed, some chairs, a table, a radio, a gardening book, several bicycles and a pair of binoculars. That was about it. His home was as spartan as a Trappist monk's but Johnny was not the least self-denying; simplicity just made him happy.

Johnny Ginger would never have left Swanbourne. Unlike Robinson Crusoe who signalled to a passing ship from his desert island, Johnny would have watched it go by. Unlike Voltaire's Candide, who left the magic land of El Dorado in order to boast about it to his friends in Europe, Johnny would have stayed put. Johnny even outclassed Henry David Thoreau, the writer of *Walden*, a classic book about the contentment of living alone in the woods. For all its literary beauty I think Walden is a bit rich. After only two years Thoreau left his log cabin and returned to the organized urbane society he had ridiculed while alone. Johnny Ginger never left; he stayed in the woods. He stayed in Swanbourne.

When I first flew back to Swanbourne from Australia I struggled to come to terms with my journey. On the road my thoughts had been as clear as the brush-strokes on a fine painting. But once I stopped, the colours began running and the canvas of my memory become confused and diluted. The thrill of movement, the ever-changing landscapes and the daily miles I had needed to clock up had given my journey a sense of purpose. But now that I was anchored, all that had gone. Even the gems of nomadic wisdom that had flashed through my mind on my travels seemed irrelevant.

My friends and family have been patient. They sense my restlessness and give me space. I still sometimes retreat into my journey, brooding over my thousands of slides and studying my diaries which are stained with blood and dirt, hibiscus tea from Cairo and coffee from Vietnam. I follow the progress of the countries I rode through in the newspapers.

Some of the news – the regeneration of Beirut and a less austere regime in Iran (plus the fact they beat America 2–1 at soccer in the 1998 World Cup!) – is heartening. Then, there's East Timor which, aided by the United Nations, has taken its first fragile steps towards independence after over twenty years of oppression. But there are sad stories too: Cambodia, so optimistic when I pedalled through, has suffered a bloody coup following the elections; Afghanistan is still firmly under the trenchant grip of the Taleban; relations between India and Pakistan are once again tempestuous; Turkey has suffered some devastating earthquakes; Italy, true to form, has already had a new prime minister; and King Hussein of Jordan has died and been succeeded by his half-British son Abdullah. I'm sure by the time you read this, the world will have already been dealt a fresh pack of kings, queens, knaves and jokers.

As the months fly by I often hear of people I met on the road. Sandrine is expecting a baby, Round-The-World-Again Dave is, predictably, cycling round the world again, Dan is working as a tour guide in Egypt, Zack is marrying a Japanese dancer, Nadav and Daniella have a baby daughter called Hagar, an Arabic name, chosen as a sign of peace, Julia and Philip have sold Penelope Pitstop and moved to Zambia to work on a game reserve, Alexandra and I rarely speak but I often think of her when Hong Kong appears in the news, Hoi has been deported by the Vietnamese police after letting former refugees stay at his home in Hanoi. He is now back in Australia. Allah only knows what has happened to Crazy Denis and his flying carpet, or the remarkable Cliff Young for that matter, perhaps he is hop-scotching up Ayers Rock.

All of the £43,000 – over twice the journey's initial target – has been injected into the wheelchair trust fund at Stoke Mandeville Spinal Unit. The generosity shown towards this inspirational place has been both astonishing and very touching.

Despite my inevitable post-travel bewilderment I am, deep down, glad to be home. I am slowly beginning to see my two-wheeled jaunt as a valuable boon to the future.

'What did you learn?' an old man asked me recently. 'You are so lucky. I never had the chance to travel. Come on, tell me truthfully, what did you learn?'

It was the toughest of questions. At the time I gave a pat answer about the world not being such a bad place if an incompetent adventurer like me could pedal unscathed halfway across it. But what had I really learnt?

I had learnt, in all my confusion of experiences, that there are two types of people in this world – rich or poor, young or old, saint or sinner it makes no difference, there are generally only two types of people – there are those who are bored with life and there are those who are not. I had sometimes been bored with life before my trip, bogged down with tepid routines and unfulfilled expectations. Bogged down with myself. My travels had helped me tap into my primitive side again. At times I had been left mad with despair, crying by the side of the road, alone and afraid, stripped of all hope. But only by plunging into these sloughs had I rediscovered life's simple and ineffable highs. My journey had taught me the joy of hot water cascading down skin caked in weeks of grime; the wonder of a red flower standing alone in a sandy wasteland; the reviving bite of an icy river on a parched throat and the thrill of freewheeling so fast your tired soul whirls like a dervish. But above all, it had taught me of strangers with generous hearts.

I could have learnt all this from Johnny Ginger a long time ago. I just never understood what he was getting at. It had taken 16 months, 12,763 miles, 56 punctures and a passport with more stamps than Henry Kissinger's to finally understand the simple value of home.

Soon after my return we had a party celebrating 200 years of Fremantles living at Swanbourne. The other villagers have just about accepted us as locals now, although I'm sure one or two still see us as Johnny-Come-Latelies. Shortly after this George Alcock, Swanbourne's oldest citizen, celebrated his hundredth birthday.

On a less fortunate note, at midnight on Christmas Eve, I was knocked off my bicycle in Knightsbridge – sod's law having survived Beirut and Cairo – and broke my collar bone. The driver was a myopic and very theatrical Italian. 'For fifty-two years I driva my car, I swear I never hitta anybody except you!' he insisted. After ten weeks in a sling I am now back on the bike – and soon I might be riding with another passenger.

Amanda and I have a baby daughter, Eliza, a six-week-old bundle of wrinkles, tears and hiccups, but quite the most beautiful thing I have ever seen. Indeed, nothing on all my travels could even touch first seeing Eliza smile.

I still dream of travel, though. I haven't been abroad for the last couple of years, but the road will lure me back sometime, even if it is for a shorter spell. But now Swanbourne, although I only visit there fleetingly, is still home. Not only for me but for my parents, for Halford, Captain Charles, Admiral Thomas,

Betsey Wynne and all the other Fremantles who have lived there over the past two centuries.

Of course, the village still frustrates me, still bewilders me and at times its tranquillity still makes me plead, 'Where are the savages?' But I love it too, this splendid place that in some ways will always be my home and, in other ways, will never be.

Swanbourne looks at its best now. It is summer and the land is alive with ripening corn and trees dense with blossom, with dive-bombing swallows and the peal of wedding bells. All that is missing is a fat, cherry-faced gardener pedalling home through the twilight, the sun shrinking fast beneath the dark penumbra of the Himalayas.